# ARENDTIAN CONSTITUTIONALISM

The meaning and function of law in Hannah Arendt's work has never been the subject of a systematic reconstruction. This book examines Arendt's work and reconstructs her ideas through political, legal and constitutional theory, and shows that her engagement with law is continuous as well as crucial to an adequate understanding of her political thought. The author argues that Arendt was very much concerned with the question of an adequate arrangement of law, politics and order—the so-called triad of constitutionalism. By adopting this approach, the author suggests an alternative interpretation of Arendt's thought, which sees her as thinker of political order who considers as crucial a stable and free political order in which political struggle and dissent can occur.

# Arendtian Constitutionalism

## Law, Politics and the Order of Freedom

Christian Volk

• HART •
PUBLISHING
OXFORD AND PORTLAND, OREGON
2017

**Hart Publishing**
An imprint of Bloomsbury Publishing Plc

Hart Publishing Ltd
Kemp House
Chawley Park
Cumnor Hill
Oxford OX2 9PH
UK

Bloomsbury Publishing Plc
50 Bedford Square
London
WC1B 3DP
UK

**www.hartpub.co.uk**
**www.bloomsbury.com**

Published in North America (US and Canada) by
Hart Publishing
c/o International Specialized Book Services
920 NE 58th Avenue, Suite 300
Portland, OR 97213-3786
USA

**www.isbs.com**



First published in hardback, 2015
Paperback edition, 2017



**British Library Cataloguing-in-Publication Data**
A catalogue record for this book is available from the British Library.

ISBN: PB: 978-1-50991-771-6
HB: 978-1-84946-584-7

Typeset by Compuscript Ltd, Shannon
Printed and bound in Great Britain by
Lightning Source UK Ltd

# *Preface*

It seems that there will be no end to the fascination with the work of Hannah Arendt. New books and articles appear at regular intervals, all attempting to interpret her writings in a new light. But what is the textual foundation of these interpretations? To which texts do we refer in our exegesis of Arendt's thought, and which texts form the basis for the plausibility or otherwise of hermeneutic claims?

A widespread assumption in academia seems to be that the work written by Arendt in English forms our textual foundation. With the exception of a few minor pieces written in German, usually from Arendt's early creative phase, it is generally assumed that the English language editions are nonetheless the 'originals'. And what appears (or is omitted) in these 'originals' is the textual basis and thus the object of the interpretation and exegesis of her work. Thus compared to the English language 'originals', the German versions of her work are regarded 'merely' as 'translations'. *Vita activa* is simply regarded as the translation of *The Human Condition*; *Über die Revolution* as the translation of *On Revolution*; *Elemente und Ursprünge totaler Herrschaft* as that of *Origins of Totalitarianism* and so on—with the result that the English 'original' must quite naturally have the last word on the textual evidence.

Yet this falls short of the mark. 'In Arendt's literary work' Marie Luise Knott rightly notes, 'the common idea of the "original" is no longer valid'. (Knott 2011: 68) Why is that the case? One reason is that Arendt's supposed 'originals', ie the English versions of the main works, were themselves always translations. The seminal publication of Arendt's *Denktagebuch*—an almost-1,200-page intellectual diary, mostly written in German—demonstrates in an impressive manner that Arendt—despite being rooted in the USA—in fact composed the vast majority of her conceptual thoughts, which would eventually be published in English, in German. Furthermore, her entire political-philosophical thoughts always referred directly to the German and European past and present—in history, politics, philosophy and literature. To exaggerate only slightly: Arendt spent all her life working on the so-called European tradition of political and philosophical thought. This tradition was her specific problem focus. Accordingly, her main concern was to take her experiences in and with 'the American' tradition of political thought and to apply it to a reorientation of the dominant European tradition of political thought. For this purpose she not only travelled frequently to Europe, but also strived to convey this reorientation of her political-philosophical thought in articles, talks and radio interviews in Germany and other European states. Arendt drafted, varied and further developed the topics of her books in these pieces—and many of these pieces are available only in German, or were in turn translated into English.

But there is another, much more decisive reason why it is a fallacy to divide the work into the English language 'original' versus the German translation: As is well known, Arendt was actively involved in the 'translation' (or: retranslation?) of her works. As a consequence, and not least through the process of translation itself (the confrontation with what was then a 'foreign text', adopting a specific perspective in order to write for a new audience, etc), almost all German versions of her main works are both more comprehensive and richer in material than the English versions, and can also stand on their own from a linguistic and stylistic perspective. Marie Luise Knott concludes that Arendt's 'American versions and German versions of her main works represent two different, albeit very closely related, originals' (Knott 2011: 68). This fact can be explicated in almost all of her key political-philosophical writings.

With a view to the differences between *On Revolution* and *Über die Revolution*, Wolfgang Heuer has shown that the German text, with its additional sections and passages, is not only longer than the English version by almost a quarter. Heuer also discovered that central topics (the analysis of Rousseau's compassion and the internalisation of the political; the role and importance of opposition; the subject of new foundation, revolution and the councils as a new form of government; the thoughts of Montesquieu and more) are treated much more comprehensively and in more detail than in the English version (Heuer 2011: 90f).

The same applies to a much greater extent to the book *Vita activa oder Vom tätigen Leben*, the German equivalent to *The Human Condition*. Hardly any major work varies so widely in its two versions as much as these two pieces (see Knott 2011: 68). In her analysis, Marie Luise Knott traces how Arendt must have approached the translation: *The Human Condition* arose from a lecture, which was then edited by an American publishing editor and released in 1958. We can see from the entries in *Denktagebuch* that a large part of the conception of the book was written in German and then translated into English by Arendt. After the publication of the English version, Charlotte Beradt, a journalist acquaintance, made a rough translation into German. Arendt worked on this rough translation for three more years, until the book was published in German in 1961. For the German version, not only were quotations checked and errors corrected; Marie Luise Knott shows that entire clarifying and explanatory passages were added, which not only made the German version much longer (by almost 40 per cent). In fact, the German version also represents, in many respects, a revision of *The Human Condition*.[1]

There are also important differences between many contributions to *Between Past and Future* and the German version *Zwischen Vergangenheit und Zukunft* (see Heuer/Rosenmüller 2011: 70-84). For example, there is a striking difference between the essays 'What is Freedom' and 'Freiheit und Politik'. The English and German versions do not only differ in their formulations. The German version of the text has five sections, while the fifth section is completely missing from the English version. Even more decisive, however, is the fact that in the German version Arendt put much more effort into providing a positive conception of political freedom. The normative content of the concept of political freedom she drafted—and this is also in contrast to 'What is Freedom', where these passages do not appear—lies in the fact that acting takes place in a 'space' provided and guaranteed by others, 'in which acting can have an impact and can become visible'(FuP: 216).[2]

The *Origins of Totalitarianism* also differs in some respects from *Elemente und Ursprünge totaler Herrschaft*, the German title. Here, too, the German text is once again longer than the English one, certainly more than the customary five to ten per cent difference that normally accrues in translations from English to German. The German version has almost 1,000 pages of pure text and is much richer in material that is expressed in longer, newly added footnotes and additional paragraphs. That which one might call the 'political-theoretical architecture'[3] of her book on totalitarianism actually unfolds to its full and understandable extent only in the German version. In our case, however, quite a different matter is of key significance: Arendt's analysis of the modern state and her consideration of Max Weber, which can be reconstructed plausibly only from *Elemente und Ursprünge totaler Herrschaft*. One reason for this is that Arendt's genealogy of the modern state begins in the part of the book concerning anti-Semitism, a section that is more comprehensive and detailed in the German rather than the English version. (In this section Arendt drafts her understanding of the modern state—and this drafting is always connected with the question of the relationship of Jews to the state and society.)[4]

[1] Roy Tsao worked out how Arendt's representation of the Greeks differed in the German and English versions (Tsao 2002). In the German version the aporia of action, questions of forgiveness and promise, the concept of the world, the concept of public sphere, criticism of Greek agonality—to name just a few subjects—are treated in much more detail.

[2] I shall outline in detail this understanding of freedom in ch 5. The German version reads here as follows: *Politische Freiheit* '*hängt daran, ob eine freie Nation den Raum gewährt, in welchem das Handeln sich auswirken und sichtbar werden kann*' (FuP: 216).

[3] See the section 'Arendt's Political-theoretical Architecture of Origins of Totalitarianism', ch 4.

[4] A brief glance at the bibliography of *Elemente und Ursprünge totaler Herrschaft/Origins of Totalitarianism* reveals that Arendt, in her considerations, refers to Weber's *Wirtschaftsgeschichte*, *Parlament und Regierung im neugeordneten Deutschland* and Weber's piece *Die Börse*.

Additionally, Arendt's analysis of Weber can be reconstructed plausibly only from the German version because the terminological proximity to and the assumption and adaption of Weber's terminology can only possibly be recognised in the German version.

What do we conclude from all of this? Well, if we wish to approach Arendt's work today with the intention of conducting an exegesis, it is not enough to focus solely on the writings in English. I am convinced that today, measured against the standards of academic probity, it is simply not possible to analyse Arendt exegetically without also being able to draw on and work with the German versions as independent writings, as 'originals'. The general question that arises, therefore, especially in view of the proliferating studies on Hannah Arendt's work, is whether we need a critical complete edition, which brings together the English and German versions, compares them and comments on them.

My book cannot provide such an overview, nor does it intend to. Nevertheless I have tried as far as possible to do justice to the fact of 'two different, albeit very closely related, originals', namely Arendt's work in both English and German. Quite apart from the fact that this book has broken new ground in focusing on the question of law in Hannah Arendt's thought, it is also the first publication to work and argue in a fundamental manner with both the English and German versions of Hannah Arendt's work. Accordingly, with each quotation I have checked whether the German passage is (more or less) identical with the English version. If that is the case, I cite the English version. If that is not the case, I cite the version that most clearly expresses the thoughts that concern me at that point. The gain for the international discussion of Hannah Arendt's work could be that, in this manner, the content of the German works might flow into the English-speaking debate, that differences become clear, and that the debate can thus receive new impulses—for example with a view to the law, or of Weber's legacy in Arendt's thought.

This book is the revised, expanded and translated version of my German book *Die Ordnung der Freiheit. Recht und Politik im Denken Hannah Arendts*, which was published in January 2010 by Nomos Verlag in the series of the section for Political Theory of the German Political Science Association. The work on this translation took a lot of time and I am glad to have received so much support from many institutions and people, all of whom I take this opportunity to thank.

First I wish to mention the Fritz Thyssen Foundation, the German Federal Foreign Office, the collecting society VG WORT and the Börsenverein des Deutschen Buchhandels (German Publishers & Booksellers Association) which, in the context of their joint initiative *Geisteswissenschaften International*, awarded my German book a prize for the translation of work in the humanities and social sciences, which financed the translation of this book into

English. I would like to thank Hart Publishing—in particular Richard Hart, Rachel Turner, Emma Swinden and Melanie Hamill, who accepted my book for publication and who gave me exemplary support. Special thanks are also due to my copy editor at Hart Publishing, Catherine Minahan. Ellen Reinolds from Nomos Verlag also deserves thanks for initiating the smooth cooperation between Nomos Verlag and Hart Publishing in terms of copyright, and for helping me so much in planning the translation.

Translating this book was a time-consuming and laborious task—especially as the German work was published five years ago, and the completion of the German manuscript lies even further in the past. Much has happened in the intervening period. I have tried on the one hand to incorporate into my work new publications that have appeared since 2010, while at the same time preserving the core of the argument and the stringency of the German book. The translator Carolyn Kelly supported me wonderfully in this endeavour. My special thanks are due to her! Apart from greater parts of chapter one, which I translated into English with the help of Claudia Mason, Carolyn Kelly translated this book for me. During months of intensive work we repeatedly reformulated, revised and rewrote various text passages. I am very grateful to her for persevering with the English text in spite of my many revisions and comments, and for successfully completing this translation with me. I would also like to thank wholeheartedly my student assistants from the university department, Sebastian Berg, Sebastian Stein, Kim Henningsen, Halima Akhrif, Franca Bülow as well as Friederike Kuntz, my research assistant, who supported this translation in many different ways.

By now I have been analysing Arendt's work for a long time. During this time I have discussed the topics of this book with various different people at various different places. The Institute for Political Science at RWTH Aachen was where it all began. I will always associate this place directly with the conversations and discussions I had with Thomas Philipp, Henrique Ricardo Otten, Richard Gebhardt, Maike Weißpflug, Amien Idries, Sebastian Rohwer, Sabine Bausch, Jürgen Förster, Thorsten Thiel, Nano Rickum, Hans Kruschwitz, Helmut König, Emanuel Richter and Verena Papke.

I then spent some time in the USA: at Yale (2006 & 2007) and at the New School for Social Research (2007). The fact that my time in New Haven would become such a fruitful phase in my career has much to do with Seyla Benhabib. She took the time to discuss key thoughts with me, she commented on drafts and she involved me in her own considerations. She has been an indispensable dialogue partner ever since. For the many conversations about Arendt, deconstruction and law, I extend my special thanks to Gaye Illhan Demiryol, Sonali Chakravarti, Alex Kirshner, Martin Blumenthal-Barby, Judith Miller, Onur Bakiner, Kush Choudhury and the other participants in the Political Theory Workshop and Political Philosophy Workshop in those times. I thank Andrew

Arato and Jerome Kohn for their invitation to the New School for Social Research in 2007 and for the numerous discussions we had, including those that took place in the colloquium at the Cardozo Law School. In particular, the conversations with Jerome Kohn and Elisabeth Young-Bruehl inspired me greatly—I will never forget their extraordinary knowledge of Arendt's work, their passion for constantly asking new questions of this work, and their willingness always to be open to and interested in new perspectives.

After many further stages in this nomadic academic life—including periods at the European Inter-University Centre in Venice, HU Berlin and the Goethe University Frankfurt—I have held the position of Assistant Professor for Political Theory at the University of Trier since 2012. There, Winfried Thaa has proven to be a friend, colleague and acknowledged expert in Hannah Arendt's thought. Our joint colloquiums have provided an institutionalised place for the research into Arendt's thought in particular, and for the further development of political theory and philosophy inspired by Arendt in general. Discussions with Winfried Thaa are an enrichment and a continual source of inspiration to me.

Helmut König once supervised this work in its doctoral phase—although he has always been much more than a doctoral supervisor. He has supported and encouraged me since my third semester. He has the very special and very rare ability to sort through the arguments of others in conversation, to separate what is important from what is momentarily unimportant, and to fish out and help to develop the central thought contained in a flood of words. With his circumspect and warm manner, always interested in both the content and the person, he removes all pressure from his dialogue partner and joins in to think about the matter at hand. By these means he creates a space of intellectual freedom in such conversations, in which one can test oneself without fear. That is surely the reason why—to borrow a famous phrase from Hannah Arendt—'everything becomes luminous' in his presence.

My first thoughts about Arendt in general and about law in her work in particular are inseparably associated with my friendship with Jürgen Förster and Thorsten Thiel. Jürgen Förster first cleared the way with his own work, which led me to think, with Arendt, about the law and its position in her work. This work took shape thanks to countless discussions about will, sovereignty, about constitutions and the human faculty of making promises. From the very outset Thorsten Thiel supported this work—like all of my works—as a friend: commenting thoughtfully, discussing intensively and criticising prudently. Along with Johanna Hoerning he is my closest and first dialogue partner in every academic, and indeed many personal, matters. I am especially grateful to him. More than I can possibly express here, I owe a great debt of gratitude to my parents, Gerda and Rainer Volk, who prepared the foundation on which I stand with their loving care and unconditional support.

Some chapters and passages of this book have been previously published in whole or in part in journals or books, often in substantially different form. The publications are:

'The Decline of Order. Hannah Arendt and the Paradoxes of the Nation-State' in Benhabib, Seyla (ed), *Politics in Dark Times: Encounters with Hannah Arendt* (Cambridge, Cambridge University Press, 2010) 172–97.

'From *nomos* to *lex*. Hannah Arendt on Law, Politics, and Order' (2010) 23(4) *Leiden Journal of International Law*, 759–79.

The completion of the final drafts of this book coincided with the birth of our daughter, Moira: our small and greatest joy. I share this joy and much more besides with Johanna Hoerning. She showed me what it means to have a truly political position, both within and beyond academic discourse. Our life, our conversations, and the way we discuss politics, philosophy, society and everything else show that it is indeed possible: to love and be loved, and yet to be free.

# Contents

# *List of Abbreviations*

| | |
|---|---|
| Arendt/Jaspers | Arendt, Hannah und Jaspers, Karl. Briefwechsel 1926–1969 |
| CD | Civil Disobedience |
| DiT | Diskussionen mit Freunden und Kollegen in Toronto (November 1972) |
| DT | Denktagebuch |
| DUR | Die Ungarische Revolution und der totalitäre Imperialismus |
| EaS | Weber, Max: Economy and Society |
| EJ | Eichmann in Jerusalem |
| ETH | Elemente und Ursprünge totaler Herrschaft |
| FuG | Habermas, Jürgen: Faktizität und Geltung |
| FuP | Freiheit und Politik |
| GEH | Weber, Max: General Economic History |
| HC | Human Condition |
| JW | Jewish Writings |
| LiP | Lying in Politics |
| LoK | Lecture on Kant |
| LoM/W | Life of the Mind/Willing |
| LR | Von der Menschlichkeit in finsteren Zeiten. Rede über Lessing |
| MuG | Macht und Gewalt |
| NuD | Nationalstaat und Demokratie |
| OR | On Revolution |
| OT | Origins of Totalitarianism |
| OV | On Violence |
| PaB | Weber, Max: Politik als Beruf |
| PRPI | Public Rights and Private Interests |
| PuR | Weber, Max: Parlament und Regierung im neugeordneten Deutschland |
| RoLR | Reflections on Little Rock |

| | |
|---|---|
| TPR | Thoughts on Politics and Revolution |
| ÜR | Über die Revolution |
| VA | Vita activa oder Vom tätigen Leben |
| WB | Walter Benjamin |
| Wg | Weber, Max: Wirtschaftsgeschichte |
| WiP | Was ist Politik |
| WuG | Weber, Max: Wirtschaft und Gesellschaft |

# *Introduction*

The key issue of future politics will always be the problem of legislation.

Hannah Arendt, *Denktagebuch* (September 1951)

HANNAH ARENDT'S POLITICAL thinking arises from confrontation with the defining catastrophe of the twentieth century, the Shoah. Hardly any other thinker of the last 100 years has thought through the consequences of the 'rupture of civilization' (*Zivilisationsbruch*) (Diner 1988) with such consistency and intensity. In contrast to many other authors of her time, Arendt's thinking does not retreat from the political sphere in the face of the crisis. Quite the contrary: she considers withdrawal from the public sphere and concern merely for one's own welfare to have been decisive factors in the establishment of the National Socialist system of rule. It is therefore notable that Arendt, at the conclusion of her voluminous work about the elements of totalitarianism, turns to the question 'What is politics?'[1]—a question that was to remain the central theme of her intellectual works until her death.

Just how fruitful this intellectual endeavour was can be seen from the fact that there appears to be no end to analysis of her work; indeed, engagement with Arendt's thoughts seems to grow in intensity, and they appear to be applied time and again to new phenomena. There are lively debates about questions regarding Arendt's justification of human rights,[2] about the interpretation of the social question,[3] about the relationship between thinking, acting and the power of judgement,[4] about foundation, revolution and

[1] Arendt addresses the question 'What is politics' directly in the context of her work on the origins of totalitarianism. The first fragment on this matter dates from 1950 (WiP: 9).

[2] The discussion has been brought forward by Peg Birmingham in her book *Hannah Arendt and Human Rights* (Birmingham 2006). Seyla Benhabib replied to this with her thoughts on 'Another Universalism: On the Unity and Diversity of Human Rights' (Benhabib 2007). At the Arendt Conference in Berlin on the occasion of her 100th birthday, Étienne Balibar (Balibar 2007) and Stefan Gosepath (Gosepath 2007), as well as Birmingham (Birmingham 2007), addressed questions of Arendt's justification of human rights.

[3] The discourse on Arendt's interpretation of the social question has been conducted at least since the Toronto Conference of 1972 (see DiT: 98ff), leading to accusations that Arendt's political thought ignored questions of social justice. I shall address this discourse in detail in ch 2, and point to a different strain of her thought in ch 5.

[4] In the field of Arendt research there is a philosophical dispute as to whether or not judgement and action, thought and judgement, and thought and action are connected. On this philosophical discourse see inter alia Barley 1990: 143; Beiner 1985: 176; Benhabib 2003: 185–93; Bernstein 1986a: 234–37; Bielefeldt 1993: 82; Bradshaw 1989: 68–71; Brunkhorst 1999; Canovan 1990: 135;

memory,[5] and about evil and banality.[6] These debates are spurred on by publications from her estate, which are released regularly, presenting in a completely new light topics that have long been considered dormant.[7] Yet with all the activity in the field of research on Arendt, it is astonishing that one question has remained (for the most part) ignored: the question of the nature and meaning of law in Hannah Arendt's thought. This forms the starting point of my work. I argue throughout this book that the question of law is a key issue in Arendt's thought.[8]

D'Entrèves 1994: 103; Gray 1979: 336; Habermas 1979: 302; Hermenau 1999; Heuer 1992: 348–70; H Jonas 1979: 355; Kateb 1984: 189; Minnich 1989: 136; Opstaele 1999: 97; Saavedra 2002; Villa 1996; Vollrath 1993; Zerilli 2005: 179.

[5] *Cf* on this point the study by Stefan Ahrens, *Die Gründung der Freiheit* (Ahrens 2005), as well as the excellent work by Jürgen Förster, *Die Sorge um die Welt und die Freiheit des Handelns* (Förster 2009). I address both works in ch 5. Additionally, see Kalyvas (2008) and Frank (2010).

[6] The discussion of Arendt's use of the banality of evil has raged since the publication of the Eichmann book. Contributions by Agamben (Agamben 1999: 70ff), Zimmermann (Zimmermann 2005: 30ff) and Bernstein (Bernstein 2007) have drawn the question back into the foreground (see on this point my remarks in Volk 2007). For the history of the reception of the Eichmann book, the two conference volumes *Hannah Arendt Revisited: Eichmann in Jerusalem und die Folgen* and *Hannah Arendt in Jerusalem* are of particular importance. On the history of the reception of the banality theory and a comprehensive overview of the literature and commentary, see also my remarks in Volk (2005: 9–20) and Volk (2006), as well as Villa (1999).

[7] Hannah Arendt's *Denktagebücher* (journals of thoughts), edited by Ursula Ludz and Ingeborg Nordmann and published in 2003, are absolutely crucial to my work. Equally important is the essay *The Great Tradition*, which was published by Kohn in two special issues of the journal *Social Research* in 2007 and 2008, as well as the volume of essays *The Jewish Writings* of 2007, which shows nicely the shifts within Arendt's approach to the concept of 'nation'.

[8] When this book was published in German in January 2010, it was the first to analyse the concept of law in Hannah Arendt's thought conceptually and systematically. Along with an article by Jeremy Waldron, which stresses the significance of 'structure, formality, and procedure' (Waldron 2005: 202) for Arendt, and thus also emphasises the value of legal questions (see on this point ch 5), Jan Klabbers and Hans Lindahl are among the few who have also examined—albeit also only in essay form—the question of law in Arendt's thought. While Klabbers, for example, claims at the beginning to be able to identify an 'intimate and reciprocal relationship between law and politics' (Klabbers 2007: 2) in her thought, he provides only a few pointers as to how Arendt's views on the Eichmann process might enrich our understanding of international law. He concludes, 'Arendt never was very clear on law, in particular on legislation. She lacked the legal background to capture some of the technicalities' (Klabbers 2007: 11). This statement is true as regards the specific implementation of legal problems, but it by no means applies to legal-philosophical questions. But this legal-philosophical dimension is revealed only by examining Arendt's political-theoretical discourse for its legal-philosophical content, or by directing attention to legal-philosophical questions. In his instructive remarks Klabbers keeps to individual references; he does not intend a systematic reconstruction. In the intervening years a whole range of studies on the legal concept in Hannah Arendt's work has appeared. Stefanie Rosenmüller's (2013a) dissertation on the position of law in Hannah Arendt's thought is certainly one of the most important of these, focusing on the question of the rationality of judicial decisions. Also worth mentioning is the anthology *Hannah Arendt and the Law* by Goldoni and McCorkindale (2012) (see, inter alia, my review of the book in Volk 2013b). For the most part, however, the question of law in Hannah Arendt's thought has been examined only in essay form. See eg Rosenmüller (2009; 2013b); Waldron 2005; Lindahl 2006; and Maxwell 2012.

There are reasons for the lack of attention to the question of the law in the field of Arendt research to date: none of Arendt's works addresses explicitly or primarily the question of the law. Arendt's analysis of law does not appear to be particularly systematic, but is instead at first glance episodic, indeed sporadic, in nature. Nevertheless, I shall demonstrate that Arendt's analysis of legal questions is indeed continuous and systematic. To date only a few of these passages have been examined in the field of Arendt research, for example her thoughts on the aporia of human rights or on the Eichmann case. Yet the focus on these Arendtian thoughts does not go beyond their relevant context in each case; it is not directed towards a comprehensive analysis of Arendt's concept of law, nor are the results analysed in that context, being seen merely as a position taken within the specific debates under discussion in each case. Thus the expression 'right to have rights' (ETH: 614) has been criticised, analysed and debated from the perspective of the moral-philosophical justification discourse,[9] critical questions have been raised as to whether human rights are aporia (Brunkhorst 1996 and Brunkhorst 1999: 95ff),[10] and Arendt's relationship to questions of democratic popular sovereignty has been problematised (Benhabib 2004: 60–69). It is a very similar matter with her thoughts on the law in the Eichmann book. Here too, Arendt's remarks on the significance of legal problems for the community, her critique of the '*nulla poena sine lege*' principle, her ideal verdict, her plea for an international criminal court, her category of crimes against humanity, all have been discussed widely and shrewdly but primarily—and most profitably—as part of the question of 'transformative justice'.[11] It is also the case with the Eichmann book that neither Arendt's legal-theoretical nor her legal-philosophical thoughts were ever drawn upon when considering the general position of the law in her thinking.[12]

The fact that it took quite a long time within Arendtian scholarship to consider reflecting upon the significance of law is due to the history of the exegesis of her work. For a very long period Arendt was regarded solely as the 'thinker of the polis' (Sternberger 1980 and Sternberger 1979). She was credited with regaining fundamental insights into the nature of the political by referring back to Greek antiquity, and was also criticised, against the same background, for romanticising antiquity (see Habermas 1977: 14f.; Springborg 1989: 12; Euben 2005: 152; O'Sullivan 1975: 228; O'Sullivan 1973). At any rate,

[9] See generally on this point Michelman 1996; Lefort 1988; Balibar 2004; Parekh 2004; Benhabib 2004; Benhabib 2006; Gosepath 2007.

[10] See also Rancière 2004.

[11] See especially Bilsky 2004 and Bilsky 2001.

[12] Linda Maxwell's deliberations mark a key exception. With reference to Arendt's Eichmann book, Maxwell elaborates 'Arendt's affirmation of law's dependence on political action' (Maxwell 2012: 104). I agree with this account, but I seek to demonstrate that there is *also* a dependence on law on the part of politics in Arendt's thoughts.

the polis was always regarded as the reference point against which to understand her thinking. In terms of Greek antiquity, her works were understood in the sense that Arendt considered the question of law to be pre-political. Evidence was purported to be found in those passages of *Human Condition/ Vita activa* in which Arendt allegedly subsumes the law, law-making and jurisdiction of the Greeks under the category of 'work' and separates it from the completely different nature of political action (VA: 241–51).[13]

Yet it proves untenable to assign to Arendt the role of an advocate for Greek antique forms of politics; a simplification proscribed by any interpretation that goes beyond *Vita activa*. Authors such as Margaret Canovan and Ernst Vollrath have always criticised such an interpretation of Arendt's work. As early as 1974, Canovan wrote that 'we have to abandon the conventional picture of Arendt judging modern politics in the light of a straightforward and unambiguous theory of action derived chiefly from an idealisation of Athens' (Canovan 1992: 138).[14] This position has prevailed in recent, more exegetic works by authors such as Tsao, Hammer and Tamineaux, who refer in particular to the importance of the Roman tradition in Arendt's thought.[15] The change in perspective from Athens to Rome made it possible to stress the moments of order safeguarding and order preservation in Arendt's thought, and to see them in the context of her understanding of the political. For Roman law is based precisely on the contractual idea: *pacta sunt servanda*. In the Roman tradition, however, contracts are not pre-political in character but rather have a genuine political core (*cf* Klabbers 2007: 10). Their political character lies in the fact that they establish a relationship between two or more persons, parties, countries, etc by means of 'proposals and counterproposals' (WiP: 109). Yet research on Arendt has not progressed any further on this point. While the idea of Arendt as a 'thinker of the polis' has now been abandoned, the consequences from the additional perspective of the Roman tradition have not been comprehensively captured.[16]

[13] See also HC: 192–99.

[14] See also Vollrath 1996: 138f.

[15] See on this point Tsao 2002 and Tamineaux 2000. Dean Hammer is quoted exemplarily at this point, who described the result of this new perspective on Arendt's work as follows: 'Only when different parts of the world appear indistinguishable can everything be indiscriminately devoured. The ability to distinguish brings with it, for Arendt, a corresponding desire to care for and preserve the things of the world. … The Romans offer just this possibility for Arendt by showing how political thinking can arise from, and evoke, a world that is sensually perceived' (Hammer 2002: 144f).

[16] Jürgen Förster's work represents the key exception here (Förster 2009). In his work the importance of institutions in Arendt's thought is reconstructed systematically and linked conceptually with her thinking. He thus goes even further than the important references made by Canovan (Canovan 1998) and Vollrath (Vollrath 1977).

If we try to understand why such an obvious step has not yet been taken, we are confronted with what is still regarded as the core of Arendt's understanding of political freedom and action: the beginning. Arendt is considered to be the 'thinker of the beginning' (Brumlik 2007: 312). Albrecht Wellmer speaks in this case of Arendt's 'revolutionary universalism' (Wellmer 1999: 130), which shows precisely no normative foundation. The various different protagonists in the field of Arendt research agree on this point of initiating unprecedented beginnings as the core idea of Arendt's political thinking—although they assess and evaluate this core idea very differently.[17] If one sees Arendt as the 'thinker of the beginning', and discerns the core of her understanding of the political in this beginning, then questions regarding the law as the 'stabilising factor' (CD: 79) of political order are of secondary importance.

Reconsidering the history of her work's reception therefore clearly reveals the key challenges for my undertaking: Any interpretation of Arendt's work that places the main emphasis on the question of the law—indeed which intends to show that it forms the centre of gravity of her thought—cannot avoid a renewed analysis of her concept of the political. With Arendt, an analysis of the law must always be accompanied by an analysis of her concept of politics as well. For it must expand Arendt's perspective as a 'thinker of the beginning' to include the problem of order and show that this is not a hierarchical relationship. In other words, such an endeavour must be in a position to unite the concept of order, as the 'fundamental category of the political',[18] with Arendt's thought.

Presenting this evidence requires me first to sketch the backdrop against which Arendt's considerations become plausible. That is her analysis of the European inter-war period, conducted mainly in *Elemente und Ursprünge totaler Herrschaft* and *Origins of Totalitarianism*. In the first chapter of this work, 'The Paradoxes of the Nation-State', I prove that the question of the political and legal order is a key issue in Arendt's thinking. For what the problem of refugees and minorities reveals to Arendt is the 'internal disintegration' (OT: 270) of

[17] In his excellent essay *The rule of the people: Arendt, Archê, and Democracy*, Patchen Markell develops an argument that corresponds to a certain degree with mine. Markell argues that democratic theorists have been too captured by the interruption/stability binary and, therefore, interpreted Arendt's remarks on political new beginnings merely as something that can only happen through interruption, rather than through practices of responsiveness: 'Correspondingly, Arendt's aim is not simply to rehabilitate those phenomena that, within that matrix, are positioned as rule's opposites: on her use, "beginning" picks out not the spontaneous disruption of existing patterns, but the sense in which action, whether disruptive or not, involves attention and responsiveness to worldly events; and what threatens "beginning" thus understood is not the enforcement of regularity, but the erosion of the context in which events call for responses and, thus, in which it makes sense to act at all' (Markell 2006: 2).

[18] See on this point the excellent study by Andreas Anter, entitled *Die Macht der Ordnung. Aspekte einer Grundkategorie des Politischen* (Anter 2007), which inspired many of my thoughts.

an order of nation-states. For Arendt this process of disintegration, as I argue in chapter one, is in the first instance a disintegration of the constitutional foundation of the nation-state—its order, so to speak. With this analysis of the inter-war period, Arendt exemplifies the impracticability of a nation-state form of government in a globalising world.

From the methodical perspective the intention is to capture the theoretical content of Arendt's description of the inter-war period by analysing the 'paradoxes of the nation-state'. This theoretical content of Arendt's analysis is manifested in the fact that law, politics and order are related internally to one another. However, in this chapter the terms 'state' and 'nation' must first be defined. The insights gained from this approach—in particular, highlighting the order problematic on the one hand as a legal problem and presenting it, on the other hand, as the central aspect of Arendt's thoughts—are accompanied by the drawback of having to adopt (temporarily) Arendt's concept of the nation-state, instead of tracing the origin of the term systematically. I counter this drawback in my second and third chapters by conducting an in-depth analysis of Arendt's concept of the *nation-state*. The subject of chapter two is Arendt's concept of the nation, or more precisely the political-theoretical dimension of this concept. The term 'nation' is used in many different ways by Arendt, but it is only by working out the conceptual dimension—I call it the political-theoretical dimension—that we can penetrate to the origin of the structural contradictions of a nation-state order. Arendt's reflection on this political-theoretical dimension of the concept of nation is conducted in her analysis of Rousseau in *On Revolution*. By explaining the context of Arendt's Rousseau discourse with the realignment of the social question for the French Revolution, her specific interpretation of Rousseau's *volonté générale* becomes clear. By these means, Arendt's discourse on pity—previously ignored in the research—attains an unforeseen political-theoretical significance: for Arendt, pity is not only the decisive emotional resource for the Rousseauean demand for 'total alienation' (Rousseau [1762] 2012: 50), but Arendt's discourse on pity is at the same time the analysis of the internal arrangement of the concept of 'nation'.

Once I have examined Arendt's concept of the nation, I turn in chapter three to her understanding of the modern state. I underline that Arendt's understanding of the state is inspired by Max Weber. Weber described and analysed, like no other author before him, the origin and nature of the Continental European state in all of its facets. I show that the modern state is 'a rationally organized institution' (*rationaler Anstaltsstaat*) (EaS: 653) for Arendt too. 'Formal-rational law' marks the core of this concept of state. In her thoughts on imperialism in particular, Arendt held the formal-rational concept of law up against the governmental practice of imperialist apparatuses of domination. In contrast to the imperialistic regime of decrees, rational law is characterised precisely by its reliability and verifiability.[19]

The two chapters belong together in so far as they complete Arendt's picture of the European nation-state. With the French Revolution, the nation as a political idea of order is united with the state as a guarantor of order to form the nation-state. This liaison between the nation and the modern, Continental European state is, as I shall demonstrate in my fourth chapter, problematic in two respects: the first section of the chapter, 'II. Popular Sovereignty and the Law' makes it clear that the national will is unsuitable as a source of law, as it deprives the law of its reliability and verifiability—its rationality, so to speak. The thesis is that the claim to absoluteness of the general will merely permits substantially undetermined law that is defined each time anew, depending on national mood and disposition. I shall present this Arendtian criticism as her legal-philosophical critique of popular sovereignty. She makes it clear that the rationality of law—in the sense of an 'impartial' and autonomous legal sphere—can be realised only on the basis of a different understanding of the political.

Yet the risk to the stability of the political order is caused not only by the nation as a concept of order, but also—as demonstrated in the second section of chapter four, 'III. Popular Sovereignty and Politics'—by the modern (Continental European) state, with its hierarchical structure and centralised power. Since the structural-hierarchical composition of the modern state does not provide any space for the political participation of its citizens, it forces phenomena such as political 'massing' (OT: 316), lack of political experience and the feeling of political insignificance. This provides the ideal breeding ground on which antidemocratic mass movements of all kinds can flourish. In short, Hannah Arendt's political thinking is a critique of the state as a hierarchical and centralised form of government and political order. However, what is crucial in this context is the fact that this structural composition is the prerequisite for how law can be rational in the Continental European tradition of political thought. In this manner the concept of law itself becomes the focus of criticism: within the Continental European tradition the rationality of the law comes along with the formalisation of politics, which itself triggers those effects that precisely undermine that which the rational law is supposed to preserve: the stability and permanence of the political order. In order for law to be 'rational', therefore, not only is a different understanding of the political required, but also a different understanding of law. The internal connection between law and politics must be acknowledged.

[19] At the same time, however, Arendt points out that it is precisely this Continental European idea of law, state and statehood that drives the European states to imperialism. *Cf* ch 3.

The task in my fifth and final chapter is to spell out the consequences of this internal connection. Arendt's interpretation of power as a fundamental condition of every community has consequences both for the concept of the political and for that of law. In Arendtian thought, law is *desubstantialised* and becomes a relational concept, a relationship-establishing concept. I shall point out that the law is not an expression of power; rather, it elucidates the existing power constellation. On the other hand, however, power is not only an 'emancipatory' (Meints-Stender 2012: 199)[20] or 'intrinsically normatively positive' (Allen 2010: 143) concept for Arendt. Quite the contrary: there are power constellations that actually inhibit diversity of opinion and plurality. By differentiating those power constellations from the ones preferred by Arendt, I shall reveal in stages the normative foundation of Arendt's understanding of the political. The very fact that Arendt demands an 'ethics of power developed on the basis of the power of judgement' (DT: 818) makes such an undertaking reasonable and important. With this in mind I argue that the normative content of her understanding of the political lies hidden in a specific form of political action—namely, 'acting with one another', which should be distinguished from 'acting for one another' as well as from 'acting against one another' (see HC: 180)—which realises in its conduct and performance the procedural requirements of the power of judgement. This specific kind of normativity of the political has consequences for the law: if law is a relational, relationship-establishing concept, then legitimate law is an enabling concept in Arendt's view. Legitimate law opens up an enabling space in which a political 'acting with one another' on the basis of the power of judgement *can be* realised by means of legally guaranteed procedures and institutions. To grasp the impact of Arendt's thoughts on the power of judgement properly, one need *not* (in the first instance) interpret them as a concept of practical wisdom, but rather consider the 'methodical procedure' (Vollrath 1987: 271) of finding judgement. It is only due to this procedure that we can speak of the 'rationality of the power of judgement' (Vollrath 1987: 253). For Arendt, the power of judgement is the reply to her search for a political type of rationality that enables a permanent, stable and free political order beyond the traditional forms of the *raison d'état*. In the course of this book I shall show that this type of political rationality arose from the deconstruction of other concepts and understandings of rationality. Rational in an Arendtian sense is not that which appears to be efficient against the backdrop of a means-costs calculation, but rather that which maintains a free political order, in and through which political conflict can be conducted. I shall illustrate that Arendt reconstructs elements and traces of the formation of this 'rationality of the power of judgement'—of a 'politics of the power of judgement' as

[20] See also Parekh 1981: 160ff; Luban 1979.

Dick Howard called it (Howard 2001: 25)—both in the foundation of and in the institutions of the American Republic. For Arendt, the American Republic differs fundamentally from the Continental European tradition due to this special type of political rationality.

Before I develop my arguments, I wish to reflect briefly on the expression contained in the subtitle of this book, 'The Order of Freedom'.[21] This title reflects those aspects of Arendt's thought that have long been regarded as irreconcilable: freedom and order. In that respect the title condenses the very core of my argument. Generally speaking, in this context order means a set of political institutions and abstract juridico-political normative principles which determine and maintain a specific form of political interaction. In other words: it is of paramount importance for Arendt to see political freedom in the context of institutionalised forms relating to ourselves and others. Accordingly, I will argue that political freedom in the Arendtian sense cannot mean the 'caesura' (Abensour 2012: 91), the specific breaking through of an order; the realisation of an as yet unrealised form of political equality (see Rancière 2002: 24–29)[22] or the 'creation of a new hegemony' (Mouffe 2007: 70). Political freedom in an Arendtian understanding does not amount to the instituting of the social (see Castoriadis 1990) or 'the extraordinary deed of collective self-institution' (Kalyvas 2008: 204). And Arendt's concept of political freedom cannot be considered part of the moral-philosophical tradition of autonomy thinking either, which, applied to democratic theory, regards freedom as the unforced identity between the individual and the collective will, brought about by rational discourse (see eg FuG: 134). During the course of this book, I shall demonstrate that Arendt's concept of political freedom can best be understood as representing the experience of having the power to act in political and public affairs.[23] Such an understanding of freedom relies on an institutionally guaranteed and perpetuated political space in which 'acting with one another' can be performed, conducted and can occur. I argue that Arendt, therefore, was very much concerned with the question of an adequate arrangement of law, politics and order—the so-called triad of constitutionalism—and considers suitable forms for the institutionalisation of conflict-ridden political action.[24] By adopting this approach, I present an alternative interpretation of Arendt's thought, which sees Arendt neither as the advocate of ancient political forms (Aristotelian communitarianism) nor fully in line with discourse-theoretical, existenialist or radical-democratic premises. In my view, Arendt is a thinker

[21] The title of the German version of this book is *Die Ordnung der Freiheit. Recht und Politik im Denken Hannah Arendts*.

[22] See also Frank 2010: 45 and 210.

[23] The German formulation is *Politische Freiheit als das Erfahren des politischen Handeln-Könnens*.

[24] Here we see the proximity to Claude Lefort's thinking, for whom the institutionalisation of conflict within society marks the core of a system of democracy. (See Lefort 1990: 293.)

of political order who is concerned with and highlights the importance of a durable, stable and free political order in and through which political struggle and dissent can happen and appear. The modern state, however, as a hierarchically structured and centralised power complex, is incapable of providing and securing such an order. Although Hannah Arendt is a thinker of order, she is nevertheless a critic of the state (see MuG: 130). Her entire political work, therefore, can be read and understood as searching for a new and alternative conception of order, new and alternative 'manifestations and materializations of power' (OV: 140) and a new and alternative organisational logic of political life. This kind of characterisation—advocating order but criticising the state—can be exemplified by her appraisal of the revolutionary institutions of order formation:

> [N]othing indeed contradicts more sharply the old adage of the anarchistic and lawless 'natural' inclinations of a people left without the constraint of its government than the emergence of the councils that, wherever they appeared, and most pronouncedly during the Hungarian Revolution, were concerned with the reorganization of the political and economic life of the country and *the establishment of a new order*. (OR: 275, emphasis added)

In addition, however, the expression 'The Order of Freedom' also refers to two further dimensions of meaning, one hermeneutic, the other relating to the history of ideas. On the latter dimension, Walter Benjamin and Hannah Arendt were friends. They conducted regular correspondence with each other and played chess together, and after the suicide of her friend Arendt published some of his works in the USA. Seyla Benhabib drew attention to the extent to which Arendt's methodical approach was inspired by Benjamin's 'fragmentary historiography' (Benhabib 2006: 158), indeed how much Arendt adapted Benjamin's thought for her own treatment of historical material. The pair's relationship has only recently been documented, impressively, in a volume with texts, letters and notes. In their introduction, the editors, Erdmut Wizisla and Detlev Schöttker, address a matter that has long occupied students of Arendt. They write:

> There is no reference to Benjamin in Arendt's work *On Violence* (1970), although she addresses questions and topics there to which he also devoted his key considerations: the first part concerns the concept of progress, which forms the core of the theses 'On the Concept of History', and in the second part Arendt refers to Georges Sorel's work *Reflections on Violence*, which Benjamin addresses in his essay 'The Critique of Violence' (1921). (Schöttker and Wizisla 2006: 41)

The reason given by the editors is that Arendt had no truck 'with Benjamin's political metaphysics and aesthetics' (Schöttker and Wizisla 2006: 41). As far as political metaphysics are concerned, this is certainly true. Benjamin's thoughts on 'divine violence' (Benjamin [1920–21] 1965: 60) in his essay 'Zur Kritik der

Gewalt' are diametrically opposed to Arendt's thinking. The fact that Arendt does not criticise him by name in her publications is probably a sign of her reverent attachment to her deceased friend. Yet at the same time it is difficult, when examining the law, to circumvent Benjamin's thesis that violence is behind *every* law—in other words, that one is always directly entangled with violence, irrespective of the form of political organisation. Benjamin is most insistent in this respect in his discussion of pacifism. The core of his argument is that pacifists' criticism of violence is restricted to compulsory military service, but does not question the legal order itself. Benjamin criticises such a view as 'naive', as it completely ignores the fact that compulsory military service is an 'application of law-upholding force' (Benjamin [1920–21] 1965: 40). Any criticism of violence must also contain a 'criticism of all authoritarian force' (Benjamin [1920–21] 1965: 40). If one ignores 'childish anarchism' (Benjamin [1920–21] 1965: 41) then not even Kant's categorical imperative is adequate for such a critique. For Benjamin, every positive law 'will certainly claim to acknowledge and promote the interest of mankind in the person of each individual'—at least if it is 'conscious of its roots' (Benjamin [1920–21] 1965: 41), ie if it refers to some kind of system of norms. The law should 'represent' and 'uphold' precisely that order contained in the system of norms. Benjamin formulates the programmatic sentence of his essay against this background:

> While this view [of order], which claims to preserve law in its very basis, cannot escape criticism, nevertheless all attacks that are made merely in the name of a formless 'freedom' without being able to specify this higher *order of freedom* remain impotent against it. (Benjamin [1921] 1965: 41, emphasis added)

Benjamin famously places this new order of freedom in the hands of Messianic violence. By using the words 'The Order of Freedom' both in the subtitle of this book and as the title of the last chapter, I refer to the fact that Arendt's thoughts on law and politics have to be conceived of as a consideration of the problem of law and violence as outlined by Benjamin. But Arendt's reply is fundamentally different in nature from that of Benjamin.

The title of my work not only refers to the history of ideas, but also has a hermeneutic dimension: according to Gadamer, 'part of understanding is that we regain the concepts of a historical past in such a way that they include our own comprehension of them' (Gadamer 1975: 356). Gadamer calls the intertwining of past and present in textual interpretation a 'fusion of horizons' (Gadamer 1975: 290). In this context he speaks of the 'hermeneutic necessity' to go beyond 'mere reconstruction' and to 'enter into the openness of the question' (Gadamer 1975: 356) in the process of understanding. In other words, to think what the author did not think. Therefore, if one sets out to interpret a thinker in the fields of political philosophy, political theory and the history of ideas, then one must not only be aware of the historical, social and political questions and problems in which the work is embedded and to which it reacts, but also reflect on one's own situation as an interpreter.[25] In this manner the reflection of hermeneutics as a method of political theory, and the 'fusion of horizons' as one of its consequences, lead back once more to Arendt as the 'thinker of the beginning': to be sure, Arendt's thought can and must also be interpreted as a consideration of beginning. It is very likely that anyone who works through the almost 1,000 pages of *Elemente und Ursprünge totaler Herrschaft*, or even the 530 pages of *Origins of Totalitarianism*, notices with some astonishment and no little emotion at the end of this story of terror and extermination Arendt's confidence in the unconditionality of 'a new beginning' and her recourse to St Augustine's *initium ut esset, creatus est homo* (ETH: 979; OT: 479).[26]

If we look at the history of reception, this kind of interpretation—Arendt's 'revolutionary universalism'—breaks implicitly with the conservative interpretation of her thought, namely Arendt as a theorist of anti-totalitarianism, which was represented by a conservative German and American elite of professors in the 1960s and 1970s and which made Arendt so unattractive as a reference for the student movement.[27] If we also realise that the scientific emphasis of Arendt as a theorist of the beginning occurred at the same time as the collapse of Soviet imperialism and the Eastern European freedom movements—which is not a new finding but a commonplace in the history of political ideas—then the significance of the 'fusion of horizons' becomes more tangible in the interpretation of her work. The revolutions in Eastern Europe were just as unexpected by the field of political theory as they were in reality. The revolutionary political new beginning had no place in the debates on system theory and questions of justice. No political author and no political theory at the time could make sense of political new beginnings in conceptual terms. In contrast to this and especially in contrast to the narrow economistic theory of revolution of the Marxist tradition, Arendt's work provided the possibility to understand in political terms this unexpected breach with the old system. The revolutions in Eastern Europe, therefore, represent the contemporary historical core located in the specific interpretation of Arendt as a thinker of new beginnings.

[25] See Benhabib 2006: 22f.

[26] See on this point also the analysis of the concept of natality by Bowen-Moore 1989.

[27] The reasons why Arendt was so unattractive for the student movement were not only her thoughts on total domination, which referred unsparingly to the terror of Soviet communism, but also because no critique of capitalism is apparent at first glance. For decades, her criticism of modernity was interpreted as a reclamation of antiquity. Works by Isaac 1992, Jaeggi 1997, Benhabib 2006, etc have shown just how oblique such an assessment actually is (see on this point also my remarks on the architecture of modernity with Arendt in Volk 2005: 60–113).

Being able to begin has not lost its validity for an interpretation of Arendt's work in 2015—and indeed how could it, against the background of the Occupy Movement or what has recently become known as the 'Arab Spring'. But the 'horizon of the present' (Gadamer 1975: 289) has also changed to some extent. From a geographical perspective the interpretation of Arendt's thought is less inspired by events in Warsaw, Prague, Budapest or Riga than it was in the late 1980s and early 1990s. Today, instead, places like Guantánamo, Lampedusa, Ceuta, the Mashriq region or the Sonoran Desert are in the foreground. The tightening of security laws in Western democracies, including the suspension of rights for suspects in the worldwide war on terror, the incapability of political action on the part of a supposed world community in the face of mass crimes, the worldwide wiretapping and monitoring of citizens, and the daily tragedies on the borders of this world, especially of 'Fortress Europe', form the horizon with which one approaches Hannah Arendt's political thought at the beginning of the twenty-first century. The belief that one might find possible connections in Hannah Arendt's work results from the knowledge that Arendt's political thought arises from the confrontation with crisis. For her thesis of lawlessness as a first step in the 'lengthy process of preparing for the extermination of humans' (ETH: 612)[28] is not only the result of theoretical reflection; this lawlessness was a real experience for Arendt, which shaped her own horizon. She lost her German citizenship in 1937 as a result of the Reich Citizens Act, and was to remain stateless until 1951. Arendt once wrote to Günther Anders that her American passport was the 'most beautiful book' that she knew (Alte Synagoge 1997: 46). The question of the *order of freedom* is therefore the intrinsic question in the life and political thought of Hannah Arendt. The aim of this book is to enrich the reception of her work by revealing the systematic significance of political order and law in Hannah Arendt's thought.

[28] See also OT: 296.

# 1

# *The Paradoxes of the Nation-State*

Whoever was ejected from the old trinity of people-territory-state, on which the nation was based, by the events arising remained homeless and stateless; whoever had lost the rights enshrined in citizenship remained rightless. Nothing that had ever really happened since the First World War could ever be repaired, and no calamity, not even the outbreak of a Second World War, could be prevented. Every event had the quality of a catastrophe, and every catastrophe was final.

Hannah Arendt, *Elemente und Ursprünge totaler Herrschaft*

For some months I have wandering around, boosted one hundred percent by an apocalyptic Schadenfreude when I think about the European porcelain shop and about the cyclone that is starting to approach its centre with mathematical precision.

Letter by Ernst Jünger to Gerhard Günther, 3 October 1930

## I. INTRODUCTION

HANNAH ARENDT'S ANALYSIS of the minority and refugee problem in the European inter-war period has found broad appeal, especially beyond the field of political theory in its narrowest sense.[1] Authors such as Michael Marrus, Claudena Skran, Gérard Noiriel or Aristide Zolberg all refer to Arendt's work in their studies on minorities and refugees. Aristide Zolberg, for instance, states that Arendt's analysis of the inter-war period 'provides the principal key for understanding how refugees come about' (Zolberg 1983: 30).[2] He concludes that in her work Arendt links the refugee and

[1] Within political theory Arendt's considerations on statelessness are mainly discussed under the scope of human rights (see eg Birmingham 2006; Benhabib 2004; Parekh 2004; Michelman 1996; Brunkhorst 1996). In their works Waltraud Meints-Stender and Wolfgang Heuer address the same issue from the perspective of the political problem of exclusion (see Meints-Stender 2007 and Heuer 2007).

[2] With regard to Arendt's considerations, Aristide Zolberg makes two modifications: as well as the ethnic heterogeneity, he points to religious differences as the cause of refugee movements. In addition, he stresses that every revolution causes flows of refugees, as the members of the old regime are driven out or flee (see Zolberg 1983: 30f).

minority problems directly to the spread of the idea of the nation-state to eastern and south-eastern states. In agreement with Arendt, Claudena Skran maintains that from the perspective of the new national governments the minorities posed a problem, 'because they do not fit within the normal parameters of a world of nation-states'. The massive streams of refugees, Skran continues, were 'by-products of efforts to achieve ethnically pure nation-states and ideologically homogeneous political systems' (Skran 1995: 29). As Michael Marrus points out, the main reason for referring to Arendt's studies by authors dealing with refugee and minority issues is that Arendt was one of the first to highlight 'the singular predicament of refugees' and to describe 'how they were reduced to a lonely, savage existence, hounded from place to place by national governments that alone accorded to people elementary rights' (Marrus 1985: 4).

Although Zolberg, Skran and Marrus emphasise an important argument within Arendt's considerations, I argue that the narrative upon which they base their arguments is problematic. With respect to their object of inquiry, all three speak of the nation-state as a sovereign actor that pursues its interests independently and which thus bears responsibility for the precarious humanitarian situation of the refugees. Yet if one considers Arendt's analysis from the perspective of political theory, that narrative of the nation-state as a sovereign actor is misleading. The refugee and minority problem, I argue, discloses the 'internal disintegration' (OT: 270) of an order of nation-states and the impracticality of its concepts in a globalised world. For Arendt, the minority problem does not demonstrate the sovereignty of the nation-state but rather its inappropriateness as a form of government and the concurrent fall of a Europe composed of nation-states. Against the background of the inter-war period, the question of the reliability, stability and durability of a political order represented by the nation-state becomes the lynchpin of her analysis.

The argument that Arendt is concerned with the problem of political order stands out for two reasons. Generally, Arendt is not considered as a thinker of order but as a thinker of contingency, of revolutionary beginning. Accordingly, Albrecht Wellmer stresses Arendt's 'revolutionary universalism' (Wellmer 2000: 224), in which 'no extra-political normative foundation secures or justifies' (Wellmer 2000: 229). If one examines her work purely from the perspective of contingency and revolutionary beginnings, it might not be apparent how one can associate her thinking with the questions on political order.[3] Irrespective of questions about order and revolution, about contingency and new beginnings,

[3] The fact that order and new beginning are directly connected with each other results from the loss of power and authority of an old order that precedes a new political beginning such as a revolution. In *On Revolution*, Arendt therefore writes that 'a revolution did not end with the abolition of state and government but, on the contrary, aimed at the foundation of a new state and the establishment of a new form of government' (OR: 265).

my evaluation might bemuse for a second reason: discussing the inter-war period from the perspective of the decline of order directly concurs with the tenor of the debates within state theory of that time. Since Bodin, the question of political order has been the central question of state theory; in the inter-war period German political thinkers in particular centred their critique of the '*System Weimar*' on the question of order—regardless of their political and ideological positions. Max Weber, for instance, says that the main purpose of the state was 'to enforce its system of order' (EaS: 55). Hans Kelsen asserts that 'the modern state is essentially a coercive order—a centralized coercive order' (Kelsen [1934] 2002: 54). For Carl Schmitt, Kelsen's strongest critic, 'public safety and order' represents not only the highest 'state interest' (Schmitt [1922] 2004: 13), but also the basis for his theory of sovereignty. Additionally, in his later work, Schmitt describes his own state-theory as 'concrete order thinking' (Schmitt [1934] 1993: 10). Rudolf Smend, a further opponent of Kelsen, defines the state as a rule that exists 'by virtue of an order' (Smend [1945] 1994: 368). For Hermann Heller, the 'question of the relation between rule and order' is the 'basic problem of all state-theories' (Heller [1927] 1971: 57).[4] Because none of Arendt's books *seems* to deal explicitly with the triad of 'state, law, and order', it is considered a remote notion to link Arendt to these discussions on state theory.

In what follows, I shall fill this void and show how far Arendt's thinking is indeed occupied with the relation between the state, law and order. However, Arendt does not reflect on political order on the basis of anthropological, moral or ethical assumptions.[5] Rather, her criticism is *immanent* and starts with the self-perception and self-description of nation-states. What does this mean? Seen from a system-analytical perspective, the nation-state is a form of government that, according to Arendt, is based on specific principles, which interact and then result in a certain form of order—the national governmental order.

[4] In his study of German state theorists who addressed the issue of order, Andreas Anter makes a valid point when he writes that '[t]he history of German ideas of order is one of yearning: the yearning for unity, integration and community' (Anter 2007: 226).

[5] Such a path was taken by Leo Strauss, for example (Strauss 1956). It is therefore not surprising that Harald Bluhm makes the first cautious attempt, in his study of Strauss, to draw the problem of order into the foreground for Arendt's thought too. At the level of the criticism of modernity, Bluhm draws the arc from Strauss via Voegelin to Arendt, and labels all three thinkers of order (see Bluhm 2002). What is questionable about Bluhm's initially convincing categorisation is that he *anthropologises* Arendt's order-critical perspective. Arendt's critique, says Bluhm, is based on a 'formal anthropology', which for its part seeks a 'reflection of antiquity, of the genuine political thought of the Greeks' (Bluhm 2002: 247). By now a number of special studies have demonstrated convincingly that the thesis of Arendt's 'Hellenistic nostalgia' (O'Sullivan 1975) must be revised. The tenor of these studies is that Greek antiquity can no longer serve as a normative backdrop to Arendt's criticism. Yet this does not remove Bluhm's 'accentuation of the problem of order' (Bluhm 2002: 248); rather, it must be located elsewhere. For the question of political order is indeed central to Arendt's thinking.

Without claiming comprehensiveness, Arendt lists, for example, peoples' right to self-determination, the identity of state and nation, the idea of democratic sovereignty of the people, state sovereignty, *Rechtstaatlichkeit* (constitutionality), etc. The principle of constitutionality is especially pivotal for the stability, security and reliability of a nation-state order. The nation-state, Arendt writes, is 'characteristically a constitutional state' (NuD).[6] In her analysis of the inter-war period she compares the actual behaviour of the European states with their self-perception and their attempts to secure peace after the disastrous experiences of World War I. Arendt comes to the conclusion that a Europe of nation-states, due to the principles of order to which it was committed and with which it attempted to grasp reality, at no time was in a position to solve or to defuse the problems posed by refugees and minorities. Because of this, the legal and political foundation of the nation-states started dissolving and—both facts are directly linked—the relationship between the different states got poisoned. This points to Arendt's assumption that within a Europe based on the principles of a nation-state order, 'a guaranteed peace on earth is as utopian as the squaring of the circle' (TPR: 229).

In this chapter I demonstrate that Arendt's assertion of the decline of a constitutional order can be determined mainly by four *paradoxes of the nation-state.* I present her argument of the 'collapse of the system of nation-state' (OT: 22), and provide tangible and concrete characteristics for the understanding of the paradoxes of the system of the nation-state. These inner contradictions—the *paradox of the right to self-determination*, the *paradox of de-assimilation and de-naturalisation*, the *paradox of rightlessness*, the *paradox of human rights*—which are a direct result of the principles of the nation-state, developed their subversive potential in the inter-war period. There is not one single paradox that justifies the claim of a Europe-wide breakdown of all national state order by itself. It also does not coincide with Arendt's idea of 'fragmentary historiography' (Benhabib 2003: 94) to try to find a closed theory or a historical chronology behind her discussion of the disintegration of order. The aim rather must be to sketch a picture in which the relation between the order-endangering potential of the paradoxes becomes apparent and thus provides an impression of the '*Totalgeschehen*' (Benjamin [1928–40] 1991: 575). However, the 'decline of the nation-state' (OT: 267) is more than just the end of a form of government. Along with the nation-state '*a whole way of life*' (WiP: 226) perished,

[6] Here I quote from *Nationalstaat und Demokratie.* The German text reads: 'Denn dass der Nationalstaat in seinem Wesen ein Rechts- und Verfassungsstaat und nur als solcher lebensfähig war, hatte sich bereits in Anfängen vorher erwiesen und sollte vor allem nach dem zweiten Weltkrieg ganz offenbar werden.' Arendt delivered this paper in a German broadcast on WDR in 1963 during a discussion with Eugen Kogon. Whenever it is appropriate, I shall also mention the German text on which my own translation is based.

and its moral standards and values, which had previously been supported by a legal-political order, vanished from public life. The collaboration of many European societies with the Nazis in the extermination of the European Jews and the 'disgracefully little resistance' (ETH: 600) encountered by the Gestapo in the national police forces of the conquered countries are only the most striking examples of these far-reaching consequences, prompting Arendt to speak famously of the 'totality of the moral collapse' (EJ: 125) in Europe. Added to this of course is the absolute rightlessness of the stateless in general and of Jewish refugees in particular, which represents for Arendt a key step in the 'rather lengthy process of the preparation for the extermination of human beings' (ETH: 612).[7] Without in the least wishing to address any questions of specific responsibility or guilt, in her view the dependencies exist between European asylum and border policy on the one hand and the immense number of victims of a National Socialist policy of extermination on the other. Not least for this reason does the decline of a Europe of nation-states take such a prominent position in Arendt's analysis of totalitarianism.

Precisely the fact that she embeds her analysis of the nation-state in the context of the elements of totalitarianism prompts questions as to method. For although Arendt sets a large amount of historical material and historical description in motion in order to work out the impracticability of a nation-state form of order, she provides no scientific or historical treatment of the inter-war period. In view of the 'rupture of civilization' (*Zivilisationsbruch*), she sees the need for a completely different treatment of history. As is known, Walter Benjamin provides her with the direction in this case. In line with his thoughts, Arendt's methods can be called 'fragmentary historiography' (Benhabib 2003: 158): Arendt gathers together '"thought fragments"' (WB: 230), analyses them, reorders them and places them in a new context of meaning, allowing the 'crystal of the total event' (Benjamin [1928–40] 1991: 575) (*Kristall des Totalgeschehens*) to form. Like Benjamin, who compares his own treatment of quotations with roadside robbers who attack and relieve

[7] Arendt states here that this process began with the explanation 'that the Jews are second-class citizens, went from the withdrawal of citizenship to the deportation to the ghettos and concentration camps, from where they were once again offered up to the world, now as the absolute rightless, in order to see if anyone would claim them: only when their "superfluity" or statelessness in the whole of humanity could be proven were they then exterminated' (ETH: 612). Arendt underlines hereby that 'the right to life' is questioned only 'when the absolute rightlessness—and that means, that nobody can be found who is willing to guarantee rights for this particular category of people—is a fait accompli' (ETH: 612). Skran comments on this point that the insight into the connection between frontier closures and the number of Holocaust victims after 1945 did not lead to a 'change in the asylum norm'. While there had been several attempts 'to incorporate in international law a "right to asylum" for individuals', it was not possible to agree on actually adopting the phrase 'to be granted'. Ultimately only the 'rule of non-refoulement' was codified (Skran 1995: 178).

the 'idler' of his convictions, Arendt also removes facts and events from their traditional context and places them in a new political narrative (*cf* Disch 1994: 188). This narrative is obliged to both the 'phenomenal character of political events and occurrences' (Vollrath 1979b: 65) and to the 'present as such' (WB: 236). The claim of Arendt's political thought to be very 'present'[8] is expressed in it. Against this methodical background, the intention is not to preserve or retell the past as it was, but rather as it appears from the present-day perspective. Historical facts do not become random as a result, but they never speak for themselves. The same also applies, in turn, to Arendt's historical remarks: these do not represent so much a factual description of historical events but instead represent illustrative political thought. The 'in some sense meaningful, symbolic' (WB: 231) nature of past events appears to the present only when it is embedded in a narrative. Arendt's thesis of the decline of Europe's nation-state order therefore should not be seen as merely *one* element in her view of total rule, but at the same time as an interventionist pointer to the fact that the nation-state is impracticable as a form of government for a globalised world. Although it might be legitimate to charge Arendt with not having described certain historical events adequately, and with limping behind the latest state of historical research with her remarks, it remains questionable as to whether anything can be gained by such a critique, because Arendt's merits reside in her conceptual conclusions.[9] In the first instance, therefore, this chapter will examine Arendt's political-theoretical argument of the decline of the nation-state, and prove that the triad of state, law and order most certainly forms the basis of her political thought. For this purpose, and fully aware that we are not concerned with historically secured findings, I shall follow Arendt's historical remarks and derive from these her political-theoretical argument.

## II. THE PARADOX OF THE RIGHT TO SELF-DETERMINATION

The first paradox that endangers the order of the nation-states may be identified as the right to national self-determination, one of the fundamental principles of the European nation-state model. Sieyès was one of the first who stipulated that 'every nation ought to be … free' (Sieyès [1789] 1988: 77). Ernest Renan sees in 'the wish of the nation … the sole legitimate criterion, the one to which one must always return' (Renan [1882] 1996: 36), and thus

[8] I refer here to the Jaspers quotation with which Arendt opens *Elemente und Ursprünge totaler Herrschaft* as well as *Origins of Totalitarianism*: '"Weder dem Vergangenen anheimfallen noch dem Zukünftigen. Es kommt darauf an, ganz gegenwärtig zu sein"' (ETH: 5).

[9] It would be of interest only if, based on a different emphasis of historical events, one were to arrive at a different narrative that questions Arendt's political-theoretical statements in general. I shall indicate such new emphases at the appropriate points in the course of this work (see ch 2).

further develops the liberating and emancipating idea of self-determination more than 100 years after the French Revolution. Since only a few nations could be accorded 'national self-determination and sovereignty', Arendt elucidates in her remarks on the inter-war period how this liberating idea of self-determination became an instrument of repression. She argues that against this background the newly established states quickly found themselves in the role of the oppressor. The 'nationally frustrated peoples' (OT: 271), on the other hand, became aware 'that true freedom, true emancipation, and true popular sovereignty could be attained only with full national emancipation, that people without their own national government were deprived of human rights' (OT: 272). Understood as a sign of national emancipation, the right to self-determination was considered a universal justification according to international law for oppressive political actions by the new nation-states, as well as for independence movements of minority groups. This dialectic of repression and autonomy coexisted with ethnic hatred that 'began to play a central role in public affairs everywhere' (OT: 268) in the inter-war period, and which reflected Arendt's assumption of the 'internal disintegration' of Europe's nation-state system.

Despite peace agreements, minority contracts and other political treaties, the European nation-states were not 'capable of bringing order to this chaos of reciprocal hate' (ETH: 561).[10] Arendt notes that in such an atmosphere of ethnic hatred, 'practical consideration and the silent acknowledgment of common interests' (OT: 278), as the idea of nation-states once envisaged, became impossible. Instantly it became apparent 'that full national sovereignty was possible only as long as the comity of European nations existed' (OT: 278). Only as long as the 'spirit of unorganized solidarity and agreement' (OT: 278) existed among the sovereign states was it possible that a balance of the different interests on the one hand and respect for the sovereignty of the other nation-states on the other could lead to a functioning political order. Without that *spirit* the situation very quickly resulted in those 'deadly conflicts' (OT: 278) that should have been prevented from the perspective of the established nation-states and against the backdrop of the experiences of the disaster of World War I. Kelsen's assertion of 'national legal order as state subjectivism' (Kelsen [1934] 2002: 345), and his theory that any idea of national sovereignty can only function if it is based on reciprocal recognition, coincides

[10] This is my own translation from the German in *Elemente und Ursprünge totaler Herrschaft*. Arendt writes: 'Selbst die Friedensverträge, welche die Nationalitäten in "Staatsvölker" und Minderheiten aufteilten, haben in dieses Chaos gegenseitigen Hasses keine Ordnung bringen können' (ETH: 561). Since some passages or phrases were added to the German version of Arendt's book on totalitarianism, I shall sometimes refer to *Elemente und Ursprünge totaler Herrschaft*. In such cases, where appropriate, I shall give the German version on which my translation is based; otherwise, I shall just cite the quotation.

with Arendt's scepticism of such things as absolute sovereignty. Nevertheless, if one perceives self-determination against the background of ethnic hatred, the first question is how, according to Arendt, the principle of national self-determination could gain such a determining influence on European politics?

Even before 1914, approximately 100 million people in Europe were denied the right to self-determination.[11] After World War I this situation was no longer tenable. For one thing, political constraints forced the established nation-states to fill the power void that ensued after the collapse of the Austro-Hungarian monarchy, the rule of the Russian Czar and the Ottoman Empire. As the old European nation-states were being confronted with independence movements in their colonies, it would have been possible to deny the ethnic groups in eastern and south-eastern Europe national self-determination only with military violence—an option that was deemed unimaginable after the shocking experiences of modern war. Arendt argues that in view of this historical-political background (a power-political vacuum and rekindled national consciousness), the peace agreements of 1919–20 were to pave the way for national emancipation of all ethnic groups and all European countries. In addition, according to Arendt, the peace agreements represented the attempt to preserve a Europe organised in nation-states, to defend the idea of nation-states as the basis of a new peace order of the twentieth century and 'to conserve the European status quo' (OT: 271). Since a different, federal, supra-national solution was not feasible, the idea of national self-determination was extended to the whole of Europe.

However, it was not possible simply to apply the nation-state theme to east and south-east Europe. None of the newly structured regions could fulfil the requirements on which traditional nation-states such as France rested; none of these territories was uni-national. On the contrary, Arendt stresses that these regions all comprised a colourful mix of ethnic groups that defined themselves as political groups. She agrees with Mussolini, who maintained that the fundamental problem of Czechoslovakia was not that it was merely Czecho-Slovakia but rather that it was 'Czech-Germano-Polono-Magyaro-Rutheno-Rumano-Slovakia' (OT: 270). The aim was to create nation-states on the grounds of the right to self-determination, yet the results were 'nationalities-states' (ETH: 567).[12] Moreover—and this is a decisive point in Arendt's considerations—the ethnic groups involved were people whose national consciousness had only recently been awakened following the example of the western nations. Instead of looking back onto a history of state-ness, and linking nationality with the

[11] Arendt takes this number from the studies by the English historian and diplomat Sir Charles Kingsley Webster (see OT: 272).

[12] The German version reads 'Nationalitätenstaaten'.

legal institutions of the state—Arendt argues in the tradition of Meinecke, distinguishing between the concept of state-nation and cultural nation—in these ethnic groups the concept of nationality 'had not yet developed beyond the inarticulateness of ethnic consciousness'. In contrast to the western understanding of nationality, 'their national quality appeared to be much more a portable private matter, inherent in their very personality, than a matter of public concern and civilization' (OT: 231). In short, in east and south-east Europe the concept of a nation-state had an ethnic connotation from the beginning.

Arendt assumed that the leading politicians of old nation-states thought or hoped that the nationality problems in east and south-east Europe could be channelled with the help of minority treaties. The minority system that they had designed warranted that the important ethnic groups could participate in administration and government, according to their proportion in the population. The other smaller ethnic splinter groups were to surrender their political rights, especially the right to national emancipation, in favour of the right to use their own language, to run their own schools, to practise their own religion, etc. Arendt stresses that the adjective 'national' was avoided at all costs when determining these minorities. Thus a 'Czech-Germano-Polono-Magyaro-Rutheno-Rumano-Slovakia' became a Czechoslovakia in which the seven million Czechs were under the auspices of the minority group comprising two million Slovaks. Describing the actual intention of the minority treaties, Arendt quotes former British Foreign Minister Sir Austen Chamberlain: '[T]he object of the Minority Treaties (is) … to secure … that measure of protection and justice which would gradually prepare them [the minorities] to be merged in the national community to which they belonged' (OT: 273).

While identifying one nation—like Poland, Romania and Lithuania—or two nations—such as Czechoslovakia or Yugoslavia—as the state's nation in order to guarantee the constitutional requirements for a national identity, European statesmen believed that decisive steps had been undertaken to secure a robust statutory future in those parts of Europe. The reality that was emerging in Europe refuted the vision Chamberlain had described. First, the minority treaties that had been designed as exceptions became the rule. There was no one region in east and south-east Europe that was not coveted by several nationalities simultaneously. Moreover, when the idea was conceived, many ethnic groups had simply not been identified. Therefore, the territorial divisions, no matter which kind, seemed arbitrary from the start. Secondly, the classifications into nations based on these divisions seemed equally artificial. One ethnic group was elevated to the status of a state's nation, whose political will was declared 'the sole legitimate criterion' and was internationally recognised with reference to self-determination, whereas the other group managed to achieve only an ethnic, religious, or language group status (see OT: 270).[13] This situation, which was deemed unacceptable by the minorities and led to separatist attempts everywhere, was accompanied by a policy of 'systematic obstruction' (ETH: 567). Looking at their own minorities across the border, many newly created states also considered the drawing of the borders unsatisfactory, which led to numerous border conflicts, some of which escalated into border wars. The border conflicts, on the other hand, spurred inner-state conflicts amongst different ethnic groups and revealed, in Pearson's words, the 'hybrid nature of the new states' (Pearson 1983: 184). Early on, it became apparent that if the constellations were 'unsuited,' *intra*-state conflicts between population and minorities, or even between minorities themselves, could very quickly lead to *inter*-state conflicts.

Arendt describes how the leading European politicians, who were worried by the increasingly conflict-ridden situation, clearly and expressly 'pointed out the "duties" the minorities owed to the new states' (OT: 272) as early as 1922, during the third assembly of the League of Nations. Here, at the latest, it was obvious what the term 'minority' actually entailed. Arendt quotes French politician Aristide Briand, who noted, '[t]he process … at which we should aim is not the disappearance of the minorities, but a kind of assimilation' (OT: 272). For Arendt, from the very beginning, the nation-state aimed at the assimilation of minorities. On this basis Arendt detects two different versions of the concept of minority. On the one hand, we see the understanding of a minority as a splinter group separated from the majority, but which is protected by the neighbour state where the minority comprises not the minority but the majority of the population. On the other hand, the idea of a nation-state minority according to Arendt was modelled on the situation of the Jews. Because Jews lived in all countries and were content with the status of a minority, they exemplified the '*minorité par excellence*' (OT: 289).

What is significant about this equation was the fact that it helped to reconfigure the concept of minority in such a way that it coincided with the expectations of the old nation-states on the one hand and the demands for absolute

[13] In all areas, whether in the later Poland, the Baltic States, Hungary, Czechoslovakia, Yugoslavia, etc, the different ethnic groups lived alongside one another in more or less separate settlements. This resulted in the fact that one ethnic group, eg the Poles, who were only a minority in Lithuania, comprised the national population in the neighbouring area. Arendt states that for all those peoples that had not been declared to be nations, and who were therefore deprived of a state territory, the contracts symbolised 'the result of an arbitrary or partisan or scheming game that allocated domination to one group and servitude to the other' (ETH: 568). Raymond Pearson reinforces Arendt's view in so far as he writes, in relation to the role of Benes und Masaryk in the creation of Czechoslovakia, of a 'clandestine campaign of back-stage lobbying of the Allies' (Pearson 1983: 150), and adds that this led to the feeling on the part of many disadvantaged minorities that they had become the victims of an intrigue.

sovereignty of the newly created states on the other. Since the Jews did not have their own state but conformed to the model of a new concept of minority, the political notion of minority changed; the term 'minority' was depoliticised; it was deprived of its 'political notion'. Such a depoliticised concept of minority was in the interest of the fundamental idea of a nation-state, as it could change a section of the population into a silent minority that had to behave accordingly towards the majority. Arendt maintains that this silent wish, which was asserted shortly afterwards in Briand's political claim for assimilation, was not fulfilled. On the one hand a depoliticised, politically non-ambitious understanding of minorities did not reflect the actual situation. It depended strongly on the minority involved as to how 'politically ambitious and 'politicised' a minority actually was. What *de facto* applied to the unprotected Jewish minorities, or to the Sinti and Roma, in all European states did not necessarily apply to the German minority in Czechoslovakia, as the crisis in the Sudetenland showed. On the other hand many ethnic groups were not happy with the situation. Most minorities defined themselves as political groups and therefore considered themselves the 'unlucky remaining rest' (ETH: 565), who, due to power-political concerns or sinister interests, were prevented from being united with their country of origin. The call for assimilation was therefore, thirdly, absolutely unacceptable to them.[14]

At the same time, the tradition of nation-state thinking that had been generally accepted since the French Revolution assumed that the people and the nation had to be the same, and that minorities were, if anything, temporary anomalies. This in turn spurred the nationalisation of minorities, because only the sustained political and permanent emphasis of their national identity could prevent the threat of absorption by the majority in the long term. In this fashion, as Zolberg maintains, the minorities changed into 'political misfits' (Zolberg 1983: 28). It is undisputed that this process of nationalisation fell on the fertile ground of an ethnic notion of nationality that comprised additional

[14] At the same time Pearson stresses that 'only loyal minorities unreasonably or gratuitously persecuted by a state exclusively on the grounds of nationality came under the League [of Nations] guarantee'. If minorities rebelled against their status and the assimilation requirements, the League of Nations understood this to be exclusively an internal matter for the 'host state' (Pearson 1983: 142). Like Arendt, Pearson also concludes that the established nation-states were concerned in the first instance with upholding a Europe organised along nation-state lines. Against this backdrop the League of Nations acted—and this is Pearson's 'chief accusation' against the League of Nations—as a 'gendarme rather than judge': '[T]he rights and wrongs of a particular minority issue were always firmly subordinated to the broader preoccupation of keeping the peace by maintaining the Versailles Settlement—... even if a minority were being scandalously abused' (Pearson 1983: 145). Therefore within the nation-state order—of which the concept of minority was just one expression—there were no means with which to guide the ever-intensifying conflicts between minorities and the citizens of the state into ordered channels.

potential for conflict. Arendt stresses in her reflections that the minority system intensified the political escalation of the nationality question. In other words, the 'means' by which the established nation-states tried to solve the nationality issue and to secure a European peace only incited further conflict. The nation-state demand for assimilation turned into the protest by the minorities and highlighted

> that the European status quo could not be preserved and that it became clear only after the downfall of the last remnants of European autocracy that Europe had been ruled by a system which had never taken into account or responded to the needs of at least 25 per cent of her population. (OT: 271)

Moreover, very early on it became clear that the older powers were not willing to consider the minorities or the minority system. From the start, the new states complained of 'an open breach of promise and discrimination' (OT: 270) between the newly created and the established states, such as France, that excluded themselves without compromise from the minority system. Arendt emphasises that this stance on the part of the older states was understandable when viewed from a national and sovereigntist perspective, because the minority treaties 'implied restriction on national sovereignty [that] would have affected the national sovereignty of the older European powers' (OT: 273). Arendt points out that not one of the older powers was prepared to accept this.[15] Thus, the potential for conflict presented by the minority system was not only evident in east and south-east Europe, but gradually affected the relationships between the new and the older powers. In this spirit, Pearson underlines how the new states were inspired 'to discriminate against minorities as a matter of national bravado, a continuous declaration of independence' (Pearson 1983: 142). The one-sided implementation of the minority system led the new states to believe that the 'spirit of solidarity' was not adopted by the older powers, and they felt forced to manifest their national sovereignty in other ways. Arendt comes to the conclusion that the 'atmosphere of disintegration' (OT: 268) created by an intentionless and aimless hate was the direct

[15] Like Arendt, Pearson also arrives at the same result in his study, namely that no state was prepared to curtail its sovereign rights: 'The host states resented the League from the outset. At a time when the new states were understandably hypersensitive about their independence, they were accorded international recognition only on condition that they signed minority treaties which clearly infringed their sovereignty. Why should sovereign states be compelled to submit to the jurisdiction of the League of Nations and Permanent Court of International Justice? More pertinently, why were the Great Powers and other states outside Eastern Europe exempt from such minority treaties? League justice seemed to most host states to be partial from its inception, with no universal or even general application of the principle of minority protection.' (Pearson 1983: 142)

consequence of the fact that no party could really be helped with the available political instruments a nation-state order could provide:

> Here, everyone was against everyone else, and especially against one's neighbour, the Slovaks against the Czechs, the Hungarians against the Slovaks, the Croats against the Serbs, the Ukrainians against the Poles, the Poles against the Jews—and so on in endless variations, limited only by the number of nationalities and state peoples … While the minorities hated the state peoples, this did not prevent them from hating equally the other minorities in the same area, and to persecute them where possible. (ETH: 561f)

Every new nation-state that attempted to gain political freedom on the grounds of international principles and which sought membership in the 'house of nations' (Kurt Tucholsky) found itself in the role of the oppressor. On the other hand, the national minorities that pursued their right to their own nation-state or sought affiliation with their country of origin were declared criminals and enemies of the state. In a situation in which every party refers to the 'dogma of state sovereignty' (Kelsen [1934] 2002: 346), communication and exchange became impossible. The ethnic hatred in the 'chronically insecure, over-ambitious and unconscionably competitive' (Pearson 1983: 185) states escalated in such a way that the minorities saw themselves confronted with the alternative, 'fight or flight' (Pearson 1983: 84), as Pearson concludes in his study. However, the end result of both alternatives was that many were driven away or fled from their home countries, creating masses of people seeking protection in West Europe (see also Pearson 1983: 184). The political and historical context in which this migration took place created a new political category that had been unknown until then—the 'stateless person'. Now, the new phenomenon of statelessness was to confront the older nation-states with massive problems as well.

## III. THE PARADOX OF DE-ASSIMILATION AND DE-NATURALISATION

The second paradox of the nation-state, the *paradox of de-assimilation and de-naturalisation*, contained in Arendt's discourse on the collapse of a Europe of nation-states, begins with the phenomenon of statelessness. Arendt attempts to prove that within the framework of the nation-state no means existed with which to restore the 'right to act' that the phenomenon of mass statelessness had brought about. The core of Arendt's critique is that the path to an agreement on international asylum and refugee regulations was obstructed by the general atmosphere of chauvinistic ethnic hatred and fear of loss of sovereignty. Therefore, the European countries, paradoxically, lost those sovereignty rights that, apart from *ius ad bellum*, had been the domain of national sovereignty, namely, 'sovereignty … in matters of "emigration, naturalization, nationality, and expulsion"' (OT: 278).

In order to unpack the *paradox of de-assimilation and de-naturalisation*, the political and legal implications of statelessness need to be explicated. For Arendt, statelessness is not only 'the newest mass phenomenon in contemporary history' (OT: 277), but also the clearest expression of 'the first great damage [of] the nation-states' (OT: 280). Before World War I, statelessness had just been an oddity that occurred where countries had renounced the citizenship of persons because they had moved to another country. During World War I 'de-naturalisation through decree' (OT: 277) had become more common in Europe. However, this was 'only' effected on naturalised citizens who had their roots in countries that had become enemy states in the course of hostilities. Even so, the political impact of statelessness was insignificant until the October Revolution; after the Revolution the millions of Russians who fled the country in the face of the revolutionary events were deprived of their citizenship by the new Government. In chronological order and in a short period of time the Russians were followed by hundreds of thousands of Armenians, Hungarians, Germans, Slovaks and Jews, who were all fleeing systematic persecution, genocide, border conflicts, civil wars, riots or pogroms, and who were forced to leave their home countries (see OT: 278). But what was the exact problem of statelessness, and how far did the 'destruction of nation-states' become apparent through it?

Although refugees are anything but unknown in history, in Arendt's view the refugees of the inter-war period were fundamentally different from those of previous ages. At no other point in time had there been such masses of people who were in a 'fundamental situation of rightlessness' (OT: 296). The fact that rightlessness followed statelessness only occurred due to the formation of nation-states. Arendt elucidates that as long as the medieval principle *quidquid est in territorio est de territorio* was valid, all persons present on the state territory were subject to the jurisdiction of the sovereign (see OT: 280). However, since with the establishment of the nation-state as the main paradigm of a political order the will of the people became the only source of law, the identity and the cohesion of a people had to be determined by the principle of exclusion and inclusion. The consequence was that a state granted legal protection only to those who belonged among the 'included', the ones who possessed citizenship on the grounds of their nationality or whose country had signed certain treaties, which ensured that the foreign citizenship was recognised in the respective countries.

The older states, just like the new ones, tried to deal with the refugee problem by 'making the problem disappear from the world through juridical interpretations' (ETH: 582). One of these, for Arendt, was the untenable distinction between refugees and stateless people. This was nothing but the 'non-recognition of statelessness' (ETH: 579) as a mass phenomenon and the attempt to declare the refugee problem a 'passing anomaly' (ETH: 582). According to Arendt, all these aspirations of the judiciary failed due to the fact that 'all refugees in effect were stateless and nearly all stateless people were virtually refugees' (OT: 276).[16] These attempts to veil the actual situation with the help of legal tricks, were for Arendt more than simple ignorance: hitherto it had been unheard of for people to lose all legal rights due to statelessness. In this new identification of statelessness and rightlessness lay the silent acceptance of the collapse of one of the oldest and nearly sacred laws of political communities: the right to asylum. The state's capacity to allow persons to stay on its territory is based on the option to expel them to neighbouring countries or to the persons' home countries. Only where the state is legally as well as factually in the position to refuse residency is it in the position to grant the right to residency. With the *de facto* stateless refugees of the inter-war period, this possibility was abolished. It was not possible to expel them because no country would take them. Since they did not belong to a state, they were 'undeportable' (OT: 276). This 'undeportability' of the refugees in particular, and the ensuing collapse of the asylum system, had consequences for the sovereignty of the nation-state when determining those who were granted permission to stay and those who had to leave the country. Arendt writes:

> The whole naturalisation system of European countries fell apart when it was confronted with stateless people, and this for the same reason that the rights of asylum had been set aside. Essentially naturalisation was an appendage to the nation-state's legislation that reckoned only with 'nationals,' people born in its territory and citizens by birth. Naturalisation was needed in exceptional cases, for single individuals whom circumstances might have driven into a foreign territory. The whole process broke down when it became a question of handling mass applications for naturalisation. (OT: 284f)

Although the solution to defusing this increasingly volatile refugee problem would have been, at least theoretically, to guarantee fundamental rights and naturalisation, Arendt points out that this possibility was blocked in numerous ways.

[16] Apart from the stateless Russian and Armenian refugees who were officially recognised as stateless persons and 'protected' by the Nansen Office—and therefore counted as a kind of 'aristocracy' among the millions of stateless refugees—most of the other refugees were *de facto* stateless (see OT: 271). Arendt cites the history of Russian refugees as an example against the thesis of a temporary anomaly. In her comments she refers to the *Refugee Report* by Sir John Hope Simpson, as well as to the research findings of Eugene Kulischer and Winfried Hadsel, who show that—apart from the first wave of Russian refugees—half a million people were still stateless after 25 years of exile, in spite of the high death rate, overseas emigration and naturalisation by matrimony (*cf* on this point exemplarily Simpson 1939). The juristic division into stateless and refugee is almost ridiculous against the background that 'in the course of one generation not one single group could be released from statelessness by means of repatriation or naturalisation' (ETH: 583).

First, it is obvious that such a naturalisation process could only be carried out on the basis of international agreements to which all nation-states would have to adhere. A single state would never have been in a position to implement such a policy on its own. But every country, as a prisoner of a nation-state order, insisted on its sovereignty, and this, complemented by the poisonous atmosphere of ethnic hatred, made an international solution to the refugee and statelessness problem unthinkable. To underline Arendt's arguments we can refer to Gérard Noiriel, who illustrated how in this time 'the asylum issue became a real problem for international law, because now norms had to be defined that could be recognised by most states' (Noiriel 1994: 86). As Noiriel highlights by referring to the French Home Secretary's views on a refugee and minority agreement that was drawn up in 1928, the general opinion was that 'social order and French security' (Noiriel 1994: 97) could only be realised unilaterally, and that any binding refugee agreement would mean a loss of sovereignty regarding security questions. Obviously this restricted any effective political action on an international level (*cf* Skran 1995: 142).

Setting Arendt's rather speculative argument aside, no bureaucracy would ever have been able to manage and organise the naturalisation of millions of refugees. Secondly, the refugees' acceptance of assimilation as a prerequisite to naturalisation was not to be assumed. Aside from the wish for national self-determination, the renaissance of nationalism also changed the refugee profile. Before this, refugees had been single persecuted individuals who fled over the frontier. Now entire ethnic groups were on the move who, due to group dynamics, were unable to assimilate. Instead they actually triggered a process of 'de-assimilation' in the already naturalised citizens with the same ethnic roots in the host countries. Arendt writes:

> Where a wave of refugees found members of their own nationality already settled in the country to which they immigrated—as was the case with Armenians and Italians in France, for example, and with Jews everywhere—a certain retrogression set in in the assimilation of those who had been there longer. For their help and solidarity could be mobilised only by appealing to the original nationality they had in common with the newcomers. (OT: 285)

What she outlines here is the transformation of an ethnic notion of nationality into a decisive political factor. This does not mean, though, that the minorities in east and south-east Europe did not have an ethno-nationalistic feeling of belonging together before. Now, however, under the situation of exile and deportation, the affiliation with an ethnic group attained new decisive importance in the old nation-states as well. When people lose all their external worldly securities, such as their rights and even their home countries, their origin becomes the central reference point and a crucial source of solidarity. For Arendt the 'humanitarianism of brotherhood'—which means nothing other than 'that the element common to all men is not the world, but human nature'

(LR: 26)[17]—has always replaced with its warmth the light of a mutual world denied to all humiliated people in dark times. Although nationality had no political significance for the now naturalised and assimilated members of the same ethnic group, and was merely a question of cultural background, these people now felt attracted by this new notion of nationality. The negative effects that the waves of refugees spawned in the already settled people and their feelings of belonging increased the fear of the old nation-states of their leading to a 'dangerous' multi-national state. This fear was not without reason and originated in the difficulties of the nation-states in dealing with other national groups; and it prevented, thirdly, any consideration of a naturalisation policy.

Nevertheless, the nation-state governments had to react to the increasing number of refugees and the accompanying process of de-assimilation. Arendt argues that when it became clear that frontiers could not be sealed completely by any means, and that ever more refugees were streaming into the countries, the governments started to revoke naturalisations already granted.[18] The problem was that de-naturalisation was just as ineffectual as naturalisation and did not really offer a solution—neither in nation-states nor Europe-wide. On the contrary, the tragedy of 'the legislation of denationalisation' (ETH: 585)[19] in the 1920s was that once a state started nullifying once-granted citizenships as a reaction to the influx of refugees, the bordering states felt forced to follow suit. The result was that the de-naturalisation laws were passed across all of Europe, and led to a 'wave of mass-denationalisation' (ETH: 585).[20] In a long footnote, Arendt depicts how in 1922 the de-naturalisation laws started in Belgium, and how states such as Turkey, Austria, France, etc followed suit (see OT: 279). The legal foundations for these 'de-naturalisation' laws were so vaguely formulated that they did not express more than the police guidelines for the treatment of 'undesirable aliens' (OT: 283). *De facto*, these are general clauses.[21]

[17] Arendt explains this 'right to the warmth of the pariah people' (LR: 26) in her Lessing Speech by taking the example of the Jews as pariah people *par excellence*, and states that the worldlessness that accompanies fraternity is conceded only to those—and even there it is not without danger—who are among the demeaned peoples. No others could afford such a lack of reality (see LR: 26f).

[18] The same assessment can be found in Skran, '[a]s government could not completely seal their borders, they used refoulement as way to return those who had crossed them secretly' (Skran 1995: 133).

[19] The German version refers to 'Denaturalisierungsgesetzgebung'.

[20] The German versions refer to 'einer Welle von Massendenaturalisationen'.

[21] The softening of the law by means of such general clauses was accompanied by a series of ordinances that, by linking naturalisation to unaccomplishable requirements, represented a *de facto* withdrawal of citizenship. Arendt reports of a decree allowing doctors to practise no sooner than 10 years after their naturalisation (see ETH: 586). Along with the French law of 1932 on the 'Protection of the Labour Market', which made residency permits for all foreigners and refugees dependent on the economic situation, reference is also made frequently in the research to the 'revision of all alien work permits' (Skran 1995: 132) in 1935. During the course of this new rule, work permits were denied or their renewal was delayed until those affected had already received their expulsion orders (*cf* on this point also Maurrus 1985: 145–49; Noiriel 1994: 98).

Far beyond referring to any actual offence, 'the laws' were couched in barely tangible terms and spoke of 'manquant gravement à leurs devoirs de citoyen belge', of being not 'worthy of Italian citizenship', or they denationalised those of the state's new citizens 'who committed acts contrary to the interests of France' (OT: 279).[22]

As the denationalisation laws spread from country to country, statelessness increased, which in turn started a process of de-assimilation to which states reacted with the further withdrawal of citizenship. This only set off the whole process again in an escalated form. Not only the living conditions of the refugees were affected by this escalation, but also the situation of the nation-states, whose scope for action declined from 'denationalisation round' to 'denationalisation round'. As more and more states followed denationalisation laws and produced ever more stateless people, the number of countries that could expel their stateless persons legally decreased. Arendt describes a spiral of denationalisation and de-assimilation or de-assimilation and denationalisation, which made the legal tools of the nation-state on naturalisation and deportation ineffectual. This highlighted clearly to what extent and under what conditions national jurisdiction could affect the international response, and how little national sovereignty was willing or capable of reacting. The importance and effect of the legal decisions of neighbouring countries on the legal and political scope of the other nation-states became clear:

> Whatever governments undertook to resist statelessness, they automatically generated new groups of real or potential stateless persons. As soon as a country was infested, so to speak, with statelessness at all, no further new catastrophic events were necessary to increase their numbers constantly; they spread like an infectious disease, for not only were those who were already naturalised in danger of becoming stateless themselves due to the arrival of the stateless; the living conditions of all foreigners were influenced decisively by these new groups of people. (ETH: 588)

The inability to find a legal and political regulation for the treatment of stateless refugees affected all those 'foreigners' who had foreign citizenship and whose residency was legalised in some form, usually with a work permit. The deciding difference between stateless people and the people Arendt called 'foreigners' (OT: 227) was deportability. Consequently, state sovereignty could

[22] In his work *Über die drei Arten des rechtswissenschaftlichen Denkens* (*On the Three Types of Juristic Thought*), Schmitt argued in 1934 that it could be very clearly discerned in Germany 'the degree to which the age of juristic positivism had ended. From all sides and in all areas of legal life, so-called general clauses advance to an extent that suspends any positive "security", undefined terms of all kinds, reference to extra-legal measures and ideas such as good morals, good faith, reasonableness and unreasonableness, good cause, etc' (Schmitt [1934] 1993: 48). Whereas Schmitt sees and celebrates in this the swansong of legal positivism, Arendt fears the collapse of an entire form of government.

manifest itself in questions of residency and non-residency for 'foreigners'. Arendt points out that the presumed advantages of statelessness were not lost on the 'foreigners', who then tried everything to obtain this status. For governments legally to manage questions of residency or deportation, it is essential to determine or to recognise the legal status of a person. However, the 'inextricable chaos' (ETH: 588) escalated so that it became more and more difficult to distinguish who was refugee, who was stateless or who was a 'foreigner,' and more and more people became 'legally undeterminable' (ETH: 581).[23] As the governments' fear of the steady increase of stateless refugees on their territories grew, the insight emerged that the refugee problem could not be solved by legal means. In the obvious knowledge of the incapacity of the nation-states in this matter, the totalitarian states consciously and systematically employed 'denationalisation' as 'a powerful weapon of totalitarian politics' (OT: 269) in order to undermine the European nation-state order.

## IV. THE PARADOX OF RIGHTLESSNESS

The refugees of the inter-war period were stateless, and as such they stood outside any legal order. Notwithstanding, the factual situation forced states to deal with the statelessness. Since the stateless refugee was not a 'juridical person' (OT: 447), the situation could not be tackled on a legal level, with the means of governance characteristic of a constitutional state. Arendt shows how stateless people endangered the 'nation-state as a legal and constitutional state ie they jeopardised it in its foundations' (NuD).[24] Arendt justifies her assertions with the fact that those stateless persons who were placed outside the pale of the law, and who represented the 'anomaly for whom the general law did not provide' (OT: 286), forced every government 'into admittedly illegal acts' (OT: 283f). The paradox that became apparent was that stateless persons whose statelessness was due to the fact that they did not fit into the national order, and even represented a danger for the order, actually managed to manoeuvre the state into a position where it acted outside its own legal order, and started 'to undermine legality in the internal affairs of the affected state and its international relations' (ETH: 592; see OT: 284).[25]

Arendt exemplifies the undermining of 'international relations' using the model of deportation practices. The concept of a nation-state order and

[23] The German version refers to 'legal undeterminierbar'.

[24] In her paper Arendt writes: 'Der Einbruch der Staatenlosen und die ihnen zugefügte schlechthinnige Rechtlosigkeit gefährdeten den Nationalstaat als Rechts- und Verfassungsstaat, d.h. sie gefährdeten ihn in seinen Grundlagen'.

[25] The German version reads, 'Legalität überhaupt im Innern der betroffenen Staaten wie in ihren zwischenstaatlichen Beziehungen zu unterminieren'.

national sovereignty inhibited the nation-state from renouncing its 'right' to deport the stateless refugees. The 'right to expel' not only mirrors the core principle of territorial sovereignty, but also expresses the state's fundamental right to national self-determination. However, it was not possible to expel stateless people on legal grounds, since no other state was there to receive them. If the respective state wanted to preserve its territorial sovereignty, it had to deport the stateless person without complying with, or even acting counter to, international agreements. The result was a steady increase of non-legal deportation practices and the increase of 'illegality in the inter-state border traffic' (ETH: 594).[26] In clandestine actions, the police smuggled stateless persons over the border into the territory of the neighbouring country. Obviously, the refugees were in breach of the immigration laws of that country and, thus, offended its rights of sovereignty. The neighbouring country, following the same logic in turn, took the stateless refugees to the next state one night later (see OT: 283f). The spread of such deportation practices revealed all too clearly that it was impossible to acknowledge the legal and sovereign sphere on the basis of the principles of a nation-state order, and that this led to the '*deadly conflicts*' it was wished to avoid after the experiences of World War I. Arendt describes a spiral of disrespect for national sovereignty jurisdictions in favour of lawless assertions of sovereignty. From the perspective of the European nation-state order, it was sovereignty that abolished sovereignty and, thus, paved the way for the next war as *ultima ratio*.[27]

In addition to the illegality of the border traffic, which Arendt marks as 'petty wars between the police at the frontiers' (OT: 284), the undermining of the *legality of internal affairs* is of defining importance in her critique. The implementation of principles of *Rechtsstaatlichkeit* (constitutionality)—meaning the separation of powers, the authority of the legal order, an independent jurisdiction, and the actual effectiveness of laws—is at the same time the implementation of a nation-state order. These principles guarantee a durable and stable state order, as well as legal reliability between state authorities and residents. In contrast, to dissolve the legality in internal affairs implies an attack on the central characteristics of the nation-state. Arendt describes how this attack took place on different levels. At the first level, *the spread of illegality in society* resulted directly from the increasing number of refugees, and was linked to the fact that people without residence and work permits were simply forced to act outside the law in order to secure their existence. Arendt explicates how an increase in illegal refugees changed everyday life in society, especially with regard to certain forms of illegality such as any kind of illicit work

[26] The German version refers to 'Illegalität im zwischenstaatlichen Grenzverkehr'.

[27] Here Arendt is in line with Kelsen, who expresses the criticism in *Reine Rechtslehre* that within the notion of state sovereignty, 'the single state is in the centre of the world of law' (Kelsen [1934] 2002: 345).

(see OT: 279). Moreover, she outlines that the 'defiance of the authority of laws' should be regarded as an 'explicit sign of the inner instability and vulnerability of existing governments and legal systems' (CD: 69).

Closely linked to the societal spread of illegality, Arendt also elaborates on the 'transformation of the juridical system' (ETH: 594). She writes:

> For then a criminal offence becomes the best opportunity to regain some kind of human equality, even if it be as a recognised exception to the norm. The one important fact is that this exception is provided for by law. As a criminal even a stateless person will not be treated worse than another criminal, that is, he will be treated like everybody else. Only as an offender against the law can he gain protection from it. (OT: 286)

Her point seems to be that the rightlessness of the stateless refugee bursts the *structure of the legal rule* on both sides: on the side of the *legal condition*, as well as on that of the *legal consequence*. Since according to Kelsen the legal rule embodies the 'basic form of law' (Kelsen [1934] 1994: 22), the *Rechtstaatlichkeit* (constitutionality) of the nation-state implodes. What does this mean in detail? Legal condition and legal consequence determine what a law contains by establishing a certain punishment for a certain crime; and in this manner, they determine and guarantee the formal character of law. This ordered union of condition and consequence 'bursts' in the case of the stateless refugee. The first 'burst' occurs on the side of the crime, the legal condition. To understand this, one has to remember that the 'right of asylum' had been a sacred right since ancient times. It was always applied when a person was being persecuted for a crime that was against the law in his country of origin but not in the country in which he sought asylum. Therefore, the asylum seeker had to prove that he had committed such an offence. Although the 'right of asylum' had become increasingly insignificant in the nineteenth century due to inter-state treaties, Arendt points out that it immediately regained its political relevance with the emergence of refugees in the twentieth century. Now the tragedy was that the modern refugees could not provide evidence that they had committed any of the required offences. They were what a refugee should never be: absolutely innocent. This kind of absolute innocence was 'the greatest misfortune' (OT: 295) for such stateless refugees, because the punishment that awaited them despite or owing to this was the 'deprivation of all rights':[28]

> Jurists are so used to thinking of law in terms of punishment, which indeed always deprives us of certain rights, that they may find it even more difficult than a layman to recognise that the deprivation of legality, ie, of all rights, no longer has a

[28] Arendt refers to the asylum policy of the US during World War II. After the French defeat, the US offered asylum to those who were in danger of being deported to Germany. To be entitled to this right asylum seekers had only to prove that they had undertaken some action against Nazi Germany. Arendt points to the facts, first, that there was not a noteworthy number of refugees who could fulfil this condition and, secondly, that those who could were not the most endangered (see OT: 294).

> connection with specific crimes. *In our times absolute rightlessness is the punishment for absolute innocence.* (OT: 295)[29]

Although the stateless refugee committed no offence, and therefore no legal condition was violated, the nation-state 'reacted' with the deprivation of all rights. By formulating a 'law' that penalised absolute innocence with absolute rightlessness, the coherence of the entire legal system was called into question and the concept of law led to an *ad absurdum*. If 'absolute innocence' was punished with the maximum penalty, what should happen to a thief?

Here the extent of the legal paradox becomes apparent, because through a theft, the stateless refugee could obtain all those legal rights that a citizen *qua* citizen was guaranteed, if a crime was committed. In other words, by committing an offence the stateless refugee again became a member of a legal-political community and regained some of his civic rights. This paradoxical reversal results from the fact that a legal process commenced that *normalised* the stateless refugee and granted him rights he previously did not have. If he did not have money, he was accorded a lawyer. Before, he was subjected to inhuman treatment by the police. After committing an offence he could complain about humiliating prison conditions and inspect the his records, obtain information, and so forth. In short, the stateless refugee 'has become a respectable person' (OT: 287). The irritating fact is that the offence against the legal order of a society put the stateless person in a position to enjoy rights he hitherto did not have, despite his innocence. While in the first case the rightlessness of the stateless refugee destroys the structure of the legal rule by realising an absurd legal condition, now it is ruined via legal consequence. The punishment for theft, burglary, bank robbery was accordance of 'civic rights'. According to Arendt, the result is that the idea of legality collapses as soon as it comes into contact with a person who has 'ceased to be a juridical person' (ETH: 609).

The corruption of constitutionality caused by an insufficient handling of the problem of stateless persons did not end with the 'reversal of the juridical principles'. Since the authorities were afraid that humane treatment would lure potential refugees and also tempt other states to expel, the police were granted exceptional powers hitherto unknown. By these means, according to Arendt, the foundation of the separation of powers was steadily undermined, and this, in consequence, promoted the 'transformation of legal relations and standards' (ETH: 597).[30] Completely detached from the political course of democratic governments, this led to a 'police-directed foreign policy' (OT: 288) that did not make the police recoil from cooperating with the Gestapo

[29] In the German version the paragraph ends with '*Absolute Rechtlosigkeit hat sich in unserer Zeit als die Strafe erwiesen, die auf absolute Unschuld steht.*' (ETH: 611)

[30] The German version speaks of 'die Umkehrung aller gesetzlich vorgesehenen Verhältnisse und Maßstäbe'.

and Soviet GPU in the 1930s. The police were allowed to choose their own methods to combat the refugee problem. With this direct power over people, they had the right to expel refugees without trial, without a judicial order and without a legal examination of the facts. This generated a fundamental shift of power within the constitutional-political structure of a nation-state. Important decisions were no longer taken within the constitutional framework and under the control of the judicature and the legislative bodies but executed by the police on the ground, without justification and without further publication (see OT: 287f). Through this 'spectral mixture' (Benjamin [1978] 1986: 286) of law-positing and law-preserving, the constitutional bodies lost their reputation and authority. As an example, Arendt describes how in France an expulsion order by the police received disproportionately higher priority and had more serious consequences than that of the Home Secretary, despite the fact that the police were constitutionally subordinated to the Home Secretary (see OT: 287f).

Meanwhile, the relationship between the 'normal citizen' and governmental bodies remained in the realm of the constitutional order. However, with every new refugee the police's 'emancipation from law and government' continued, leading to a process of 'gradual transformation into a police state' (OT: 287f).[31] Besides an almost unlimited and arbitrary domination and a new 'form of lawlessness, organised by the police' (ETH: 599),[32] this situation

[31] Arendt's thoughts on the police and the police state can also be seen as a change in the phenomenology of the state and of governing. This change also forms the basis of Foucault's work on the history of governmentality. Arendt's distinction between a police state and a constitutional state can be found in Foucault in the differentiation between a 'legal-juridical mechanism' and the idea of a 'security dispositive', between the state as a sovereign domination of the law and that which he calls raison d'état (see Foucault 2004: 22f). Whereas in the system of laws, all things that are forbidden are codified, the essential function of the security dispositive is to 'respond to a reality so that this answer suspends, checks, limits or regulates that reality to which it is responding' (Foucault 2004: 76). The security dispositive is concerned with controlling reality by setting its elements in motion. Although the goal of the raison d'état is the 'wellbeing of the state' (Foucault 2004: 379), Foucault points out that under the security dispositive one encounters a de-substantialistic concept of state that regards the state as the practice of governing. It has detached itself from any kind of finality and operates in an 'open historicity' (Foucault 2004: 376). 'The state', writes Foucault, 'is a practice' (Foucault 2004: 400). A central means of this practice is the police. Such a type of government is not indifferent to laws. But there are moments and events during which the raison d'état can no longer serve the laws and liberates itself from them out of a certain necessity. As I shall demonstrate below with Schmitt, Foucault also has a substantially undefined concept of order and sees only a power logic in operation. In contrast to Foucault, who regards the history of the nation-state merely as a chapter in the history of the disciplining and formation of the subject, Arendt certainly does emphasise the moments of (political) freedom that can be found in this world of order, the loss of which can have catastrophic consequences (see on this point Foucault 1994 and Foucault 2006), as well as the essay by Dolan about Arendt, Foucault and the problem of the 'normalisation of people' in modern societies (Dolan 2005: 375).

[32] The German version reads 'eine Form polizeilich organisierter Gesetzlosigkeit'.

contributed to the massive undermining of the legal order of the nation-state, and also explains why there was 'disgracefully little resistance from the police in those countries the Nazis occupied'.[33]

Of course, one could argue with Carl Schmitt that to suspend constitutionality on nearly all levels of the political system demonstrates the state's claim to sovereignty. However for Arendt, Schmitt's attempt agrees with the traditional metaphysical approach to politics and its need for an Archimedean point, while at the same time he completely ignores the historical, social, societal, political, moral and legal dimensions of the idea of nation and nation-state. Certainly, Arendt would agree that police conduct as well as the systemic shifts within the state resulted from the jeopardised order brought about by the refugee problem. However, unlike Schmitt, Arendt takes the liberal and constitutional characteristics of a nation-state structure very seriously and criticises those systemic shifts. If we follow this discussion further, we have to ask what Schmitt considers a political order to consist of? Who is the sovereign? Who can declare a state of emergency and abrogate constitutionality for the sake of public safety and order? These questions lead further into the work of Schmitt and away from my attempt to explain Arendt's argument of the collapse of the nation-state. Nevertheless, when questioning Schmitt about these issues, one is confronted with plenty of inconsistencies and contradictions in his work. His definition of the concept of order varies from a catholic theological design in his early work (see Schmitt 1914: 7), to a cultural-national concept in *Crisis of Parliamentary Democracy* (see Schmitt [1923] 1991: 88f), to a racist, national socialist one in *Über die drei Art des rechtswissenschaftlichen Denkens* (Schmitt [1934] 1993: 23).[34] Without doubt, Schmitt had always deemed man to be *subjectum* (*cf* Meuter 1994: 491), but subjected to whom and by whom remains completely unclear. Hermann Heller had already criticised the concept of sovereignty in Schmitt's work in his sovereignty paper in 1927. Heller states that Schmitt is 'inherently contradictory and not tenable' (Heller [1927] 1971: 89). Apart from his 'inadequacies in reference to international law' (Heller [1927] 1971: 89), it also remains unclear to Heller who should

[33] Arendt's account of the shift within the function of the police has a striking though unacknowledged affinity to Walter Benjamin's considerations in 'Zur Kritik der Gewalt'. Like Arendt, Benjamin also points to this '*gespenstische Vermischung*' ('spectral mixture') between law-positing and law-preserving within the police.

[34] Especially in this work from 1934, Schmitt distances himself decisively from decisionism and describes his juristic mind set as a 'concrete understanding of order'. Whereas for the decisionists—in Schmitt eyes, Hobbes is the prototype of this juristic way of thinking—both the order and the norm are justified and created by the decision (see Schmitt [1934] 1993: 23f), in the concrete understanding of order every decision is itself subject to the order. In the concrete understanding of order, every decision is the 'result of a previously existing order, a reestablishment, not an establishment, of order' (Schmitt [1934] 1993: 23).

act as the sovereign in Schmitt's theory. Heller supposes that for Schmitt the *Reichspräsident* takes up this position, but, as Heller continues, Schmitt actually avoided a clear answer (see Heller [1927] 1971: 89f). In *Der Hüter der Verfassung*, some years later, Schmitt explicitly repudiated the assertion that the *Reichspräsident* could be the sovereign (see Schmitt [1931] 1996: 132). From Arendt's perspective the polemical remark springs to mind that the problem faced by many state theorists, namely to define the sovereign—and Heller did not satisfactorily solve it at all[35]—was due possibly to the political situation of the inter-war period and the fact that there was nobody in a position to execute the alleged rights of sovereignty unilaterally.

In the undermining of constitutionality and the threat of an imminent police state, Arendt sees systemic changes to the extent that a decline of the nation-state order appeared conceivable—an order that had *also* once begun with the wish to realise political freedom. She concludes that since the peace treaties of 1919–20, refugees and stateless people 'have attached themselves like a curse to all the newly established states', bearing for both, the new as well as the old nation-states, 'the germs of a deadly sickness'. For Arendt, it becomes clear 'that the nation-state cannot exist once its principle of equality before the law has broken down. Laws that are not equal for all revert to rights and privileges, something contradictory to the very nature of nation-states' (OT: 290).

## V. THE PARADOX OF HUMAN RIGHTS

> If I knew something that was useful to me and harmful to my family, I would banish it from my mind. If I knew something useful to my family but not to my Country, I would seek to forget it. If I knew something useful to my Country and harmful to Europe, or else useful to Europe and harmful to the human race, I would regard it as a crime.
>
> Montesquieu, *Mes pensées*

The paradox of human rights, one could elaborate on the basis of Arendt's considerations, expresses the danger that threatens a nation-state order by the *non-realisation* of human rights. The liberal and free democratic content of the nation-state found its most distinct expression in the declaration of human rights. Therefore, it is not surprising that the French Revolution started with the declaration of inalienable rights, which became the pillar of its constitution. In her examination, Arendt maintains that the traditional understanding of human rights could not be realised within a nation-state logic. Apart from the humanitarian consequences, Arendt argues that with an obvious

[35] *Cf* the illuminating critique by Otwin Massing (Massing 1993: 58ff).

political disregard of human rights, the nation-state loses a central legitimation principle of its order. '[M]ass-statelessness' (OT: 298), the rightlessness of the refugees, their difficult humanitarian situation and their illegality revealed that the moral and liberal aspects of a nation-state constitution and the talk of inalienable human rights 'were mere prejudice, hypocrisy, and cowardice' (OT: 269). Hereby the nation-state not only disavowed the enlightened and liberal idea of human rights, but also ridiculed 'the political apprehensions of the fully developed nation-states' (OT: XVII) and the 'conscience of the nation' (OT: 133), thus undermining the authority of an entire political order. The result was that supporters of a nation-state order, such as politicians, parliamentarians, journalists, intellectuals, etc, lost their power to convince people in the political debate about the interpretation and evaluation of events and developments. They thus missed the opportunity to highlight the vital differences between an authoritarian form of government on the one hand and a constitutional government on the other, and to warn of the consequences of a systemic shift that the radical left-wing or right-wing parties and movements would create. But why does Arendt believe that the liberal principles of human rights can never be guaranteed within a political order based upon the idea of nation-states?

First of all, her discourse on human rights confronts us with the irritating assertion that the situation of stateless refugees cannot be understood within the framework provided by the traditional understanding of human rights. Arendt argues that one cannot speak of the loss of human rights if one is deprived of this or that fundamental legal entitlement usually considered to be a human right. In this case one is proclaiming only individual rights that are designed to guarantee a constitutional minimum within a political community (see OT: 295f), However, the stateless refugees did not belong to any community, and therefore no laws existed for them at all. Together with their nationality they lost their 'place in the world which makes opinions significant and actions effective' (OT: 296). They had to rely on either the 'charity of private people or the helplessness of public bodies' (OT: 296). Arendt sarcastically calls their freedom of movement '*Hasenfreiheit*' (ETH: 613) (freedom of a hare), meaning that such freedom is illusory, and refers to the freedom of speech as 'a fool's freedom because what [such a person] thinks or says is of no interest to anything or anyone' (OT: 296). In short, Arendt considers this rightlessness to be the real 'human rights' violation. She points out that the authors of the human rights declaration had not realised that these individual rights were based on the right to be a member of a political group. But why had nobody thought of such a right? To what should human rights react if not to rightlessness?

In order to answer these questions that lead directly to the centre of the contradictions in the traditional concept of human rights, we need to look at the dimensions of the human rights declaration. Arendt distinguishes *four* dimensions. The first, the *moral-enlightenment dimension*, emphasises the fact that man liberated himself from all historical, societal, or religious authorities. It was no longer God or tradition that justified the state and its laws, it was the human being and his dignity that set the standard for right and wrong (see OT: 290f). In the second, *historical-functional dimension*, Arendt speaks of the 'historic implication' (ETH: 602)[36] of human rights. With the abolition of holy certainties through secularisation and the collapse of traditional customs and habits, human rights were expected to replace old guarantees and certainties. From then on human rights were to safeguard something 'that could not be guaranteed politically or that had never been guaranteed politically' (ETH: 602). With this, the idea of human rights 'acquired a new connotation' (OT: 293),[37] and its thoughts of freedom, especially the postulation of inalienable rights for all human beings, changed in the political area to a 'kind of additional law for those who had nothing better to fall back upon' (OT: 293). The tragedy of this change was that only those who were already powerless in the public realm called for human rights. Arendt specifies that not one important political figure or group referred to the human rights idea in its argumentations. The consequence was that human rights remained politically ineffectual as well as insignificant. Although this train of thought is pivotal for Arendt's political justification of human rights—which would open another discussion[38]—the third dimension of human rights is crucial for our considerations here. This *political-legal dimension* indicates that human rights were interwoven with the people's sovereignty and, therefore, were meant to be realised in the civil rights. Arendt writes:

> Man appeared as the only sovereign in matters of law as the people was proclaimed the only sovereign in matters of government. The people's sovereignty (different from that of the prince) was not proclaimed by the grace of God but in the name of Man, so that it seemed only natural that the inalienable rights of man would find their guarantee and become an inalienable part of the right of the people to sovereign self-government. (OT: 291)

If one looks at the fusion of people's sovereignty and human rights against the background of the moral-enlightenment dimension of the human rights idea,

[36] The English text only speaks of 'another implication of which the framers of the declaration were only half aware' (OT: 291). The German versions speaks of a 'geschichtlich sehr wesentliche Sinn' (ETH: 602).

[37] Arendt differentiates between the 'idea of human rights' and 'human rights'. By doing so, she reflects the difference between principle and content, which is characteristic of the philosophy of the 18th century.

[38] Elsewhere I have argued that there is a political justification of human rights in Arendt's work (see Volk 2008).

this fusion is confusing. Had the intention of the human rights declaration not been emancipation from all traditional authorities and recognition of man as the only standard? Yet the talk of a connection between human rights and people's sovereignty suggests that the isolating absolutism of man would not remain for long. The human being was categorised directly into the order and context of a political community, namely the nation, and the right to inalienable rights became dependent on the people's sovereignty. On the one hand, this 'curious conversion' (ETH: 604) was the result of the structural design of the concept of human rights. On the other, it was linked to the historic origins of the nation-state. To speak of the structural design of human rights, I want to point to the specific subject of examination, namely the concept of man. Due to this concept of man as an 'abstract human being' (ETH: 604), human rights were granted on the grounds of human dignity and nature. For Arendt, the problem with this approach lies in the fact that the 'abstract human being' was at no time and at no place a reality. Even indigenous people lived together in some form of human community, and humans were known at best as men and women. Arendt, therefore, arrives at the bemusing conclusion that the idea of human rights in this individualistic and abstract version was not operational in legal-political terms. The idea had to be changed in such a way that the concept of human rights could encompass the 'plurality of human beings' (ETH: 604)[39] and, by doing so, apply to the condition of a political community. With the means of the historical-political facts of the eighteenth century, plurality could be realised only if the individualistic-abstract concept was identified with the people. At first sight it is not directly clear why an individualistic-abstract concept of man was politically not practicable. Why is identifying an individual with the term 'the people' superior to the abstract concept of man? *Concreteness* and *objectivity*. Although the proclamation of inalienable and indispensable human rights emancipated human beings from traditional historical hierarchies and annihilated feudal privileges, to believe in the nature and dignity of a human being is no more concrete than to believe in history (see OT: 297f). Yet a citizen of a state was visible and perceptible. Above all, that citizen had a concrete authority that could deal with civic rights, in whatever form. In sum, man was set as an absolute on the basis of philosophical consideration. But because no authority could realise

[39] The German text reads: 'Die Paradoxie, die von Anfang an in dem Begriff der unveräußerbaren Menschenrechte lag, war, daß dieses Recht mit einem "Menschen überhaupt" rechnete, den es nirgends gab, da ja selbst die Wilden in irgendeiner Form menschlicher Gemeinschaft leben, ja, daß dieses Recht der Natur selbst förmlich zu widersprechen schien, da wir ja "Menschen" nur in der Form von Männern und Frauen kennen, also der Begriff des Menschen, wenn er politisch brauchbar gefaßt sein soll, die Pluralität der Menschen stets in sich einschließen muß. Diese Pluralität konnte nur wieder aufgeholt werden im Sinne der politischen Gegebenheiten des 18. Jahrhunderts, indem man den "Menschen überhaupt" mit dem Glied eines Volkes identifiziert.'

the abstract absoluteness, this 'idea of human rights' fell so low in the political arena that it finally came to rest in the lap of national sovereignty. The sovereign nation-state was the most powerful and most important political agent and the only authority that could guarantee any sorts of rights. This fact changed those inalienable and indispensable rights to which everybody should be entitled into rights that the respective state granted its citizens. In the case of the nation-state they were the civic rights of the nation.[40]

Apart from this internal explanation for the merging of human rights and sovereignty, Arendt also proposes a directly linked historical-political explanation. Human rights were anything but inalienable and indispensable. On the contrary, the French Revolution in particular demonstrated that they must be fought for in battles against an absolute monarchy. At this point we can speak of the *historical-political dimension* of the human rights idea. From the start, human rights were the result of national freedom struggles and, consequently, were connected to a people's right to self-determination. On the basis of historical experience, one was convinced that only the sovereign will of one's own people was in a position to guarantee human rights. The rights had been procured in battles against despotic usurpations and were proclaimed inalienable and indispensable in every civilised state. No other authorities were required to establish them. Hence, one believed that those peoples that still had to suffer under despotic or tyrannical rulers 'had not yet reached that stage of civilisation' (OT: 291).[41] The human rights concept stigmatised these regimes as illegitimate, and committed every thinking person to protest. This way, human rights functioned as a criterion that distinguished the civilised world from the uncivilised and the wild 'rest'. Rightlessness was not only a sign of the lack of civilisation; the assertion also prevailed that rightless persons did not exist in the civilised world.

In Arendt's view this belief was misleading. At the latest, when millions of refugees moved from one European country to the next it became apparent how deceptive the assumption of inalienable and indispensable rights in the civilised world, organised into nation-states, actually was. Even more, it illustrated

[40] Étienne Balibar and Julia Kristeva point out that this shift can already be found in the *Déclaration des droits de l'homme et du citoyen 1789*. While Article 1 of the Declaration of the Rights of Man and of the Citizen states that 'human beings' are and remain free and equal from birth, Article 6 suddenly refers to 'citizens'. Kristeva comments: 'One will note the talent of the drafters: the word "citizen" appears in a sentence where *rights* turn out to be civic *duties*—citizens will "work toward". And it is on account of this give-and-take of obligations and enjoyments that *man*, having become a *citizen*, will be protected as well as, in case of an offense, punished.' (Kristeva 1991: 149) At the same time, however, this passage underlines the fact that human rights were inconceivable anywhere other than in the context of the nation-state.

[41] In this sense one can read in John Stuart Mill, for example, that those peoples who suffered under despotic rulers were themselves still 'barbarians' who had not yet reached the 'maturity of their faculities' (Mill [1879] 2006: 16).

that a human rights guarantee was infinitely far away and that a nation-state order could not create the necessary requirements. The only guarantee that could be given was a guarantee for civic rights for the citizens of the same nation. Arendt argues that the reason why one could only include the 'plurality of human beings' in the concept of human rights from the eighteenth to the twentieth centuries by linking the individualistic-abstract concept of man with that of a people, results from the centuries-old belief in state sovereignty which the nation-state also followed. Probably it is going too far to generalise Carl Schmitt's provocative words, '[w]hoever invokes humanity wants to cheat' (Schmitt [1932] 2002: 54), as being the statement of a whole era, but they do express the core idea of a political order that recognises the sovereign will of a nation as the 'the sole legitimate criterion'. Within the political logic of the nation-state the term 'humanity' cannot be a 'political concept' (Schmitt [1932] 2002: 55) for Arendt either. Although the term does exist on a moral or a moral-philosophical level, as Kant's *Zum ewigen Frieden* ([1795] 1999a) shows, it never played an important role in political thinking.[42] In order to realise anything that resembles a human right and to guarantee every human being a place in the world, the term *humanity* must become a political concept—a concern to which Arendt's work is committed.

However, the sovereignty principle of a nation-state order is diametrically opposed to this concern. Arendt's criticism of this is not morally, ethically, anthropologically but purely *politically motivated.* Her assumption of a 'collapse of the system of nation-state' manifests itself as a massive loss of legitimation and authority in the paradox of human rights. Whereas the paradoxes centred attention on the domestic and the inter-state undermining of a nation-state order in Europe, here Arendt's criticism was that due to the politics of the nation-state, 'the mere phrase "human rights" … became for all concerned—victims, persecutors, and onlookers alike—the evidence of hopeless idealism or fumbling feeble-minded hypocrisy' (OT: 269).[43]

[42] Accordingly, Seyla Benhabib argues that in Kant's political thinking, 'exclusionary territorial control' is 'an unchecked sovereign privilege … which cannot be limited or trumped by other norms and institutions' (Benhabib 2004: 67).

[43] It has by now become commonplace, when thinking about the role of human rights in Hannah Arendt's thought, to assume that Arendt 'furtively' concurred with 'the ideas of Burke' (Kristeva 1991: 152 or 1993: 45) and 'was driven to resurrect the nation-state, even though her own analysis had already shown with perfect clarity where that could lead' (Fraser 2004: 257). Yet two key points are often overlooked here: first, Arendt criticises Burke and the entire English constitution massively for not integrating human rights in any form. In her view, precisely their absence and the constant emphasis on the 'right of an Englishman' were responsible for the formation of a very particular and politically noxious racial doctrine (see ETH: 390). Secondly, the thesis that Arendt wanted to reconstruct the nation-state overlooks Arendt's criticism of the concept both of nation and of state, including her conceptual reconsideration of the establishment of political communities. Arendt's thought advocates order but criticises the state on the one hand, and is cosmopolitan and non-nation-state-oriented on the other (see ch 4 and ch 5).

If one assumes that the liberal concept of the nation-states manifests itself in the 'idea of human rights', in the 'faith of the enlightenment' (Kristeva 1991: 152)—and Arendt does—then a '*whole way of life*' losses its authority, credibility and persuasive powers. Trying to convince the world of the liberal and free democratic potential of this form of government becomes a farce.

With Arendt's thesis of the 'collapse of a Europe of nation-states', the question of the stability of a nation-state order shifts to the centre of the examination in this chapter. I follow Arendt methodically in so far as I have examined the theoretical implications of four different phenomena. The benefit of doing so was to be able to demonstrate the problem of order, including its connection to questions of law, state and politics, to be key issues in Arendt's thought. However, this insight was possible only at the cost of terminological concessions. Specifically, I mean that central concepts such as 'nation' and 'state' were not elaborated and worked out theoretically but rather set. This deficit will be remedied in the next two chapters, where the political-theoretical content of Arendt's concept of nation and state will be thoroughly examined and reconstructed.

# 2

# *The Concept of the Nation in Hannah Arendt's Thought*

A great enthusiasm for the 'new specimens of mankind' (Herder) filled the hearts of the heroes of the French Revolution who were not only concerned with the liberation of the French nation, but who hoped to liberate all peoples under the colours of the tricolour, and make them into nations. This is what '*fraternité*' meant, and it was supposed to spread across the entire earth, for: '*La raison est de tous les climats*' (La Bruyère). And yet precisely in the very century that liberated the nation and became enthusiastic about the idea of mankind, we find the first seeds of the concept of race that destroyed the nations and annihilated the idea of mankind that had been born of the nation.

Hannah Arendt, *Elemente und Ursprünge totaler Herrschaft*

## I. INTRODUCTION

A BRIEF LOOK at the extensive literature on research into the nation and nationalism suffices to suggest just how ambitious it is to attempt to develop *one* single definition of the concept of 'nation'. Though it is not disputed that the nation embodies the key political 'idea of order' (Anter 2007: 238) in the modern age, there is no agreement on the actual substance of the concept of the nation. Andreas Anter highlights that fact that, despite their differences, attempts at a definition, such as those by Anderson, Fehrenbach, Gellner, Wehler, Furet or Hobsbawm, at least agree that there can never be *one* definition of 'nation' (*cf* Anderson 1996, Fehrenbach 1997, Gellner 1995, Hobsbawm 1991). For instance, Hobsbawm states in his classic text on nations and nationalism that it is pointless to define the term 'nation' because of the ambiguousness, inconstancy and vagueness of the criteria (see Hobsbawm 1991: 19). In order to take due account of this inconstancy and ambiguousness, research into the nation and nationalism has distinguished not only roughly three phases in which nations were formed (see Schieder 1991: 65–86), but also three versions of the concept of the nation, which (might) in turn arise within these phases.[1]

[1] Stefan Breuer, for example, points to the fact that in the revolutionary period alone a distinction would have to be made between two different versions of the concept of the nation in

Arendt attempts to address this complexity of the idea of the nation by observing the concept from very different perspectives, depending on the problematic context to which the term is applied. The concept of the nation is reflected from a *historical-political* perspective throughout large sections of Arendt's *Origins of Totalitarianism*. A *historical-political* perspective means that two factors that had been separate during the eighteenth century, national belongingness and the state apparatus, merged with the advent of the French Revolution. In her view, national liberation movements took hold wherever

> nations entered the scene of history and were emancipated when people had acquired a consciousness of themselves as cultural and historical entities, and of their territory as a permanent home, where history had left its visible traces, whose cultivation was the product of the common labour of their ancestors and whose future would depend upon the course of common civilization. (OT: 229)[2]

Like Hobsbawm, Arendt also emphasises the historically and culturally motivated self-conception of a crowd of people as a unit. This self-conception was allowed to form wherever people resided in a common area, cultivated the land, and thus generated a certain degree of permanence and symbolic continuity, which could create unity across generations. Arendt locates the idea of national belongingness primarily in a rooted farming class, and considers the emergence of nation-states as marking the end of migratory movements. While state structures went through a much longer development, albeit one that started earlier, national consciousness developed only much later, before ultimately advancing suddenly in the nineteenth century to become a decisive political factor.

Arendt also demonstrates a *political-phenomenological* manner of observing the nation. 'Nation' is defined here as a 'politically emancipated people' (NuD)—in contrast to a people determined by culture, language or religion. We might say that the *political-phenomenological* version of the concept of the nation acts as a kind of working definition that reveals nothing about the conceptual structure of the term—other than the fact of its being applied to a politically emancipated people. In principle the *political-phenomenological* concept of the nation is used only when Arendt—without seeing the need to provide any conceptual clarification—intervenes in political debates of the time.

relation to France: individualistic-territorial and holistic. Towards the end of the 19th century, with Barres and Maurras, this territorial holistic understanding of nation turned into an ethnic one (see Breuer 1998: 196).

[2] Arendt thus adopts the comments by Delos in his book *La Nation*. In her review for *The Review of Politics* in 1946 she writes: 'What now follows is a highly welcome clarification of some of the basic notions of historical writing. A people becomes a nation when "it takes conscience of itself according to its history"; as such it is attached to the soil which is the product of past labor and where history has left its traces. It represents the "milieu" into which man is born, a closed society to which one belongs by right of birth' (Arendt 1946: 139).

Yet neither of the approaches described helps us to probe those structural contradictions that Arendt establishes on the basis of the inter-war period and then attempts to position against the nation as a political concept of order in general. This is very clear from Arendt's proposition that the nation is always associated with a demand for homogeneity. In her examination of the problem of refugees and minorities she demonstrates that the nation-state of the inter-war period cannot deal with ethnic heterogeneity and is brought down by this fact. Her analysis is useful in the sense that it names those consequences for the nation-state that come about when the problems of the stateless persons, refugees and minorities are not addressed: the undermining of the character of the rule of law and the political order. Yet a very crucial intermediate step has been completely neglected thus far, namely, the question as to why the nation-state cannot handle heterogeneity. This silence is no coincidence; a glance at Arendt's book on totalitarianism provides only a very unsatisfactory answer. It is claimed there that the nation-state cannot handle heterogeneity because it is based on homogeneity. As to why the nation-state is based on homogeneity, whether it was always thus, and indeed what is meant by homogeneity in the first place, Arendt remains for the most part silent in *Elemente und Ursprünge totaler Herrschaft/Origins of Totalitarianism.* This silence prompts Hauke Brunkhorst to accuse her of ignoring the important differentiation—defined by Meinecke—between the state-nation and cultural nation. I have already dismissed this claim in the previous chapter. Arendt most certainly does formulate this distinction. Yet Brunkhorst's objection is not yet rebuffed. Quite the contrary: to take up Brunkhorst's argument, it might be possible to find passages in the *Elemente/Origins* that do indeed refer to the difference between the cultural nation and the state-nation. However, one could argue in line with Brunkhort that Arendt does not draw any conclusions from these passages for her understanding of 'nation'. Instead she lumps the different phenomena together, and thus misjudges the democratic and human rights-preserving potential of the French concept of nation. Brunkhorst writes:

> The self-conception of the French Republic was, like that of the Revolution of 1789, *assimilatory* and *juristic* in nature, culminating in imperialism, but never ethnic. The French human rights policy was never interested in an organic family of peoples with different historically-shaped constitutions, but instead in the historically blind demand to make all people French and to instil them with a French style of republican constitution. (Brunkhorst 1996: 338)

For Brunkhorst, Arendt views the nation solely from the perspective of a German, cultural-national and ethnic concept of homogeneity. This concept, however, cannot be applied one-to-one to France, Brunkhorst argues. To do so would be to neglect the juristic-democratic notion of the French concept of nation (see Brunkhorst 1996: 338f). Similarly, Ingeborg Maus argues that Arendt overlooks the fact that the people and the nation of the French Revolution are not based on a supposedly natural, substantial or historically developed identity. Arendt's interpretation falters, according to Maus, on the fact that 'the sovereignty of the people's will in the 18th century was considered just as universalistic as the idea of human rights itself, which is why they were able to connect' (Maus 1994: 204).[3]

Below I argue that the accusations levelled by Brunkhorst and Maus are misconceived. But to demonstrate this I shall not take the historical path, attempting to show that political belongingness is somehow inseparable from ethnic belongingness, also in France. I shall not confront Brunkhorst and Maus with any contrary historical interpretation: instead I shall demonstrate that Arendt denounces, with the accusation of homogeneity, the key consequence of *the manner of forming national political will.* I call this problematisation of the concept of nation *political-theoretical*, and shall therefore refer in future to the political-theoretical dimension of Arendt's concept of the nation.[4] My proposition is that homogeneity, or the demand for homogeneity on the part of the (French) nation, means for Arendt a homogeneity of the 'emotional mood' (ÜR: 99). Based on Arendt's unconventional interpretation of Rousseau's '*volonté générale*' (general will), I shall prove that Rousseau's demand for *aliénation totale* (Rousseau [1762] 2012: 50), which is the prerequisite for the formation of the general will, can only succeed on the basis of a specific 'emotional mood', which Arendt calls 'patriotism of the heart' (ÜR: 124).

How should we understand that? The *aliénation totale*, ie the self-restraint and relinquishing of all of one's interests for the sake of the common good, becomes a new political virtue and demands that the individual engage in a battle against himself, which can be conducted successfully only thanks to the emotional power of the right inner feeling or mood. How this emotional power arises, and how it helps to bring about the required self-restraint, is explained by Arendt in her discussion of pity. Arendt's analysis of pity is an analysis of the 'functionality' of the 'patriotism of the heart'. Arendt believes that the 'patriotism of the heart' is nothing less than the nucleus of the political-theoretical

[3] Similar arguments have been presented more recently by Jean L Cohen (see Cohen 2007: 307ff) and Jason Frank (see Frank 2010: 48ff). For a historical account in line with this argument see Brubaker 1994.

[4] Political-theoretical means that Arendt examines the specific form and presentation of a term in political life. In contrast, political-philosophical means the examination of the terms themselves. In this context, Arendt's *Vita activa/The Human Condition* could be called a political-philosophical work. In *Vita activa/The Human Condition* Arendt runs through the history of ideas, led by the questions as to how and why various different thinkers thought this way about the political and not in another way, and how the concept of the political relates to other terms. In contrast, *Über die Revolution* is, for example, a political-theoretical work, which deals primarily with the actual features of concepts in political life. The specific use of terms such as revolution, will, constitution, freedom, nature, etc are examined and dissected. Added to this is a clear focus on the functioning of political institutions. A political-theoretical perspective questions how the content of terms is presented concretely in 'political everyday life', and how this 'everyday life' itself in turn affects the content of terms.

version of the concept of nation, and the most explicit expression of the emergence of an *internalisation of the political* as a consequence of Rousseau's general will of the nation. Only those who can demonstrate the same purity of heart, who are homogeneous in relation to the 'inner life of the soul' (ÜR: 124), belong to the citizenry. Against the background of such an understanding of politics based on the *volonté générale*, only those who identify with the general will and take it as the 'supreme direction' can belong to the citizenry (Rousseau [1762] 2012: 50). I shall demonstrate Arendt's claim that it is impossible to reach an understanding with all those who seek something else, due to the inner composition of the 'patriotism of the heart'. The roots of Arendt's homogeneity theory can be found here: the battle against oneself becomes the battle against others. By these means, the mechanism of inclusion and exclusion, which forms the basis of the national, is established and becomes its central modus for the creation of identity and solidarity.

I have said that Arendt's book on the elements and origins of totalitarianism is 'for the most part' silent on this alternative understanding of homogeneity. 'For the most part' only because Arendt leaves a trail in *Elemente/Origins* that leads the reader to another thinker who pioneers a different approach to the concept of nation. That other thinker is Heinz Ziegler.[5] On the way to the aforementioned political-theoretical dimension of the concept of nation, which can clarify and reveal the origin of the internal contradictions, dysfunctionalities and inadequacy of the nation as a political concept of order, Arendt follows the remarks in Heinz Ziegler's study of the nation, published in 1931, in terms both of method and, in part, content. By method I mean the following: Ziegler's book on the nation hinted already, with its subtitle 'A Contribution to Political Sociology', at the analytical approach that would be taken. He writes:

> [W]e are concerned solely with the social or practical validity. We want to know: how and why does the concept of nation have an impact, how can it influence the behaviour of the masses, how can it mobilise individuals, how can it determine our consciousness and what are the consequences of all of that. We thus observe the nation as an idée-force. The point of interest is effectiveness, and social commitment, and not the theoretical value of this idea, the validity or invalidity of which remains a question in itself, on which our study cannot comment. It is perhaps important to emphasise this point, as there is the common misconception that such a sociological analysis of an ideological concept intends, at the same time, to relativize its validity in a normative sense. We believe that is not the case: instead it addresses a completely different problem, namely that of *social validity*, in other words the effectiveness and social commitment of such an idea. (Ziegler 1931: 15)

[5] Heinz Ziegler's study on the modern nation was published in 1931 (Ziegler 1931). Arendt draws extensively on this study in *Elemente und Ursprünge totaler Herrschaft/ Origins of Totalitarianism.*

The perspective suggested by Ziegler for his study of the nation is one that questions the political-social situation that determines the 'emergence and assertion of the nation as a form of legitimation' (Ziegler 1931: 69). In addition, Ziegler wishes to examine which ideological content the 'social commitment' managed to create and how this is composed. It is precisely this focus on the political-social situation of the revolutionary period that Arendt chooses in her substantive examination of the nation as a concept of order. Under which historical-social conditions did the nation become a central political concept? Why did it fit this situation so well? How and by which means did it deal with this historical-social situation? Which elements are still effective in the present-day concept of 'nation', and how do they determine the duration and stability of order?

Ziegler's approach is excellently suited to Arendt's own methodical understanding. Precisely, the conceptual analysis, the examination of the origins of a term, its different contextual integration and substantive modification, is beholden to the insight that historical-political experiences condense and solidify into concepts. Certainly the concept of 'nation' existed well before the French Revolution. But it was only with the Revolution that it became such a key concept within the political sphere. The question of when and in which circumstances a concept comes to shape reality is closely linked to Arendt's understanding of political theory and the history of ideas.

My thesis is that Arendt worked out this *political-theoretical dimension of the concept of nation* in her examination of the French Revolution. A series of intermediate steps is required in order to reveal the significance of this dimension of the concept of nation: to start with, section II. of this chapter attempts to give a new thrust to Arendt's contentious analysis of the social question in France. First I shall show that the French Revolution, according to Arendt, also makes a 'promising start' (ÜR: 93), with attempts to facilitate solidarity and belongingness by discursive-democratic means. However, this beginning proves to be a 'mere fiction' (OR: 68). Not only is it confronted by traditional ideas of 'how' a stable state order works, but the social question also demands a fundamentally different *consensus universalis*. By tracing how and to what extent the misery in France largely shaped questions regarding the constitution, political forms of organisation and—not least—political legitimation for Arendt, I provide a political-theoretical foundation for Arendt's thoughts on the social question. Her discourse on the social question is a reflection on the failure of the creation of a constitution in revolutionary France. Applied politically-theoretically, her discussion of the social question is therefore a discussion of the fact that France's social structures called for a different type of consensus building. In this historical phase the nation, in the theoretical vestment of Rousseau's *volonté générale*, rose to become the political *idée-force* of the age, as solidarity and identity could be formed, according to his thoughts on the general will, in a manner different from that of discursive-democratic participation. Precisely, this was the 'political-social function of the nation' (Ziegler 1931: 58).[6]

Section III of this chapter will address the question as to how precisely this other kind of solidarity and identity construction takes place, and which consequences it has for the conceptual framework of the political-theoretical dimension of the concept of nation. The central focus here is on Arendt's Rousseau interpretation. The key term for understanding this interpretation is Rousseau's 'total alienation', the absolute relinquishing of one's own interests as the basis for employing the general will as the 'supreme direction'. Yet Rousseau was aware that this alienation could not take place without difficulty. Accordingly he refers constantly to the 'opposition' (Rousseau [1762] 2012: 60), a battle against one's own private interest. This battle—and this is the point of Arendt's Rousseau discourse—was only possible on the basis of an 'emotional mood', which sufficiently motivates the combater in his battle against himself. This 'emotional mood' is fed by 'pity',[7] which—conceptually speaking—allows an emotional solidarity with 'the destitute', 'the oppressed' and 'the exploited'. At the same time, however, pity alters the perception of reality enormously. I shall show precisely what Arendt means conceptually by pity, and how the virtue of selflessness occupies the energetic centre of the concept of nation, thus making the nation fundamentally an 'irrational' concept of political order.

A brief word on my method is perhaps due at this point, before I present my differently weighted interpretation of Arendt's book on revolution: Arendt's thoughts on the French Revolution should not be understood in the sense of a historical or political-historical treatment. As such they are simply sub-complex—pace Arendt. A whole range of outstanding historians have pointed to the fact.[8] Hannah Arendt is also not Quentin Skinner—and that also applies to a certain extent to her Rousseau interpretation. It should be noted at this point also that she does not do justice to Rousseau's numerous, multifaceted and often contradictory thoughts, nor does she aim to. However, in this chapter I do not consider it my job to defend Rousseau against Arendt, or to point to the deficits and reductions in her interpretation of the French Revolution. Rather, I am more concerned with tracing Arendt's political narrative of

[6] Accordingly, Arendt does not overlook the discursive-democratic moment at the root of the concept of nation, but merely does not equate it with the *volonté générale* or the political content of the concept of nation. In order to regulate political matters in a discursive-democratic manner, according to her theory, the people do not need the idea of a nation as motivation. In reply to the question as to what can induce the individual to participate in the common political good, Arendt suggests a handful of reasons. It might be any one of a 'desire' to be politically active, 'worry' or 'interest'.

[7] For Arendt's discussion of the concept of 'pity', see OR: 65–91.

[8] See on this point my remarks in section II.A below.

the French Revolution—and Rousseau takes a very prominent position in this narrative. By these means I shall be able to tease out the political-theoretical arguments that are embedded in this narrative, gain new insights and thus reveal the structure of Arendt's argumentation.

## II. ARENDT AND THE SOCIAL QUESTION—A POLITICAL-THEORETICAL READJUSTMENT

### A. Revolution and Discourse

Much has been written about Arendt's book on revolution. She is usually accused of not representing the two Revolutions—the American and the French—adequately. While she ignores fundamental achievements of the French Revolution, it is claimed, she idealises the American.[9] Hobsbawm, for instance, asks whether Arendt's description in her book *On Revolution* could be of any interest to the historian. His answer is unambiguous:

> The answer, so far as the student of the French and most other modern revolutions is concerned, must be no. I am not able to judge her contribution to the study of the American Revolution, though I suspect that it is not great. (Hobsbawm 1977: 201f)[10]

Yet this dichotomous comparison is misleading, as it ignores and forgets what Arendt identified as an achievement, also attained by the French Revolution: the discursive-democratic moment. Although Arendt found that a new political type of rationality was realised with the American Revolution and did, in fact, contrast this with the Continental European tradition of politics and statehood, the simple dichotomy of a good *versus* bad new beginning conceals the qualities worth preserving of both Revolutions. I shall therefore suggest a differently weighted interpretation below. It is an interpretation that sees Arendt's analysis of the American and French Revolutions more as an attempt to emphasis the discursive-democratic and the civil-society potential at the foundations of both. Such an interpretation places the primary focus on the question as to how and under what conditions the political-democratic promise of both Revolutions can be preserved in a modern world. To interpret Arendt's comments merely as the negation of the French path misses the

[9] For example, Friedrich Jonas wrote as early as 1979, '[t]he American Revolution is therefore a good new beginning, the French a bad one' (F Jonas 1979: 273).

[10] Jonas takes the same line and argues that whoever seeks to learn more about the phenomenon of the revolution is set to be disappointed, as political, social and historical questions are treated with astonishing superficiality (see F Jonas 1979: 274). More recently, Lisa Disch posed the question how Arendt could 'glorify the American Revolution and revile the French?' (Disch 2011: 350).

intention of the book. What is more, if the drawing of a clear front between both Revolutions prevents us from reflecting on the 'promising start' (ÜR: 93) of the French Revolution, then a key dimension of the book is lost: Arendt's analysis of the concept of nation. For this dimension of *Über die Revolution/On Revolution* reveals itself only if we also take the French new beginning seriously. Therefore, we should take as our starting point the view that both Revolutions arose, according to Arendt, from the 'hatred of tyranny' and aimed to create a permanent polity that enabled freedom. Arendt writes on this point in *On Revolution*:

> To be sure, the men of the French Revolution had been inspired by hatred of tyranny, and they had no less risen in rebellion against oppression than the men who, in the admiring words of Daniel Webster, 'went to war for a preamble', and 'fought seven years for a declaration'. Against tyranny and oppression, not against exploitation and poverty, they had asserted the rights of the people from whose consent … all power must derive its legitimacy. Since they themselves were clearly politically powerless and hence among the oppressed, they felt they belonged to the people, and they did not need to summon up any solidarity with them. If they became their spokesmen, it was not in the sense that they did something for the people, be it for the sake of power over them or out of love for them; they spoke and acted as their representatives in a common cause. However, what turned out to remain true through the thirteen years of the American Revolution was quickly revealed to be *mere fiction* in the course of the French Revolution. (OR: 68, emphasis added)

When reading this quotation most Arendt interpreters pounce immediately on the distinction between the battle against oppression on the one hand and that against exploitation on the other hand. Her book is conventionally interpreted as claiming that the French Revolution certainly was interested in the establishment of liberty in its early phase, but then entered the treacherous terrain of the social question. This leads us back to the notorious subject of the relationship between political freedom and social liberation, a subject traditionally believed to be generally underdeveloped by Arendt in the first place. Supported by the starving masses, Julia Kristeva believes that Arendt sees the promising start 'destroyed' (Kristeva 2001: 121) by Robespierre's revolutionary apparatus. Hannah Pitkin is not sure whether Arendt blames the poor or perhaps the revolutionary leaders for the failure of the Revolution. With Arendt there is uncertainty

> as to whether it was the biologically driven poor or the sentiment-driven leaders who ruined the Revolution […]; sometimes both; and sometimes no one, as when she says that 'the shift of emphasis' in the French Revolution, from founding freedom toward alleviating suffering, 'was caused … by the course of the Revolution' itself, which seems no explanation at all. (Pitkin 1998: 221)

Pitkin thus concludes that Arendt's book on revolution, while it does present some brilliant insights, is ultimately 'profoundly incoherent' (Pitkin 1998: 219) and 'extraordinarily confusing and confused' (Pitkin 1998: 225). Seyla Benhabib comments that a mixture of manipulation and ideological necessity—Robespierre's philosophy of the natural law of the 'noble savage'—led to an alliance between the people and the Jacobins, which ends ultimately in the 'the replacement of political diversity' (Benhabib 2003: 162). Since the Toronto Conference of 1972 it has become customary in the academic literature to claim that Arendt makes an untenable distinction between the political and the social. This distinction is said not only to disregard the political dimension of social processes and emancipation movements, but also makes her thinking unfit for the analysis of present-day modern social and political orders.[11]

Without doubt, *On Revolution* contains passages that might document Arendt's disparaging attitude towards questions of social justice. Yet at the same time a number of passages suggest the opposite. Quite apart from the special situation of the black population, Arendt stresses, for example, that the comparison between the American and French Revolutions is 'unjust' and 'detrimental' to an understanding, precisely because in America people had never been confronted with such blatant social inequalities as they had in Europe. According to Arendt, the American Revolution never had to deal with the pressure of mass destitution, as was the case in Paris on a daily basis at the turn of the nineteenth century. For this reason, in her view, nothing could be more

> unjust or detrimental to a true understanding of these matters than to judge and condemn the men of the French Revolution from the perspective of the successful American Revolution. The success in America was due not only to the statesmanlike spirit of the 'founding fathers', albeit this spirit was at a very high moral and intellectual level.… The reason for the success as well as for the failure was the same: America was not subject to the curse of poverty. The establishment of freedom could only succeed because the 'founding fathers' were not obstructed by the

[11] See inter alia Bernstein 1986b: 238–59; Benhabib 1995a: 94; Cohen 1996: 165; Guggenberg 1993: 97–118; Höffe 1993: 23; Thaa 1997: 700–04. Jason Frank supported this reading once again more recently (see Frank 2010: 50). Such a critique of Arendt is justified insofar as one gets the impression that social justice can only be delivered technocratically, that is, via experts, administrators, and managers—an impression which would clearly contradict Arendt's own reflections on the nature of political acting under conditions of plurality. Here, for sure, one has to argue with Arendt against Arendt. Furthermore, her remarks in *The Human Condition*—but also from her critique of the workers' councils towards the end of *On Revolution* (see OR: 274)—seems to suggest that for Arendt the economic realm, in sharp contrast to the political realm, is not a sphere of freedom and not a sphere where citizens can have political aspirations. One important consequence of this sharp division between the economic and the political is the ruling-out of calls for economic or workplace democracy and democratisation, a long-standing theme for socially-concerned critical theorists. However, this common and to some extent well-put criticism needs to be careful not to condemn Arendt's approach to social questions so radically that it fails to grasp the political and political-theoretical dimensions of Arendt's socioeconomic considerations. (*cf* Volk 2015)

> *politically unsolvable social question*; but this foundation could not be universally valid in matters of freedom, as the entire rest of the world was and remained dominated by the misery of the masses. (ÜR: 85, emphasis added)[12]

Accordingly, the 'curse of poverty' was the key difference. No revolution of the time could have circumvented or solved this problem. The problem could not be solved politically in Europe because a certain technical standard, which would have made it possible to supply the urban masses with food, had not yet been reached. Very quickly it becomes clear that if we exaggerate too much in defending Arendt's position, we soon begin to highlight the fateful nature of the two Revolutions, with a Malthusian complexion. Furthermore, historians such as Robert Nisbet have shown convincingly how unsustainable it really is to limit the social question to Europe.[13]

On the other hand, however, it appears to me that political-theoretical, sociological and historical research has focused so much on this aspect that it no longer notices a central thought in *On Revolution*. The criticism attacks Arendt's treatment of the social question so radically that it can no longer admit the radicalness of Arendt's thoughts: Arendt's discourse of the social question in France emphasises the problem of a lack of *consensus universalis*, part of which was expressed in the failure of a permanent constitution. The Jacobins formulated an answer to the lack of a *consensus universalis* within French society that voices the core of the concept of nation. Precisely because the idea of the nation—in its political-theoretical version—was able to formulate a 'suitable' answer, it became the '*idée-force*' of the time. In other words, what Arendt does in *On Revolution* is nothing less than reflect in a political-theoretical light the socioeconomic situation in France at the time of the Revolution. In support of this change in perspective with regard to the social question there is a small and yet key reference, which can be found in the quotation above about the motivation of the revolutionaries and which I already highlighted there. In this passage Arendt describes the promising start of the French Revolution as a 'mere fiction':

> [T]hey spoke and acted as their representatives in a common cause. However, what turned out to remain true through the thirteen years of the American Revolution was quickly revealed to be *mere fiction* in the course of the French Revolution. (OR: 68, emphasis added)

The promising beginnings of freedom were therefore not suppressed, nor were they ruined, destroyed or otherwise halted in their development, as Pitkin,

[12] Parts of this passage can also be found in *On Revolution*—though not in this cohesive form. See OR: 54f.

[13] Robert Nisbet questions the limitation of the social question to Europe, and also criticises Arendt's opinion that the French Revolution was more influential than the American (Nisbet 1979: 245–56).

Kristeva and others would have it; the promising start had something fictional, unreal about it from the very beginning. What was unreal, fictional about this start was the idea that a 'common cause', a *consensus universalis*, had been reached, in whatever form. Behind this unreal, fictional nature of a merely ostensibly promising start, a different view of the book *On Revolution* opens up. However, before we can penetrate to this other perspective, we must first ask what it was that made the beginnings of the French Revolution appear so promising in the first place?

According to Arendt, what was seemingly auspicious at the beginning of the French Revolution was the fact that sections and popular societies had emerged in which solidarity and belongingness could be experienced by means of a discursive-democratic process of opinion making. Arendt reports discontent at the fact that the 48 sections of the Paris Commune were authorised only to elect delegates and to send representatives of the people to the National Assembly. They constituted themselves as regular 'self-governing bodies' (OR: 242). In the early phase of the French Revolution a number of so-called *sociétés populaires* were founded, whose only task—Arendt reverts here to Albert Soboul's book on Robespierre—was to

> discuss the laws to be passed, obtain clarity on the existing laws, monitor all public offices … and instruct their fellow citizens on the true principles of the constitution, and to place the constitution in the public light, without which it could not survive. (ÜR: 307)

According to Arendt, Robespierre was one of the leading advocates of this form of political-discursive opinion making: if the objective of the Revolution was the preservation and conquest of freedom, then the clubs and the popular societies were the only places in which this freedom could be practised. Although Robespierre's attitude was to change abruptly as soon as he seized power with the Jacobins, in that early phase he glimpsed, according to Arendt, the 'the first manifestations of freedom and public spirit' (OR: 245) in the debates of the popular societies. In contrast to the widespread belief that Arendt misjudges the achievements of the French Revolution and 'minimizes the new political spaces created by the people and for the people—the revolutionary societies, the clubs, the municipal councils and militia, women's associations' (Benhabib 2003: 163), she reports with great enthusiasm that these sections and popular societies thoroughly embodied political freedom. She quotes extensively from the statutes, for it is here that we see how the people organised themselves, ie how they regulated changes in office, installed the president and vice-president, and determined the frequency of sessions:

> [T]he president and half of the secretaries are replaced every month, so that all members have the chance to hold office. And what is the purpose of the society? It 'deals with everything that concerns freedom, equality, unity and indivisibility of

> the republic, in order to enlighten themselves and especially to inform themselves on the respect due to the laws and decrees that are promulgated'. This was achieved by exchanging opinions: 'Opinions are conscientiously respected as long as they do not infringe public order. A speaker may not be interrupted for any reason.' If 'he digresses or gets tiresome, the audience stands up. As soon as six have risen, the president must consult the assembly'. (ÜR: 311)[14]

The free political-democratic core of the French Revolution can be found in this type of discourse among the citizens. Political enlightenment is conducted here, and the political representatives are controlled democratically. The sections and popular societies provided a forum in which real opinion making was possible and the French people could gather political experience for the very first time. It is therefore not surprising, according to Arendt, that the 'immortal constitution' was praised so highly in such societies, and called 'sublime' (OR: 246), since it was this that guaranteed each of them the right to political participation within the newly created sections. If they had continued generating belongingness and solidarity within the citizenry in this manner, then a constitution would have been constituted which, according to Saint-Just, '"would have changed everything if … they would have conducted themselves according to their own proper spirit"' (OR: 246). But it turned out to be a 'mere fiction' that the democratic procedures of the sections and popular societies constituted the *consensus universalis* in France.

## B. Sovereignty and Misery

The central thesis of this entire chapter will be to claim that instead of the consensus on the democratic procedures for forming political opinion, as described by the sections and popular societies in Arendt's account, a different kind of solidarity and identity construction prevailed in the course of the French Revolution. The logic of this other kind of identity and solidarity formation constitutes the notional core of the concept of nation—or, to put it more precisely, its political-theoretical dimension of meaning. However, before I can tease out this other kind of identity construction, a number of intermediate steps are necessary in terms of conceptual clarifications and descriptions of political-social context. A first and important step here is the question as to why, according to Arendt, the sections and popular societies were not retained? Or more precisely, what was so fictional about this supposed consensus and libertarian impulse? Two key answers to this question can be found in Arendt's work: first, the lack of political experience among the revolutionaries and the fact that they fell into the western tradition of

[14] See also OR: 246.

thinking in terms of hierarchical state organisation and sovereignty; secondly, the specific configuration of the French misery.

With regard to the first reason, Arendt's claim is that discursive-democratic spaces are incompatible with the idea of sovereignty and thus with the accompanying hierarchical structure of the state. While Arendt takes the view in the case of the American Revolution that the loss of political significance of the town halls—of those spaces in which the 'political spirit of the revolution' (ÜR: 298) was at home—was the result of a '"tragic oversight"' (OR: 238),[15] she derives this loss of political significance in the case of the French Revolution directly from the handed-down idea of the structural make-up of the Continental state. Arendt explains this assessment based on the shifting esteem for the sections and popular societies on the part of Robespierre and Saint-Just: before Robespierre and Saint-Just each held the reins of state authority in their hands, they were both convinced that the popular societies, clubs and sections were the only places in which political freedom could become reality and be exercised by the citizens. What is more, both assumed that the formation of the 'public spirit' (OR: 243) that occurred there was a vital question for the stability of the community, and adjudged the persecution of the popular societies by the National Assembly or the regional parliaments to be the greatest '"crimes against the Revolution"' (OR: 243). Their attitude changed the moment they seized power. From then on Robespierre spoke only of the '"so-called popular societies"' (OR: 243) and disparaged all associations apart from the Jacobins as '"bastard societies"' (OR: 250). For Saint-Just the popular societies were engaged only in planning the great '"conspiracy"'. The reason for this 'turning about' (OR: 243) of principles was, from Arendt's state-critical perspective, the adherence to the idea of a 'mercilessly centralized power apparatus'. Arendt argues that if one were truly of the opinion that power could exist only 'under the condition of centralization of power, the societies, each a small power structure of its own, and the self-government of the Communes were clearly a danger for the centralized state power' (OR: 248).

As soon as the French revolutionaries fell in line with the Continental European tradition of 'state absolutism' (ÜR: 203)[16] out of a mixture of a lack

[15] In this case Arendt cites approvingly the assessment by Lewis Mumford that the lack of constitutional institutionalisation of non-parliamentary, political spheres of action was a '"tragic oversight"'. This oversight can be explained, says Arendt, on the one hand by the fact that the Americans considered the political spirit that had formed in the pre-revolutionary period to be so self-evident that they did not see the necessity of conserving it in any form. On the other hand, the town halls—the epitome of this political spirit—remained completely untouched by the Revolution, so that nobody ever considered institutionalising them constitutionally. The consequence of this oversight was that the local town and village councils suffered great losses of power and influence in everyday political business and that—sooner or later—that place of the specific political spirit of the Revolution was lost.

[16] See also OR: 154.

of political experience, philosophical conviction and conventional ideas of legitimation, and made the representation of the people into a '"monopoly" of the state' (OT: 251), they thus adopted the idea that power is at its greatest when it is monopolised and centralised at one point. Against this background, different centres of power, such as those represented by the sections and popular societies, equated to a loss of power and were therefore considered 'fatally dangerous'.

The 'danger' posed to the Continental European state by the sections and popular societies that emerged in the course of the Revolution resulted from two features, according to Arendt: their 'non-partisan character' (OR: 250) on the one hand, and their federal orientation on the other (see ÜR: 314). Because these societies lived precisely from the convergence of political interests and exchanges on the political questions of the day, opinions were formed during discourse, and differed from day to day and subject to subject. This principled openness and undeterminability, the conflictive spirit and the unforeseeable result were in stark contrast to the idea of the uniformity of a people, which had now taken the place of the king on the throne. The multiplicity of opinions that were repeatedly formed and re-formed within these discursive-democratic spaces, depending on place, time and subject, served to underline the fact that there was no such thing as a unanimous will that could have been represented or symbolised or otherwise made noticeable. Against this background, according to Arendt, it became clear that if 'the people' really were to 'govern', fundamentally different state structures were needed, and a totally different idea of statehood from that which monopolised all power at the top would be necessary. Furthermore, the federal orientation of the sections indicated the existence of very different 'sources of power' on the same territory, which was not at all directed or controlled by the state. The sections thus contravened the 'majesty of the sovereign state' (ÜR: 27).[17] Arendt concludes that, irrespective of the form taken by these discursive-democratic spaces in detail, whether as popular societies or sections, town halls, or workers', soldiers' or students' councils, they produced as a result of their features the 'seeds of a new revolutionary organisation of the state' (ÜR: 319) or the 'feeble germs of a new form of government' (OR: 252). These 'seeds' or 'germs' were incompatible with the localisation and definition of power in the traditional understanding of the Continental state and were smothered at once. One can therefore say that the hope—based on the western idea of state and sovereignty—that it might be possible to institutionalise discursive-democratic spaces permanently, is a 'mere fiction'. The new type of political rationality emerging in the discursive-democratic spaces demands a kind of

[17] See also OR: 16.

structural organisation of political order fundamentally different from what the traditional statist approach could provide.[18]

The line of criticism presented is certainly of great importance for Arendt's thought. For this reason I shall address her critique of state directly in chapter four. But with regard to our analysis of the concept of nation, we should focus on another of Arendt's arguments for the time being: the misery of the masses. For this misery emphasises a different kind of 'fictional' feature of the sections and popular societies of France, which is seminal for Arendt's understanding of the concept of nation.

What is fictional about the idea that the sections and popular societies could form the basis of the *consensus universalis* with their discursive-democratic methods of opinion forming and decision making is the fact that the majority of the people of France—in the first instance the so-called 'wretched masses'—were *de facto* excluded from this *consensus* from the very beginning. The wretched masses did not destroy the spaces of practised political freedom; they never belonged to them in the first place. Driven by the destitution that subjected the masses to the 'the absolute dictate of their bodies' (OR: 54), all their thoughts and strengths were expended solely on a daily battle for survival. What is interesting here is Arendt's view towards America and the narrative she builds upon it. Severe poverty also existed in America, albeit not with the same degree of misery as in Europe. What is decisive now is the comment that poverty in America was not a social problem, as in Europe, but rather a political problem (see ÜR: 86).[19] How can the distinction between a social and a political problem be understood?

In contrast to Europe, the problem of poverty in America was the fact that it 'automatically excluded [the poor] from active participation in government—though, of course, not from being represented and from choosing their representatives' (OR: 63). The parenthesis is of central significance; Arendt thus stresses that the majority of the American population supports the basic parliamentary order, despite poverty. It is a different situation in France. Just as for Arendt the fight for civil rights by the black population is a fight against the constitution—as a manifestation of the 'original crime' (CD: 91)—a basic political order that is based on sections and popular societies becomes the enemy of the destitute masses. The main difference, of course, is that the exclusion in the first case is racist in character and the second is socio-economic. But apart from that, the wretched masses of France find themselves in a politically 'similar' situation at the end of the eighteenth century. They too, *de facto*, did not belong to the political citizenry or to the constitutive people who could assemble in

[18] *Cf* ch 5.

[19] For the English version see OR: 63.

the sections and popular societies. This consideration opens the door to the political-theoretical core of the social question: in contrast to America, where poverty facilitated political competition between different parties, the solution to the social question in France must become a state objective. The negotiating and political debating in the sections and popular societies about the future and the next political steps are no longer capable of reaching a majority. The reason for this lies in the different configuration of poverty in each case and its different magnitude on both sides of the ocean. In contrast to America, where there was 'only' poverty, the misery in France demanded immediate satisfaction. The poverty in America, in Arendt's narrative, robbed large sections of the population of active political participation, but did not demand a totally different political form of government. Instead the poor in America were left with the well-founded hope that their situation would improve over the course of time, and this hope was enough for the time being. They lived in poverty, but not under the oppressive misery that prevailed in Europe. Accordingly, they entrusted their interests to political representatives, who could then represent their specific interests and concerns in parliament. It was a different matter in France: there, misery threatened life and existence on a daily basis; misery arose there with an intensity that demanded an immediate reaction:

> Poverty is more than deprivation, it is a state of constant want and acute misery whose ignominy consists in its dehumanizing force; poverty ['misery' would be more exact here] is abject because it puts men under the absolute dictate of their bodies, that is, under the absolute dictate of necessity as all men know it from their most intimate experience and outside all speculation. (OR: 54)

Although Arendt abandons the previously postulated separation of misery and poverty here and presents a different configuration of poverty—poverty as misery, we could call it—it is still clear that an inevitable, 'acute', 'irresistible' and 'absolute' improvement to the material situation was necessary for the population of France. If we leave aside the fact that Arendt's historical references are questionable and in most cases not shared by historians, Arendt's argument here is that against such a background, the emphasis of the newly won political freedom, which could indeed be enjoyed in the sections and popular societies, was simply meaningless. Misery not only made every discussion superfluous—for it is impossible to discuss anything in the face of the direct consequences of hunger and the bitterest misery. Its immediate appeasement is a basic human need, and thus stands apart from the spectrum of subjects to be negotiated politically, precisely because there is no alternative. Arendt says that the only thing capable of consensus for these people was the satisfaction of their needs. In other words, only the direct satisfaction of needs and the removal of misery could form the basis of the *consensus universalis*, and therefore had to become the highest political priority.

## C. Misery and Consensus

For Arendt, mass misery was of fundamental importance for the further course of the French Revolution. If the point of the sections and popular societies was to promote political belongingness and solidarity within society by means of discussion, listening and being listened to from various different positions, the 'truly interminable suffering of an inestimably large number of people' (ÜR: 114) exposed this intention as a 'mere fiction'. The majority of the people were *de facto* excluded from these spaces from the outset due to the socio-economic situation. In the historical moment in which the concerns of these people also became public concerns upon the advent of the Revolution, it emerged that the necessary *consensus universalis* did not exist. In other words, that society was still very far removed from the constitution as a political entity. Accordingly, Arendt writes:

> In France the downfall of the monarchy did not change the relationship between rulers and ruled, between government and the nation, and no change of government seemed able to heal the rift between them. The revolutionary governments, in this respect not unlike their predecessors, were neither of the people nor by the people, but at best for the people, and at worst 'usurpation of sovereign power' by self-styled representatives who had put themselves 'in absolute independence with respect to the nation.' The trouble was that all chief difference between the nation and its representatives in all factions had very little to do with 'virtue and genius,' as Robespierre and others had hoped, but lay exclusively in the conspicuous difference of social condition which came to light only after the revolution had been achieved. (OR: 69)

This passage is an excellent example of how Arendt obscures the problem to be addressed by means of terminological confusion. Not only are the terms 'nation' and 'people' used identically here, but additional dimensions are introduced with the state and government, which are apparently intended to reflect the same problem. But they do not. What resonates in all of these allusions, but gets confused, is the question as to what constitutes a political unit from a more or less undefined crowd of people on the one hand, and its legal-political constitution on the other. Although both questions usually blur in practice, in a political-theoretical observation a very clear distinction must be made between the formation of a group from a large number of individuals, and the determination of the structure with which this group is authorised to act as a whole. Although Arendt is not at all clear in her terminology, she has the first of the two problems in mind here. In the quotation above Arendt speaks of a rift between rulers and ruled. The rift results from the very different social conditions, and places the revolutionary government in a similarly unfavourable light as that with which the legitimatory deficit of the monarchical power structure had been detected.[20]

[20] See also Frank 2010: 44.

Politically this is expressed in the fact that the new revolutionary government 'were neither of the people nor by the people'. Arendt's terminological imprecision becomes particularly pronounced at this point, because the definition of 'the people' is used very specifically here to mean the wretched people. This passage would not make any sense otherwise, since most of the revolutionaries did not come either from the nobility or from the church. The wretched people, according to Arendt, do not recognise the revolutionary elites as their equals. The reason for this is the completely different social condition, which made it impossible to produce 'unanimity, on one occasion at least' as demanded by Rousseau for the creation of a constitution. As is well known, Rousseau explains the necessity of establishing unanimity on 'one occasion at least' in the fifth chapter of the first book of the *Social Contract.* He argues against Grotius that one must examine the act that creates 'the true foundation of society', by which means 'a people is a people' (Rousseau [1762] 2012: 49), before examining how the people subject themselves to a king.

In Arendt's interpretation of the first years of the Revolution, the lack of a 'true foundation of society' becomes the central political problem.[21] No sustainable basic political consensus could be formed within French society—and that appears to be the political-theoretical argument upon which Arendt's narrative is based at this point. In her view, the lack of approval for the constitution was simply an expression of the fact that there was no such thing as *the* consensus, which was supposed to be symbolised by the constitution and awaken the people to 'existence and life' (Rousseau [1762] 2012: 66). For Arendt the 'rift' is compelling proof of the fact that the common political objective, which was supposed to be expressed in a moderate constitution by the establishment of a space for discursive-democratic opinion making, was a mere chimera and not capable of consensus. The fundamental consensus, that which according to Rousseau gives 'the body politics existence and life' (Rousseau [1762] 2012: 66), had to take a different form. The failure of the constitution revealed the

> inescapable fact ... that liberation from tyranny spelled freedom only for the few and was hardly felt by the many who remained loaded down by their misery. These had to be liberated once more, and compared to this liberation from the yoke of necessity, the original liberation from tyranny must have looked like child's play. (OR: 69)

The sections and popular societies become irrelevant, replaced by the need for liberation from necessity and misery. This shift becomes inevitable, according

[21] According to Arendt, this lack of a French nation is expressed historically most clearly by the fact that the Girondists did not manage to pass a viable and generally accepted constitution. Arendt mentions numerous reasons for the failure, but in light of the political events, the Constitution of 1791 remained a 'piece of paper' (OR: 122) because it did not get the approval of broad sections of the population—in the first instance, of course, that of the wretched masses.

to Arendt, because no other substantial interest could find a power base within French society.[22] Arendt seeks to make clear that a state could be established in France only with the support of the wretched masses. For this to happen, however, the interests of this stratum of the population would immediately have to become the leading interests of a future or incipient community. That is the 'practical' (ÜR: 310) background, which the revolutionary institutions sacrificed in favour of the traditional, Continental European structure of the state. The revolutionaries take on 'the corps of the absolutist administration, as it corresponds well to the new demands for the calculability of state action and the uniform control of mass behaviour' (Ziegler 1931: 86).[23] The legitimatory gap between rulers and ruled was to be closed by declaring the liberation from need and misery to be the highest state goal, the national interest. Yet the switch in course from discourse and procedures to a substantial interest had great consequences not only for the development of the political community: in the very first instance it formed the internal framework of the concept of nation. Historically, Arendt dates this switch to the Jacobins' seizure of power. Arendt sees in this event the advent of that stage in which the concept of nation became the decisive political concept of the time and formed its specific political-theoretical content, which is examined in the following sections. The political-theoretical dimensions of the concept of nation were formed at a time and under socio-economic conditions when society threatened to break under the conflicting interests, on the one hand, and debilitating misery on the other.

If we ignore questions of historical exactitude and reflect on Arendt's discussion of the social question from a political-theoretical perspective, we can see, astonishingly, that it is not as far removed from Habermas's critique as he believed in his review of *Über die Revolution*. Habermas comments critically:

> We can discuss sensibly the conditions of political freedom only in the context of an emancipation of rule. This category of rule may not separate political power from social power, but must instead show them both for what they are: repression. Under the conditions of social dependence, the best right to political freedom remains ideology. (Habermas 1981: 227)

Arendt should have expressed it just as clearly, because it is also her view that the structural forces of social inequality can be studied most precisely from

[22] Arendt writes on this point: 'By these means the leading men of France learned a lesson in human need, which they would not forget for a long time. But one shouldn't overlook the fact that the people also received its first lesson in human dignity and freedom in the same period. An enormous appetite for debate, instruction, mutual enlightenment and exchange of opinion developed in the popular societies and sections of the Commune, and this appetite was practically free of intent in a sometimes directly touching manner; the primary intention was certainly not to exert pressure on the rulers' (ÜR: 315). See also OR: 249.

[23] See on this point ch 3 and the comment that very similar assessments of the French Revolution can also be found in Burke, Hegel, Tocqueville and Weber. *Cf* also Benhabib 2003: 161.

the mass misery of France in its politically destructive consequences. Despite the political revolution, striking social inequality continues to perpetuate the relationship between rulers and ruled, and 'exposes' the 'promising start' as a 'mere fiction'. It is undisputed that the 'curse of mass misery' (ÜR: 204) is only one reason, together with the lack of political experience, philosophical conviction and handed-down ideas of legitimation, for the failure—according to Arendt—of this beginning and of the idea of enabling solidarity and a feeling of belongingness by means of a discursive-democratic process. Nevertheless, Arendt is convinced that political freedom and equality without social rights is a fiction that—sooner or later—shatters in the face of reality:[24]

> While it is true that national equality, on which the new state form was based, had prevailed to such an extent that for the most part the former ruling groups had been politically disempowered and the formerly oppressed classes were politically liberated, albeit with the loss of the economic protection of the old order; however *in its concrete effect, equality was reversed immediately due to the emergence of class society*, whose main feature was that one always remained in the class into which one was born, with very few exceptions. *True equality*, such as that which the Jacobins in the French Revolution demanded and wanted to carry out by means of the state-secured establishment of a society of small entrepreneurs, came about only in America, under very different circumstances. The conditions in the new continent, in which there was a natural surplus, which was simply waiting to be developed and realised, *made it possible to add the equality of all before the law, based socially on the opportunity given to all at birth.* The fundamental contrast between a form of government based on equality and a society in which the inequality of circumstances at birth is solidified in classes, prevented both the formation of real republics and the emergence of a new political hierarchy. (ETH: 49f, emphasis added)[25]

There can be no clearer rejection of all those critics who accuse Arendt of ignoring the social dimension of politics and the political. Taking the example of equality, a fundamental political category, Arendt explains what it means when the political-legal guarantee is faced with social conditions that question on a daily basis the propagated equality in the political process. In its 'concrete effect', political-legal equality is reversed and political freedom made impossible. A succession of political thinkers have accused Arendt of ignoring those problems that are of key political importance: matters of distribution and questions of justice. Albrecht Wellmer summarises this view pithily when he claims, supposedly in contrast to Arendt, 'that the problems Marx confronted are still our—political—problems' (Wellmer 2000: 235). I do not wish to dispute that her reply at the aforementioned conference in Toronto, which

[24] *Cf* on this point in particular my comments on the internal link between politics and law in ch 5.

[25] A similar, yet not identical and less explicit passage can be found in OT: 12f.

is usually taken as a starting point for the criticism, does little to elucidate the problem (*cf* DiT: 90f). It is a different matter, however, with the above comments: 'true equality' can only exist where one is liberated from the acute needs of the life process and is able to lead a life that can, to a certain extent and at certain times at least, emancipate itself from the demands of the life process. In her response to a contribution by Charles Frankel, Arendt stresses that '[b]efore we ask the poor for idealism, we must first make them citizens: and this involves so changing the circumstances of their private lives that they become capable of enjoying the "public"' (PRPI: 106 f).[26] In her thoughts on the prerequisites for political equality, Arendt seems to be much closer to Marx than Habermas, Wellmer or she herself would like to admit (see here also Disch 2011: 351).

Arendt's critique, which she develops in her thoughts on the French Revolution, takes two directions and works on two levels: it is *first* a criticism of the manner in which the processes of power formation were organised in France under Jacobin rule in the course of the emergence of the social question. At the point where the concerns of the 'wretched masses' became public concerns and when it was clear that no state could be established without this majority of the population, the interests of this stratum of the population were placed directly among the main interests of an incipient community. The idea of 'acting with one another' in the discursive-democratic institutions (sections and popular societies) in the early phase of the Revolution—the 'promising start' of the French Revolution—transformed into a condition of 'acting for each other'. Liberation from need and misery became a principle of 'acting for each other'; it was declared to be the highest priority of the state, to be in the national interest. The consequences are well known: the suppression of all discursive-democratic spaces, the establishment of an understanding of politics based on sovereignty in the tradition of an absolutist *potestas legibus soluta*, the Reign of Terror and the failure of the Revolution in the foundation of freedom. However, this interpretation of the Arendtian critique—that the pressure of need and misery changes the political mode of action in which processes of power formation operate—is only the first part of her critique of power. Taken alone it remains incomplete and is incorrect. For Arendt's critique of power in her thoughts on the French Revolution is, *secondly*, a critique

[26] In her assessment of social justice in America, however, Arendt is anything but clear. In the *Denktagebuch* she writes in 1952 that 'human dignity has been restored' in America due to the 'actual power of organised labour', the 'relative abolition of the classes', the 'removal of misery' and the 'market situation that has been achieved, in which labour has become the most expensive "good"' (DT: 202). At the same time we read in a letter to Jaspers in 1946 that the USA is a country that is based on the 'fundamental contradiction' between 'political freedom' and 'social servitude' (Arendt/Jaspers: 67).

of the idea that discursive-democratic procedures could have led *at all* to the foundation of an order of freedom—given the social and economic relationships of rule and exploitation. Against the background of conditions of need and misery, sections, popular societies, councils and similar places of political experiences of freedom are extremely elitist, exclusive and excluding—and the plea inherent to them for an open and rational debate could easily degenerate to an ideology.

The consequence for the subject of nation building is that, in her political narrative, Arendt assumes that the social structures demanded a substantial initial consensus of a different kind, thus at the same time providing the Revolution with its new objective. At this moment, the nation becomes a central political concept and formulates its political-theoretical dimension of meaning. Instead of discursive-democratic procedures, the men of the French Revolution aspire to substantial, pre-discursive or supra-discursive commonalities.

## III. THE CONCEPT OF THE NATION AND THE *VOLONTÉ GÉNÉRALE*

### A. Arendt, Rousseau and the French Revolution

> Rousseau's '*volonté générale*' is perhaps the most murderous solution to the squaring of the circle, namely the fundamental problem of all Western political philosophy, how to make a singularity out of a plurality—in Rousseau's words: 'réunir une multitude en un corps' … What makes this solution so murderous is the fact that the sovereign is no longer one or a number of persons who rule over me, but he instead, as it were, sits within me—as the 'citoyen' opposed to the 'homme particulier'. In the '*volonté générale*' each man does indeed become his own executioner.
>
> Hannah Arendt, *Denktagebuch*

During this historical phase, and against the background of the situation described above, Rousseau's ideas on the *volonté générale* developed an unexpected persuasiveness. His thoughts were 'so extraordinarily convenient' to the revolutionaries because, with Rousseau's help, a number of people could be formed into a 'many-headed one' (OR: 72), precisely *without* a discursive-democratic process. His 'consensus of the heart' (Habermas 1990: 171) did not require a discourse to generate solidarity and identification within the community. Rather, general will could form best of all wherever 'citizens had no communication among themselves' (Rousseau [1762] 2012: 60). According to Arendt, what occurs *theoretically* with Rousseau and attains an unexpected plausibility *in practice* in the French Revolution, due to the social situation, is the *internalisation of the political*. With Rousseau, the identity and solidarity-establishing power comes from the heart: the last thing it needs is discourse. This internalisation of the political reaches the core of the political-theoretical dimension of Arendt's concept of the nation. In addressing Rousseau and his ideas on the *volonté générale*, Arendt spells out this political-theoretical dimension. I argue that the most important aspect of Arendt's Rousseau discourse is that her interpretation of the *manner* in which the general will is formed describes the nucleus of her political-theoretical understanding of nation. To exaggerate somewhat, Arendt's Rousseau interpretation therefore provides nothing less than the key to her understanding of the political history of the nineteenth and twentieth centuries.[27] With Rousseau the nation becomes a homogeneous united will with a claim to absoluteness, which is always, in every legislative act, identical to itself.

It is therefore no coincidence that Arendt's examination of Rousseau takes place specifically in *On Revolution*. Rousseau is the theorist of the French Revolution. And not only did this Revolution mark the birth of the nation as a central political factor; in addition, Rousseau's idea of a unanimous general will became historical reality for the first time and experienced the expression of its content. The necessity of liberating the masses from poverty and misery, in Arendt's interpretation, was so obvious that it was bound to become the uniform interest of the Third Estate, and indeed also concerned all those with 'hearts and minds' (ÜR: 87). Although Arendt emphasises that the men of the Revolution took up the cause of the wretched masses in the first instance out of power-political necessity—no state would have been possible without the support of the masses—she certainly takes the moral impulse seriously. Accordingly, she evaluates the attempt to free the masses from misery and poverty, and the accompanying facilitation of a 'dignified life', as a logical consequence of the human dignity inherent in the declaration of human rights. Indeed Rousseau was not the first to note that a functioning order must also be able to facilitate liberty if it is to fulfil the criterion of legitimate rule. Thus the first specification of the *volonté générale*, in Arendt's view, is to improve the national welfare. Naturally, the substance of a national will is bound to change over the course of time and appear on the world's stage in ever-changing costumes. But what remains the same in all of these appearances, according to Arendt, is the *manner* in which national interests are presented to mass effect. What exactly is meant by the term 'manner'?

The justification with which we ascribe a general will to the French Revolution lies in the fact that with this will the people became an object of the political public sphere, reduced to their purely biological needs by the prevailing misery, where each resembled the others in their hunger. Within this historical

[27] See on this point also my remarks on 'Arendt's Political-theoretical Architecture of Origins of Totalitarianism' in ch 4.

context, Arendt finds that Rousseau's thought on the general will attains a degree of empirical foundation. She comments on this as follows:

> The 'malheureux' whom the French Revolution had brought out of the darkness of their necessity and their misery were a multitude only in the merely numerical sense. Rousseau's image of the 'multitude … united in one body' and driven by one will was an exact description of what they actually were, for what urged them on was the quest for bread, and the cry for bread will always be uttered in one voice. Insofar as we all need bread, we are indeed all the same, and may as well unite into one body. (ÜR: 120)[28]

Two things are expressed in this point: first, it is underlined that talk of unanimous will did in fact have a real reference to the everyday existence of a certain section of the population. In all, according to Arendt's narrative, 'the "malheureux"' expended great energy day after day in order to secure somehow a means of subsistence. Though numerous, they were united in their fate of being engaged in a relentless battle against hunger. To Arendt, the common social circumstances of absolute destitution and the resulting common interest legitimise talk of the wretched masses as a homogeneous unit.[29] Secondly, the passage is revealing because in relation to these masses—and only here—Arendt agrees with Rousseau's identification of interest and will, which can be traced throughout all of his political-theoretical statements in the *Social Contract*. Being 'urged on' by hunger does indeed become a 'cry'. Here the interest, seen as a manifestation of the real, temporal position of the individual in the social structure, coincides with the will.

Even if the accordance between will and interest is correct in the case of the destitute masses, Arendt argues that the same does not by any means apply to the rest of society. The difficulty that arose from the required identification of the national will with the will of the wretched, was that not only did the structure and objectives of the Revolution bring change by these means, but also that all actors appeared in a new light due to the substantiation of the political objectives. According to Arendt, the revolutionaries, in bringing about liberation from tyranny, were still acting in their own interest. After all, they themselves had been politically unfree under the absolutist monarchy—and this now changed abruptly. For Arendt, the revolutionaries came from completely different circles and belonged to a totally different social stratum from the class of population they claimed to represent. They were mostly embedded in the bourgeoisie, like Robespierre, who came from a family of lawyers, or Saint-Just, whose father was a cavalry officer. Their lives and works had nothing in common with the

[28] See also OR: 89.

[29] According to Arendt, the 'political danger of poverty' (ÜR: 120) lies in this reduction to the purely biological life process which, when it attains such prominence as in revolutionary France, destroys all plurality, allowing the wretched to speak with *one* voice.

starving masses of France. But if the general will reflects the nation, and coincides with the interests of the destitute, then strictly speaking neither the majority of the revolutionaries nor the rest of society belongs to the nation.

It soon becomes very apparent that this problem has nothing to do with the typical dilemma of representative rule. Rather, the problem is that, with the liberation of broad strata of society from poverty and misery as the new objective of national politics, will and interest remain separate for the rest of society. This generates the task of convincing the rest of society to recognise the interests of the wretched masses as an overreaching, national interest, and to make it the 'supreme direction' of its own actions. The answer to this, as provided by Rousseau, is 'total alienation'. In the next section I shall demonstrate the significance of 'total alienation' in Rousseau's thoughts on general will, and in the process—with Arendt—highlight the question as to the prerequisites for this alienation. By these means attention is drawn to a discourse that has received hardly any notice so far in comments about Arendt's book on revolution: the discourse of compassion.

## B. General Will and Alienation

Rousseau is a theorist of freedom, whose ideas should guarantee freedom for all individuals. At the same time he recognised that human plurality is condensed into very different interests, which is likely to make it difficult to organise a form of coexistence that allows each to attain his rights. The success of this coexistence is suggested by the term *volonté générale*. For in order to form such a society, each individual must waive his interests and rights and abandon himself 'entirely' (Rousseau [1762] 2012: 50). Only by these means is it possible to create the same basic conditions for all, and to such a complete extent that interests can never come into conflict. Rousseau calls this act 'total alienation', and its theoretical content lies in the reduction of plurality[30] or, more precisely, in its elimination. The act of 'total alienation' reduces the number of persons with different interests to one single person: Rousseau calls it the 'public person' (Rousseau [1762] 2012: 50). He ascertains that this public person, in executing his will, at the same time realises his interest.[31] However, neither

[30] Rawls's 'veil of ignorance' (Rawls [1971] 1998: 36) follows a similar objective. He is also concerned with reducing the plurality of perspectives by 'liberating' the individual from his specific position in the social order. In this manner he can reach his two fundamental principles of justice (see Rawls [1971] 1998: 81ff).

[31] If there is only one person left in the realm of the political, the meaning of the concept of interest also dissolves, for 'between' whom can there 'be' anything, as suggested by the phrase *inter-est* (see HC: 182). Then it is indeed irrelevant whether the interest thus understood can be identified with the will, or whether it maintains its independent meaning.

the abandonment of one's own interest nor the identification of the will with means of action can readily be understood. With regard to the individual interest, Rousseau speaks of an 'opposition', while Arendt even calls it a 'rebellion' (OR: 69) and refers in her interpretation to a footnote in the third chapter of the second book of the *Social Contract*:

> 'Each interest,' says the Marquis d'Argenson, 'has different principles. The agreement of two particular interests is formed by opposition to a third party's interest.' He might have added that the agreement of all interests is formed by opposition to each one's interest. If there were no different interests, the common interest would scarcely be sensible since it would never encounter obstacle: everything would run by itself, and politics would cease to be an art. (Rousseau [1762] 2012: 60)

For Rousseau, opposition to individual interests is a central prerequisite for generating a uniform and homogeneous will. Drawing a frontline against a third party creates the necessary 'agreement'. Here the opponent is not in fact the interlocutor, who might have something to interject, but rather, as a 'third party', he is a means to agreement, and thus solely negative. Yet the central problem is the question of how this 'total alienation' can be brought about in the first place. In other words, how can the 'opposition' of individual interest be overcome? What can motivate the individual to renounce all of his interests for the sake of the public person that is to emerge?

It is generally assumed with Rousseau that a union between free and equal individuals comes about in a contract for rational reasons. Other parts of the *Social Contract*, in contrast, indicate that Rousseau was most certainly aware of the 'fiction of the contractualist tradition' (Habermas 1998: 116) of his thoughts and the possible limitations that accompany them. Bruno Schmid addresses such passages and points out in his Rousseau book, entitled *Sittliche Existenz in Entfremdung* (*Moral Existence in Alienation*), that while Rousseau, with his understanding of *aliénation*, ostensibly picks up on a central concept of political and legal-philosophical tradition, he accentuates it very differently (Schmid 1983). Alienation in the legal-philosophical tradition of contractarianism, Schmid argues, means the act of law by which the individual alienates his rights to the sovereign. With Rousseau, however, such a purely juridical obligation on the part of the citizen does not suffice to provide the body politic with a sustainable foundation. Schmid thus sees Rousseau as relying on affective sources:

> The bond of the individual to society must be conducted, in his view, at an affective level. On the other hand, the extent of this affective bond may not be subject to vagary; it must have the character of a binding, comprehensive committal. (Schmid 1983: 408)

According to Schmid, this 'comprehensive committal' points to the 'anthropological dimension of "aliénation"' (Schmid 1983: 404), which enables a new kind of existence for people, based completely on the community. However, it is unclear from Rousseau's work how people can be motivated to adopt this kind of *aliénation.* At first glance, the solution for Rousseau seems to lie in virtue. However, as Schmid questions critically, 'how can a person who does not yet know virtue decide in favour of "*aliénation*"?' (Schmid 1983: 417). Ultimately, Schmid solves the problem of motivation by rejecting the utilitarian trait in favour of a theological-ethical one, and gives the '*religion civile*' as a basis for motivation to adopt alienation—albeit with certain theory-coherent reservations (see Schmid 1983: 419–65).

Like Schmid, Ulrich Preuß also focused his attention on, what Schmid calls the 'unsolved problem of motivation to "*aliénation*"' (Schmid 1983: 415). In contrast to Schmid, Preuß points to a pre-political trait in the *Social Contract,* which undermines the social contract idea of the unification of free and equal people. According to Preuß, Rousseau does not rely on reason or civil religion, but instead on the unifying power of ethnic homogeneity. Here Preuß refers to the chapter ten of the second book of the *Social Contract,* in which Rousseau asks what kind of people is best suited for legislation (Preuß 2006: 385). This shows, Preuß argues, that Rousseau also has greater confidence in a people 'finding itself already bound together by some union of origin, interest, or convention' (Rousseau [1762] 2012: 77). Preuß therefore concludes:

> His assumption of a preconstitutional union and coherence of the people would limit the validity of his contention that his construction of the social contract generates the solidarity which binds a multitude of individuals to a social group. More important for our contemporary problems is the question of whether the constitutional state presupposes some minimum degree of prepolitical sameness and homogeneity of the constituent power. (Preuß 2006: 385)

I do not wish to discuss Preuß's thoughts on ethnic homogeneity in Rousseau's work, but simply acknowledge his and Schmid's indication that Rousseau himself is unclear on the manner in which the creation of a nation might succeed and how permanent it might be. In other words, whether a state can indeed be created only with a group of people that already demonstrates a minimum amount of pre-political equality and homogeneity? Preuß's and Schmid's thoughts are so valuable in this context because they direct attention to the question as to which conditions are necessary for the required alienation, and the accompanying identification with the general will, to succeed at all. Like Preuß, Arendt also doubts that Rousseau was satisfied with the rational solution. But instead of searching for passages that expose him as a secret theorist of *ethnic* homogeneity, she opts for a different method: by working out the logic of the affective dimension in Rousseau, Arendt names both the origin of the homogeneity claim and the cause of the modus of inclusion and exclusion in the national construction of identity and solidarity.

According to Arendt, Rousseau is aware that the required '*aliénation totale*', the battle of the individual against his individual interests and the identification of the individual will with that of the nation, cannot be achieved simply with rational reasoning. What is needed instead is much more the 'pleas for passion, for the heart, for the soul, and especially for the soul torn in two' (OR: 75) which is aroused by pity:

> To partake in the body politic of the nation, each citizen must rise and remain in constant rebellion against himself and his own interests. Compassion with others, which after all certainly contradicts one's own interest, is the *emotional mood*, so to speak, in which this rebellion against oneself and the submission to the general will can be realised in the simplest and most natural manner. (ÜR: 99f, emphasis added)[32]

This passage is of fundamental importance to understanding the political-theoretical dimension of Arendt's concept of nation, as it expresses, in a very condensed form, the manner in which national identity is created and how the required 'act of showing solidarity' (ÜR: 94) should be: identity is generated by means of a constant rebellion against oneself. Solidarity in the context of nation, in contrast, means an act of identifying one's own will with that of the general public. Both constructions—that of identity and of solidarity—are naturally connected to each other in the sense that the required act of showing solidarity can only succeed where one has already ceded one's own interests. Both the generation of identity and the act of demonstrating solidarity are supported, borne and driven by an 'emotional mood', namely compassion, which allows one to maintain virtuous self-control. Nussbaum thus notes in her thoughts on Rousseau that compassion, according to Rousseau, represents 'the root of each successful citizenry' (Nussbaum 2000: 149). Although the pointer to pity/compassion still requires more detailed clarification, Arendt argues that Rousseau's demand for an '*aliénation totale*' represents a reinterpretation of the concept of virtue: thus the object of virtue is no longer the *res publica*; rather, 'virtue meant having the welfare of the people in mind, identifying one's own will with the will of the people' (OR: 68).[33] From that point on, according to Arendt, it became customary to 'equate' virtue 'with selflessness' (OR: 74). In other words, self-restriction or selflessness and the abandonment of one's own interests for the benefit of the general will become the badge of a good citizen.

However, before we can begin to scrutinize the constructions of identity and solidarity at the level of the nation, the way in which pity/compassion works must be examined more closely. This is the only means by which not merely to complete Arendt's answer to Rousseau's 'unsolved problem of motivation',

[32] Parts of the passage can also be found in OR: 73f.

[33] Arendt speaks of Robespierre here, but Robespierre 'preached a virtue that was borrowed from Rousseau' (OR: 74).

but also to take a decisive step towards Arendt's (political-theoretical) understanding of the nation: the *way in which pity works* is nothing less than a description of what Arendt, following Robespierre, calls the 'patriotism of the heart'. The patriotism of the heart, however, forms the core of the concept of nation and the phrase as such epitomises the internalisation of the political which works alongside this concept.

## C. The Internalisation of the Political

### *i. From Compassion to Pity*

Arendt's discussion of Rousseau's concept of pity in *On Revolution* is inspired in many points by Nietzsche's strong criticism of a 'philosophy of pity' (Nietzsche [1881] 1972b: 109). Even at the point where Arendt distances herself from Nietzsche and counters his one-sided plea that pity is a 'sin' (Nietzsche [1882] 1972c: 306) with a more balanced elaboration of this type of emotion, she still seems to accept Nietzsche's lament of 'how clumsily with this one word does language fall foul of such a … polyphonous organism!' Arendt separates the '*simple*' (Nietzsche [1881] 1972b: 106) German term '*Mitleid*' (pity) into the English expressions 'pity' and 'compassion'. In the German version of the book *Über die Revolution* compassion is used to mean 'true (co-)suffering', '*wirkliches Mit-Leiden*' (ÜR: 108) or simply in the gerund as 'suffering' (*Mitleiden*). Pity (*Mitleid*), on the other hand, is the feeling generated by observing suffering from a distance.

Arendt's intensive and condensed discussion of pity in *On Revolution* is heavily pre-suppositional and difficult to understand without reverting to central concepts in her work. The discourse on pity becomes clear in its political-theoretical significance only when one realises the function that the concept, in her view, had for Rousseau; the extent to which compassion becomes pity, arising from this function; and ultimately which mechanisms are brought to bear behind the concept of pity. A look at the *The Human Condition* is essential for this purpose. There, Arendt refers to Rousseau as the theorist of intimacy, who prepared the way for the 'modern individual' (HC: 39) with his 'rebellion of heart … against the demands of the social, against what we would call today the conformism inherent in every society'. In order to understand Rousseau's flight into the sphere of intimacy, one needs to realise that he withdraws from a society that is already in the middle of a process of disintegrating. The private sphere was precisely that area which had been considered until then a safe place of retreat for the individual:

> The first articulate explorer and to an extent even theorist of intimacy was Jean-Jacques Rousseau … He arrived at his discovery through a rebellion not against the oppression of the state but against society's unbearable perversion of the human heart, its intrusion upon an innermost region in man which until then had needed no special protection. (HC: 39)

Accordingly, Rousseau's protest was one that began to argue from the inner human depths, from the heart—as a symbol of the feelings. And this starting point for the rebellion was by no means coincidental. For the place that had remained untroubled by public exposure for centuries now threatened increasingly to fall victim to the emergence of society. Rousseau recognised that the relentless advance of the social would, in the final instance, not stop at the inner human depths, the intimate.[34] Whether he was also aware, on the other hand, of the common nature of attacker and defender is doubtful. For, taking account of the unfathomability of the social, Rousseau's rebellion retreated to a region that possessed no place in the world. Just as society, which is nowhere and thus everywhere, cannot be localised—as the home was once the symbolic expression of the private or the *agora* that of the public—the place of protest becomes similarly worldless with the retreat to the subjective emotional life (*cf* Volk 2005: 64–72).

According to Arendt, man—thrown back radically upon himself and ensnared in his emotional life—loses the ability to perceive reality outside of himself. His senses, his moods, his inner conflicts, his feelings, in brief his individual desires and needs become the only determining aids to orientation for him. From the insistence on subjective need, 'reality does not lie in the public presence of others, but rather in the *greater or lesser urgency of needs* to whose existence or non-existence nobody can ever testify except the one who happens to suffer them' (HC: 56, emphasis added).

With Rousseau, reality is not attained from a '"testimonial" concept' (Saavedra 2002: 120) but rather from an emotion diagram. That which is felt is real. That which is felt more intensely is even more real. Anything that invites projection while at the same time promising an intense feeling is set up to provide the desired result. Reality thus degenerates into idiosyncratic projection. The feeling of the individual is the final aim and, as a consequence, shapes the world in such a manner that it can also be grasped with its one-dimensional instrument of perception. Of importance here are those affects that arouse the heart, as this, according to Arendt, allows one to experience one's own body as the first outside world. Desire, pain and everything else contained in the range of emotions are those internal senses whose greatest stimulation leads to self-affirmation (see DT: 509). At the same time, however, it is precisely these emotional stirrings that separate one from the whole world that exists outside oneself. In an increasingly uncertain world that has lost its secure standards as a result of revolutions, secularisation, economic progress and scientific discoveries, the intensification of one's own feelings serves as a supposed proof or guarantee of the fact that one can at least be sure of oneself. Timid self-affirmation in the form of 'I feel, therefore I am'.

[34] See on this point Rousseau's distinction between the *amour de soi* and *amour propre* (Rousseau [1755] 1995: 169).

Thus Rousseau's discourse of pity must be understood precisely from the motivational basis just outlined, which represents a key component of Arendt's critique of modernity. If we take this view, it becomes clear that 'the moral tarantula Rousseau' (Nietzsche [1881] 1972b: 13) is not terribly interested in the misfortune of others, but rather places his hope in the 'movement of one's own heart' (ÜR: 112),[35] which is prompted by the sight of the suffering of others. In 'Menschliches, Allzumenschliches' (Human, All too Human), Nietzsche seems to take this aspect into consideration when he writes that the 'thirst for pity is a thirst for self-enjoyment' (Nietzsche [1878] 1972a: 486) which seeks to be satiated. Taking this 'thirst' as a starting point, the substantial content of the term *compassion* changes for Rousseau, and turns compassion into *pity*. Arendt argues:

> In this sphere of intimacy, however, it was not passions—the emotion of suffering in view of powers or events outside of the individual—that were decisive, but rather feelings, sentiments and emotions, in brief everything that could be aroused by the newly-discovered scale of the stimulus of the heart. Compassion therefore was discovered and understood as a self-reflecting feeling, and the feeling of passionate emotion at the suffering of others is, of course, pity, in the common sense. (ÜR: 112)[36]

In the English version, pity is defined as 'the sentiment which corresponds to the passion of compassion' (OR: 83). Accordingly, pity means this 'passion of compassion' and no longer compassion itself. Thus when Rousseau speaks of pity, he is not thinking of 'true suffering', understood as being directly affected by the specific, obvious suffering of a concrete individual. Rather, he means an emotion that affects the entire range of feelings, through which pity is enabled in the first place. As Rousseau makes clear in his essay 'On the Origin of Languages', precisely the capacity for empathy should prevent one from feeling only oneself and thus permanently obstructing successful and lasting solidarity with others. (see Rousseau [1781] 1981: 186)[37] Arendt, in contrast, argues that due to the status, meaning and function that compassion has in Rousseau's thoughts—as an intense feeling for the purpose of self-affirmation—compassion changes its internal arrangement and turns into pity. By means of its function as a seismograph of reality, compassion becomes consolidated

[35] See OR: 83.

[36] The passage in *On Revolution* reads: 'In this sphere of intimacy, compassion became talkative, as it were, since it came to serve, together with passions and with suffering, as stimulus for the vitality of the newly discovered range of emotions. Compassion, in other words, was covered and understood as an emotion or a sentiment, and the sentiment which corresponds to the passion of compassion is, of course, pity' (OR: 83). Elsewhere Arendt speaks of the 'loquacity of pity' (OR: 81).

[37] Rousseau there writes: 'Whoever is without empathy feels only himself; he is alone amongst the human race.' (Rousseau [1753] 1981: 186)

and transformed into pity. Whereas in 'true suffering' the distance between the person specifically suffering and one's own person is practically extinguished, leading to an 'awkwardness with words' (OR: 81) that causes one to express oneself rather by gestures and looks, Rousseau's pity maintains a distance from the very beginning.

Only by distancing himself can the individual become excited, with fiery speeches and agitation, by the image he has created. For the image of the destitute masses of France as '*le peuple, les malheureux m'applaudissent*', in Robespierre's words, or, in those of Sieyès, '*le peuple toujours malheureux*' (ÜR: 95) is a projection—for Arendt, this is beyond any doubt. Only by distancing themselves could the men of the Revolution manage to lose themselves in fiery speeches and agitation about the suffering of others, who had long been allowed to appear only in a 'depersonalised' (OR: 80) manner as the poor, '*toujours malheureux*'. Depersonalisation had also been mentioned already by Nietzsche. In his 'Die Fröhliche Wissenschaft' (Gay Science) he highlights the fact that 'it belongs to the nature of the emotion of pity to divest unfamiliar suffering of its properly personal character' (Nietzsche [1882] 1972c: 473). To be more precise, then, one does not suffer with the sufferer but rather with what one has created, the suffering object. Because this suffering object is merely an internal image projected outwardly, one ultimately suffers with oneself, becomes intoxicated by one's own words, images, etc, and delights in the feeling that one has generated within oneself. One is transfixed by one's own feelings and emotionality.

Accordingly, the concept of pity for Arendt must be seen as a kind of place holder, which stands for the capability to identify with a prepared object—in the case of the French Revolution this meant the wretched masses, for whom the Revolution created access to the public sphere and through whom the great misery was visible to all—in such a manner that one's own heart is set, so to speak, in motion. It is therefore conceivable that the mechanism—increased visibility, projection, stimulation of the heart, identification—also takes effect with a very different object. To put it another way, that the 'emotional mood', the 'passionate compassion' not only ignites for social topics, but is also—as later in the Napoleonic Wars—sparked by contrasting pairs such as liberator and oppressor, friend and enemy.[38] For pity, in the first instance, means the excitement of one's own heart; one becomes excited by the excitement. With regard to Arendt's Rousseau discourse and the question of the motivation to the '*aliénation totale*', pity means a capability for suffering that disperses both 'petty egotism' and 'callous reason', and creates an emotional disposition that allows one to establish the general will as the supreme direction and to act accordingly.

[38] See on this point also Nietzsche [1882] 1972c. There, Nietzsche refers to pity as an 'admittedly secret desire'.

It has already been pointed out in the course of addressing the '*aliénation totale*' how the concept of virtue changes with Rousseau. Whereas in the Roman tradition it had always been connected with and related to the outer world, the *res publica*, with Rousseau—according to Arendt—it centred solely on the individual self. Selflessness, self-restriction, become the foundation of the concept of virtue. The remarks have shown that this selflessness and self-restriction are possible only thanks to the motivating power of pity. Thus it is revealed that the virtue of selflessness, according to Arendt, had always been linked to a high emotional charge. To put it differently: in Arendt's Rousseau interpretation, service to the community is a service that draws its strength from the heart. This changes not only the concept of virtue for Rousseau but also, as a logical consequence, the understanding of patriotism. Patriotism, understood as service to the public cause, becomes 'patriotism of the heart', which is concerned with the purity of one's own heart—as this is now seen as the prerequisite for being able to serve the community.[39]

If we summarise roughly the considerations above, we can establish the following: by reflecting the social question in a political-theoretical light, we reveal Arendt's conviction that no state could have been created in France by discursive-democratic means. Underpinned by the misery on the streets of Paris, Rousseau's thoughts on the *volonté générale* developed immense plausibility

[39] A completely different interpretative appreciation of Rousseau's thoughts on pity can be found in Martha Nussbaum's work. Precisely, the 'compassionate imagining of oneself in the other's position' is 'of great importance for good citizenship in a world in which we unavoidably encounter the other, the stranger' (Nussbaum 2000: 147f). This capability, Nussbaum continues, must be urgently cultivated if one wants to erect a political order that respects the difference in the other beyond mere lip service. It is thus fundamental to apply Rousseau's thoughts on pity, for he argued convincingly that the view of the suffering of others has a special power that tears us out of our selfishness: 'The view of suffering has this power because it reminds us of our own vulnerability and makes us aware of the adversities that could happen to us. In our curiosity about the quality of life, catastrophes and hazards stimulate our thoughts much more powerfully than placid or happy events. For this reason the painful forms the basis for our attachment to the other.' (Nussbaum 2000: 150) Specifically, Nussbaum's conclusion that the painful becomes the basis of our solidarity with the other, would have prompted massive criticism from Arendt. For example, in her Lessing Speech she quotes Cicero in opposing the affective character of pity (LR: 30): '"Or, are we unable to be open-handed without pity?" In other words, should human beings be so shabby that they are incapable of acting humanly unless spurred and as it were compelled by their own pain when they see others suffer?' Now it is most certainly not the case that Arendt denies or cannot acknowledge the 'mimetic impulse' (*cf* Adorno [1966] 1997c: 281) upon observing the suffering of others. She merely rejects its capability to organise political solidarity and to establish permanent order. For sincere compassion for the suffering of the specific other can never be generalised without the actual impulse to destroy compassion for the specific suffering of a person. In addition, this 'real compassion' is always silent and, according to Arendt, is expressed only by gestures and glances, as she illustrates in her thoughts on Jesus' silence in Dostoyevsky's 'The Grand Inquisitor' and Billy Budd's stammer in Melville's work (see OR: 77). The reason for the muteness of real compassion is that, as with love, all distance between the specific sufferer and the truly compassionate (co-sufferer) is dissolved. The world that lay between the two and via which one could have communicated disappears. Precisely for this reason, according to Arendt, true compassion can never be of political significance.

and persuasiveness at this historical point in time. The establishment of a general will, formed according to the interests of the wretched masses, was only possible if the rest of society could be convinced to waive its own interests. Selflessness and total alienation are the key words.[40] But this battle against oneself, against one's own interests, could only be conducted, according to Arendt, with pity as a motivating power. Looking to her statements in *The Human Condition*, we can see what function pity played for Rousseau, and how compassion is consolidated into pity by these means. The motivating power of pity arises from the fact that the object, with whose interests or will one is supposed to identify, is prepared in such a manner that it stimulates one's own heart. But to what extent was this functionality of pity of significance to the French Revolution?

### *ii. Pity and the Concept of Nation in the French Revolution*

When assessing how significant pity was to the French Revolution, one should perhaps consider where the object for which one should have pity is politically formed and where the 'conscious forming' of pity, ie its public display, was 'declared to be the cardinal virtue of the political'. What is meant here is the shaping of the content of the concept of nation and its identification with Sieyès' '*toujours malheureux*'.

When it became clear with the failure of the constitution that, as Arendt claims, there was a lack of a suitable body politic, the question of both power and legitimation arose anew. Initially, all actions that were compatible with the political will of the people appeared to be legitimate. But who or what is the people? And what is its political will? Arendt writes on this point:

> The words *le peuple* are the key words for every understanding of the French Revolution, and their connotations were determined by those who were exposed to the spectacle of the people's sufferings, which they themselves did not share. For the first time, the word covered more than those who did not participate in government, not the citizens but the low people. The very definition of the word was born out of compassion, and the term became the equivalent for misfortune and unhappiness—*le peuple, les malheureux m'applaudissent*, as Robespierre was wont to say; *le peuple toujours malheureux*, as even Sieyès … put it. (OR: 69f)

[40] Although Arendt does not extensively cite the passages in the *Social Contract*, she most likely thought of those passages in which Rousseau rejects common discussion, the exchange of opinion and consultation in the constitution of the general will—and indeed even considers the exchange of information to be damaging: 'the more concord reigns in the assemblies, that is to say the closer opinions come to unanimity, the more the general will also predominates; whereas long debates, dissensions, disturbances, signal the ascendancy of particular interests and the decline of the State' (Rousseau [1762] 2012: 123). The alienation enabled by pity prepares the way to making the true needs and necessity of the general will 'universally seen'. The first man to propose them '*only states what all have already sensed*' (Rousseau [1762] 2012: 121, emphasis added).

Similar to the transformation of compassion to pity with Rousseau, a (sincere) compassion for the suffering of the people also consolidates itself and solidifies in the concept of nation among the men of the Revolution. From now on the people are conceived of only as a suffering mass, leading to the claim for the self-renunciation of all, for '*aliénation totale*'. It thus becomes clear how '*le peuple*', as the political version of the people, was in Arendt's view a product of the revolutionary elite, who attempted 'to achieve solidarity with the unfortunate and the miserable' (LR: 29) with the help of the passion of compassion. There is no doubt that the masses were united with regard to their misery. But according to Arendt, they did not represent a political unit with the corresponding feeling of togetherness. The differences between the individual professions and social strata of the Third Estate were, according to Arendt, so weighty that there can be no question of an all-encompassing consensus of interests. However, by equating 'the people' with the destitute masses, and thus raising the interests of these masses to the order of national interests, the path was prepared for the people to assume the moral status that is expected of legitimate decision-makers. In addition, by these means the men of the Revolution justified their efforts for those interests that were not directly linked to their own social position and origin.[41]

[41] As well as the transformation from compassion to pity, described above, Arendt senses a further possibility for pity to very much manifest itself politically. The consequences, however, would not be any less fatal: 'As a rule, it is not compassion which sets out to change worldly conditions in order to ease human suffering, but if it does, it will shun the drawn-out wearisome processes of persuasion, negotiation, and compromise, which are the processes of law and politics, and lend its voice to the suffering itself, which must claim for swift and direct action, that is, for action with the means of violence.' (OR: 82) I think that we can interpret this passage as a reply to Benjamin's thoughts on 'pure divine violence' (Benjamin [1920–21] 1965: 60). Arendt's talk of 'direct action', of the violent action of true compassion when dealing with the world, corresponds in my view with Benjamin's remarks on 'pure immediate violence' (Benjamin [1920–21] 1965: 59), the 'holy manifestation' (Benjamin [1920–21] 1965: 60) of a 'violent truth' (Benjamin [1920–21] 1965: 62), recognising in this violence not a means, but rather direct action or the manifestation of justice. As is well known, Benjamin regards this holy manifestation of a divine violence as the only way out of the eternal recurrence of oppression and violence. Arendt, in her silent criticism of Benjamin, certainly does not follow the (misleading) path of Derrida, who even goes so far as to claim that he recognises in Benjamin's thoughts a harbinger of the final solution, for which he has been criticised (Derrida 1991: 123f; and the criticism by Lindner 1997). The core of Arendt's critique is most likely directed at the apolitical monism of Benjamin's thought, which radiates from his work on violence. Violence against others is justified from the Archimedean point of an idea of justice. This violence does not claim victims but takes them. The founding act of Benjamin's order is, according to Arendt, thoroughly without communication, and will never be able to free itself from this lack of communication. The reason for this is that Benjamin operates with ideas of the absolute good, of a divine justice, to which one either aligns oneself or which one rejects. No diversity of opinion is possible. 'For the good', she writes, 'the good deed is self-evident' (ÜR: 110). All forms of the absolute—whether good or evil—must end in violent disaster in the political sphere, because they lack communication due to their absoluteness, and cannot admit plurality.

Arendt finds that the obvious reason for the selection of the interests of the wretched masses as a source of legitimation is a mixture of disillusionment about the corrupt conduct of the wealthy nobility and Rousseau's thoughts on the good, unspoilt nature of man in his natural state (see Rousseau [1755] 1995: 91ff). Because of their destitution, according to Arendt, this stratum of the population fits smoothly into the empty space created by the elimination of religious institutions, and is now given the task of providing human dignity with a secular face. The wretched masses were the embodiment of the absolute good, and thus symbolised that higher moral order to which the entire Third Estate, the new French people, were (supposedly) obliged in spirit. The constituent power is sanctioned morally by this higher order. Even more, it serves as impulse and justification for the actions of the revolutionaries, who were, to cite Nietzsche again, 'one … in their belief in the morality of *common* suffering' (Nietzsche [1886] 1972d: 106). According to Arendt, this is the decisive point for understanding the French Revolution in general and Rousseau's 'teachings' (OR: 75)[42] for the Revolution in particular. Neither can be understood if one does not take 'into account the crucial role compassion had come to play in the minds and hearts of those who prepared and of those who acted in the course of the French Revolution' (OR: 74).

> The magic of compassion was that it opened the heart of the sufferer to the sufferings of others, whereby it established and confirmed the 'natural' *bond between men which only the rich had lost.* Where passion, the capacity for suffering, and compassion, the capacity for suffering with others, ended, vice began. Selfishness was a kind of 'natural' depravity. *If Rousseau had introduced compassion into political theory, it was Robespierre who brought it on to the market-place with the vehemence of his great revolutionary oratory.* (OR: 76, emphasis added)

Compassion was to restore the lost bond between the social strata, and in this function it turned into pity. For this purpose it appeared necessary to exhibit compassion consciously, as it is of course impossible to see into the heart of the individual.[43] By these means, the presentation of passionate compassion

[42] Arendt writes: 'It is as though Rousseau, in his rebellion against reason, had put soul, torn in two, into the place of the two-in-one that manifests itself in the silent dialogue of the mind with itself which we call thinking. And since the two-in-one of the soul is a conflict and not a dialogue, it engenders passion in its two-fold sense of intense suffering and of intense passionateness. It was this capacity for suffering that Rousseau had pitted against the selfishness of society on one side, against the undisturbed solitude of the mind, engaged in dialogue with itself, on the other. And it was to this emphasis on suffering, more than to any other part of his teachings, that he owed the enormous, predominant influence' (OR: 75).

[43] Added to this is certainly also Rousseau's thoughts on the lack of empathy among the nobility, clergy and the upper bourgeoisie. Naturally, the men of the Revolution wanted to evade this accusation at all costs. In *Emil*, Rousseau asks: 'Why are kings without pity for their subjects? Because they count on never being mere men. Why are the the rich so hard toward the poor? It is because they have no fear of becoming poor. Why does the nobility have so great a contempt for the people? It is because a noble will never be a commoner.' (Rousseau [1762] 1979: 224).

became the 'cardinal virtue of the political' with the Revolution. Only those who agitated passionately for the benefit of the wretched masses seemed truly to seek solidarity with the nation. The consequence, according to Arendt, is that hypocrisy and mistrust on the part of those acting and spectating become one of the unintended effects of such a brand of politics based on feelings. The history of the Jacobin Terror is too well known for it to be necessary to detail it again here. I shall simply mention briefly that Rousseau's virtue of selflessness is not the same as the passionate exhibiting of compassion, Robespierre's revolutionary virtue of pity. However, I shall demonstrate in the next section that Arendt certainly sees a connection between the two.

It becomes clear at this point how Arendt deduces or sees the development of the definition of the general will from the historical-political situation. On the one hand, the external social circumstances delegitimised the sections and popular societies in their original form, and on the other hand the hierarchical structure of the Continental European concept of state could not admit any other centres of power (such as sections and popular societies). As a result, the general will could also not be defined by means of a discursive-democratic process within the citizenry. It was more or less imposed. Making the interests and needs of the wretched masses of France the general will of the nation, to which all political actions had to be orientated, originated on the one hand from a power-political necessity. All of the leading revolutionary powers felt compelled to take this step. On the other hand, this imposition derived its legitimation from pre-political considerations based on natural law of the higher moral value of the destitute people, and served as the source of those emotions that are necessary in the rebellion of the individual against his own interests. The choice of the wretched masses as the bearers of the *volonté générale* was therefore anything but arbitrary; it arose from the socio-historical constellation within French society. That is a central strand in Arendt's narrative of the French Revolution. By taking this path in defining the *volonté générale*, she once again follows Heinz Ziegler, who also suggests socio-historical and political-historical analyses of the relevant time when defining the national will. He writes accordingly, in his thoughts on the relationship between nation and *volonté générale*:

> And it is now of crucial importance as to which form of social association is identified with this category [*volonté générale*] *in the course of the actual political events*. For that group declared to be the *bearers of the volonté générale* [emphasis added] must be given this sovereign, state-forming unity that is contained within the term *volonté générale*. (Ziegler 1931: 99)

According to Arendt, the interest of the wretched masses advanced during the course of the Revolution to become the 'bearer of the *volonté générale*', and provided the embodiment of a national general will for the first time in history.

Power-political necessity and moral-philosophical considerations combined to produce this result. Over the next hundred years new constellations with different agents would declare a different complex of interests to be the national will, designating them in turn as the 'bearer of the *volonté générale*'. Other phases in which the general will experienced clear contours and a dominant and clearly discernible formulation of content most certainly included the age of imperialism, when economic expansion became the national interest, and the inter-war period with its policy of national homogeneity. I shall address the consequences for law and order at a later stage.[44] Beforehand, however, the comments made thus far about Arendt's concept of nation must be reduced to a clear common denominator, while at the same time clarifying the questions, raised at the beginning, regarding homogeneity and the exclusion of the other which, according to Arendt, accompany the concept of nation.

### *iii. The New Virtue and the Exclusion of the Other*

According to Rousseau, the virtuous citizen of the nation is the one who alienates himself totally and waives his own interests for the sake of the general will. Only when the individual gives up all of his interests in political matters as a private person, and the *bourgeois* is transformed into a *citoyen*, is it possible for him to recognise the true interests of a community and to form the *volonté générale*. Once the general will has been discovered, it must be identified with one's own will. This identification of each individual's own will with the general will produces the identity of a community. The concept of solidarity is a separate matter. In this context it means that one should also act in accordance with the general will. Only then has solidarity been reached with one's fellow citizens. But what about those who do not wish to consent?

If we take on this question of the relationship between Arendt's Rousseau discourse on the problem of homogeneity and exclusion of the other, we must warn immediately against rashly reaching the wrong conclusion: the rebellion against myself, against my own interest, does not lead inevitably to a battle against others.[45]

[44] See ch 4.

[45] At any rate an *internal* reason can be given for Freud's theory of projection, which makes a battle against others out of the battle against myself. Clear indications of this can be found in Freud's thoughts on projection in his work *Beyond the Pleasure Principle*: 'There will be a tendency to treat them [inner excitations] as though they were acting not from within but from without, in order for it to be possible to apply against them the defensive measures of the barrier against stimuli (*Reizschutz*). This is the origin of projection, for which so important a part is reserved in the production of pathological states.' (Freud [1920] 1999a: 29). However, this psychoanalytical figure of argumentation merely looks at the form, according to which the exclusion of the other is to be carried out. So while one attains valuable conclusions about the Janus face of self-restriction, at the same time, valuable historical and political-moral questions threaten to get lost.

Rousseau and the traditional interpretation of his work do not point to any internal connection from which a rebellion against myself might extend to a battle against the deviating attitude of others. Rousseau argues *externally*: the battle against the deviating others arises from the moral significance of the general will; it is not a direct consequence that arises from the logic of the battle itself. The demand for the total alienation of the individual is nothing less than the demand on all, and therefore every person must agree to give up his own interests; otherwise no individual will be prepared to take this step. That is not meant psychologically—though it could certainly also be interpreted so—but pragmatically: I waive my rights and my interests only if the others do the same. For Rousseau, consent to the social contract, ie the first and fundamental 'yes' to the general will, at the same time means submitting oneself to each subsequent announcement of the general will. Thus people of a different opinion are merely tolerated upon the conclusion of the social contract. They are 'foreigners among Citizens' (Rousseau [1762] 2012: 123) and must live with the fact that they are not considered when determining the general will. As soon as the state has been formed, submission to the sovereignty results from the place of residence in a 'free State' (Rousseau [1762] 2012: 124)—in other words, in states which are in line with Rousseau's theory of a social contract. There are not only pragmatic reasons for this, deriving from the idea of the social contract itself; the required submission to the general will is also connected to its immanent moral content:

> When a law is proposed in the People's assembly, what they are being asked is not exactly whether they approve the proposal or reject it, but whether it does or does not confirm to the general will, which is theirs; everyone states his opinion by casting his ballot and the tally of votes yields the declaration of the general will. Therefore when the opinion contrary to my own prevails, it proves nothing more than that what I took to be the general will was not. If my particular opinion had prevailed, I would have done something other than what I had willed, and it is then that I would not have been free. (Rousseau [1762] 2012: 124)

In the moment when the general will is expressed, one learns whether one's own opinion was right or wrong—wrong in the sense that it differed from the true interest of the nation. The only thing left to do in such a situation is to obey accordingly and to force oneself to be free. For Rousseau's fundamental idea is that the general will cannot damage anybody and its existence implies an obligation. But what happens with those who nevertheless do not comply? They become a 'rebel and a traitor to the fatherland' (Rousseau [1762] 2012: 64) and must be destroyed, or at least banished. Rousseau's reason, however, is *external*, for it refers back to a certain formulation of the content of the idea of freedom and therefore does not result from the *modus of the construction of solidarity* itself: one is free only if one follows the general will. The particular opinion, which originates in the individual will, is an expression of estrangement. While it might be possible to refuse to follow the general will, it is morally indefensible and equates to a meaningless existence:

> The pressure on the illegal individual will of the law-breaker is merely the externalised reshaping of the wayward particularity by the general and just law that is desired by all. The success of coordinating the generalisation of complete democratic will-formation, based on consent, is repeated externally in the forced strategic adjustment. (Kersting 1996: 175)

Arendt does not follow this traditional Rousseau interpretation for the precise reason that it locates the reason for the exclusion of others in the understanding of freedom and does not derive it from the logic of alienation and a virtue of selflessness. Certainly, Rousseau's concept of freedom gets its moral content precisely from the alienation of all members of the incipient community. But according to the traditional Rousseau interpretation, it is not the modus in which the alienation occurs that motivates the pressure placed on deviants, but rather the simple assumption that a life without such a freedom is meaningless.

Contemporary authors prefer the traditional Rousseau interpretation. All those who, like Ingeborg Maus, feel obliged to the tradition of Rousseau's thought, try to minimise the 'crushing burden' (Kersting 1996: 155) of his concept of freedom and believe that they can rehabilitate Rousseau by these means.[46] Maus argues against Arendt that Rousseau is the wrong person to accuse when it comes to a critique of the concept of nation, as 'the Continental democratic nationalism of the 18th century' represents 'nothing other than constitutional patriotism' (Maus 1994: 209).[47] But what do Rousseau's thoughts on the *volonté générale* have to do with a constitutional patriotism? It is anything but plausible. With Rousseau, the sovereign will is characterised precisely by the fact that it cannot be bound. Even if one meets Maus half way in her *Kantianisation* of Rousseau and allows that the sovereign will is expressed 'not counter to the general law ..., but through the general law' (Maus 1994: 209), that is still not constitutional patriotism. Constitutional patriotism makes sense as a concept only when the law is granted *a certain* autonomy—if necessary, even against the will of the people. Otherwise, law always becomes 'situational law' (Schmitt [1922] 2004: 19). From a constitutional or legal-theoretical

[46] Albeit certain differences in the concept of sovereignty, the subject of equiprimordiality or the extent of the contract-theoretical argumentation movement impel authors such as Maus, Brunkhorst or Habermas to a juridification of Rousseau, based on Kant. The most extreme ideas in this direction are surely those of Ingeborg Maus. In many passages of her Kant interpretation she is keen for her convincing comments on Kant to extend to Rousseau. With the much too frequent use of certain expressions without sufficient argumentative support, such as 'Kant's (or also Rousseau)' (Maus 1994: 7) or 'Kant's (like Rousseau's)' (Maus 1994: 9), Maus turns the Genevan into a Kantian.

[47] Similar also Herb 1989: 196–209.

perspective, Rousseau postulates exactly the opposite to constitutional patriotism. The autonomy of law does not exist in his thinking.[48]

There is no doubt that Arendt—like Schmitt (see Schmitt [1923] 1991: 20)—remains silent about the rational-legal strand in Rousseau's *Social Contract.* Her interpretation in *On Revolution* presents Rousseau as a political thinker who prefers 'feeling' what is right over discourse. If one looks at other passages in her work—especially the *Denktagebuch*—it becomes clear that she certainly did acknowledge the contractual character of Rousseau's thought (see DT: 260). In *On Revolution,* Arendt shifts Rousseau very close to Robespierre. The main reason for this is her methodical approach and her key question. As was made explicit at the outset with the reference to Ziegler, Arendt is concerned with the 'practical validity' of the idea of nation. How and why did Rousseau's general will become the core of the concept of nation? The extent to which this approach does justice to the theoretical content and the versatility of Rousseau's thought is a different matter. Measured against the quality criteria of the history of political ideas, Arendt's interpretation and treatment of Rousseau is one-sided. The same applies to her interpretation of the French Revolution. None of the debates in the course of the Revolution about a different, non-Rousseauian understanding of a people's sovereignty, which places the focus on the aspect of restriction and divisibility of rule, finds its way into Arendt's discussions. Some examples would include Constant's plea for a system of representatives, Sieyès' critique of an absolute sovereignty or Sismondi's separation of the sovereignty of the people and the sovereignty of the nation. From the perspective of the history of ideas, *On Revolution* might be seen as a questionable contribution. Nevertheless, despite all the justified criticism, we may not lose sight of Arendt's specific question. For she is concerned with working out, by means of the Rousseau discourse, a specific manner of constructing identity and solidarity within the political community. Arendt identifies this manner as a feature of the concept of nation, and it helps her to formulate an answer to the question, so central to her, to wit, why one 'never found a device by which to transform this idea [meaning a concept of the nation as a part of the human family which is divided into nations] into a working concept in the world of sovereign states' (OT: 40f). In other words, the merits of this Rousseau interpretation are in working out a systematic argument—and not in its adequacy in terms of the history of ideas.

For this reason, Arendt is not satisfied with the traditional interpretation of Rousseau. In reply to the question of homogeneity and exclusion, she focuses on the mode of political action and power, and places the modus of how alienation should take place at the centre of her unconventional interpretation. Her argument is that selflessness as a virtue leads to the exclusion of the other.

[48] On the relation between the *volonté générale* and law, see ch 4.

To explain this theory it is worth pointing out again that, according to Arendt, the interests of the wretched masses not only formed the general will from a power-political necessity, but this was also flanked by the moral-philosophical assumption of the 'good poor'. What is now decisive is that the interests of the wretched are not only 'good' in terms of moral-philosophical consideration, but must also be so in terms of affect. The affective dimension needs a coherent, clear and pure object of identification, since only such an object is able, due to its nature, to induce intense inner feelings. According to Arendt, talk of 'the poor' and 'the suffering' already abstracted from all of the special features of the individual human. Everything that might be confusing or contrary, anything that could disrupt or question one's own design, is removed. 'The masses', completely 'depersonalised', exist so purely only in an idea that can be applied at will—just as the inner emotions require. But no such purity exists. Such an idea, as expressed in Sieyès' epochal description of the people as '*toujours malheureux*', or in '*les misérables*', famous in the nineteenth century, abstracts equally from the justified and unjustified, from the just and unjust declarations of will. Yet those who put forward different, but no less reasonable and justified interests do not see it that way. In the required purity the affective dimension knows only one criterion of judgement: Are you for me or against me? Do you correspond with my image or not? It implies the exclusion of all those who do not fit in with the image demanded. The nature of the image is accompanied by its absoluteness. Only the highlighting of a Third Estate, which is formed on the natural-law idea of the higher value of the destitute and thus justified in speaking of the 'absolute good', enables the intensification of its own emotions and the renunciation of its own interests. Only the preceding moral absoluteness enables the establishment of the interests of the wretched masses as the 'supreme direction'.

Even if we suppose that Robespierre really did become a victim of the passion of compassion, then

> his compassion would have become pity when he brought it out into the open where he could no longer direct it towards specific suffering and focus it on particular persons. What had perhaps been genuine passion turned into the boundlessness of an emotion that seemed to respond only too well to the boundless suffering of the multitude in their sheer overwhelming numbers. By the same token, he lost the capacity to establish and hold fast to rapports with persons in their singularity; the ocean of suffering around him and the turbulent sea of emotion within him, the latter geared to receive and respond to the former, drowned all specific considerations, the considerations of friendship no less than considerations of statecraft and principle. (OR: 85)

In examining the function of pity with Rousseau, it was made clear where Arendt considers the 'boundlessness of their sentiments' to have come from, and how revolutionaries and other political agents were 'so curiously insensitive to reality in general and to the reality of persons in particular' (OR: 85). The intensive stimulation of the inner senses serves as the only medium for giving meaning and direction. We see, therefore, that the 'patriotism of the heart', which drives the virtue of selflessness, is thoroughly lacking in communication and proves itself to be unable, precisely because of its postulated purity of heart, to communicate with others who want something different. Either they feel the same or they do not. The patriot of the heart can neither allow himself to be confused by the opinion of others, nor can he relent and acknowledge the other, complete with his interests and opinions, because that would always lead to a reduction in his strength, which he desperately needs in his rebellion against his own interests. Accordingly, Arendt is convinced that pity, understood as a description of the energetic centre of patriotism of the heart and

> in contrast to solidarity, does not look upon both fortune and misfortune, the strong and the weak, with an equal eye, without the presence of misfortune, pity could not exist, and it therefore has just as much vested interest in the existence of the unhappy as thirst for power has a vested interest in the existence of the weak. Moreover, by virtue of being a sentiment, pity can be enjoyed for its own sake and this will almost automatically lead to a glorification of its cause, which is the suffering of others. (OR: 84)

The patriotism of the heart has already cleansed the glorified object of its identification of all contradiction and heterogeneity, and prepared it in such a way that it can be reduced to one single factor. Only when we know that we are absolutely on the right side and engaged on behalf of 'good' can we forsake our own position in the world for the sake of a suggested entity. Two instances, an affective stance and absolute good, merge together and adjust the exchange with the other: the affective stance is not all aimed at convincing, but rather at feeling. It wants to lose itself in emotion, in order thus to retrieve itself in the accompanying intensification of the inner life. Only by these means can the 'egoistical' individual interest be overcome. In correlation, the compassionate person is focused on the misfortune, or misfortunate, which he needs just as much as the power-hungry person need the weak (see ÜR: 113). If the idea of 'acting for the other' leaves the private sphere, where this type of action can identify itself precisely by means of its specific immediacy, and establishes itself as an ideal in public political life, then this type of action loses its normative quality. Surprisingly swiftly, in the political arena this motivated 'acting for the other' soon turns into and unmasks itself as 'acting for oneself'. Furthermore, the 'onset of absolute good' always means the end of the discussion. Good becomes a simple fact that one can either acknowledge or, indeed, renounce. To demand of 'absolute good' that it must prove itself to be so, would undermine its immediate validity. It would almost be like demanding that God prove his identity, which would make God not the most supreme and absolute, but rather the obligation of identification.

Accordingly, Arendt assumes that, in dealing with other people, good can only rely on being recognised through feeling, as 'it can neither persuade with words nor argue' (ÜR: 110).[49]

If we transfer these considerations to the question of the political-theoretical dimension of Arendt's concept of nation, we can establish the following: in her political-theoretical dimension of meaning, 'nation' means a community that aims to create its identity and solidarity by means of the patriotism of the heart. In other words, the passionate rebellion of each individual against his interest is the basis for employing a general will of the nation of whatever kind or content as the 'supreme direction'—in the case of the French Revolution the content of the general will arose, according to Arendt, from the interplay between the power-political necessity and the moral-philosophical assumption of the good poor. Within a nation this general will can 'in fact only work if it remains unbroken and indivisible in itself'. The reason for this is that understanding between people, who can engage in public debate only by fighting passionately against their own interests, becomes impossible. No further discussion is possible between two such extremely emotionally charged stances. Each step towards the other diminishes the passionate capacity for suffering in the rebellion of the individual against his own interest. As a result, there can be 'no possible mediation between people whose will is for different things, as there is between people with different opinions' (ÜR: 96).[50] For Arendt, the national general will is nothing but a 'subjective, ephemeral state of mind' (ÜR: 204).[51] It is the expression of the fact that the nation leads to the internalisation of the political. By working out the potential for exclusion that accompanies this manner of constructing political identity and solidarity, which is hidden in the affective understanding of the political and which constitutes the motivational core of the understanding of nation, I believe that we shall discover one, if not the central, contribution by Arendt's book *On Revolution* to political theory and the history of ideas.

According to Arendt's Rousseau interpretation, the homogeneous will is the result of an emotional alienation. By means of pity, the individual is able to free himself from his own interest and to employ the general will as the 'supreme direction' of action. Contrary to the interpretation by Preuß, Arendt does not read Rousseau from an ethnic perspective, but rather emphasises the anthropological foundation of pity:

> The goodness of man in a state of nature had become axiomatic for Rousseau because he found compassion to be the most natural reaction to the suffering of others, and therefore the very foundation of all authentic 'natural' human intercourse. (OR: 74f)

[49] See also OR: 82.
[50] See also OR: 71.
[51] See also OR: 156.

Accordingly, the capacity for compassion specifically does not depend on ethnicity but is instead intrinsic to each person. The anthropologically-based capacity for compassion is, according to Arendt's Rousseau interpretation, the 'essential foundation' for constituting the general will and, as highlighted by Kersting, can in principle even be expanded in a 'cosmopolitical direction' to a 'global social contract' (Kersting 1996: 161)—at least all those who feel the right thing belong to this world.

In contrast, homogeneity in the works of Carl Schmitt, who also refers to Rousseau, is interpreted in a directly ethnic—in places racial—manner and presupposed in the political process. In the political sphere, therefore, an already-present homogeneity is merely recovered, manifested and perpetuated. Arendt's assumption of the internalisation of the political—due to the patriotism of the heart—suggests, on the other hand, that the main task of the citizen is absolute alienation. The fight against others is a consequence of this internalisation. With Schmitt, in contrast, the fight becomes the purpose. It is the existential affirmation of one's 'own form of existence' (Schmitt [1932] 2002: 27). Whereas in Arendt's Rousseau critique the homogeneity of the will develops from the motivating emotionality, with Schmitt it precedes in principle the political. For him, the political begins only with the battle between conflicting, ethnically homogeneous entities. Only by shifting to the ethnic level can Schmitt establish any link at all between Rousseau's 'individualism' and his comments on collective action. For only by leaving aside the liberal part of Rousseau's thought, or by doubting its motivating and mobilising power, can the obligation of reciprocity no longer serve as a useful reason.[52] Schmitt confronts the obligation of reciprocity with myth.

[52] Schmitt follows a clear goal with his separation of liberalism and democracy. He wishes to prove with this separation that democracy and dictatorship are compatible. Even more, that in certain circumstances dictatorship is necessary for the creation of 'true democracy' (Schmitt [1923] 1991: 37). As Schmitt considers democracy to mean that a homogeneous will is present, dictatorship is given an educational mandate. For the identity between the ruled and the rulers that is necessary for a Schmittian democracy depends in the first instance on the democratic will of the people: according to Schmitt, the problem of a democracy is the question of its will formation (see Schmitt [1923] 1991: 36f). If the community fails to form a homogeneous will, then that power with the means to form a will is obliged to become educationally active. Dictatorship, says Schmitt, is therefore a consequence of educational theory. Democracy is suspended in order to allow a 'true, as yet to be created democracy' (Schmitt [1923] 1991: 37). This does not mean that democracy is abolished. On the contrary, Schmitt regards dictatorship as a period of transition in which the 'democratic identity' prevails and only the will of the people can be the measure of all things. Dictatorship is not the opposite of democracy, but rather its democratic preparation. Arendt also sees or emphasises the connection between democracy, understood as the rule of the majority will, and dictatorship: 'What saved the nation state from immediate collapse and ruin was the extraordinary ease with which the national will could be manipulated and imposed upon whenever someone was willing to take the burden or the glory of dictatorship

For him the myth of a community of fate with a common origin, a common race, language, culture and tradition symbolises that 'national energy' that awakens the 'sensibility of being different' (Schmitt [1923] 1991: 88) and introduces the individual to the community. The same myth is the most powerful symptom of the 'decline of the relative rationalism of parliamentary thought' (Schmitt [1923] 1991: 89).

With due respect to the rightful criticism of Arendt's book *On Revolution*—and in the course of the chapter I have referred repeatedly to the relevant passages—none of Ingeborg Maus, Hauke Brunkhorst or Jason Frank has acknowledged these shifts in Arendt's discourse on homogeneity. Instead they assume that Arendt's critique of the homogeneity idea of the French nation understands this homogeneity erroneously in Schmitt's sense—and therefore ethnically. According to Brunkhorst, both Arendt and Schmitt identify the concept of nation with ethnic homogeneity. Frank also assumes that 'Arendt follows Schmitt's analysis … but then comes to the very opposite evaluation' (Frank 2010: 49).[53] But that would mean that the difference between Arendt and Schmitt is 'only' that she criticises ethnic homogeneity, while he defends it (see Brunkhorst 1996: 338–41). It should be clear from the explanations presented here, however, that Arendt does not operate at the ethnic level at all in the discussion of homogeneity. Rather, she works out the requirement for homogeneity from the internalisation of the political, which accompanies the nation, and thus formulates it as the central consequence of *a specific manner* of political action and will formation.

In all subsequent remarks focusing on the political-theoretical dimension of meaning in Arendt's concept of nation, the nation is synonymous with an emotionally highly-charged unity. Such a unity operates with criteria of 'purely good' and 'purely evil', ever-changing in their specific concrete content.

upon himself.' (OR: 162) The constitutional avalanches in the course of the French Revolution show that a community that believes it sees more than a legal fiction in the idea of a unified people's will is 'built on quicksand' (OR: 162). It may well be that this will is identical with itself, even with the most glaring contradictions. But according to Arendt it will not succeed in providing the coexistence with a certain permanence, stability or planning security, as it declares everything it once wanted to be invalid if it changes. In brief, it does not create order, but rather the chaos that prompts one to roll out the red carpet in gratitude for the coming dictator. Thus the assessment and categorisation of dictatorship differs greatly: for Schmitt, dictatorship is an educational means and thus a necessary step for the creation of true democracy, ie it represents national identity for him. For Arendt, on the other hand, dictatorship is the inevitable result of the fiction of a unanimous political will. In her eyes, dictatorship is the necessary consequence of the (false) attempt to establish a general will in a pluralistic society.

[53] It is therefore not decisionism that Arendt rejects in the figure of constituent power, but rather, as I shall show in ch 4, the irrationality of law, which takes as its starting point the will of the nation.

This justifies calling the idea of the nation an 'irrational potency' (Ziegler 1931: 30) and assuming it to be a dysfunctional political concept of order. My explanations in chapter four will demonstrate—both from the perspective of law and the perspective of the institutional-political implementation—how and why each state and each political order that is erected upon the national will 'as a foundation is built on quicksand' (OR: 162). Beforehand, however, we must clarify what exactly Arendt understands by the concept of state.

# 3

# *Law and the Modern State—Hannah Arendt on the Trail of Max Weber*

I had a remarkable dream last night. We were at Max Weber's together. You—Hannah—arrived too late, were received with rejoicing. The staircase led through a gorge. It was the same apartment as ever. Max Weber had just returned home from a world trip, had brought back political documents and artworks, in particular from East Asia. He made us a gift of some of them, giving you the best, because you understood more of politics than I.

Karl Jaspers to Hannah Arendt, 20 April 1950

I read a lot more by Max Weber—prompted by your dream, in fact. I felt so idiotically flattered by it that I was ashamed by myself. But this mastery of austereness cannot be achieved, at least not by me. Something dogmatic always remains hanging with me somewhere. (That's what happens when the Jews venture into the writing of history.)

Hannah Arendt to Karl Jaspers, 25 June 1950

## I. INTRODUCTION

HANNAH ARENDT'S UNDERSTANDING of the modern Continental European state is inspired by Max Weber. She follows Weber in her thoughts on the essence and structure of the modern state, and interprets the 'state as a rationally organized institution' (EaS: 653).[1] Its central feature is the rationality of law: more precisely, the formal-rational understanding of law. In the course of reconstructing Arendt's concept of the modern state I shall explain what this formal-rational understanding of law involves and how it differs from other conceptions of law. Furthermore—and more generally—I shall demonstrate that Arendt orients herself in relation to Weber in her comments on the state and modern statehood.[2]

[1] For the German version see WuG: 394.

[2] So far only a very few authors have examined the significance and influence of Weber's thought on Arendt's work. Peter Baehr delivered an instructive study on the friendly and philosophical-

When we begin to reconstruct Arendt's understanding of the Continental European state, we are confronted by a fundamental conceptual problem: Arendt is very ambiguous when using the term 'state' or 'nation-state'. On the one hand, Arendt's concept of the nation-state covers the combination of two elements thus far separated, national belongingness and the state apparatus (ETH: 487). Elsewhere, in contrast, the concept of the nation-state appears in its state-theoretical version, and is used by Arendt to distinguish a certain form of political organisation from other forms of organisation such as absolute or constitutional monarchy. In such passages the nation-state stands for the monopolisation of state power and the disentanglement of the state from the nobility (see ETH: 60). At the same time she sees the nation-state as a legitimatory counterpoint to the monarchy, which embodies the equality of all citizens before the law, only to accuse the nation-state elsewhere in her work of irrationality in dealing with the law.[3] As if all of this were not confusing enough, Arendt also speaks, without indicating clearly what precisely she means, of a 'nascent nation-state' (ETH: 46), and she replaces this term with the 'modern national state'. And still there is no end to the confusion surrounding the concept of the nation-state. For if we ask about its origins, it is written in one place that the nation-state originated 'in France during the course of the French Revolution' (NuD), thus making the French Revolution 'the very birth of the modern nation-state' (OT: 230). Elsewhere, however, she claims the exact opposite: the origin of the nation-state should be dated back to the seventeenth century. She states explicitly that 'the nation-state did not begin with the French Revolution' (ETH: 46).

The terminological chaos is huge. There is no other option, therefore, than to define for each single quote what is meant by nation-state in each case. It seems that the use of the term 'nation-state' is a matter of emphasis: when Arendt speaks of the *nation*-state, she does not so much mean the legal-governmental structure but rather the legitimising authority of political decision making; the national will. In this respect the origin of the *nation*-state does indeed coincide with the French Revolution. When, however, Arendt emphasises the nation-*state*, she directs attention to a political-legal structure that had developed and expanded gradually during the course of the Peace

scientific interrelationship between Jasper, Arendt and Weber. He concludes that Arendt's deep affinity with Jaspers prevented her from criticising Weber, who was a close friend of Jaspers, more severely (see Baehr 2001). For a comparison of the methodology of Weber and Arendt, see Parvikko 2004 and the critical response in Baehr 2005. In an essay, Kari Palonen compares Arendt's and Weber's view of representative democracy (see Palonen 2006).

[3] On the one hand, Arendt's work contains assertions such as that the nation-state is 'in its essence a legal and constitutional state', 'and only viable as such' (NuD). Elsewhere, in contrast, she criticises that the nation supplants law in the nation-state, thus endangering the stability of order (see ETH: 488).

of Westphalia—the origin of which can therefore be dated back to well before 1789. It is likely that the multidimensionality in Arendt's use of terms is due to her essayistic style, and it should be seen as a rejection of the traditional systematic of philosophical or political-philosophical thinking, which has become, to borrow a phrase from Adorno, 'dilapidated in its foundations' (Adorno [1931] 1997a: 340). (It is certainly too short-sighted to derive any general insignificance of her political-theoretical and philosophical work from this.)[4] However, a systematic reconstruction of Arendt's understanding of the Continental European state must clearly separate and name the conceptual dimensions. In my subsequent remarks, therefore, I shall refer to the 'modern state' when I mean the political-legal structure of the nation-state that Max Weber refers to as the 'rationally organized institution'. When I use the term 'nation-state', I shall either draw attention to the 'emphasis', as suggested above, or clarify the context of the term.

## A. In Which Line of Tradition to Think About the State? Neither Hegel nor Elias

In the only detailed analysis of Arendt's understanding of the state that I know, Roy Tsao points to another line of tradition: instead of Weber's, he emphasises Hegel's legacy in Hannah Arendt's thought. Tsao's assumption that Arendt's 'underlying conception of the state bears a striking, though unacknowledged affinity to that of Hegel' (Tsao 2004: 105) is based primarily on two key parallels that he claims to identify between Arendt and Hegel. The first parallel consists, according to Tsao, in the belief of Arendt and Hegel that the state has a socially integrative function. Tsao writes:

> Like Hegel, Arendt believes that the basic challenge confronted by the modern state in sustaining its people's allegiance to a single political community lies in the conflicting, particularistic interests that arise with the emergence of a market-oriented, 'bourgeois' society. With more than a century's hindsight, Arendt takes a different, and darker, view of the forms those conflicting interests had taken. Even so, her account of the syndromes of political alienation that resulted from the European state's historical failure to contain and surmount those conflicts may be regarded as an imaginative extension of the underlying concerns that led Hegel to lay great stress on the socially integrative function of political institutions. (Tsao 2004: 108f)

It is beyond dispute that both Hegel and Arendt problematised the relationship between civil society and the state. Yet while Hegel adheres especially to the classical demand of the French Revolution, and expects from the members of the state precisely that duality between their existence as *bourgeois* and as *citoyen*,

[4] This position was taken by Russell Jacoby (see Jacoby 2007: 262 and 266).

Arendt seems more to follow Marx's critique in his early works, and to doubt the very possibility of this duality.[5] Tsao himself recognises this discrepancy between Hegel and Arendt, but classifies them very differently:

> Arendt, too, defines the issue with reference to the French duality of bourgeois and citoyen. Only for her the decisive fact is the failure of the two sides to fuse, leaving the bourgeois without any civic orientation. (Tsao 2004: 119)

While Tsao attempts to minimise the discrepancy by using the word 'only', it has to be pointed out that completely different approaches to the problematic relationship between the state and society are being expressed here. Although Arendt does not follow Marx's critique of the state, she is at least convinced that in the context of a Continental European understanding of sovereignty, it is not possible simply to remove the potential for political conflict that is concealed in the duality of *bourgeois* and *citoyen*. Furthermore, another point in Tsao's interpretation seems problematic: in speaking of the supposed significance of political institutions for Hegel's thoughts on the state, Tsao is alluding to Hegel's remarks on the transition of civil society to the state. Here Hegel says that corporations and self-regulatory organisations should represent the 'system of needs', as Hegel characterises society, before and in respect of the state. However, it must be apparent here that Hegel advocates forms of organisations in which the belongingness is connected with the profession, and which for this reason must serve the interests of a certain clientele.[6] It remains completely unclear how those fundamental conflicts of interest that poisoned the political climate throughout the nineteenth century should be balanced out by these means. It is precisely Arendt's criticism that the citizens in the nineteenth century themselves determined only their socio-economic position, and that they lacked any political sense of community. The contribution that self-regulatory organisations could possibly have made for a stronger political awareness among citizens remains incomprehensible. At best they function along the principle of representation, similar to that of the

[5] See Hegel [1821] 1986: 409. Hegel writes there: 'The particular interest [of the bourgeois] truly should not be put aside or even suppressed, but rather brought into accordance with the general interest, by which means both it [the particular interest] and the general interest are preserved. The individual, subject to his obligations, finds in their fulfilment as a citizen the protection of his person and property, the consideration of his particular welfare and the satisfaction of his substantial being, the awareness and feeling of being part of the whole, and this fulfilment of obligations as services and businesses on behalf of the state constitutes his preservation and his existence … Everything depends on the unity of the general and the particular in the state.' Marx doubts precisely this possibility of unity on the basis of a bourgeois society. On Marx's critique of the political suitability of the bourgeoisie, see inter alia Marx [1842] 1961a and Marx [1844] 1961b).

[6] See Hegel [1821] 1986: 393–98. See on this point Marx's excellently written polemic against the Prussian parliament in his work *Debatten über das Holzdiebstahlsgesetz* (Marx [1842] 1961a).

party system. However, in contrast to the party system—criticised heavily by Arendt in its Continental European manifestation—Hegel's professional self-regulatory organisations are also contrary to the principle of free organisation and the free recruitment of equal citizens to political interest groups, which is at least possible with parties.[7]

Tsao's second parallel, the maintenance of legal order, is also not really substantial:

> The consonance between Arendt's arguments and Hegel's is no less striking with respect to her claims about the state's still more fundamental function of sustaining a rights-based legal order. Like Hegel, Arendt holds that the reciprocal recognition of rights among the citizens of legally constituted political community is an indispensable condition for an individual's attainment of full human agency, so much so that a life spent outside such a community is in a sense not fully human. (Tsao 2004: 109)

If we ignore the problematic statement that a life spent outside the community is, according to Arendt, 'not fully human', then the claim about 'the state's still more fundamental function of sustaining a rights-based legal order', as a supposed parallel between Hegel and Arendt, is such a platitude of state-theoretical and legal-philosophical thought that parallels could be constructed with almost every thinker of the nineteenth and twentieth centuries who has ever thought about the state. The reference to Kant would be very obvious; but the leading legal philosophers and state theorists of the nineteenth century also come into question: Savigny, Stahl, Treitschke, Gerber, Laband, Jellinek, etc, who were in principle all concerned with laying a firm foundation for the determination of the legal essence of sovereignty.[8] Much more decisive, and much more revealing, however, is the question as to what exactly is meant by 'law' here? What kind of autonomy is granted to the law, and what are the consequences for the systemic structure of the state? Tsao's treatment

[7] This leads us to another, quite pragmatic objection: if the party has already emerged as a central institution from the state and statehood over the course of history, whose state-theoretical function—at least ideally—is specifically the integration of citizens into the state, why should one then retreat back to the position before this development process and emphasise a problem that no longer exists in the form presented? Why not examine an author who, like Max Weber, is in tune with the times and has presented an analysis of the party, including its socially integrative usefulness? The party is intended, after all, to fill the gap between the state and society—and here, precisely, in Arendt's view, is where it has failed. One reason among others for this is the idea of representation itself, on which, however, Hegel's self-regulatory organisation is also based.

[8] See Hennis 2003: 15. Similarly, Möllers establishes right at the beginning of his impressive study of the concept of state, 'The self-description of German public law as *state* law, which with a few exceptions has no parallels in the public law of other countries, is only the most visible expression of the large significance held by the concept of the state in German teachings on constitutional law.' (Möllers 2000: 1)

contains many interesting insights, but his thesis that Hegel is Arendt's model in determining the essence of modern statehood isn't fully convincing. By this I mean not only that Hegel does not appear even once in the bibliographies of *Elemente und Ursprünge totaler Herrschaft* or *Origins of Totalitarianism* (only Hegel's historical-philosophical approach is mentioned in passing);[9] it is also the lack of substance of these supposed parallels and the accompanying randomness that render Tsao's assumption unconvincing.

More so than with Hegel's state philosophy, there is a much closer affinity—at least to some extent—between Arendt's thoughts on the origins of (modern) statehood and those of Norbert Elias. Although there are only a few speculative indications, this connection is worth examining briefly, as it highlights the different argumentative core of Elias and Weber—and thus also leads to a directional decision in the attempt to reconstruct Arendt's understanding of Continental European statehood. In the *Elemente/Origins*, Arendt does not refer to Norbert Elias's work *The Civilizing Process*, which was published in Basle in 1939. That is not surprising, as the two-volume work remained more or less unnoticed for many years, with a second edition printed only 30 years later. One indication that Arendt's thoughts on the modern state had a certain proximity, at least in terms of content, to Norbert Elias's 'sociogenesis of the state' (Elias [1939] 1997: 132) and his thoughts on the 'monopoly mechanism' (Elias [1939] 1997: 151), might be the emphasis with which Arendt accentuates the transition that allowed nobles and feudal lords to become princes and monarchs (see on this point ETH: 45–55). This transition involved precisely that paradigmatic shift away from focusing on the management of one's own sinecure alone, and the observation of rules befitting the appropriate social status above everything else, which included, among other things, the refusal to avail oneself of foreign, ie primarily Jewish, capital for the purpose of financing. The feudal lords became political rulers, who entered the fight for the two key monopolies, that of taxation and that of power (Elias [1939] 1997: 151ff). In order to be able to prevail in this fight, or to maintain the monopoly position that had been attained, a standing army, which had to be fed and clothed, was just as important as a constantly expanding number of civil servants to monitor the increasing number of administrative tasks. At the same time, it is revealing that for Elias this process of selection could only have begun where 'migration came to an end' and a 'firmly rooted peasant class' (OT: 229) was able to establish itself. In the formation of an established

[9] Roy Tsao argues that Arendt attended Kojève's famous Hegel seminar during her years in Paris. He then concludes that it is plausible 'to suppose that such ideas of Hegel's could well have been somewhere in the back of her mind when she came to write *The Origins of Totalitarianism*' (Tsao 2004: 111). I do not want to dispute that Hegel might indeed have been 'somewhere in the back of her mind'. However, solid and substantive parallels can be established much more clearly with Max Weber.

farming class, Arendt, too, sees the central, state-forming difference between the Western European people and those of Southern and Eastern Europe. Again, she appears to be in line with Elias, since it was the coincidence of this increase in population, the 'consolidation of land ownership and the difficulties of external expansion' (Elias [1939] 1997: 142), which, according to Elias, intensified the internal competition for land in the first place. Elias spells out in detail how, in a society with the pressure of competition and the 'drive for land' (Elias [1939] 1997: 142), it is not enough merely to preserve that which has already been attained. Whichever of the feudal lords and knights wished to hold onto their rank and reputation had to accumulate more and more. The result was the territorial state. In addition, Arendt sees the increased financial needs of the princes as being 'determined by exclusively political factors' (ETH: 61), thus essentially putting the case for the monopoly mechanism. The argumentative core of a theory on the origin of the (modern) state based on the 'monopoly mechanism' is marked by the autonomous nature of a political system that forces the princes to bear ever more tasks. New ruling techniques, complete with an entire power apparatus, were formed during the course of these new tasks, which replaced the vanities of status with rational considerations of expediency. This is also the birthplace of the 'idea of the reason of state', which would become for a long time the central 'technique of politics' (Ziegler 1931: 85). Here, however, is where the—admittedly somewhat speculative—parallels between Arendt and Elias end. Accordingly, I shall demonstrate below that it is Max Weber whom Arendt follows in her thoughts on the origin and nature of the modern state.

## B. An Initial Plea for Max Weber

A first and important hint that Arendt got her understanding of the state from Max Weber is that he is mentioned, with pertinent works, in the bibliography of *Elemente und Ursprünge totaler Herrschaft/Origins of Totalitarianism*.[10] Furthermore, Max Weber seems to be the impulse behind countless sections of this work: from the critique of parties and parliament, to his thoughts on economic history and his examination of the law.[11]

[10] In *Elemente/Origins*, Arendt refers not only to the *Wirtschaftsgeschichte* and *Parlament und Regierung im neugeordneten Deutschland*, but also to Weber's treatment *Die Börse*. It is also clear from other writings and records—*Denktagebuch*, early pieces on Antisemitism or letters to Jaspers in the 1930s (Arendt/Jaspers: 52) and Blücher—that Arendt engages herself intensely with Weber's thoughts on the state from an early stage.

[11] Arendt must at any rate have studied Weber already in the early 1930s. On the one hand, references are made to Weber's *General Economic History* and his religious sociology in an early treatment of anti-Semitism (see JW: 74, 115). On the other hand, Arendt notes that she borrowed the term 'pariah people' for the Jews from Weber (JW: 276).

While there are numerous agreements between Weber and Elias, the core of their argumentation nevertheless differs: whereas the formal rationality developed, in the case of Elias's monopoly mechanism, from the intrinsic logic of power politics, Weber sees the triumph of rationality as going directly hand in hand with the all-encompassing economic process of transformation. This difference can be illustrated with the distinction between the feudal lord and the prince, which can also be found in Weber's *General Economic History* (GEH).[12] For in contrast to Elias, Weber places the switch from feudalism to princely rule in a very different context. Without narrowing Weber's thoughts down to a base-superstructure-economism, it can be asserted that Weber sees the emergence of the modern state as being closely interwoven with the economic structure in general and the development of capitalist action in particular.[13] Due to the intertwining of the state and the economic structure, formal rationality was able to become the engine of the societal, social, cultural and in particular political development of the Occident.

The emphasis on the interdependence of economics and politics, on the establishment of capital accounting and the structural changes in statehood, tallies with Arendt's actual motivation to address the question of the origin and nature of the state in the first place. How should this be understood? A central problem in reconstructing Arendt's idea of the modern state is that there is no explicit examination of *the* state. In brief: at no time does a state-theoretical analysis become the explicit object of her consideration. Instead, her interest in the conditions enabling the emergence of the (modern) state and its structure lies in and is conveyed by her thoughts on the political and social role of Jewry in Europe, and her thoughts on imperialism. In the context of her analysis of anti-Semitism, Arendt traces the shift from the Court Jew to the European Jew, who acted as state financier and broker between the European powers. The emergence of modern statehood is of key importance here, as it led to the demand for capital that could only be supplied, according to Arendt, by Jewish financiers due to their social position. The resulting close interrelation between Jewry and the modern state provided, in turn, fertile ground for the politicisation of the Jewish Question, and represents

[12] Everything points to the fact that this is where Arendt got this differentiation, as she lists the *General Economic History* in her bibliography. Moreover, in the field of Weber research, the *General Economic History* is considered to be the 'final version of his thoughts on the state' (Anter 1995: 204).

[13] Weber uses the term 'capitalism' not only in defining an economic and socio-historical era, which generally begins with industrialisation; he also means a kind of capitalist action that places money and later capital accounting to the fore, leading to the formation of a culture that is based solely on calculatory considerations and which dispenses with each person, as well as any other postulate, that is 'alien to the system'.

an important mosaic piece in the overall picture of German and European anti-Semitism:

> If we want to understand clearly the connection between the Jewish Question and the nation-state on the one hand and anti-Semitism on the other, we must bring to mind the emergence of this international role of the Jews in the system of the nation-state. (ETH: 65)[14]

Because my study does not concern anti-Semitism but rather the idea of statehood, the object here is to extract the state-theoretical content from Arendt's thoughts on the relationship between Jewry and (modern) statehood, and to draw this content together into a coherent whole. This shall be done in section II of this chapter. In the process, questions about the origin of statehood and the conditions of its emergence will be raised and answered: What contributed to the formation of the state as a political guarantee of order? What, in Arendt's view, constitutes the essential characteristic of the state and the modern state? On which understanding of law is the modern state based? Where can Arendt's ideas be positioned in the state-theoretical and state-sociological literature? Then, in section III, I shall turn my attention to the law. Here, I shall first clarify what Weber meant by 'rational law' and how it differs from other understandings of the law. I shall work out criteria of rational law, with the help of which I shall then look at Arendt's work. More precisely, Arendt's critique of imperialist forms of rule will be examined from a legal-theoretical perspective. It should become clear that this critique was formulated against the background of a formal-rational understanding of the law.

Peter Baehr, one of the few authors who have addressed the importance of Weber's thought for Arendt's work, arrives at the conclusion that 'Weber did not significantly influence Arendt, if by "influence" one means that she reflected seriously on his work and then applied it to her own' (Baehr 2005: 130). My work in this and subsequent chapters will prove the exact opposite. Arendt's view of the Continental European constitutional state is influenced to a significant degree by Max Weber. However, and in this point I agree with Baehr to some extent, I shall show that 'Arendt was anti-Weberian on all vital political axes of her thought' (Baehr 2005: 130). Ultimately, she will develop completely different concepts of both law and of the political—differing from, even directed against, Weber's political and legal understanding (*cf* on this point chapter five). But what Arendt does take from Weber is the idea that the law contains an intrinsic rationality that is of fundamental importance for a durable and reliable political order—a political order in which political struggle and dissent can happen and be experienced. Arendt follows Weber

[14] With this in mind, Arendt points to the fact that Herder referred to the Jewish Question as the State Question. (ETH: 143).

in claiming that the law can form its specific rationality only as long as it remains autonomous to a certain extent from extra-juridical postulates. The problem with Weber's understanding of the law, however, is that it can retain this autonomy only at the price of the dichotomy of politics and law. This is the point where Arendt's critique of Weber begins, and where she reveals that such a dichotomy infiltrates both trust in the law and the stability of the polity (*cf* on this point the second part of chapter 4).

## II. ON THE ORIGIN OF THE MODERN STATE

### A. State and Modern State in Weber

If we follow Stefan Breuer, Weber's concept of the state produces (only) superficially a problem of definition. For although Weber blithely uses the term 'state' for political associations in antiquity, for those in Pharaonic Egypt, in Assyria and Phoenicia, although he speaks equally of the state in Confucian China as in his comments on feudal Japan or the Peru of the Incas, a common strand can be recognised here. For Breuer, there are no terminological shortcomings concealed behind the extensive use of the term 'state'. Rather, an important insight can be attained into a central differentiation in Weber's thoughts on the state: the differentiation between the state and the modern state (see Breuer 1993: 207). Breuer suggests using the (slightly modified) classical Weberian triad to define the state, but for the modern state we need the concept of association (*Anstalt*). Breuer argues:

> Statehood exists also without rational statutory order, without a concept of association, on the basis of relationships of rule and domination that rest on charisma or tradition. A political association … should be called a state when its existence and the validity of its order can be guaranteed within a definable geographical territory by a rule that avails successfully of the monopoly of legitimate physical force so as to maintain this order. *The state becomes a modern state when the feature of the political operation of the association is added.* (Breuer 1993: 214, emphasis added)

Whereas Weber defines the state primarily by the monopoly of violence, the *modern state* is characterised by the fact that it has become an operative association (*Anstaltsbetrieb*). But what does Weber mean by 'association'? What does it mean when a state has transformed into an 'operative association'? Weber defines the state as an association within his 'basic sociological terms' and explains it as follows: 'an organization which imposes, within a specifiable sphere of operations, its order (with relative success) on all action conforming with certain criteria will be called a *compulsory organization* or *association*' (EaS: 52).[15]

[15] For the German version see: WuG: 28

From Andreas Anter three key criteria can be found, which should help to illuminate the definition of Weber's concept of the association: the state as an association is *first* an organisation with a rational statutory order. In this manner, according to Anter, the modern state for Weber is equipped indirectly with the criterion of rationality. For in contrast to the arbitrary rule of the despot, the modern state is based on a rational statutory constitution with rational statutory law, as well as an administration and bureaucracy that must orient themselves to rational statutory rules when exercising power. Thus rule and law are predictable (see Anter 1995: 47ff). *Secondly*, the statutory order applies to each person within the association. Nobody can evade it and privileges—especially those of the nobility—become obsolete. The statutory order is, *thirdly*, an imposed order. Like Hume (and after him Hegel), Weber rejects the 'hypostatisation of the regulative idea of the social contract'.[16] The state is not based on agreement, but rather on imposition. Its specific feature is violence. Although the last criterion, violence, inevitably forms part of any definition of the state *à la* Max Weber, Weber experts such as Breuer or Anter recommend placing greater emphasis on the first two criteria for an adequate understanding of the modern state: the 'constitutive feature' (Anter 1995: 188), the 'elementary feature' (Anter 1995: 206) or the 'main feature' of the 'institutional state' of the concept of the modern state, is the 'existence of a rational statutory order' (Breuer: 1993: 202).

In his *Wirtschaftsgeschichte (General Economic History*, Weber remarks that such a 'rational state' existed 'only in the Occident' (Wg: 289).[17] Only there could one find a combination of 'formal juristic thinking' (GEH: 342)[18] as a consequence of 'two-fold rationalization' (GEH: 341)[19]—secular and spiritual—on the one hand, and of the capitalist economy, by which Weber means primarily the application of money or capital accounting, on the other. For the most part, all other cultural circles—Weber explains it in his *General Economic History* using the example of China—remained bound to traditional forms of rule, which made the law and the administration of justice, with institutions such as the ancient Chinese brotherly aid, unpredictable. With such unpredictable law, according to Weber, capitalism cannot flourish. Instead capitalism requires a law that ignores all ritual-religious and magical aspects, and that allows it to be calculated reliably like a machine (see GEH: 342; Wg: 293). But how does Weber explain the transition from traditional rule to legal rule?

The decisive contribution to the transition was made by the economic structure. Without addressing this complex development in detail, it can at

16 Weber [1922] 1973: 335.
17 For the English version see GEH: 339.
18 For the German version see Wg: 292.
19 For the German version see Wg: 291.

least be said that the ruling structure of feudalism greatly expedited market orientation and money calculation, and thus contributed to the 'development of individualized production' (EaS: 375). Individualised production results in the disintegration or subdivision of households, and with it the demise of so-called 'original modes of market regulation' (EaS: 83).[20] This forced people to make exact calculations, which in turn had to be oriented towards bartering opportunities, needs, competition, etc. Accordingly, the money calculation of feudalism gradually transformed into capital accounting, which Weber calls the 'highest level of rationality, as an instrument of calculatory orientation of economic action' (EaS: 108).[21] Over time the formal rationality of capitalist economy, ie the world view based solely on calculatory considerations, ignoring all persons and postulates (ethics, politics, religion) that are 'alien to the system', extended to all areas of life. I follow Stefan Breuer here, who regards Weber as rejecting pure economism and emphasising the legal, political and religious 'room for manoeuvre' of 'Occidental feudalism' (Breuer 1982: 129). Economic development would not have been possible without this leeway. Nevertheless, with Weber the economic structure can be considered to play a central role in the transition from traditional to legal rule.

## B. Arendt and the Genealogy of the Modern State

### *i. Accentuation of the Economic Structure*

A first indication of Arendt's approximation to Max Weber in her thoughts on the modern state is that she tackles the issue of economic structure. Weber's reference to the 'qualitative individuation' (EaS: 80/WuG: 42) of the commercial and agrarian structure is addressed by her in so far as she too places the emphasis on the necessity of capital accumulation within a company for the emergence of modern statehood: as no social class was willing any longer to cover the financial needs of the state, due to growing private economic engagement, the state was forced to distance itself ever more from all social classes and estates, and to ensure its own financial survival. According to Arendt, it was the economic imperative—and this includes things such as amortisation, equity requirements, etc—which prohibited private companies from acting as permanent, state credit grantors. Quite apart from the fact that, over time and in the long term, the state demand for capital could not have been borne by only a few companies, the requirements of an expanding private economy forced entrepreneurs to direct their capital into their own companies (see ETH: 54ff). Arendt illustrates this idea with the example of the Fuggers, from

[20] See German version WuG: 44.

[21] For the German version see WuG: 58

Augsburg, once Europe's richest and most influential bankers: while they had provided credit to the ruling princes in the sixteenth century, it would never have occurred to them to establish a specific state credit. The Fuggers, according to Arendt, saw themselves as a commercial company, and were therefore reliant on large sums of equity (see OT: 16).[22] On the other hand, the expansion of private companies naturally led to an increasing demand for juridification, for police and military protection. In addition, the disintegration of households and house communities eventually led to greater calls for social and charitable aid. The state also came under increasing pressure from this side, but could no longer rely on sufficient financial support from the estates.

For Arendt, only Jewish lenders were in a position to fill this funding gap, as they had (or were) kept away from all private economic activity due to their religious, social and cultural independence:

> Thus the Jews were the only part of the population willing to finance the state's beginnings and to tie their destinies to its further development. With their credit and international connections, they were in an excellent position to help the nation-state to establish itself among the biggest enterprises and employers of the time. (OT: 17f)

This not only led to an ill-fated interdependence between the state and Jewry—an interdependence that Arendt traces in detail and which, in her view, prevented the Jews from flourishing in society. Of similarly key importance for the emergence of the modern state is the fact that private Jewish individuals were able, due to their abstinence from commercial activities, to amass savings. As a counterpoint to the typical class or estate-related formation of society, a Jewish society within the society, a '"nation within the nation"' (OT: 11) was formed, which itself was to become, in turn, the precondition of the inter-European, supra-territorial, Jewish network. It was this Jewish network that enabled in the first place the provision of those immense amounts of capital on which the European states were dependent. Conversely, Arendt argues that this is the reason why the governments did everything to block Jews' path into private business:

> After the French Revolution, which abruptly changed political conditions on the whole European continent, nation-states in the modern sense emerged whose business transactions required a considerably larger amount of capital and credit than the court Jews had ever been asked to place at a prince's disposal. Only the combined wealth of the wealthiest strata of Western and Central European Jewry, which they entrusted to some prominent Jewish bankers for such purposes, could suffice to meet the new governmental needs. (OT: 14f)

Thus, over time, the Court Jew became the great 'Jewish State Banker' (OT: 11), whose most significant representative was the Rothschild family.

[22] For the German version see ETH: 57f.

Far removed from private commercial involvement, 'large Jewish capital' was concerned almost exclusively with providing government bonds and securing the international exchange of capital.

### *ii. The Development of the State into a Political Power and Business Concern*

Arendt's thoughts on the emergence of a 'special sphere of state business' (OT: 17) for the formation of the modern state form another parallel with Weber. She argues that due to the increasing functions of regulation and control that had to be borne by the state, the demand for capital grew to unknown dimensions. Thus, Arendt puts forward the thesis that it was the absolute monarchies in the age of mercantilism who prepared the modern state. For the monarchies were increasingly reliant on a regular income and safeguarded finances. Without doubt, feudal lords, too, had required money and credit, but these were usually for one-off purposes and special projects. In contrast, the 'fight of the monarchies for secure finances' (ETH: 57), and their unprecedented 'need for state credit' (ETH: 46), was systemic. Although the absolute monarchies also tried to satisfy their financial needs by means of war and plunder in their early phase, these methods were soon joined by 'the new device of tax monopoly' (OT: 16). The previous sources of income were 'insufficient', 'completely unsecured and unpredictable' (ETH: 57). Such sources of income would have facilitated the satisfaction of the limited needs of a feudal lord at best, but not those of a state budget (see ETH: 57). Arendt describes the consequence of this permanent shortage of capital as follows:

> By the end of the eighteenth century it had become clear that none of the estates or classes in the various countries was willing or able to become the new ruling class, that is to identify itself with the government as the nobility had done for centuries. The failure of the absolute monarchy to find a substitute within society led to the full development of nation-state and its claim to be above all classes, completely independent of society and its particular interests, the true and only representative of the nation as a whole. (OT: 17)

In the quotation above, the nation-state means the nation-*state*, with its political-legal structure. This new form of government could not merely rest on the 'claim' of being independent of all classes; it had to actually complete the detachment. It is of great importance to our discussion that what Arendt discusses here with 'above all classes' and 'complete independence' can be termed, in line with Weber, 'the development of the state as a political power'.[23] The increase in income on the one hand and the rise in revenue-rais-

[23] GEH: 347. For the German version see Wg: 297. On Weber's concept of the power-state, see also Anter 1995: 137–46.

ing power on the other are its conditions. Entirely in line with Weber's formation of the power-state, Arendt outlines how the state turned into a monopolist in a number of very different areas. She describes how the monopolisation of tax collection under lease came about in France, along with military instalments. In Prussia, metal stamping and the mint were nationalised, as was porcelain manufacture. In Bavaria the mines, salt, tobacco and the lotteries came under strict state control and served as a main source of income (see ETH: 61). This 'special sphere of state business' within the economy became necessary, as the financial expense of administrative tasks and the civil service grew considerably.

When all attempts by the absolute monarchy to ally itself with any of the large classes in society failed—Arendt gives as an example the futile battle of the French state, going back to the fifteenth century, to win the favour of the guilds (see ETH: 57)—'the state chose to establish itself as a tremendous business concern' (OT: 17). Jewish providers of credit were the main financiers of this 'tremendous business concern' until the nineteenth century. Here, too, Arendt follows Weber's remarks in his *General Economic History*. And in that work, mercantilism is described as the era that transformed the state into a 'capitalistic commercial enterprise' (Wg: 296).[24] This not only means the centralisation and monopolisation of decision-making authority, which accompanied the formation of the power-state, but also evidence of the 'formal relationship' (Breuer *et al* 1982: 135) between the state and enterprises.

### *iii. The Functional Importance of the Bureaucracy*

This formal relationship aims at the continuous conversion of the entire administrative state system, which adapts itself almost completely to the formal rationality of a capitalistic economy. Stefan Breuer described this 'adequacy' as follows:

> Just as in the economy, where the care of certain social groups was no longer performed under the aspect of material postulates but only according to the ability to pay, there was also in the administration—and every rule is expressed as administration—a radical renunciation of material patrimonialism in favour of a form that radically eliminates the ethical and/or political maxims and aims for a depersonalisation of office-holding. (Breuer 1982 *et al*: 135)

The 'radical renunciation' of the traditional and the transition to legal rule also occur in politics, the law and administration. Along with the establishment of formal law, which I shall address in detail in the next section, the spread of a rational bureaucratic administration, in which the specialist

[24] For the English version see GEH: 347.

knowledge of the civil servants is central, is surely one of the most outstanding achievements. It is therefore not surprising, upon a thorough reading of *Elemente und Ursprünge totaler Herrschaft*, how little attention Arendt devotes to the state's monopoly of the use of force in her comments on statehood. She mentions it, but the 'outstanding achievement' (ETH: 114) of the modern state or its 'greatest achievement' is the establishment of a 'non-party political, neutral civil service' (ETH: 104), with its 'aspiration … to become the representative of the whole nation to get exclusive power, to take possession of the state machinery, to substitute [itself] for the state' (OT: 38).

Arendt delineates how the civil servants in Prussia not only fought against the privileged treatment of the nobility, but actually advocated the equality of legal status for Jewish people—which did not necessarily correspond with the wishes of the King. The reason was that the civil servants expressed 'the principle of the nation-state' (ETH: 88) or the 'spirit of the … nation-state' (ETH: 89), where 'nation-state' once more means the political-legal structure of a modern state. But what is meant by the terms 'spirit' or 'principle' of this state? The civil servants were in the very first instance 'servants of the nation as a whole' (OT: 154). They were independent of all social interests and devoted solely to the state: 'It was not the King who spoke through them, but the anonymous monarchy.' (ETH: 88) The 'anonymous monarchy' is the formal monarchy that sets a form of rule that is oriented strictly towards statutory principles against the material ruling style of the King. In the words of Max Weber, it is the 'reduction of modern office management to rules (EaS: 958),[25] which leads to its 'depersonalisation'. The civil servants were completely 'independent of special economic privileges' and totally 'uninfluenced by reasons of state' (ETH: 87). It is significant to note that Arendt contrasts the rationality of the civil service with the economic interests on the one hand and with the *raison d'état* on the other, as both undermine constancy, calculability and predictability. By setting not only the economic interests but also the *raison d'état* against the rationality of the civil service, Arendt again follows Weber on the narrow path of his remarks on different forms of rationality. For Weber also distinguishes between the statesman and the civil servant not only in terms of responsibility, specialised qualifications, etc (see on this point PuR: 340–48); in his sociology of domination he also emphasises their different types of rationality. While the civil servant displays formal rationality, shown in the 'subsumption under general concepts', Weber's reference to the 'reason of state' means a material rationality, the '*leading* spirit' (PuR: 334) of the statesman, which is expressed in the 'considering of means and ends' (see WuG: 565). The question of the nature and form of the symbiosis of both types of rationality is certainly the unsolved problem in Weber's political

[25] For the German version see: WuG: 552 u. 562.

thought. I shall address this at a later stage (*cf* on this point the second half of chapter four and chapter five). Here, however, it is simply important that Arendt—like Weber—considers the rational character of the state to be secured through the 'professional honour' of the civil servants and emphasises their 'absolute independence' (ETH: 345) and isolation from all materiality. Precisely, the 'enlistment of an independent civil service'[26] was the 'project of the nation-state' (ETH: 345). For this could exist in its independence only when a group had been formed—of specialised civil servants—that served the national interest, detached from all social strata. From a state-theoretical perspective, this independence was due to the transformation of the state, as described above, into a 'tremendous business concern'. But it is also possible to observe this urge for independence from the perspective of the nation. Specifically, the emancipation of the state from all social classes reveals the prerequisite that allowed the state to become the 'symbolic representative' of the nation. It was the civil servants, with their battle against privilege and for the legal equality of all citizens, who drove forward the process of rationalisation in the state, thus initiating the transition from absolute monarchy to the modern state.

### *iv. The French Revolution and the Genesis of the Modern State*

The emancipation process of state rule, ie the establishment of an independent civil service and a functioning administrative apparatus, entered the phase of its completion with the French Revolution. Arendt even sees 'the only undeniable achievement to this day' (NuD) of the French Revolution in the catalysing impulse to complete the modern state:

> The body politic of the nation-state came into existence when no single group was any longer in a position to wield exclusive political power, so that the government assumed actual political rule which no longer depended upon social and economic factors. The revolutionary movements of the left, which fought for a radical change of social conditions, had never directly touched this supreme political authority. (OT: 38)

In her assessment of the contribution of the French Revolution to the development of modern statehood, Arendt follows Tocqueville.[27] Like her, Tocqueville

[26] ETH: 114. Breuer highlights the fact that the loyalty of the civil servants to the state emerged precisely from the structure of the civil service: the expert and specialised knowledge attained is tailored entirely to the organisation and is of value only within the organisation, while outside it is completely useless. Leaving a civil service career, which already begins very early and provides for slow advancement through the hierarchy, is very costly and risky. In order nevertheless to make the civil service attractive, people are enticed with 'social security', 'legally fixed pension entitlements' and 'protection against arbitrary dismissal'. This, however, is also accompanied by 'strict access restrictions' (Breuer 1998: 183f).

[27] *Cf* on this point also Benhabib 2003: 161f.

sees in the removal of absolutist monarchy and all the rest of the old feudal order the prerequisite for a forced bureaucratisation of the entire state.[28] In addition, with the establishment of the civil service, the modern state and its institutions also free themselves from the vagaries of alternating political directions. For no political grouping would be in a position to shoulder the tasks and demands arising for the state without the help of a 'non-party political, neutral civil service' (ETH: 104). All parties, according to Arendt, were reliant on the civil service apparatus, 'without which no modern state, irrespective of its character, can function' (ETH: 105). With this 'appreciation' of the functional importance of the civil service she also follows Max Weber, who famously referred to the professional civil service in his writings on religious sociology as the 'cornerstones of the modern state',[29] and who considered its historical development to coincide with the history of modern civil service. Also closely connected to this is Arendt's state-theoretical reception of the French Revolution. With her assertion that no revolutionary movement had infringed upon the independence of the state apparatus, Arendt joins the traditional line taken by Alexis de Tocqueville, Max Weber and Heinz Ziegler. In their thoughts on the French Revolution, all three emphasise the continuity of the administrative structure. Tocqueville, for example, highlights the fact that while the Revolution removed absolutism and the feudal order, the entire administrative apparatus was still adopted seamlessly (see on this point Tocqueville [1856] 1969: 39–46, 58–61, 166–74). Max Weber argues similarly in *Economy and Society*: compared with the period of the First Empire, 'the ruling apparatus remained essentially the same'[30]—despite the Revolution. Ziegler also concludes in his political-sociological study of the concept of nation that the complete administrative apparatus remained 'relatively untouched' by the Revolution. He writes:

> The revolutions do not destroy anywhere, but rather take from everywhere and increase the body of absolutist centralisation, as it corresponds well, technically, with the needs for the calculability of state action and for a uniform guidance of mass behaviour. (Ziegler 1931: 86)

As well as the accentuation of the economic structure for the history of the emergence of the modern state, the formation of the state as a political power (*Machtstaatsbildung*), the description of the modern state as a 'tremendous business

[28] *Cf* on this point Tocqueville's famous statement: 'The centralization of administration is an institution of the old regime and is not the work of the revolution, or of the Empire, as is said.' (Tocqueville [1856] 1969: 39)

[29] Weber [1920-1921] 1972a: 3. See also Andreas Anter's excellent remarks on the 'archaeology of the state' and his description of the history of the state as a history of civil service. (See Anter 1995: 172–84.)

[30] WuG: 571. Weber appraises the Napoleonic *Code Civile*, in contrast, as 'the third of the world's great systems of law' (EaS: 865).

concern' and the stress on the functional importance of bureaucracy, Arendt thus also follows Weber in the state-theoretical classification of the French Revolution.

The decisive parallel with Weber, however, is provided by her conception and understanding of law and legal rationality. As for Weber, Arendt, too, determines the modern, Continental European state by its 'character of a rational legal institution'.[31] The 'internal rationalisation of law' (Freund 1987: 12), which, according to Weber, was primarily the work of professional jurists, fits in with the general rationalisation process of the Occident (*cf* Schluchter 1979).

In this manner, the law became the central element of control. It is therefore not surprising that Arendt looks at the Continental European state from the perspective of the law. Precisely against the background of the constantly menacing 'thoroughgoing nationalisation of the state' (Ziegler 1931: 296)—which then came about in the inter-war period—it was the 'legal structure' (ETH: 488) of the state that was able to generate a minimum of stability and order. Even though Arendt severely criticises the structural composition of the Continental European state, its accompanying concept of the law, and the closely connected ideal of stability that prepared the ground for the advance of national forms of identity and solidarity, she commends the juridification of social and political relationships as an essential achievement of the modern state. Below I shall show to what extent Arendt assumes Weber's idea of rational law in her examination of the Continental European state. She spells out all historical-political conflict situations and events, such as the Age of Revolution, Imperialism, the Dreyfus affair, the refugee and minority problems of the inter-war period, as legal conflicts, respectively as conflicts with the law. Beforehand, however, we must clarify what Weber understands by rational law.

## III. ON THE RATIONALITY OF LAW

### A. What is Rational Law? A Look at Weber's Sociology of Law

If we scrutinise Weber's understanding of the law from the perspective of his sociology of domination, we detect that the concept of law serves Weber as a criterion for differentiating his idea of legal rule from patrimonial and charismatic forms of rule. For Weber, legal rule is characterised by the fact that the

[31] ETH: 490. The prerequisite for the emergence of a legal state order is the deprivation of power and dispossession of those with their own means of coercion by a central authority. Weber lists three factors that, in combination, lead to the emergence of legitimate legal order: economic development, monopolisation of violence, monopolisation of law (see Anter 1995: 190).

law is created by means of formal, correct statute, and is thus no longer reliant on the validity of higher principles. However, instead of acknowledging only formal-rational law as law, like the legal theorist Kelsen, Weber's perspective on the sociology of law distinguishes four types of law. These four types are formed from the combination of the pairings rational/irrational and formal/material.[32] Patrimonial or charismatic rule also produces law, according to Weber, but not a formal-rational law.

In my reflections on Weber's understanding of the law I refer specifically to that section in *Economy and Society* that contains the core of Weber's legal thought and which Alberto Febbrajo calls the 'famous passage, and the most difficult to interpret' (Febbrajo 1987: 60). One of the reasons why this passage is so difficult to understand is that the terms *rational* and *rationality* have dual meaning. In one place 'rationality' is used as the *determination of the quality of the law as a whole*, which can differ according to 'the extent and the nature of rationality' (EaS: 655). At the same time, however, Weber uses the term 'rational' as a *criterion for describing the internal structure of the law*. For this purpose, the short word 'rational' is placed in quotation marks at the beginning of the section (see EaS: 655).[33] Being 'rational' in the sense of its internal structure, the law can then be one of two different 'types'. First, it can be 'rational' with regard to the determination of 'decisive reasons' (WuG: 395) for the judgment in an individual case. This determination is always 'rational' when one adheres to the 'generalization, ie in our case the reduction of the reasons relevant in the decision of concrete individual cases to one or more "principles", ie legal propositions' (EaS: 655) when assessing a fact. Normally, according to Weber, the reduction is determined by an analysis of the facts of the case, in which exactly those elements are carved out that are considered relevant for a legal judgment.[34] Irrational 'law-making and law-finding' (EaS: 655) occur when *no reference is made* to any kind of system of norms. In such cases, the only determining factor is the personal feeling of the kadi or oracle—in Weber's example. Additionally, the second way in which the law can be 'rational' is when norms that are decisive for the judgment are able to be systematised. By '"systematization"' (EaS: 656) Weber understands the creation of a system of norms that is logically clear and without contradiction, and in which all conceivable cases can be subsumed seamlessly.[35] By fulfilling the criteria of

[32] See WuG: 395ff or EaS: 655ff. On the relationship between Weber and Kelsen, see Bobbio 1987.

[33] For the German version see WuG: 395.

[34] Weber speaks here of 'legal rules', and demonstrates with the quotation marks that he has already taken it a step further. For by rights he should speak of legal norms, which must then be converted into legal rules. Rödig describes in detail the relationship between legal norms and legal rules. He calls the legal rule the 'outer substrate of the legal norm' (Rödig 1986: 46).

[35] Weber naturally refers to English law as an exception, yet assumes that systematisation will prevail in the modern world (WuG: 396).

'*generalising*' and '*systematising*' legally relevant norms, the law becomes verifiable and therefore also predictable. Verifiability and predictability are decisive factors in whether or not one can speak of a 'rational' law. 'Rational' law is no longer—as, for example, in kadi justice—the result of a spontaneous, possibly sentimental emotion, but is instead based on accessible norms, in the best case even legal propositions, to which reference is made in the solving of legal problems.

Along with the distinction rational/irrational, Weber makes another, no less essential differentiation on the determination of 'the extent and the nature' of the rationality of law: the differentiation between formal and substantive law. At the centre of this division is the question of the *systemic positioning of the system of norms* (see EaS: 656f).[36] Two answers are possible here: either 'law-making and law-finding' refer to a juridical conglomerate of norms that corresponds with the criterion of 'an extraordinary measure of lucidity as well as a precise intelligibility in its provisions' (EaS: 865) and, accordingly, uses legal technical methods when deciding on legal problems; or 'law-making and law-finding' rely on extra-juridical 'norms of a different qualitative dignity' (WuG: 397), on 'norms' which are 'different from those obtained through generalization of abstract interpretations of meaning' (EaS: 657). In the first case Weber speaks of formal law, the so-called 'jurisprudence of concepts',[37] which takes account of 'only unambiguous general characteristics of the facts of the case' (EaS: 656f). When naming the legal technical methods, Weber distinguishes between two varieties of formalism: the 'formalism of the "external characteristics"', and the formalism 'which uses logical abstraction' (EaS: 657). He regards the formalism of the external characteristics as 'the most rigorous type of legal formalism' (EaS: 657), directed only towards external characteristics such as the spoken word, a signature or a symbolic act with a fixed meaning. In the case of logical abstraction, however, the legally relevant characteristics are determined by means of interpretation, in order to then create or apply fixed legal concepts in the form of strictly abstract rules (see EaS: 656f). If one refers to an extra-juridical system of norms in the course of solving legal problems, both types of formalism described above are negated. In this case, Weber speaks of material law and the 'jurisprudence of interests'.[38] Instead of

[36] For the German version see WuG: 396f.

[37] The term 'jurisprudence of concepts' (*Begriffsjurisprudenz*) goes back to Savigny and refers to the 'productive powers that exist in the juristic systems, which have developed by means of the legal text itself' (Coing 1969: 335). For Savigny and the so-called Historical School, the primary task is to fathom the legal institutes, rules or concepts that arose historically and to move from them to principles. The inductive approach can be seen as a core element of the jurisprudence of concepts (*cf* Seelmann 2001: 66ff).

[38] The term 'jurisprudence of interests' originated in Bentham's utilitarian ethics. Accordingly, an action is 'correct, a law is just, when it causes the greatest happiness to the greatest number of people (so-called utility principle)' (Coing 1969: 49).

legal norms and the legal technical methods specific to them, ethical imperatives, utilitarian rules of expediency, political maxims, religious source interpretations, etc are called upon to solve legal problems.

The point of Weber's legal sociology now lies in the fact that the two pairings thus attained, rational/irrational and formal/substantive, can be hybridised, thus producing four ideal-typical combinations:[39] one speaks of an *irrational-material* law, when the law-finding and/or law-making is entrusted exclusively to the personal emotion, ethical considerations or political estimations of a person who somehow holds power (*material*), and who does not refer to a fixed system of norms (*irrational*). The law is *irrational-formal* when the judge observes the formal rules of procedure and pronounces his judgment accordingly (*formal*), but who, when determining the sentence, for example, bases his decision on the revelation, the oracle or some other surrogate (*irrational*). *Material-rational* law is given when the law is based on norms that derive from extra-juridical sources (*material*), but where its interpretation is calculable by means of certain 'techniques' (*rational*): in other words, when the ruling on legal problems is based on an exegesis of the Bible or the Quran, on ethical, utilitarian or political maxims. The greatest degree of rationality, according to Weber, is contained in *formal-rational* law. Here, decisions are based on systematised legal rules and orient themselves towards abstract, juristically developed concepts. In legal conflicts, norms are consulted (*rational*) that have been systematised in a juristic manner (*formal*).

Whenever Weber applies the terms 'rational law' or 'legal-rational law', he refers to the formal-rational law embodied by modern legal systems. Accordingly, a rational constitutional state should be understood as a state that adheres to the 'generalising' and 'systematising' of its legal basis of measurement when finding and making law—with all of its accompanying systemic consequences, eg the separation of powers—but which on the other hand, however, also reverts to a well-composed juristic system of norms and the corresponding legal-technical methods when deciding upon legal problems. Weber specifies the methodical-logical rationality of formal-rational law based on five postulates that are indispensable for juristic work: *first*, each specific legal decision must be the application of an abstract legal rule to a specific case; *secondly*, a decision must be found from the relevant abstract legal rules using the means of legal logic; *thirdly*, the valid objective law must be seen as a complete system of legal rules; *fourthly*, anything that cannot juristically be construed rationally

[39] The discussion in the field of Weber research about the interpretation of his legal sociology is certainly not yet concluded. In my explanation of the four hypotheses I follow not only Weber but also the comments by Freund (Freund 1987), Febbrajo (Febbrajo 1987), Rossi (Rossi 1987) and Schluchter (Schluchter 1979).

must be regarded as irrelevant; and *fifthly*, the common social action of people must, without exception, be seen through the lens of the legal rules and, consequently, be evaluated either as an application or as an infringement of the same (see WuG: 397).

I have already pointed above to the function of bureaucracy for the internal and external rationalisation of the law. When Arendt, like Weber, speaks of the civil service, which was responsible for transforming monarchy into a modern state, she means nothing other than that the foundation and establishment of legal rules that result from and are justified almost completely by legal logic itself. The personal influence of the ruler on the legal system is driven back ever further (see ETH: 91, or OT: 38).

Having outlined Weber's understanding of the law, the question arises as to the extent to which these considerations on rational law can also be found in Arendt's view of the Continental European state. Here we must place our central focus on those criteria that determine the 'type and extent' of the rationality of law: besides the criterion of the verifiability and reliability of those reasons that are crucial for deciding on legal problems, these criteria include the systemic location of the norms, respectively the system of norms, and the application of the relevant (legal) technical methods. In the following chapter I shall show that Arendt follows these Weberian criteria in determining the legal character of the modern, Continental European state. Beforehand, however, an argumentative diversion is required, as the legal concept of the modern state appears only in mediated form with Arendt. What is meant by 'mediated form'?

Arendt does not work out the legal character of the modern state in a comparably systematic manner to Weber. The specific legal character of the modern state can be construed, with her, only via her analysis of its counterpart, 'bureaucracy as a form of rule' (ETH: 519). For in Arendt's description and critique of 'bureaucracy as a form of rule', she orients herself exactly towards those criteria that Max Weber also suggested for the 'type and extent' of the rationality of law. In this way, 'bureaucracy as a form of rule'—which should not be confused with the 'bureaucratisation of existing civil service apparatuses'[40]—counters the rational-formal legal understanding of the Continental European state. Or, to put it another way, the opposite of 'bureaucracy as a form of rule' is the rational-formal law of the modern constitutional state.

[40] ETH: 519. Arendt also refers to this differentiation in *Origins of Totalitarianism* when she writes, 'government by bureaucracy has to be distinguished from the mere outgrowth and deformation of civil services (which frequently accompanied the decline of nation-state—as, notably, in France)' (OT: 244).

## B. Arendt and Rational Law

### *i. Bureaucracy as a Form of Rule and the Materiality of Law*

In her remarks on bureaucracy, Arendt distinguishes strictly between 'bureaucracy as a form of rule', which she identifies in Imperialism as well as in the despotic bureaucracies in Austria-Hungary and Tsarist Russia, and the 'bureaucratisation of existing civil service apparatuses', which Arendt explains with the example of France.[41] Despite certain similarities, the fundamental difference is the fact that the civil servants in France, the so-called *ronds-de-cuir*, did not rule the country at any time. The French state apparatus may well have been 'a useless organism whose only purpose appears to be chicanery' (OT: 244), but nobody could claim seriously that it had cloaked itself in that 'aura of pseudo-mysticism' (OT: 245) that was the typical product of the Russian and Austro-Hungarian bureaucracies. If one questions further the precise reasons for this 'pseudo-mystical aura' of the bureaucratic rulers, it can be seen that Arendt explains this expression in a legal-philosophical manner: 'Juristically speaking, and in contrast to the rule of law', says Arendt, 'bureaucracy represents the regime of decree' (ETH: 516);[42] 'People ruled by decree never know what rules them because of the impossibility of understanding decrees in themselves and the carefully organized ignorance of specific circumstances and their practical significance in which all administrators keep their subjects.' (OT: 244) The latter passage already suggests the two directions in which Arendt's analysis of 'bureaucracy as a form of rule' will take us, and at the same time names the main source of the 'pseudo-mystical aura', namely 'incomprehensibility' and 'secretiveness' (see ETH: 518). The 'specific circumstances and their practical significance', which motivate a decree, are treated like the 'greatest state secrets' (ETH: 518). They result solely from the considerations of expediency on the part of a political elite, to which the people have no access and which therefore remain incomprehensible. Materialisation meets a lack of verifiability of decisions, thus creating an

[41] Distinguishing very clearly between both forms of bureaucracy, she writes in the German version of her book on total domination: 'Bureaucracy is a form of rule in which administration replaces government, decrees replace law and the anonymous domain of an office replaces public-legal decisions, for which a person can be made responsible and held to account. In this respect, bureaucracy has hardly anything to do with the civil service apparatus, without which the nation-state cannot manage and without which no modern state of any description can function.' (ETH: 405)

[42] The English version says (OT: 243) 'Legally, government by bureaucracy is government by decree.' By adding 'in contrast to the rule of law' in the German version, Arendt shows once again more precisely that she analyses and criticises bureaucracy as a form of rule (also) from a legal-theoretical perspective.

atmosphere of ignorance about who or what actually governs and rules. This results in the 'pseudo-mystical aura' of a regime ruled by decree.

Although it might appear that the decree itself is responsible for this ignorance, and that the 'pseudo-mystical aura' derives essentially from the decree itself, we need to clarify that decrees within a constitutional state are by no means the same as those in a decree regime: decrees are a part of every democratic constitutional state. Not only would each parliament be overwhelmed if it had to clarify every single legal matter down to the smallest details of its technical implementation and administrative execution; even more important is the fact that in many respects, parliamentarians do not have the necessary expertise that one hopes to find among civil servants. It is therefore too simplistic to find the cause of the pseudo-mystical aura of a system of bureaucratic rule in the decree itself. The difference between decrees and a 'regime of decrees' lies much more in the fact that the decree is embedded in the overall formal-legal system of a state, and it is only from this that the relevant administrative unit experiences the 'scope, content and purpose' that sets the limits to the decree and empowers it. In brief, the legislator must set the precise limits within which the executive may make laws. With this in mind, Arendt emphasises that the administrative civil servant is confined to a system of constitutional power separation that places him in permanent relation to 'the law-making activity of the statesman on the one hand, and the law-interpreting activity of the jurists on the other' (ETH: 526). Before official political action can be taken in the modern state, the legality and constitutionality of this action must be reviewed. One commonly speaks of decrees as 'laws in the material sense', as decrees need not go through the entire legislative process; but this does not mean that law, as such, is materialised. Rather, the decree derives its validity solely from the lawful reference to the rationally and formally correct law of a community.

It is quite a different matter in a 'regime of decrees'. Here the relationship between decree and legal system is reversed: the decree, according to Arendt, replaces the law completely: 'Actions are constantly taken before their legality is reviewed.' (ETH: 527) But we must once again stop at this point for the sake of terminological precision. For it is only half the truth to claim that the decree takes the place of the law. Rather, decrees appear clothed as the law, and thus change the entire concept of law itself. It is clear that Arendt had these upheavals in mind from those passages in which she equates, in terms of the legal concept, bureaucratic rule with despotism, and remarks that 'in despotism … all "laws" [should be seen] as the direct discharge of an overpowering omnipotence' (ETH: 516f). By placing '"laws"' in quotation marks, Arendt seems to point to the loss of the formality of the law in a regime of decrees. For if we speak of decrees in a constitutional state as 'laws in a material sense', but embedded in formal-rational law, in a 'regime of decrees' all law is materialised by means of the corruption of the concept of law. Arendt makes this clear when she writes, 'The power that serves only the execution and upholding of the law in constitutional states, here becomes, in a command, the direct source of order.' (ETH: 516)[43]

The (material) law of bureaucratic rule is contrasted here with the (formal) law of the constitutional state: while it is a typical feature of legal rule in a rational institutional state that the state authorities and organs can only execute that which has proven its compliance in every respect with the legal order, in a decree regime the only thing that counts is the simple ability to issue statutes. Accordingly, in the case of a materialisation of the law, the 'intermediary stages between legislation, issuance and application' (ETH: 518)[44] disappear. The executive makes the laws; and in doing so, it ignores the benchmarks that Weber highlighted for the preservation of the 'formal character of law and law-finding'( EaS: 774): the separation of powers.

### *ii. Bureaucracy as a Form of Rule and the Irrationality of the Law*

According to Weber, it is the separation of powers that preserves the sphere of law-making and law-finding from (complete) occupation by material postulates—whether political, religious, economic or whatever kind. The separation of powers establishes the freedom required to form the 'abstract formalism of legal certainty' (EaS: 811), and thus creates the prerequisite that the entire legal apparatus can be set up like a 'technically rational machine' (EaS: 811). The advantage Weber sees in the legal apparatus as a 'technically rational machine' is the holding of a 'pacified contest' (EaS: 811) of interests on the basis of fixed and steadfast rules of play. The claim is that legal formalism is accompanied by the greater stability and rationalism of coexistence—rationality understood here as a determination of the quality of the entire law. In the decree regime, in contrast, the only 'yardstick for the value' of a law, according to Arendt, is the question whether it is 'applicable or not applicable' (ETH: 518).

> Since the people it ['it' meaning bureaucracy as a form of rule] dominates never really know why something is happening, and a rational interpretation of laws does not exist, there remains only one thing that counts, the *brutal naked event* itself. (OT: 245, emphasis added)

Because only the 'brutal naked event' counts in terms of whether something is legal or not, the need for any legal-technical methods is obviated. Both the 'formalism of the "external characteristics"' and that of 'logical

[43] In words to the same effect, but less precise, it says in the English version, 'and this means that power, which in constitutional government only enforces the law, becomes the direct source of legislation' (OT: 243).

[44] For the English version see OT: 244.

abstraction'—ie of achieving a 'rational declaration and interpretation of laws'—lose their validity in law-finding and law-making. They are replaced by the simple fact of the decision, for which accountability and justification are no criteria: in the decree regime, the decision does indeed become a 'specifically juristic element … in absolute purity' (Schmitt [1922] 2004: 19), because the only thing behind the law of a bureaucratic system of rule is the ability 'to control its outward destinies' (OT: 245) and those of its citizens. The rationality of the formalism of legal-technical means is detached from the 'immediate emanation of the state monopoly of force' (ETH: 320). Laws thus become the 'direct discharge of an overpowering omnipotence' (ETH: 517).

Along with the rational declaration and interpretation of laws, Arendt points to the fact that laws in a modern, Continental European state must be able to be traced back to a transparent legislating authority. In the regime of the decree, in contrast, pure anonymity dominates: 'Decrees moreover remain anonymous (while laws can always be traced to specific men or assemblies), and therefore seem to flow from some over-all ruling power that needs no justification.' (OT: 243)

Besides the transparency of the source of law, Arendt's talk of anonymity also spans the arc to those criteria of verifiability and reliability that I mentioned above as indicators of the inner core of the law and which should answer the question as to whether or not reference is made to existing norms when deciding on legal problems. For while a clear reference to an existing system of norms can always be discerned in a legislating assembly, that does not apply to the regime of decrees: in a legislating assembly, the reference can be recognised by the fact that, as a *pouvoir constitué*, it is itself embedded in a constitutional order, which both empowers and constrains it. Therefore, all of the laws it passes must not only remain within a certain framework, guaranteeing already by these means a certain reliability, but they must also be able to be substantiated and justified against the background of an existing legal order, which guarantees their verifiability.

By contrasting the Imperialist apparatuses of power in the colonies with the constitutional institutions of the motherland, Arendt draws attention to a series of further aspects that shape the modern Continental European state, but which are completely perverted in the governing practice of colonial apparatuses of rule. One of these aspects is the existence of clearly understandable legal rules or principles which are, according to Weber, part and parcel of the reliability of the law. To clarify a legal conflict, the legal rules or principles that are addressed or infringed by the facts of the case are examined.[45] The statutory principles

[45] Weber writes on this point: 'This process of reduction is normally conditional upon a prior or concurrent analysis of the facts of the case as to those ultimate components which are regarded as relevant in the juristic valuation.' (EaS: 655)

should be clear, simple and understandable to all. It is quite a different case in the normal issuing of decrees in the colonies: Arendt argues that '[t]here are no general principles which simple reason can understand behind the decree' (OT: 244). Rather, law-making and law-finding are oriented only towards the imperative of the moment, while 'only an expert can know in detail' its 'ever-changing circumstances' (OT: 244). By placing the negation of principles and legal rules at the centre of her criticism of bureaucratic rule—a system in which nobody knows why something is happening just now, or why this way and not that—Arendt contrasts it with the manifest image of a practice of law-finding and law-making in the modern, Continental European state that is based on legal rules and which guarantees reliability and verifiability.

Closely connected with the unclear principles of a regime of decree is its 'contempt for law' (OT: 243). Legality, according to Arendt, means the 'permanence of laws with general validity' (ETH: 459). Legality means that not everything can just be made into law, but that each new law must fit without contradiction into the existing legal system. Precisely this demand nourishes justified fear among the advocates of the regime of decree—Arendt refers in this context to Pobedonostsev's *Reflections of a Russian Statesman*—that laws are '"snares"', because they inhibit the immediate execution of administrative power due to the multitude of possible interpretations that precede each action and '"restrictive prescriptions"' (OT: 248) within the law. In constitutional states, Arendt summarises, the administrator has 'eternal contempt' for 'the supposed lack of freedom of the legislator, who is hemmed in by principles, and for the inaction of the executors of law, who are restricted by its interpretation' (ETH: 517).

The legal process takes a very long time in modern states due to the separation of powers, formal procedural requirements and systematic checks, while decrees can be issued 'in rapid succession' (ETH: 459). Furthermore, in a system of bureaucratic rule, legal decisions can be made in a completely 'disorderly' manner and can differ greatly 'from case to case' (ETH: 459). The reason for this is that no consideration need be made of a coherent overall context of all legal decisions. As everything can be decided without reason or justification, without the obligation to fit in with the overall legal order, Arendt compares the law-making and law-finding of bureaucratic regimes of rule with the 'state of emergency': 'The state of emergency justifies in exceptional cases that which is the norm in despotism, namely the concentration and limitlessness of power over the subject.' (ETH: 516)[46]

[46] The diction in the German version of this passage is very reminiscent of that of Carl Schmitt.

In a regime of decrees and under the rule of a material-irrational concept of law, the state of emergency has become the normal standard (*cf* Benjamin [1940] 1961: 272; Agamben 2005). In states with a formal-rational legal order, on the other hand, law-making is not arbitrary. It is based on formalism, which must orient itself towards the systematisation of the legal rules. Therefore the systematisation of law can be observed from two different perspectives. First one can address the systematisation from the aspect of an existing and perfected system of norms. In this case, one examines it from the level of the inner core of the law. On the other hand, however, the systematisation can also be seen under the postulate of a well-composed body of law, in which every decision and each new law is logically clear and can be integrated without contradiction. The objective is to create a seamless system, in other words an apparatus that can function like a technical machine.

If we view Arendt's remarks on the Imperialist rule apparatus purely from the legal-theoretical perspective, certain terminological allusions to Carl Schmitt's thoughts on the state of emergency and the 'nature of the state and the law' (Hofmann 1964: 68) can hardly be denied. In a certain sense the legal-theoretical dimension of Arendt's imperialism analysis makes explicit those consequences that would arise for the normal state if in fact, as Schmitt believes, 'all law is "situational law"' (Schmitt [1922] 2004: 19). If, in other words, the '*only* criterion for the value' (ETH: 518, emphasis added) of a law were its applicability. What would it mean for the normal state of affairs if the rational declaration, interpretation and justification of laws were to become irrelevant as legitimation criteria, and only the decision as such counted? Arendt's talk of the dominant anonymity of the legislating authority and her reference to the 'pseudo-mystical aura' of the entire system is probably also directed against Schmitt's theory of sovereignty. All his life, Schmitt was unable to say who exactly the sovereign was and where the basis for his decision lay. The sovereign shows himself only in the moment of decision—and thus underlines that he is also *de facto* able to make this decision.[47] With her distinction between power and violence, between willing to and being able to, Arendt would fundamentally attack Schmitt over the course of her works and would attempt to provide evidence that under the condition of plurality, Schmitt's notion of sovereignty cannot lead to any stable political community or to any permanent order. Although Arendt, like Schmitt, questions the completely depoliticised idea of rationality on the basis of the formal-rational concept of law of the modern Continental European state (*cf* also Ahrens 2004: 88–105, and chapters four and five of this book), her criticism is not

[47] *Cf* on this point inter alia Hermann Heller's critique (Heller 1971: 87ff) and my remarks on it in ch 1.

based on 'metaphysical conviction' (Schmitt [1922] 2004: 14),[48] but is instead genuinely politically motivated.

If we follow the arc once more back to Arendt's interpretation of the modern state, we realise that she classifies its understanding of the law as an attempt to assert verifiability, reliability and stability against the arbitrary decisions of a sovereign power:

> The bureaucrat, who does not feel subject to any law, but rather to the powers of the administrative machine, has no other choice but to confront each situation with a separate decree and to shun binding agreements and generally valid laws; for agreements and laws, irrespective of whether they are good or bad, just or unjust, contain a stability that can only stand in the way of the maelstrom of magical powers; laws and agreements always tend to establish permanent communities and political bodies *in which nobody can play God*, because they must all obey the law or are bound by an agreement. (ETH: 460, emphasis added)[49]

It becomes clear once again from this passage that Arendt reinforces a very particular understanding of the law and stresses it with the example of the modern state: namely the formal-rational understanding. For against the background of a material-irrational understanding of the law, nothing could be said against recognising decrees, edicts, etc as laws—irrespective of whether or not they can be altered at will by each sovereign. Therefore what Arendt alludes to in the first instance with her talk of the 'generally valid' laws that 'all' must obey is the general character that necessarily accompanies a formal-rational understanding of law. Only against the background of such a legal conception do laws and decrees differ in the sense that the latter are applicable only to certain persons or populations—and without consideration of normal legal process—and other persons or groups of people are excluded from them.[50] The remarks have shown that the general character of the formal-rational

[48] *Cf* on this point also Schmitt's critique of Kelsen and Weber in *Der Hüter der Verfassung* (Schmitt [1931] 1996: 38).

[49] For the English version see OT: 216.

[50] It is notable that both Weber and Arendt refer to Friedrich II to illustrate the general character of formal-rational law. Weber introduces him into his *General Economic History* and points to the fact that Frederick the Great 'hated' jurists (Wg: 292, or GEH: 342), as they continuously applied his materially-oriented edicts in their formalised manner, thus making them subject to purposes that he did not wish to know about. Arendt speaks of Friedrich II in order to illustrate the discrepancy between the formalism of the Prussian civil servants and the material interests of the King. Quite apart from the fact that the civil servants were very active in advocating the abolition of privileges for the nobility, they demanded the political equality of the Jews. They were not motivated by any ethical postulate of humanity, but solely by the aspect of generality of a legal system that can only function properly if the legal rules apply unrestrictedly to all citizens in a community. The Prussian civil servants recognised that the preservation of the system of privilege for certain Jewish citizens, and the accompanying rejection of fundamental rights for the rest of the Jews, represented an attack on the law's character of generality, and thus at the same time a danger to the rights of all. However, Frederick the Great, continues Arendt, reacted with horror to the demands of his civil servants, as he was worried about his finances. (See OT: 30f, or ETH: 87ff.)

law according to Weber is based on the fact that a decision is reached for each case with the methods of legal logic and taken from the relevant abstract legal rules. The legal logic ensures that each case is examined solely with a view to which legal rules apply to it, respectively which legal rules have been breached. As a legal rule is constructed from legal conditions and legal consequences, the legal consequences always take effect, regardless of the person, as soon as the legal conditions are fulfilled. According to Weber, under the rule of formal-rational law, all actions take place either at the level of the application and execution of legal rules, or at that of infringements of these rules. The method of 'logical generalisation' leads to the fact that the status and name of a person are completely ignored. The remarks in this chapter show clearly that Arendt follows Weber's view that only the autonomy of the legal system can form a rationality that is specific to the law, and thus guarantee reliability and verifiability, and with it order.

Nevertheless, Arendt's view that no authority can play God in this understanding of the law is confusing, ie that there can be no such thing as sovereignty beyond the statutory law. For here Arendt does not reveal where her trust in the rational law comes from, that it requires no source outside of the law. The only explanation might possibly be found in Weber's idea of the logical rationalism of legal formalism which, like a machine, drives forward the production of future law. If we follow Weber in this respect, we may not overlook that fact that for him, too, the state is based principally and primarily on violence. If demanded by the political interests of a Weberian statesman, then this violence also becomes active beyond the law.[51] Within the Continental European tradition of statehood and sovereignty, the 'God' beyond the law has not been abolished but at best restrains himself. Because only a precarious balance between formal and material rationality is possible upon this restraint, Arendt's critique of the law starts at this point. With the quotation above, however, she still lies quite a distance from her later legal-theoretical, legal-philosophical and constitution-theoretical views and insights, and believes erroneously that the problem of sovereignty in the modern (Continental European) state has already been solved. Because this is not the case at all, and neither the legal, nor the state or political understanding of legal-rational rule can be compatible with Arendt, it is necessary at this point to read Arendt against

[51] The trouble with Schmitt's argument is precisely that the sovereign is active in a state of emergency both outside of and inside the legal order: the suspension of law for the sake of the law (see Schmitt [1922] 2004: 14 and Agamben 2004: 7–41). With her remarks above, Arendt disregards this problem and falls back behind her own critical considerations. In principle, however, it is of a different quality whether one points to the fact that violence is behind rational law, and can invalidate the law in a state of emergency; or, like Carl Schmitt, whether one feels obliged by this circumstance to interpret the nature of law based completely on this rupture, and to interpret all law as 'situational'.

Arendt. This is the only way to escape the dead end into which her uncritical thoughts on the stabilising function of the law outlined in the quote above lead, and to penetrate to a key topic of her political thinking: her critique of sovereignty.

In his thoughts on nationalism, Carlton Hayes established that the 'God' beyond the law did not disappear with the French Revolution but had simply taken on a different form: 'The will of the nation is God.' The nation, according to Hayes, 'can seize everything and destroy anything, for above it there is no law' (Hayes 1949: 69).[52] Hayes, to whom Arendt also refers in her work, thus expresses what Arendt considers to be 'Rousseau's original contribution': the assumption that the political community can possess a will just as much as the individual:

> Rousseau comes to this assumption by means of the peculiar problem of the law which, in its generality in a double sense, in that it applies to all and to none, precisely corresponds with the generality of the '*volonté générale*', which is common to all and yet is not the sum of individual votes. It is as if he were the first to recognise that this product of the people, namely the law in its generality, is confronted by no subject whose product it is. He finds this subject in the '*volonté générale*'. The '*volonté générale*' as a source of the law in its generality replaces the 'ius naturale' (which cannot exist, according to Rousseau) and the commands of God.' (DT: 260)

Under the changed legitimatory auspices since the French Revolution, the *volonté générale* has become the epitome of sovereignty, more precisely of the sovereignty of the people. In the following chapter it will be shown that the sovereignty of the people on the one hand undermines the law with its substantive 'vagueness', and on the other hand triggers political pathologies among the citizenry when attempting its political-institutional implementation. Arendt's critique of sovereignty will serve as our starting point in examining the development of her own understanding of the law and politics.

[52] In her book on totalitarianism, Arendt refers to a whole series of works by Hayes on nationalism and totalitarianism. (see on this point ETH: 989.)

# 4

# *Hannah Arendt's Critique of Popular Sovereignty*

## I. INTRODUCTION

WHEN THE NATION became the 'dominating principle of order for political communities' (Anter 2007: 238) with the French Revolution, the question arose as to how this new principle of order could merge with the almost 150-year history of the state and statehood. In other words, how the nation, as a concept of order, fits together with the state as a 'guarantor of order' (Anter 2007: 247)—and forms the *nation-state*? This question of the relationship between state order and national will marks a key starting point in Arendt's political-theoretical work. In various different ways she repeatedly addresses the problem of the unfortunate liaison between state and nation. In conceptual terms, she condensed these thoughts about the state and the nation in her critique of popular sovereignty. For popular sovereignty implies that the will of the people should form both 'the origin of the laws' and 'the source of legitimate power'. Arendt's critique of popular sovereignty addresses both points equally, and is therefore both legal-philosophical and political-institutional in nature.

Against this background, this chapter is divided into two principal sections. In section II, Arendt's legal-philosophical critique of popular sovereignty is introduced: the claim to absoluteness of the *volonté générale* demands a law that is indeterminate of content and can thus be defined anew and arbitrarily—depending on the national mood and disposition. Precisely, this revokes the reliability, stability and verifiability of the law, in other words its rationality. The legal-philosophical critique of popular sovereignty makes it clear that the rationality of law can be realised only on the basis of a different and new understanding of the political. Section III concerns Arendt's political-institutional critique of popular sovereignty: the institutional realisation of popular sovereignty, ie the Continental European, democratic constitutional state, is accompanied by numerous political pathologies, such as the political 'massing of individuals' (OT: 316; see also ETH: 680), mistrust and a lack of political experience. Since this structure of the constitutional state forms, at the same time, the prerequisite for law to be rational in the Continental European tradition of political thought, the concept of law itself becomes a target of Arendt's criticism.

## II. POPULAR SOVEREIGNTY AND THE LAW

> The crimes against human rights, which have become a speciality of totalitarian regimes, can always be justified by the pretext that right is equivalent to being good or useful for the whole in distinction to its parts.... A conception of law which identifies what is right with the notion of what is good—for the individual, or the family, or the people, or the largest number—becomes inevitable once the absolute and transcendent measurements of religion or the law of nature have lost their authority.
>
> Hannah Arendt, *Origins of Totalitarianism*

Below I shall explain my thesis that Arendt's legal-political criticism of popular sovereignty is aimed at the quality of the *volonté générale* as a source of law. The core of my argument is that the *volonté générale* as the source of all law procludes only material-irrational law, which is incompatible with a stable and reliable political-democratic order. In order to explicate her critique, Arendt reverts to Delos' phrase, according to which the nation gradually conquers the state.[1] What precisely is meant by this conquest? *Who* or *what* is conquered, and *how*? And why is the *volonté générale* necessarily accompanied by an irrational concept of law?

In order to be able to answer these questions, we must examine, as a first step, the *political-theoretical architecture* of Arendt's book on totalitarianism. Only by these means is it possible to present Arendt's talk of the 'conquest' as a 'battle' between different notions of political order, which in each case accompanies its own way of understanding law, politics and the interrelationship between the two. It already becomes apparent in this manner that law and politics are connected internally in Arendt's view. The subsequent section about the sources of juridification is intended to underline the fact that Arendt's interpretation of nation and law is anything but one-dimensional. Far from suggesting that the nation is, from the outset, a chauvinistic concept that is incompatible with the rule of law, Arendt emphasises that precisely the idea of the equality of all before the law and the obligation to reach 'understanding and agreement within the family of the nation' (ETH: 293) are directly connected to the idea

[1] See OT: 230. Arendt writes in this passage of the '"conquest of the state by the nation"'. One of the theories presented by Delos in his book, *La Nation*, is that the nation corrupts the legal institutions of the state. Arendt reviewed this book for *The Review of Politics* in 1946 (see Arendt 1946).

of the nation. Why, asks Arendt, has one 'never found a device by which to transform this idea into a working concept in the world of sovereign states?' (OT: 40f; see also ETH: 110). Section II.C, about the quality of the *volonté générale* as a source of law, should provide an answer to this question: no state order can be achieved with such an undefined law. Taking this insight as our starting point, we then make a foray into the depths of the ramifications of nation and law. This examination culminates in a discussion of the question as to whether the internalisation of the political, which according to Arendt constitutes the core of the *nation*-state way of understanding the political (see chapter two), leads to an ethnicisation of the political. If that is the case, the internalisation of the political is responsible for the huge potential for ethnic exclusion on the part of national politics. With regard to the primary question of the nature of an Arendtian Constitutionalism, this chapter should demonstrate that law is indissolubly dependent on the way of understanding the political, and that therefore the rationality of law cannot—as Weber and many others assume—be solely a matter for the law itself.

## A. The Political-theoretical Architecture of Arendt's book on Totalitarianism

In order to understand Arendt's analysis of the relationship between nation, popular sovereignty and the law, we need to examine the political-theoretical architecture of the *Origins/Elemente*. What precisely is meant by the political-theoretical architecture? The political-theoretical considerations in Arendt's book on totalitarianism contain *four* different *paradigms of notions of political order*, each of which represents very different ways of understanding the relationship between law and politics: besides the formal rationality of a modern administrative government as a paradigmatic notion of political order, we also find, secondly, the material rationality of the *raison d'état*. Both were tackled and driven back in the nineteenth and early twentieth centuries by the *volonté générale*, another paradigm of the notion of political order. The material rationality of the *raison d'état*, which Arendt circulates under the term 'Machiavellian raison d'état',[2] is replaced—especially in foreign affairs during the period of imperialism—by the 'Hobbesian raison d'état'[3] as the fourth paradigm. The Hobbesian *raison d'état*, which no longer has anything to do

[2] DT: 509; see also Machiavelli's famous thoughts on the *raison d'état* in Machiavelli 2001.

[3] As the Hobbesian *raison d'état* plays a minor role in this chapter, I shall sketch it only briefly here. Machiavellian *raison d'état*, which was connected with the concept of the state from the outset, is confronted with another concept of political wisdom with imperialism and the, as Arendt calls it, 'Political Emancipation of the Bourgeoisie' (OT: 123). Arendt traces this other concept back to Hobbes, who in her view anticipated the logic of a liberal competitiveness

with Hobbes himself, experiences its climax in the power-accumulating logic of total domination.

The first paradigm, I call it the formal-rational way of understanding the political, was introduced in the previous chapter by referring to Max Weber's thoughts on the rational institutional state. In most cases, when Arendt speaks of the modern state, she means the form of rule that is expressed primarily by rational administration. The 'rule by nobody' (HC: 40), by a bureaucratic machine, is the most extreme form in which this paradigm can be realised. Conservative thinkers such as Weber have sometimes emphasised the large contradiction between the state as a rational administrative machine and material, statesmanlike *raison d'état*, and sometimes the compatibility of both, depending on their mood. While in his parliamentary writings, for example, Weber declares it to be a vital political matter to restrict the power of bureaucracy, in his sociology of domination he assumes that the *raison d'état* of the administrative machinery 'mostly provides a specifically applicable content,

paradigm clearly and in its consequences. Under this new paradigm, which I call Hobbesian *raison d'état* because of its origin, politics become a permanent process of power accumulation, to which even the state must subject itself. In her *Denktagebuch*, Arendt speaks of the 'Hobbesian subjectification of the Machiavellian concept of power' (DT: 26). The new imperative becomes politically effective for the first time in imperialism: 'When the accumulation of capital had reached its natural, national limits, the bourgeoisie understood that only with an "expansion is everything" ideology, and *only with a corresponding power-accumulating process* would it be possible to set the old motor into motion again.' (OT 144, emphasis added) Just as in the process of accumulating capital neither a stable adjustment nor the halting of the process is possible without massive and almost self-destructive annihilation of capital, it is all the more so the case in power processes. The Hobbesian paradigm transfers the logic of accumulation to the political sphere, where it makes the accumulation of power the imperative of all political action. In this manner, naturally, the state is also made to serve and downgraded to an instrument. This downgrading is shown very clearly in the dissolution of the legal concept and its replacement by the decree. The legislative and judicative become meaningless; and even the executive is little more than a mere cog in the large gear of the logic of accumulation. The replacement of the Machiavellian *raison d'état* as a rational canon of political action by the Hobbesian *raison d'état*, which Arendt calls a 'process of revaluation' (OT 138), initially took place only at the level of foreign policy, and its duration was restricted to the phase of imperialistic policy. It was only in a system of total domination, with the concentration camp as its most distinct place, that this paradigm achieved completion. Then, admittedly, it no longer has anything to do with Hobbes' thought. Hobbes, according to Arendt, describes the ascent of the bourgeoisie correctly when he argues that its 'existence is essentially tied up with property as a dynamic, new property-producing device' (OT 145). Once formed against the background of an individualism of competition, the Leviathan should ideally, according to the liberal understanding, guarantee the protection of the individual. But from the very outset, a mechanism is immanent to this means-and-ends rationality with the principle of competition, which develops its own intrinsic logic, which bursts open the narrow framework of instrumental rationality and makes the accumulation process of power absolute. Ultimately, all individual rights to protection are also removed domestically, the individual is drawn into a permanent process of power accumulation, and the state with all of its institutions is abolished. See also Volk 2007.

and in dubious cases is the determining factor' (WuG: 565; see also EaS: 979). As Arendt's thoughts about politics and law start precisely at that precarious relationship between formal and material rationality, it is not surprising that the kind of *raison d'état* demanded by Weber from every political leader forms a paradigm of its own for Arendt: the 'Machiavellian raison d'état'.

In this chapter, however, the conflict between the formal rationality of an administrative state and the material rationality of the *raison d'état* is eclipsed by a further political paradigm, the national general will. In describing the gradually expanding general will as a new paradigm of the political, Arendt refers repeatedly to Delos' phrase concerning the nation conquering the state. A key task of this section of the chapter will be to interpret this expression from a legal-philosophical perspective, while exposing the problem of the establishment of a different, a national understanding of law. Conquest, as will be shown, means in the first instance that the rationality of law is undermined by the national will and makes the law irrational. The formal-rational character of the law is replaced by a 'legal form' that encompasses everything that benefits the nation under law. This is where the core of Arendt's legal critique of popular sovereignty lies. At the same time, however, it can be seen that this legal critique turns into a critique of the ways of understanding the political.

Once again it is Heinz Ziegler who very clearly identified the consequences of the new paradigm for the law:

> What is meant is the dissolution of the objectivity and absoluteness of the state idea of classical rationalism. The belief manifested here in an objective legality and doctrine of order deriving from it withdraws, and the subjective *volonté* is accentuated instead of the general *raison*. This leads ultimately to the justification or at least the acceptance of every claimed will. (Ziegler 1931: 271, emphasis added)

Besides the substantial accordance with regard to the criticism of the legislating suitability of a national general will, the consistency in the language used by Ziegler and Arendt is striking, and once again stresses the claim that Ziegler's work influenced that of Arendt. By linguistic consistency I mean the fact that in January 1955 Arendt described the point of this paradigm shift using very similar words. We read in the *Denktagebuch*: 'The Machiavellian raison d'état ends in Rousseau's "*volonté générale*"—but what a shift in accentuation! From the state to society, and from reason to will.' (DT: 509)

Strictly speaking, it is not quite correct to speak of the 'end' of the 'Machiavellian raison d'état'. Even after 1789 and up to the beginning of the age of imperialism, Continental European politics remain for Arendt to a broad extent understandable and explicable in the context of the 'Machiavellian raison d'état'. Yet with the French Revolution, the *volonté générale*, the sovereignty of the national general will, comes increasingly to the fore as a paradigm. The decisive difference between the 'Machiavellian raison d'état' and *volonté générale* on the one hand, and their respective relationship to formal-rational law on the other hand, reveals itself in the aspects of reliability, calculability and restrictedness. Arendt expresses this difference by comparing the conceptual pairs state/reason and society/will. According to Arendt, with Rousseau's *volonté générale* the idea of the 'wise rule' of a 'genius statesman' is confronted by the highly emotionalised, morally sanctioned majority will of society.

There is no doubt that the law, based on the Western idea of sovereignty, is in constant danger of being broken or suspended—the Machiavellian *raison d'état* by no means forms an exception in this tradition, but indeed establishes the rule itself. If, however, we review briefly the remarks above on the origin of the modern state, it becomes clear just how closely integrated the monarchs of 'modern' states already were in the demands and logic of an expanding and expansionist statehood towards the end of the eighteenth century and the beginning of the nineteenth.[4] What guided this form of rule was not personal vanity or individual discretion, but rather the 'rationality of the power chess game' (Ziegler 1931: 264), embodied in the idea of the *raison d'état.* At the very beginning of the standard work on the history and idea of the *raison d'état*, Friedrich Meinecke writes: 'Raison d'état is the fundamental principle of state conduct, the state's first law of motion. It tells the statesman what he must do to preserve the health and strength of the state.' (Meinecke [1924] 1929: 1)

Meinecke does point to the fact that each state has a 'particular structure' and a 'particular environment'. However, this by no means opens the floodgates to the arbitrariness and personal emotion of the ruler. Rather, according to Meinecke, the '"intelligence" of the state' consists in understanding oneself and one's environment, and using this understanding to derive an 'ought and must' (Meinecke [1924] 1929: 1f), principles to guide the stateman's behaviour. By these means the monarch becomes an enlightened monarch, the despot becomes an enlightened despot. Arendt adopts these thoughts on the *raison d'état* for her own considerations of the political quality of an enlightened monarchy and an enlightened despotism.[5] Accordingly, with reference to Meinecke's *raison d'état*, she writes, 'The enlightened despotism was based on

[4] In his parliamentary writings Max Weber stresses the fact that the king—if he is not a born politician—usually does not rule himself. If he does so then not only his crown is at stake, but also the existence of the entire state. According to Weber, an absolute monarchy should be governed ideally by a cabinet, consisting in part of expert administrators, and in part of politically experienced and loyal persons. The rationality of the *raison d'état* and the stability of the state would arise from this cabinet on the one hand and from the expert bureaucracy on the other. (See PuR: 337f.)

[5] When Arendt speaks of the enlightened monarchy, she wishes to point to the potential for rationality of *raison d'état* thinking. Because this material rationality represents the legal source of an enlightened monarchy, the term 'enlightened monarchy' has always had a legal dimension of meaning. When, on the other hand, she speaks of absolute monarchy, which need not necessarily always be less enlightened, this suggests that Arendt is pointing to the state-theoretical dimension of the monarchical ruling apparatus, ie its hierarchical structure, with an absolute king at its head.

Rohan's "kings command the peoples and interest commands the king", an idea that forms the basis of all theories of raison d'état.' (ETH: 489; see also OT: 230)

The underlying idea of reverting to the *raison d'état* against the background of the discourse on sovereignty is that the 'normativity' of *raison d'état* thinking is also reflected in the law; it shapes the law and, what is more, it establishes the rationality of the *raison d'état* itself as a significant source of law. If we say that the *raison d'état* represents the legal source of an enlightened monarchy then we assume a concept of law that is based on the materiality of political deliberations of expediency, which guide the process of law-finding and law-making. Although Arendt leaves no doubt in her thoughts on imperialism that this process of law-finding and law-making very soon leaves its rational path, seen from a legal-philosophical perspective, the idea of the *raison d'état* is based on a certain conglomerate of norms, which makes both political action and—crucially—the legal process reliable and verifiable *to some degree*. At least, more reliable than popular sovereignty based on the *volonté générale* could ever be. Precisely in this sense, we find in Ziegler that

> [t]he ideal guidelines that are decisive for this behaviour are specified in a rational canon. One orients oneself above all on deliberations of expediency, and a splendidly realistic doctrine of the technique of politics takes the foreground. The prince, as the "manager" of this organisation, the individual actions of this rule, they appear justified if they can prove themselves before the tribunal of this ratio … (Ziegler 1931: 85)

The fact that the formal rationality of a judicial apparatus and the material rationality of a cabinet oriented on the *raison d'état* are not completely incompatible, and in their symbiosis have, to a large extent, shaped the nineteenth century politically, is precisely a result of the *raison d'état* itself. For the analysis of the 'particular structure' is aware of the relationship of the state to other states, and develops from this certain strategic principles. Furthermore, *raison d'état* thinking is also aware of the significance of the rule of law as a guarantee of internal order in the state. Even if the idea of the *raison d'état* repeatedly and arbitrarily—depending on the political situation—ignores the law, it is most certainly aware of the importance of an independent rule of law for the stability of the state.

The fact that Arendt shares this assessment can be explained briefly by her depiction of Georges Clemenceau during the Dreyfus affair: Clemenceau, whom Arendt considered to belong to the political protagonists of a 'Machiavellian raison d'état', scoffed that against the background of French history, it could not seriously be the case that a single man, Alfred Dreyfus, could be condemned without recourse to the law (see ETH: 213). He repeatedly highlighted the importance of the rule of law and the legal institutions of the state, and emphasised, according to Arendt, that they meant that 'an infringement of the rights of one man was an infringement of the rights of all'

(OT: 113). Clemenceau was therefore aware that the loss of authority experienced by the courts in the Dreyfus affair marked the 'beginning of the end of the nation state' (ETH: 216).

If we examine the political history of the nineteenth and early twentieth centuries against the background of Arendt's political-theoretical architecture, the Dreyfus affair represents only one historical moment at which the 'secret conflict between state and nation' (OT: 230), between the formal rationality of a judicial apparatus and the emotional *volonté générale*, once again erupted and dictated the battle between different paradigmatic notions of political order. Repeatedly, according to Arendt, 'the times of quiet and restoration were only the pauses in which the current had gone underground to gather force to break up to the surface again'—such as in 1830, 1832, 1848, 1851, and 1871—inciting the political awareness of the citizens and undermining the legal state institutions. Yet it only became apparent with the Dreyfus affair just how rotten these state institutions had become from the regular frothing up of the national will. This affair was the 'dress rehearsal' (ETH: 213), and gave a foretaste of the 'disintegration of this form of government' (OT: 275) which was to take place in the inter-war period. The character of a 'dress rehearsal' for the later internal disintegration was a result of the fact that no court in France had sufficient authority any longer 'to truly administer justice' (ETH: 216). After an immense back-and-forth, and more than 10 years after being charged with espionage, the Jewish General Staff officer was acquitted eventually by the Court of Cassation (see ETH: 214ff). But, Arendt argues, because the decision was made by this particular court, it meant that the previous judicial decisions could only be confirmed or annulled. It was not possible to initiate proper appeal proceedings, resulting in a proper acquittal. Nothing more than a judicial error was repaired. Thus Arendt reminds us that 'Dreyfus, therefore, was never really acquitted in accordance with the law, and the Dreyfus case was never really settled' (OT: 90), never confirmed, and the judgment was never accepted by a vast majority of the French people. Accordingly, she writes:

> And the fact that a legal judgment in this matter was never acknowledged remains, in fact, most decisive. It means that no court in the France of the Third Republic had sufficient authority to truly administer justice. Clemenceau knew that this was the end of the rule of law, just as he knew that the end of the rule of law must inevitably mean the beginning of the downfall of the nation-state. (ETH: 216)

Arendt considers the courts' loss of authority to be the decisive factor in the Dreyfus affair. For the loss of authority is an expression of the fact that the viewpoint 'the law is that which benefits the nation' had established itself as a social truism. A parliament or a government that introduced *raison d'état* considerations contrary to social attitudes and values, or a court that relied solely on the juristic facts of a case when adjudicating a legal problem, would no longer be acknowledged. This is the point where the 'constantly precarious balance between nation and state, between the people's will and the law, between national interest and legal institutions' began to tip with 'great swiftness'. And it tipped to the advantage of a 'demagogically incitable people's will' and an 'increasingly chauvinistic nation'.[6] Historically, however, 'great swiftness' is not measured in months or years. Therefore one must realise, according to Arendt, that this process of the internal disintegration of the state, which turned the state—as a 'legislating apparatus and institution for the protection of rights'—into an 'instrument of the nation', and which ultimately puts the nation 'in place of the law',[7] was completed over two to three decades. The conflict was decided in favour of the nation, and the 'supremacy of the will of the nation over all legal and abstract institutions, was universally accepted'[8] and applied throughout Europe. Here it became clear just how little the legal sphere can be isolated in the long term from the political culture and mentality of a community, and thus how much the impartiality of law *also* depends on the notion and understanding of the political. In other words, it depends on how politics is conceived and understood.

If we now return to the 'Machiavellian raison d'état' as a paradigm of the political and recall the chaos of the inter-war period as described in chapter one, then it is precisely that bit of *raison d'état* reliability which Arendt holds up against the *volonté générale* as a paradigm of the political. Even though the law does not fulfil the criterion of formality, it is nevertheless not irrational under the paradigm of the 'Machiavellian raison d'état'. Quite the contrary: with the *raison d'état* as a source of law, the law follows a means–end rationality that is based on a 'rational canon'. Law is that which benefits the state—and although Arendt cannot relate either to the underlying concept of rationality, which perceives politics merely in terms of a 'power chess game' and sees some kind of 'technique' in action, or to the utilitarian 'legal form', the law thus becomes more controllable and predictable than a law that depends solely on the personal emotions of the ruler or the national mood. From Arendt's

[6] ETH: 576. Arendt's remarks more or less follow the same line in OT: 275.

[7] ETH: 488. In *Origins of Totalitarianism*, Arendt writes concisely: 'This meant that the state was partly transformed from an instrument of the law into an instrument of the nation.' (OT 230)

[8] OT: 275. Max Weber was occupied with similar worries. In his sociology of domination he writes: 'Not only any sort of popular justice—which usually does not ask for reasons and norms—but also any intensive influence on the administration by so-called public opinion—that is, concerted action born of irrational sentiments and usually staged or directed by party bosses or the press—thwarts the rational course of justice just as strongly, and under certain circumstances far more so, as the star chamber proceedings of absolute rulers used to be able to do.' (EaS: 980) However, when it comes to suggestions as to how the undermining of the rule of law should be prevented, Arendt and Weber each take a different view.

legal-philosophical perspective, what we have in the case of the 'Machiavellian raison d'état' is material-rational law.[9]

## B. Arendt and the Sources of Juridification

Arendt's interpretation of the relationship between nation and the law is just as multidimensional as her thoughts on the idea of the *raison d'état* and the associated ideas of politics and law. Like Tocqueville, she sees as the most important achievements of the French Revolution the fact that the professional civil service was liberated from the yoke of feudalism, that the internal and external processes of rationalisation of law were driven forward, and that the development towards a modern state was completed. In this respect, Arendt writes:

> The great achievement of the French Revolution was not equality as such…, as the *equal status of all before the increasingly powerful state apparatus* was already well on the way towards realisation. The revolutionary achievement was that this equality before the state became an *equality before the law*. (ETH: 46, emphasis added)

The equality of all before the state was the product of the increasing *étatisation* of rule. Arendt speaks in this context of an 'emerging nation-*state*' (ETH: 46). Because the state could no longer rely on a single class to satisfy its financial

[9] Precisely because of the underlying idea of the political, the supposed advantage of the 'Machiavellian raison d'état' over the *volonté générale* is a Pyrrhic victory. The 'championing' of this perspective serves primarily here to illustrate the different types of law. Arendt's criticism of the 'Machiavellian raison d'état' is in the first instance a political criticism; in Arendt's view, this Machiavellian paradigm fails with imperialism. For it emerges there that its principles, its 'rational canon' demand consequences—such as imperialistic expansion—that threaten to destroy precisely the cornerstones of the state. Yet this expansion was necessary against the background of a Machiavellian idea of *raison d'état*, as economic losses would otherwise have resulted. Arendt emphasises that those 'statesmen, who thought primarily in terms of the established national territory' (OT: 125) such as Bismarck, Clemenceau, etc, engaged only reluctantly in imperialism; yet at the same time, they could hardly act any differently in view of their way of understanding politics, political order and the order of things as such. For in the tradition of the Machiavellian *raison d'état*, the state and its preservation were, for these statesmen, ends in themselves. While they resisted replacing political considerations with economic ones, and thus reversing the hierarchy of value, at the same time they were unable to conclude proper international agreements due, for example, to ideas of state sovereignty. Arendt stresses that only such agreements would have provided the opportunity to prevent one nation-state after another from feeling driven to imperialism. In any case, because of the narrow political understanding of those statesmen, they had little option, according to Arendt, other than to pursue an imperialistic policy if they did not want to lose 'touch with reality' completely (OT: 124). Arendt therefore concludes that, from the perspective of the leading statesmen of that age, 'it seemed that the only alternative to export of power was the deliberate sacrifice of a great part of the national wealth', coupled with 'greater losses than the economic body of any country could sustain' (OT: 136). Here, in this apparent compulsion to imperialism, which according to Arendt was a result of the Machiavellian *raison d'état*, is where she sees the actual tragedy of the nation-state unfold: 'The tragedy of this half-hearted opposition was not that many national representatives could be bought by the new imperialist businessmen; worse than corruption was the fact that the incorruptible were convinced that imperialism was the only way to conduct world politics.'(OT: 132)

needs, it emancipated itself from all non-state interests and established the *raison d'état* alone as the sole guideline of its actions. However, the independence of the state from all classes and the accompanying *de facto* 'equality of all citizens before the … state apparatus', reveals nothing about whether, or to what extent, the law ruled. It has been pointed out, consequently, that the *raison d'état* as a source of law refers to the materiality of the law, and thus cements the dependence of the law on power-political principles. At the same time, with the development of modern statehood, the system of the separation of powers becomes more differentiated. According to Arendt, this process is deepened with and because of the French Revolution. A differentiated and deepened system of the separation of powers allows the juristic interpretation of general laws to become a pillar of the entire political system. Only by these means can the 'equality of all citizens before the law' be safeguarded. In addition, the Revolution led to the fact that the concept of citizenship was extended to all professions and classes, the concept of the legal subject was firmly anchored in the state and social structure, and thus the formal side of the law was aided in overcoming its material side.

This summary of the almost 200-year history of the development of modern statehood already suggests that Arendt regarded the increasing juridification of the state as emerging from two sources. On the one hand, the moral content of the so-called 'individualistic-liberal concept of nation' (Breuer 1998: 194) is given positive legal expression with the French Revolution. Arendt refers to this legal positivisation of the moral-enlightening substance of the French Revolution in the course of her analysis of human rights. The *Déclaration des Droits de l'Homme* defined the rights of man as the 'inalienable heritage of all human beings', and the nation 'was at once declared to be subject to laws, which supposedly would flow from the Rights of Man' (OT: 230). Although Arendt criticises elsewhere both the structure of the traditional understanding of human rights and the nation-state context in which they were embedded from the outset, she most certainly acknowledges the achievement of the French Revolution, namely, that it defined and transformed the enlightening content of the era in legal-positivist terms. Even more, she repeatedly refers to the balancing and pacifying idea of a 'concept of a "nation among nations", all of which belong to the family of mankind' (OT: 40). For Arendt, the 'new national idea' (OT: 163) is anything but chauvinistic in terms of its origin; from the very beginning it has humanitarian characteristics and is accompanied by a high moral content. This content becomes clear in the ideal concept of the boundaries of national laws:

> The nation, however, conceived of its law as an outgrowth of a unique national substance which was not valid beyond its own people and the boundaries of its own territory. On the other hand, the nation implies that another national law begins beyond its boundaries and that communication and agreement within the family of nations formed by humanity are both possible and necessary. (ETH: 292)

It becomes clear at this point what is meant by references to the 'equality of all before the law': because each citizen of a country identifies with the law, can approve it, and thus must participate equally in the process of law-finding and law-making, national laws can never be transferred to the neighbouring country, for such an expansion would breach the ethical and moral foundations of one's own state. Furthermore, the obligation of 'communication and agreement within the family of nations' is also derived from the idea of the equality of all before the law, as this is the only way politically to realise the idea of human rights. If the history of the nineteenth and twentieth centuries were not so shocking, one could call it a tragedy. Unfortunately, it is much more than that, and the main focus of Arendt's thought is to work out the reasons why the history of the nation became a history of war, racism, displacement and annihilation.[10] How can it be explained? Why did the people never find 'a device by which to transform this idea into a working concept in the world of sovereign states?'

Besides the moral-enlightened substance that prevailed with the Revolution, Arendt outlines a second source from which the juridification of rule arises: the occidental process of rationalisation, according to which the positivisation of individual law results from the logic of an increasing *étatisation* of rule itself. Arendt examines this aspect primarily in her thoughts on the position of the Jews in the modern state. Here, the legal equality of the Jews is described as a consequence of

> the political and constitutional structure of the new state body, which could function only under the conditions of the legal equality of all citizens; as such it had to be implemented in the course of the liquidation of the feudal order, and as quickly and radically as possible. This will have led to a rapid assimilation of the Jews, as the old Prussian administrators and their successors, the Reformers, relentlessly demanded. (ETH: 47)

[10] The concept of nation is connoted much more positively specifically in her writings for the journal *Aufbau* in the 1940s. For example, in the article 'What is happening in France?' of 25 September 1942, Arendt claims that the 'sudden burst of outrage among the French people … against the planned mass deportation of Jews out of Vichy France' (JW: 176) was due to the 'first signs of a reawakening of national awareness': the French people 'have "merely" become sensitive to shame and do not want to have the same thing happen on French soil that has happened in Germany, Poland, Romania, and Hungary' (JW: 177). In another article for the journal *Porvenir 3* from 1942, Arendt argues that the current situation of the Jews provided a chance 'for a new orientation of Jewish national politics', and for the first time in history placed the Jewish people in a situation where they 'can appeal directly to other peoples in regard to our just claims to national emancipation—that is, to Palestine' (JW: 261). Both the extent of the National Socialist system of extermination—Arendt learned of Auschwitz 'only' in 1943, and said herself that this day was 'decisive' (see Arendt [1964] 1998c: 59)—and the intensive examination of questions of the nation and nationalism, building on that, would lead to an altered evaluation of the political suitability of the concept of nation.

Here Arendt places the 'old Prussian administrators' in the same context as the French idea of the state-nation, which demands the legal equality of all citizens in a community. Quite irrespective of the fact that this juristic elite could not prevail against either the cultural-national understanding of the rights of citizens or the *raison d'état*-related thoughts of Frederick the Great, Arendt places the main focus on the structure of modern statehood—or more precisely, she highlights the juristic civil service as the catalyst for legal equality. The *étatisation* of rule is accompanied by the increasing juridification of the state. The French Revolution forced the bureaucratisation of the administrative and civil service apparatus. On the basis of economic and administrative factors, the modern state becomes increasingly an 'institution for the protection of rights' (WuG: 519; see EaS: 908). General, subjective laws do not result from the arbitrary concessions of a state instance of power, but rather are the consequence of the 'intensification of the institutional and organisational character of the state' (Breuer 1998: 162). From this perspective the equality of the citizen is a by-product of administrative, juridified rule. Laws order, prohibit or allow certain actions, and thus regulate the subjective expectations of the individual. Moreover, the general character of laws counters an exclusive, particular allocation (WuG: 398). In that respect, according to Arendt, the equality of all citizens before the law has *one* key source in the rationalising process of rule. Against this background and from this perspective, the achievement of the French Revolution lies not so much in the realisation of the moral substance of the Enlightenment, but rather in the fact that the feudal order was removed violently, thus paving the way for a progressive objectification and juridification of the state. In emphasising the occidental rationalising process of rule as a source of equality, Arendt once again follows Max Weber. Weber also argued that the jurists not only influenced the development of the law, but that the entire 'revolution of political management in the direction of the evolving rational state has been borne by trained jurists' (PaB: 522). Accordingly, Weber concludes that the 'birth of the modern occidental "state"' was mostly the work of *jurists*' (Weber [1915–19] 1972b: 272).

Regarding the question of the juridification of individual rights, the enlightening-liberal part of the Revolution—and moral idea of the nation—on the one hand, stands opposed to the structural history, on the other hand, in the work of Hannah Arendt. In places it looks as if Arendt gives more weight to the process of rationalisation. The reason seems to be that the modern state forms institutions which, according to Arendt, can 'function only under the conditions of the legal equality of all citizens' (ETH: 47). Seen from this angle, the rule of law would not be the result of political demands by the citizenry, but instead a fundamental condition for the existence of the modern state. If that were the case and Arendt did indeed give priority to the structural history over the democratic intervention of the citizens, then she would be mistaken in the same way as is Weber. Changes to the principle of legitimation are certainly not the result of 'a silent metamorphosis of the state' or due to the 'self-conversion of the rulers to "objectivity"' (Breuer 1998: 162). They are the result of political protest.[11]

## C. Nation and Law

> Avoir pris la Bastille, guillotiné Louis XVI et fait des révolutions sans nombre—pour aboutir à l'impossibilité de juger un homme suivant le Code—quelle ironie!
>
> Clemenceau, *Contre la Justice*

### *i. The Indefiniteness of the Law*

An apparent inconsistency in Arendt's interpretation of the French Revolution is that she on the one hand acknowledges its achievement, but on the other hand identifies the idea of popular sovereignty as the moment that was diametrically opposed to the new legal guarantees. For according to Arendt, the idea of popular sovereignty continues the absolutist tradition of a *potestas legibus soluta*, and thus undermines the autonomy of the law that had just been attained.

The starting point of Arendt's legal-philosophical criticism of popular sovereignty coincides with the moral-legitimatory aspect of her talk of the equality of all before the law. She writes:

> Hence, when the men of the French Revolution put the people into the the seat of the king, it was almost a matter of course for them to see in the people not only … the source and the locus of power, but the origin of all laws as well. (OR: 156)[12]

[11] Without doubt there are passages in her thoughts on the nature of state and statehood in *Elemente und Ursprünge totaler Herrschaft* that emphasise the structural history in the alteration of the principle of legitimation. It may well be that this was due to a central topic of the book, the genesis and alteration of forms of rule, or that it was an expression of the influence exerted on her by Weber's ideas. However, if we examine this problem in the context of her overall work, it would be wrong to view Arendt as subscribing entirely to the Weberian tradition described here. Quite apart from the fact that such an interpretation is difficult to reconcile with Arendt's political concept, there are places in many of her writings in which she specifically emphasises the importance of protest for the reshaping of laws (see here also Maxwell 2012). For example, in 'Civil Disobedience' Arendt writes, 'The whole body of labor legislation—the right to collective bargaining, the right to organize and to strike—was preceded by decades of frequently violent disobedience of what ultimately proved to be obsolete laws.' (CD: 80)

[12] In her translation into German, Arendt highlights the role of the will in even clearer terms, when she writes: 'Hence, when the men of the French Revolution put the people into the seat of the king, the consequence is not only that the source of all legitimate power lies with the people, but that *the will of the people must form the source of the law*.' (ÜR: 204, emphasis added)

By putting the people in place of the King, the French Revolution continued the tradition of the idea of sovereignty. It is inherent to this idea of sovereignty, which is expressed in talk of the *absolute* monarchy, to establish the sovereign as the basis of all law. Seen historically, Arendt argues, the will of the King represents God's will on Earth, and thus symbolises both the source of the law and of power. From this supposedly 'divine origin' the absolute monarchy derives the claim to be a *potestas legibus soluta*—a power that is subject to no laws. The end of monarchical state sovereignty and its replacement by popular sovereignty by no means represents the end of the idea of sovereignty as such. It is true that talk of popular sovereignty marks the end of the political suppression of the people by the monarch and guarantees the political participation of all citizens in decision making. In brief, the people become the source of all legitimate power. However, the fact that the people at the same time also claim to be the 'origin of all laws' means that the French Revolution joins, according to Arendt, the state-theoretical tradition of absolutism and establishes the will of the people beyond all legal boundaries—with a paradoxical result: while on the one hand the Revolution shakes off the feudal yoke and makes the 'complete' juridification of rule possible in the first place, on the other hand it places the will of the people above the law, thus freeing them, so to speak, from being bound to a constitution. But precisely the claim that the *volonté générale* has the right to 'flout the law' undermines 'every trust in justice and the law' (ÜR: 115). The *volonté générale* was authorised to do so in the new national world of ideas precisely because it itself marked a new absolutism, due to its moral universal content (*cf* on this point my remarks in chapter two). This feature of popular sovereignty can be found most clearly in Rousseau, when he says that it is 'contrary to the nature of the body politic for the Sovereign to impose on itself a law which it cannot break' (Rousseau [1762] 2012: 52). It is astonishing how the conventional state structure, including its hierarchical design, has already become second nature to Rousseau, and how this structure forces him to call for a sovereign who is above the law.[13] On the other hand, Rousseau could only argue in this manner because the general will is, in his view, 'always … good' (Rousseau [1762] 2012: 60), thus justifying the priority of politics over the law.

The decisive question now, which leads us to the centre of Arendt's legal-philosophical critique of popular sovereignty, is how can this claim of the general will to be a *potestas legibus soluta* be implemented legally? As I shall

[13] By questioning the state structure in her critique of popular sovereignty, Arendt emancipates herself implicitly from all those thinkers, such as Weber or Ziegler, who inspired her in numerous passages in her work. For precisely this kind of criticism of popular sovereignty points to a critique of the tradition of Continental European state thinking from which none of Rousseau, Weber or Ziegler is excepted.

demonstrate below, Arendt argues that such a way of understanding the political as that expressed by Rousseau's *volonté générale*, cannot be reconciled with an autonomous legal sphere. For in the law, the claim to sovereignty of the general will can be established and realised only by means of formulating *general clauses within the law*. A law that has its origin in the national will is therefore neither reliable nor verifiable. Under the rule of the general will, the law thus becomes irrational.

As outlined above, we are dealing with an irrational concept of law when legal problems are decided upon 'without making reference to general norms' (Freund 1987: 329). In judgements by a kadi or oracle, for example, the decisive reasons cannot be understood precisely because the decision is made according either to personal emotions, or to an obscure inspiration or intransparent interpretation. It is a very similar matter when the *volonté générale* becomes the source of the law. For Rousseau, the general will is always what it ought to be just because the will *is* (see Rousseau [1762] 2012: 52). For Sieyès, it does not matter 'what a nation's will is, it suffices that it has a will. All forms are good and its will is always the highest law' (Sieyès [1789] 1988: 83). As well as the characterisation of the *volonté générale* as a *potestas legibus soluta*, the 'is' and 'ought' identified by Rousseau and Sieyès also express the irrational feature: the very existence of the will justifies what it ought to be. To put it another way, simply making reference to the existence of the will justifies the decision. Thus the attention of our examination must shift briefly to the will, particularly to the manner of its formation.

The remarks in chapter two have shown that the formation of the *volonté générale* occurs at a place that lies hidden and which cannot be shared with others: the pure heart. This kind of internalisation of the political has tremendous consequences for the act of judging persons, social groups or political constellations: what is right or what is wrong, what is just or unjust, arises from a highly emotionalised, idiosyncratic projection—which is itself, in turn, the prerequisite for a successful *aliénation totale* (see OR: 69f). Rousseau's general will is thus revealed as an emotional will.[14] Good and bad, just and unjust are

[14] From the perspective of Arendt's reflections on the will, the same applies in effect to Rousseau as to Kant. Arendt writes on this point: 'The only great thinker in these centuries who would be truly irrelevant to our context is Kant. His Will is not a special mental capability distinct from thinking, but practical reason, a *Vernunftwille*' (LoM/W: 149.) Accordingly I refer to the will in Rousseau as an 'emotional will'. It is therefore important to be careful, particularly in discussing the will. Arendt does not regard the *volonté générale* as will in the proper sense. In her book about the will, in the second part of *Life of the Mind*, neither the name Rousseau nor the term *volonté générale* is mentioned even once. For Arendt the *volonté générale* is an 'emotional will', the 'subjective, ephemeral' character of which is the result of its affective formation. The *volonté générale* does not describe an individual, intellectual capacity. Even if we accept Rousseau's definition of the community as a 'public person' (Rousseau [1762] 2012: 50), for Arendt the 'will' of this 'person' is not the cause of itself as it is the core for the will as a mental activity. Rather, the irrational perception of reality of a community formed along the lines of a *volonté générale* is

not the result of an understandable decision that can be verified using norms, rational justification or free debate. An understanding of law, or a concept of law that could be brought into accordance with such an understanding of the political, necessarily lacks any *objective determinateness*. And it is exactly this non-determinateness of judging criteria that led Arendt to conclude that, with Rousseau's *volonté générale*, 'the laws themselves were understood to be commandments' (OR: 190).

The phrase 'law as commandment' can be traced back to Hegel,[15] and in this respect, Arendt does indeed follow him. In his legal philosophy Hegel demands 'that the law, in order to be a law and not a mere commandment …, must be in itself determinate'. The lack of determinateness of a commandment is expressed in such formulations as 'thou shalt not kill' or 'thou shalt care for thy own well-being and that of thy family', etc. According to Hegel, no law can be formed with such an 'indistinct generality' as that displayed by the commandments mentioned. For a law is characterised precisely by a 'determinate, objective limitation', by which means one can determine what is a crime and what is not. It appears to be an anticipation of Arendt's critique of the legal quality of Rousseau's general will when we realise what infiltrates, according to Hegel, 'such a determinateness':

> Here again the will holds to the abstract good; and every absolutely existing and valid mark of the good and bad, of just and unjust, is superseded by and handed over to the feeling, opinion, and liking of the individual. (Hegel [1821] 1986: 272 (§140))

the result of a highly emotionalised rash conclusion: giving up one's own position and one's own interests, ie *aliénation totale*, is possible only by means of an affective solidarity with the supposed 'absolute good'. The key problem with Rousseau, as Arendt sees it, is less the will than the formation of the will. All problems with the will result from its formation. At the same time, however, Arendt criticises that tradition of political-theoretical thought which constitutes the will as the energetic core of the political. But Arendt's criticism of this is not a criticism of the will as such, but instead of the ideas of sovereign action, of '[replacing] acting with making' (HC: 220), as the supposed core of the political, which accompanies the conceptual transfer of the will to the political. This can be seen from the fact, for example, that Arendt considers this idea of sovereign action to have originated with Plato, although with Plato there was no such thing as 'will' in the proper sense of the word, ie as the faculty by which a person decides or initiates action, due to the concept of time in antiquity (see LoM/W: 11–19). According to Arendt, the (problem of a free) will was discovered only with Paul the Apostle and Christianity. From there the metaphor of the will found its way into political jargon, and from then on it denoted a sovereign and self-determined unit that arranges the world according to its ideas. If, however, one applies the will metaphor to a political community then one is constantly suspected, in Arendt's view, of wanting to conjure up a unity that does not exist, of describing a unanimous impulse to act that can serve as a supposed Archimedean point and postulates the end of plurality, at least in the short term, and of presenting knowledge about oneself, the other and the consequences of political action which one can never have. In very different contexts, Jürgen Förster and Patchen Markell have drawn attention to this political-philosophical critique of sovereignty that accompanies the will metaphor (*cf* Förster 2009 and Markell 2003).

[15] I would like to refer here to an essay by Henrique Otten (Otten 2001), which had a decisive influence on my view at this point.

In the case of Arendt's thought, the individual of whom Hegel speaks and who is left here to define what is good—and thus what should be law—is Rousseau's 'public person' (Rousseau [1762] 2012: 50). The undefined categories with which this 'public person' must judge right from wrong, turn the law into a commandment, thus stunting all verifiability and reliability. The law becomes 'irrational'. What is or is not a crime—to stay with Hegel's example—is defined anew from case to case, based on feeling and liking. Hegel writes that the 'subjective opinion' becomes the 'rule of the law' (Hegel [1821] 1986: 272 (§140)). He takes the same line here as Arendt, who criticises that with the *volonté générale*, a 'subjective state of mind' (OR: 156) decides what is right and what not, plays 'havoc with justice and [makes] light of laws' (OR: 86).

One could now argue that such a concept of law cannot be reconciled with Rousseau's *volonté générale.* After all, Rousseau explicitly stressed that the 'object of laws is always general' (Rousseau [1762] 2012: 67). However, the decisive problem of Rousseau's understanding of the law is that he identifies the law with the 'public interest': 'I therefore give the name "Republic" to every State that is governed by laws …: for only in such a case does the public interest govern' (Rousseau [1762] 2012: 67). If one indeed wishes to make the 'public interest' the sole criterion of the law, ie allow it to 'govern', then the consequence for the specific legal implementation is that one must set general clauses instead of a law, the content of which is defined. Why and to what extent, according to Arendt, is the sovereignty of the general will accompanied by general clauses? If the general political will is always what it ought to be simply because the will is (Rousseau); if the will is always the 'highest law' (Sieyès), then no law can or may be enforced against it (see Rousseau [1762] 2012: 52). Such a claim of primacy of politics and the general will, however, can be implemented in a legal system only with the help of general clauses. How exactly does that happen?

According to Franz Neumann, the defining feature of the general clause is that it primarily upholds the generality criterion of modern law. *De facto*, however, general clauses represent 'only a veil … with which individual measures are obscured',[16] and which therefore undermines the equality of all before the law. As Neumann argues, wherever 'fundamental principles or important

[16] Neumann 1970: 14. Thanks to the 'advance of the general clause', Schmitt already celebrates the swansong to legal positivism and writes: 'As soon as terms such as "loyalty and belief", "good manners", etc refer not to individualistic, bourgeois society, but to the interest of the entire people, the overall law does indeed change, without a single "positive" law having to be altered.' (Schmitt [1934] 1993: 49) Referring to the core of this process of formulating general clauses within the law, Schmitt writes that the general clauses can establish 'to an extent that suspends all positive "security" …, indefinite terms of all kinds, references to extrajudicial standards and ideas such as good manners, loyalty and belief, reasonableness and unreasonableness, important reason, etc', in place of the rationally defined law.

elements of the legal system are under the rule of such general clauses' one can no longer speak of a 'rule of general laws' (Neumann 1970: 14). Everything can take legal form in such a legal system. Thus the law completely loses its autonomy. In our context, that means that the claims to sovereignty by the general will can only be integrated in the legal system by undermining the postulate of legal definiteness and determinateness of a legal rule. This postulate of definiteness is undermined or infiltrated by incorporating a legal rule that is deliberately kept completely indefinite, in other words a general clause. In practice, such an infiltration is made by incorporating an additional, completely undefined provision, such as 'reasons of public safety and order' into a law—for example a law of residency for foreigners—along with a number of definite criteria such as the independent securing of subsistence, no prior convictions, language skills, etc. With this in mind, Arendt, in the course of her critique of the nationalising of the law in the inter-war period, highlights the fact that in the case of key juristic problems and legal decisions, 'legally intangible formulations' were used, such as '"grave infringement of obligations as a Belgian citizen"', '"behaviour that is unworthy of Italian citizenship"', or '"interests … that are detrimental to France and its security"' (OT: 279; see also ETH: 586). With the help of general clauses, both the indeterminateness of the content and the national will's claim to sovereignty are translatable into legal codes. By these means the general will also gains exclusive access to the very place where justice is administered. If no such general clause is built in, legal claims must also—where all other criteria are proved to be fulfilled—be asserted against the supposed 'public interest'. As this is not reconcilable with the general will's claim to sovereignty, but at the same time a legal order is naturally indispensable, general clauses are incorporated. The law thus becomes the plaything of political interests, and the idea of justice degenerates into the mere command of the sovereign. To be very clear, of course there are general clauses in every legal system—for very different and sometimes good reasons. The problem is that an understanding of the political, the core of which is marked by the sovereignty of the general will and which postulates the rule of the public interest, is compatible only with a law that consists substantially of undefined and undetermined legal rules and general clauses.

Furthermore, these passages help to illustrate to what extent law and politics are interrelated in Arendt's view. It is not very original to argue that Arendt condemns Rousseau's idea of the *volonté générale*. What is novel, however, is to highlight the systematic legal- and constitutional-theoretical considerations embedded in this critique: the prevalent paradigm of politics, ie the way in which political opinion and decision-making are understood and perceived within a political community, has a massive influence on the chance to uphold the legal rationality. Arendt's Rousseau discourse reveals the internal connection between maintaining the stabilising function of law on the one hand and the configurative structure of the concept of politics on the other. The radical-democratic version shaped by Rousseau—the primacy of politics—endangers not only individual legal claims, according to the classical interpretation; rather, under the dictates of the claim to sovereignty by a general will, the legal system as a whole becomes rotten. In order for law to contribute to a stable political order, a completely different, *law-accommodating understanding of politics* must be developed and the claim of the primacy of politics must be abandoned.

### *ii. Arendt on the Abrogation of the Law During the French Revolution*

Arendt points to the undermining of the rule of law by the nationalising of the law not just in her remarks on the 'denaturalisation laws' of the inter-war period.[17] The relationship between the nation and the law is also addressed in her reflections on the Jacobin rule. In brief, in her view the problem of nation and law is as old as the *nation*-state itself. Although Arendt emphasises in her writings on the French Revolution that, 'measured against the immense sufferings of the immense majority of the people, the impartiality of justice and law, the application of the same rules to those who sleep in palaces and those who sleep under the bridges of Paris, was like a mockery' (OR: 86), she sees the abrogation of the law laid out in the idea of the national will. Arendt identifies this abrogation of the law in the first instance in the application of completely undefined criteria.

The first example that can be found in *On Revolution* is the conviction of King Louis XVI. Arendt does not dispute that he had to be convicted; however, she by no means agrees with the type of indictment. This condemned Louis XVI as a traitor—and not as a tyrant, which Arendt believes he was (see OR: 86f). While a tyrant is characterised by the fact that he passes law to which he himself is not subject, and in addition usually suppresses his own people by the cruellest means, treason takes place at a very different moral level and tends to refer to a sly offence against the community. The tyrant is an oppressor who will not acknowledge that a legitimate political order can only be based on the consent of the citizens—but at the very least with the acknowledgement of fundamental freedoms and rights. The charge of treason in the case of Louis XVI, on the other hand, was based on his having surrendered the supposed common will of the nation to other interests. A provable and understandable charge of having rejected fundamental rights and having violently upheld a repressive form of government is transformed into an infringement of the supposedly insufficient national ethos. Instead of cogent criteria, a randomly formulated and poorly defined category is applied in order to judge the case.

[17] *Cf* on this point my remarks in ch 1.

Arendt's next example takes the same direction: her criticism of the 'laws of Ventose in 1794' (OR: 43). These laws on the confiscation of property might possibly be justifiable as a response to the devastating humanitarian situation in France at the end of the eighteenth century—although those who advocated the confiscation of property were the very same people who had declared the right to own property to be a human right only a short time before. However, Arendt considers it problematic that apart from the Church and expatriates, 'suspects' (OR: 43) were also relieved of their property, which was then bequeathed to the 'unfortunates'. But in the context of the French Revolution, 'suspects' were all those who were lacking the supposedly correct ethos.

In both cases the judgment criterion refers to an insufficient inner attitude. The consequence, once again, is a loss of legal determinateness and definiteness. That is no coincidence in the context of the French Revolution: a political world view for which the idea of the *volonté générale* is crucial means that the purity of the heart becomes the proof for the individual that he represents the common cause. The reinterpretation of the concept of virtue, which was, according to Arendt, the necessary consequence of the *volonté générale* as a new paradigm of the political, led to an 'internalisation of the political'. In Arendt's view it was precisely this concept of virtue, relocated to the inner being of man, which was the reason why the French revolutionaries repeatedly reverted to the simile of the mask, which was to be torn from the faces of supposed traitors in order to reveal to the public their inner depravity. But Arendt believes that in this way they dissolved the concept of the juristic person—a fundamental principle of every rule of law (see OR: 102).

Since the Latin term *persona*, which originally denoted the mask worn by actors on the Ancient stage, became a fixed juristic term, the double function of the mask is expressed for the first time in its political-legal dimension (*cf* on this point also Manthe 2003). In Rome the difference between a citizen and a private person was that the citizen was regarded as a juristic person. This meant that he was granted a 'mask' by the law. This mask of the law allowed him to appear in public without having to surrender his inner being, his subjectivity. The mask served as a medium that hid the face, but which at the same time was built in such a manner 'that his own voice would be able to sound through':

> The point was that 'it' is not the natural Ego which enters a court of law. It is a right-and-duty-bearing person, created by the law, which appears before the law.' Without his persona, there would be an individual without rights and duties, perhaps a 'natural man'—that is, a human being or homo in the original meaning of the word, indicating someone outside the range of the law and the body politic of the citizens, as for instance a slave—but certainly a politically irrelevant being. (OR: 102f)

What Arendt is trying to say with her thoughts on the mask and the concept of *persona* seems to be as follows: by drawing solely on the ethos, attitude and basic beliefs, and not on the facts as judgment criteria in legal matters, the Jacobins dispensed with the idea of the legal person. The manner of use of the terms 'suspects' and 'traitors' testifies to this. It was not the person who was granted rights and obligations, but exclusively those with the proper ethos. If one did not share the right ethos—or more precisely if one was suspected of not sharing it—one had no rights. This was accompanied by the reversal of the proof of innocence—according to Arendt, 'the great maxim of all civilized legal systems'. The accuser no longer had to produce evidence of guilt, but rather the accused was required to prove his own innocence. But because innocence means possessing a pure and uncorrupted heart and subjecting oneself completely to the *volonté générale*, proof of innocence was impossible. For a pure heart 'cannot be proved but must be accepted on faith' (OR: 82); confessions, however, made in an atmosphere of mistrust, have always been suspected of being pure lies.[18]

### *iii. From the Internalisation of the Political to Its Ethnicisation*

In her treatment *Strangers to Ourselves*, Julia Kristeva draws attention to the undoubtedly disconcerting and tragic aspect of the French Revolution wherein, at the beginning of the Revolutionary Wars, the 'suspects' were in the first instance foreigners (see Kristeva 1991: 154–63). Kristeva traces the development that led to the demand by the Committee of Public Safety on 18 March 1793 that a law be passed to allow the criminal prosecution of foreigners, and for all foreigners to be banned from the Republic. Robespierre would later join in this demand, and he for his part also called for the expulsion of all foreign generals who had led the French army to that date (see Kristeva 1991: 157). At the same time the Committee on Public Safety pleaded 'Let us drive the English from our territory!'; and the representatives, according to Kristeva, yelled 'All of them! All of them!' (Kristeva 1991: 158), A short time later a

[18] Questions of ethos naturally still play a role in the modern administration of justice. However, this can never be separated from the actual offence committed, which is also considered in the judgment. By ignoring the actual actions of a person and believing that one can take his inner constitution as a criterion of judgment, this leads to an implicit reinterpretation of what a crime actually is. The crime becomes a vice: 'There is a fundamental difference between the crime and the vice, into which society assimilates the crime. Crimes are committed by free people, who can be brought to account for their misdeeds. Vices are imposed upon people by means of a fatal, natural disposition. Thus the often narrow-minded moralising attitudes that in earlier times judged and condemned vices as crimes, without any so-called "psychological understanding", demonstrated so much more respect for the human being, for the freedom of people, than the human "understanding" of modern psychologists, who demean people to a mechanism that functions automatically according to the law.' (ETH: 203f) While talk of a crime acknowledges that a criminal is a person who could have acted differently, a vice indicates a 'natural fatality, like a club foot or a hunched back' (ETH: 204).

law was passed in the National Convention that provided the basis for the arrest and confiscation of the property of all those foreigners who came from countries with which the Republic was at war, and who were not yet resident in France prior to 14 July 1789 (see Kristeva 1991: 158). This law reads like a poor parody of the Citizenship Act of April 1790, respectively its formulation in Article III, Part 2 of the Constitution of 1791. For in this document, naturalisation was defined as follows:

> All persons having been born of foreign parents outside the kingdom and who have settled in France will be recognized as French and, after having taken the civic oath, allowed to exercise the rights of an active citizen, after residing five years in the kingdom, provided they have furthermore acquired real estate or married a French woman, or founded commercial establishments, or received from some cities letters patent or burgess, contrary regulations notwithstanding, which are hereby abrogated. (cited after Kristeva 1991: 155)

How can it be that within only a few years, an attitude towards foreigners such as that expressed in the Constitution of 1791, and representing the spirit of the *Déclaration des Droits de l'Homme*, was transformed into a mood that placed all foreigners under general suspicion?

Although Kristeva places this question to the fore of her examination, her reply remains relatively vague: in her view it is the wrongly understood and naive universalism of the Enlightenment which was unable to integrate foreigners. Instead, that which is foreign about the other is suppressed and can once again break out with a hostile complexion in times of crisis. What is expressed here, according to Kristeva, is the 'violence and strangeness of the subjective facet of cosmopolitanism' (Kristeva 1991: 142). Building on this, Kristeva formulates her theory that the cosmopolitan and emancipatory claim of the Revolution can only have a chance of being realised if the foreign is recognised in ourselves. By means of an 'ethics of psychoanalysis' (Kristeva 1991: 192), she seeks to lay a new political foundation for the treatment of the foreigner. Although Kristeva's analysis provides valuable insights into the Janus face of the Enlightenment, it seems to me that there is a psychologisation of the political at work here that identifies worldly plurality with emotional plurality. The treatment of the foreigner within oneself is still a treatment of *one's own* foreigner, while the foreigner within a political and social community really is another.[19] There is a divide between psychological economy

[19] I refer here to Kristeva's syllogism, in which she concludes, against the background of the foreigner within oneself, that we are all foreigners. If we would only acknowledge this foreigner within us then there would no longer be any foreigners, Kristeva seems to promise. For wherever everyone is foreign, nobody is foreign anymore (see Kristeva 1991: 192). Instead of a political examination of the conflictive plurality of human forms of existence, she makes a large plea for tolerance. That at least is how I understand Kristeva's demand to recognise 'our uncanny strangeness' (Kristeva 1991: 192).

and worldly political and social events, which arises from the intrinsic logic of each sphere and which cannot be closed simply by terminology. Furthermore, Kristeva has no answer to the question as to why only *foreigners* came under suspicion. For, according to Kristeva's line of argument, my neighbour—of the same nationality—can hardly be any less foreign to me. All Kristeva can point to, ultimately, is *that* foreigners came under suspicion, and she explains this—retrospectively—by means of their apparently disreputable foreignness.

Therefore, I shall embark on a different path with Arendt in order to explain this drastic shift within the first years of the Revolution.[20] In a first step I introduce a proposal from 1793, 'hospitality certificates' (cited after Kristeva 1991: 158), which were intended to free the foreigner from general suspicion following a detailed examination of his civic ethos. An armband bearing the name of the country of origin and the word 'hospitality' was to make this foreigner visible to all. We encounter here once more the motivation described above to place the ethos, the inner attitude—and not the acts—at the centre of attention. This time, however, the ethos test was of course demanded only of those who were not of French origin. This raises the question as to whether *ethnicisation of the political* could be connected in some way to the *internalisation of the political*? And that seems to me to be precisely Arendt's assertion.

With the French Revolution, the idea of a good citizen was conveyed to the inner being of the person. For the nation, patriotism is patriotism of the heart: it is not so much the acts as the inner purity of the individual that is decisive for judging his quality as a citizen. For the justified possibility of a passionate identification with the will of the nation can arise only from purity. The gap between the demand for the emotional purity of the individual on the one hand and the emphasis on common lineage on the other is bridged by the fact that the common lineage provides the patriotism of the heart with the opportunity to take an external, worldly form, while at the same time addressing its configuratory specifications, ie emphasising a homogeneous, similar inwardness. How can we understand that? Just like the patriotism of the heart, the common lineage also draws its community-forming strength from something that lies hidden. But this hidden aspect is now objectified, so to speak, by birth, and can therefore be transferred to a tangible world. With a common lineage

[20] The fact that Arendt also has this shift in mind is shown by this passage: 'A great enthusiasm for the "new specimens of mankind" (Herder) filled the hearts of the heroes of the French Revolution who were not only concerned with the liberation of the French nation, but who hoped to liberate all peoples under the colours of the tricolour, and make them into nations. This is what "*fraternité*" meant, and it was supposed to spread across the entire earth, for: "*La raison est de tous les climats*" (La Bruyère). And yet precisely in the very century that liberated the nation and became enthusiastic about the idea of mankind, we find the first seeds of the concept of race that destroyed the nations and annihilated the idea of mankind that had been born of the nation.' (ETH: 358)

one assumes that one is connected by a pre-political, intangible internal band, but that this band, at the same time, is manifested in the world by the fact of birth.

This idea of the switch from the national general will to a national lineage can be explained forcefully using Renan's thoughts on the nature of the nation. In his famous speech on the question '*What is a nation?*', Renan highlights the daily plebiscite as a feature of the nation: 'A nation's existence is, if you will pardon the metaphor, a daily plebiscite, just as an individual's existence is a perpetual affirmation of life.' (Renan [1882] 1996: 35)

One cannot accuse Renan of being a deliberate advocate of an ethnically connoted concept of the nation. Quite the contrary: particularly in the question of the status of Alsace-Lorraine, he sets out his idea of the nation as a unity of will against the cultural-nationalistic view of the German publicist David Friedrich Strauß (see Renan [1882] 1995). It appears all the more puzzling, therefore, that when we pursue the question regarding the prerequisites for the formation of the will, we encounter a definition by Renan of the nation as a family, connoting lineage:

> A nation is a spiritual principle resulting from the profound complexities of history—it is a spiritual family, not a group determined by the lay of the land.... A nation is a soul, a spiritual principle.... One is the possession in common of a rich legacy of memories; the other is present consent, the desire to live together, the desire to continue to invest in the heritage that we have jointly received. (Renan [1882] 1996: 33f)

Soul, will and family apparently form the core of Renan's concept of nation: the precondition of the 'common will' lies not in itself but in the 'soul', which guides and motivates it. This soul, which is shaped by the 'common glories' of the past and by the history that has been experienced, is embodied in the 'family', in an ancestral community. Although this is a family that places the conscious 'will' at the forefront—thus setting itself fundamentally apart from tribal 'ideas of nation'—the soul, as the precondition of this will, is shaped by history, and is therefore somewhat removed from individual access. If this very special kind of soul is placed before the will then it is above all necessary for all those who now wish to contribute to shaping the will of the nation to carry this common soul within them. If, based on this consideration of Renan's analysis of the nation, we return to the question raised above as to why foreigners in particular had to prove they had the right ethos, and were the first to come under suspicion, then precisely the soul as the precondition of the common, national will provides the key to the answer: the required 'emotional, character-related' (ETH: 204) attitude, the identification with the national soul, was believed to be held by those who had lived through this common history, or by the children of those who had done so. This is also how the decision by the Convention to expel all foreigners who settled in France in

1789 is to be understood. When political affiliations are fed for the most part by an inner, hidden strength, there is a desire to symbolise this inner, hidden strength in some way. Thus the nation as a family, which has lived through a very specific history, acts as a symbol. It is not out of the question that other people might join this family—and one can join this family—but the family certainly knows who belongs to the 'narrower circle' and who does not. In other words, every form of the internalisation of the political and the identification of the soul as the origin of the will is accompanied by the danger of ethnicising political matters.

I wrote above of the fact that Renan's understanding of the nation as a family places the will in the foreground and thus sets itself fundamentally apart from the tribal idea of nation. This addendum is of fundamental importance, as it lays the foundation for being able to differentiate thoroughly between 'Western nationalism'—also in its 'perverted chauvinistic form'—and 'völkisch nationalism' (tribal nationalism) (ETH: 481). For not even the chauvinistic expression of Western, French nationalism, as represented in the '*nationalisme intégral*' (ETH: 481) of Maurras and Barrès, is ever manifested as such that people who are perhaps of French ancestry, but who were born and have grown up in a different country without any knowledge of the French language, history or culture, are declared to be French simply due to the 'mysterious qualities of their "blood"' (ETH: 481). Although the will owes its origin to a common soul, which is itself in turn at home in the national family, the expression of the will is indispensable. For precisely the expression of the will makes it clear to the outer world what distinguishes individuals from one another. In *völkisch* or tribal nationalism, an expression of the will that is outwardly visible was and is completely superfluous. There the 'soul' is *not* the product of a verifiable history oriented on events of the past, but rather a 'national quality' (ETH: 482), which results ultimately from the common 'blood':

> [T]he difference between even the most violent chauvinism [of Western nationalism] and this tribal nationalism [is] still the fact that one is at least concerned with the world and its tangible realities, with the actual, factual achievements of a nation in all areas, whereas the tribal one, even in its mildest forms (for example, the German youth movement) is introverted, and begins to see the human soul as the 'embodiment' of general national qualities … Chauvinistic megalomania continues to point to something that really existed in the past and merely tries to elevate these national realities into a pseudo-mystical realm, beyond human control; tribalism, on the other hand, adheres from the outset to non-existent, imaginary ideas, and does not even attempt to take the past as its verification, but instead proposes to realise these ideas fully in the future.… Tribal nationalism can always be recognised by the fact that it principally measures and judges everything that belongs to the visible existence of its own nation, its traditions, its political institutions, its culture, by this imaginary yardstick of 'blood'. (ETH: 482)

For Arendt, the difference between Western and tribal concepts of the nation is the most relevant difference of all. Only a tribal nationalism could, based on the conditions of its constitution, develop such racial hatred as that which released such a previously unforeseen potential for annihilation. The 'trinity of people, state and territory' (ETH: 107f), which forms the foundation of the Western concept of the nation, is queried by tribal nationalism.[21] This can be seen merely from the fact that the idea of a blood community transcends territorial boundaries and makes out of a people, as a historically formed unit, a tribal community. In contrast, the Western concept of the nation is connected directly with the state and its institutions. The remarks on the relationship between law and nation have shown that the French Revolution helped the modern state to prevail precisely by removing feudalism completely, and thus further propelling a juridification of the state. In addition, with the Revolution the 'equality of all before the law'—thus a qualitative expansion of the 'equality of all before the state'—invokes the political agenda. It therefore seems paradoxical that the relationship between nation and law takes a different aspect, which undermines both the newly-attained rationality of the law and the legality of political action. Arendt therefore writes, reflecting the exciting conflict situation at the basis of the nation-state,

> [t]here is no question that this development of the conquest of the state by the nation has always been a danger specific to the nation-state. Because this form of state at the same time means the creation of a constitutional government and was based essentially on the rule of the law against arbitrary despotic administration, it was also the danger that proved fatal to this form of government. (ETH: 575)

This tension in the basic structure of the nation-state prompts Arendt to speak of the 'precarious balance between nation and state, between the will of the people and the law, between national interest and legal institutions' (ETH: 575f). We have seen how this 'precarious balance' tips in the inter-war period and turns the state, as a 'legislating apparatus and institution for the protection

[21] Arendt distinguishes not only between Western nationalism and tribal nationalism, but also between tribal nationalism and 'race thinking'. National Socialism transformed tribal nationalism—which had always had a dominant position in Germany, as well as in Eastern and Southeast Europe—into race thinking. Arendt highlights the fact that everything racial is always tribal, but not everything tribal is always racial. The great danger of the tribal is its worldlessness and its speculative tendency. Race thinking exaggerates this immediately with a scale of values that divides the world into higher and lower races. This instantly makes race thinking 'political'. The communication between political entities, as contained in the idea of the nation, is impossible on the basis of race thinking. Accordingly, Arendt speaks of 'anti-national race thinking' and assumes that racism is 'everywhere a factor that is opposed to nationalism and which undermines it and every form of patriotism'. Racial ideologies are the only ones that 'truly struck at the heart of the nation-state, together with nationalism, with its denial of the principle of equality and the solidarity of the nations, which was guaranteed by the idea of humanity' (ETH: 357).

of rights', into an 'instrument of the nation': 'The nation takes the place of the law' (ETH: 488).

In section III. of this chapter, Arendt's critique of popular sovereignty will be presented as a critique of the structural composition of the Continental European state. My argument is that Arendt also detects order-endangering features in the structure of the modern state. The analysis will show inter alia that the state is in danger of being conquered by the nation precisely because the idea of the nation provides the only way in the modern state to generate identity and solidarity within the citizenry. One criticism, therefore, will be that the conversion to the national is also a reaction to the fact that the modern state did not develop or allow any political institutions within which a political culture and mentality could have emerged on the basis of a discursive-democratic process. However, if we recall Max Weber's thoughts, precisely this structural-hierarchical composition was a precondition for the rule of rational law. Now, in questioning the structural composition of the Continental European state, the concept of law becomes the focus of the criticism. While the legal-philosophical critique of popular sovereignty ultimately becomes a critique of the way of understanding the political, the critique of the institutional and structural composition of the state ultimately questions the concept of law. This is not a dialectical gimmick, but rather a reference to the internal connection between politics and the law.

## III. POPULAR SOVEREIGNTY AND POLITICS

*Adelbert Reif*: What concept of the state do you have?

*Hannah Arendt*: I don't actually have a different concept of the state, I just see the necessity to change this concept of the state.

Hannah Arendt in an interview with Adelbert Reif, 1970

The key problem of the Continental European state is the localisation and description of the nature of political power. Each depends directly on the other. As far as the nature of power is concerned, the Continental European state institutionally establishes a conviction which has been a commonplace of political thought since Plato: the identification of power with violence. In this way the 'effectiveness of command' (OV: 37) becomes the essential feature of power, and domination (*Herrschaft*) becomes the fundamental category for all considerations of political community. For domination means in the first instance a condition that guarantees that the will of the ruler or rulers, ie the command, can be enforced permanently upon the ruled. With this in mind, the concept of domination is a crucial pillar in Max Weber's famous definition of the state, which describes the 'state' as 'a relation of men dominating men, a relation supported by means of legitimate (ie considered to be legitimate) violence' (PaB: 507). If one assumes that power and violence are identical, and that domination represents the essence of each state, consequently, only a state in which the ordering will is undivided and the resources for its enforcement are centralised and monopolised can be described as 'powerful'. In brief: where power is concentrated in a single place. This idea of the place and nature of power leads Arendt to write—with regard to the structural composition of the Continental European state—of 'state absolutism' (ÜR: 203), which was embodied memorably for centuries in the image of the king as sovereign. With the French Revolution, this structural composition of the state becomes the central problem. While the question of legitimisation was posed afresh with the Revolution, and the supposed God-given nature of the absolute ruler was declared to be invalid, a tight grip was nevertheless maintained on the traditional concept of the state. The people placed itself on the King's throne. This produced the difficulty as to how the newly postulated rule of the people could be brought into compliance with the structural composition of the state. According to Arendt, at the level of legitimisation, 'a highly ingenious means' had been found with Rousseau's thoughts on the *volonté générale*, 'to put a multitude into the place of a single person; for the general will was nothing more or less than what bound the many into one' (OR: 72). But in her view that did not answer the question as to how this supposed general will was to be formed and defined. In other words, how was the rule of the people to be implemented politically and institutionally?

For Arendt, the parliamentary party system represents 'to this day the only form … in which popular sovereignty can attain validity in a nation-state' (NuD). However, as I shall demonstrate below, this political-institutional form develops political pathologies in modern mass democracies, which can be read from the behaviour of the citizens. For Arendt, these pathologies result from '"*Praxisentzug*", the suspension of action' (OV: 81) and '*Machtfremdheit*' (unfamiliarity with power) (ETH: 540), as central consequences of the political structure of the modern state. Therefore, we must conclude that Arendt's critique of parties and parliament is, at the same time, a critique of the state, namely in the sense that she raises the problem of the position of power within the state and the relationship of the citizens to this power.[22] But that

[22] The assumption that Arendt's critique of party and parliament is also a critique of the state is reinforced by the fact that the political systems of the United Kingdom and the USA are excluded, for the most part, from this criticism. Even more: Arendt's critique of party and parliament starts precisely with a contrast between the Anglo-Saxon system and that of Continental Europe. With a view to the European inter-war period, Arendt argues that although Britain had a 'distinct imperialistic tradition' (ETH: 530) and that the consequences of mass society could be much more readily seen there than in Germany or France, no mass movement had ever succeeded in exerting true political influence there. Therefore, the decisive question for Arendt is

is not all: the formal-rational concept of law needs precisely this structural composition in order to develop its ordering potential within a community. I argue that Arendt's critique of party, parliament and the state not only radically questions the traditional basic conditions for the formation of rational law, but also fundamentally challenges the essence of the concept of law itself.

In order to be able to explain this thesis, I shall first present Arendt's understanding of mass society, and examine its relationship to the Continental European representative system. In doing so, I address Arendt's accusation that parliamentary democracy impels the 'gigantic massing' (OT: 316) of its citizens, instead of trying to break open this 'massing' in the sphere of politics. For Arendt, the 'massing' is expressed in the mentality, common across all of society, that the individual is politically insignificant. Afterwards, I illustrate how this feeling of political insignificance develops into a mistrust against all other political institutions of the state. The key problem with this mistrust is that the '*Legalitätsglauben* (belief in legality)' (WuG: 19, see also EaS: 37), as a central pillar of democratic order, is called into question. Both, insignificance and mistrust, can endanger the democratic order in the sense that they trigger the rise of anti-democratic mass movements, as the last section of the chapter will point out. What becomes evident here is that 'the

to what extent the 'conditions of mass society' also lead to 'the formation of mass movements' (OR: 274)? While the British two-party system could manage without any decisive change in 'political institutions' (OT: 252), mass movements found much more 'fertile soil' (ETH: 540) in the multi-party system of the Continent. According to Arendt, this more fertile soil consisted in the fact that there was, in truth, a different understanding of the state behind this formation of the representative system. While in the vertical composition of the Continental European state all power is centralised at the top of the state, the two-party system is based on a horizontal state structure, which is associated with a 'radically different concept of power' (OR: 272). Implemented institutionally in the political system, this other principle of power is expressed in the fact that—*first*—the governing party in Britain is not only identical to the Government, but also 'that, temporarily, the party in power becomes identical with the state' (OT: 252). The consequence is that all branches of administration are oriented towards this identification of party with state, and cannot be conducted in a non-partisan manner. In the Continental party system, in contrast, each party is only part of the whole, the nation, which for its part is represented by the state. While theoretically the idea is that all parties form this whole together, in reality, however, this imagined whole shrinks into one unit comprising the ministries and other state units of administration, which can then certainly confront or oppose the individual parties and even the government. In this case the power of the state lies in the administrative apparatus (see OT: 252ff). Closely connected to this—*secondly*—is the fact that the Opposition in Britain itself is acknowledged as a kind of 'institution of government' (OR: 271), which embodies power and to which falls the task of ensuring the 'integrity of the whole' (OT: 252). The 'essential difference between government and state' (OT: 252), ie essential to the Continental European state, is omitted in this way. Furthermore—*thirdly*—because of the 'function of the party in the overall body politic' and its 'relationship to power', 'power as well as the state remain within the grasp of the citizens organized in the party' (OT: 252).

progressive loss of authority corresponds to an equally progressive threat to freedom'.[23] For the apolitical mentality of the citizens as a consequence of mistrust and insignificance threatens to capsize into an anti-democratic attitude. In short, the Continental European state produces pathological and destabilising forms of political behaviour.

## A. Politics in Mass Society

There is no doubt that the problem of the masses and the pathologies of a mass society are of central importance in Arendt's thinking. Nevertheless, the topic of masses and mass society needs to be analysed carefully. Without the ambition to cover Arendt's concept of the masses in all its dimensions, I shall discuss the term in three different ways. First, Arendt speaks of a mass society when she means the—more or less neutral—sociological assessment that one can no longer speak of a class society merely by taking a look at modern societies and the dissolution of the class structure. The term 'mass society' then attempts to capture the changed social, cultural and socio-economic conditions, by which means the traditional patterns of identity and values start to dissolve with time. As a consequence, attitudes, interests and life plans can no longer be understood within the previous habitual template of a class society (see OR: 274ff). Besides the sociological use, there is, secondly, the concept of the modern masses. This concept refers to the selflessness and isolation of modern people, who feel increasingly superfluous in the face of social and economic modernisation. The access to the concept of the modern masses not only fits in with the classical critique of modernity, which was predominant among many intellectuals in the first half of the twentieth century, but it also underlines the strongly normative impact of Arendt's concept of the masses. Selflessness and isolation describe the 'psychology of the European mass man' (OT: 315). In order to reinforce the social relevance of this mentality, Arendt speaks in some places in her work of the *mass* society—not so much in the sociological sense, but seen rather as a society of modern mass men. I shall indicate clearly by means of italics what is meant in each case. Thirdly, Arendt's analysis of the masses is directly connected to her thoughts on the

[23] Arendt [1956] 2000b: 162. This sentence and the entire paragraph in which Arendt considers the connection between authority and freedom is missing in the English version of 'What is Authority'. Arendt concludes this paragraph with a sentence that is opposed to any radical democratic interpretation of her thought: 'Our question: What was authority?, which assumes that there is no longer any true authority in the political field, would correspond to the question that we can no longer discuss, namely: What is freedom, actually, under modern conditions?' (Arendt [1956] 2000b: 163)

'architecture of the modern world' (Volk 2005: 60). Against this background a specific 'mentality of the modern age'[24] develops from the overriding position of the life process. In this mentality of the modern age, logical reasoning assumes the all-important position. It ensures that the individual perceives, designs and evaluates her environment solely from the perspective of her subjective needs. In brief, Arendt also discusses the subject of the masses under the aspect of a *specific mentality*. The reason for this prior terminological differentiation is that Arendt uses all three versions of the term 'masses', each as an argument against the system of democratic-parliamentary representation.[25]

With the disappearance of class society, which has always had a Janus face[26] for the modern nation-state, the modern state was confronted with completely new political difficulties. These difficulties resulted primarily from the phenomenon of the modern masses and the accompanying 'problem of loneliness' (ETH: 682). Loneliness, according to Arendt, is a general phenomenon of the modern age and results primarily from the competitive pressure of capitalistic societies. Arendt argues that loneliness can already be perceived as a social mood in a class-based competitive society, although there it can be channelled and limited by the social framework. Loneliness appears as a pervasive current only with the disintegrating process of class society. But why is loneliness a 'problem', and what makes the 'problem of loneliness' a political problem?

Loneliness means for Arendt not only isolation or strict individualisation in the sense of being abandoned by others. The term 'loneliness' means that this being abandoned by others has transformed into a state of being 'deserted by my own self' (OT: 476). The core of loneliness, and thus the specific mentality of the modern masses, lies in this self-abandonment, which Arendt refers to as 'selflessness'. With this mentality, the belief is expressed that 'oneself does not matter, the feeling of being expendable' (OT: 315). The attitude that one is 'superfluous' (OT: 475) is reflected in the political in a specific lack of interests and a worldlessness that is diametrically opposed to the representational principle of the parliamentary system. Accordingly, Arendt writes in her chapter

[24] In my work *Urteilen in dunklen Zeiten* I write of an 'architecture of modernity', which can be worked out from Arendt's thoughts. This mentality plays a key role within this architectural structure of modernity. (See Volk 2005: 92–113.)

[25] In this section only the first and last versions of the term come into play. The mentality of a mass society will be the subject of the subsequent section III.B.

[26] On the one hand class society guarantees 'the only social and political stratification of the European nation-states' (OT: 312), and thus facilitates a minimum of democratic freedom. On the other hand, the rigid belongingness to a class prevented the development of anything like a political awareness of responsibility for the state as a whole across broad stretches of the 19th century—in some passages Arendt even speaks of a latent but 'permanent civil war' (OT: 230) as a result of class differences.

on the masses in *Elemente und Ursprünge totaler Herrschaft* with reference to the inter-war period:

> One could no longer motivate these people to engage in political and revolutionary acts by saying to them that they had nothing to lose but their chains; they had already lost much more than the chains of misery and exploitation when they were robbed of their interest in their own wellbeing. *Their material misery was usually quite tolerable thanks to the social security of modern states, but that did not give them back the lost relationship to a common world. With the loss of the common world the massed individuals had lost the source of all worries and cares that not only make human life troublesome, but which also guide and direct it.* They were in fact not 'materialistic' and no longer reacted to materialistic arguments because even purely material advantages had lost much of their meaning in this situation. Compared with their worldlessness, Christian monks appeared rooted in the world, full of interest for secular affairs. (ETH: 679, emphasis added)

Arendt makes it clear how the feeling of being superfluous to world affairs, to the social and political coexistence of people in the here and now, is reflected in a general lack of interest. This lack of interest on the part of the modern masses leads to worldlessness and becomes a political problem, because the traditional parties are no longer able to further integrate the modern masses politically. In Continental Europe, the representative system in general and the party as an organisation for the representation of political interests had their historical origins in a society that provided 'more or less candid and objective' (ETH: 667), definable profiles of interest that could be derived from the social position and which could be represented programmatically by the relevant parties. Arendt's argument seems to be that, in a *mass* society where no interests can be further discerned, the idea of interest representation is deprived of its basis.[27] Without doubt the mistake made by Arendt here is that she defines representation solely as identity or interest representation. She fails to see the political-configurative dimension of representation, ie the 'constitutive character of representation for the formation of political alternatives' (Thaa 2011a: 143).[28] Having said that, if we assume that the central function of a parliamentary democracy is the formation of the will, and thus the generation of legitimacy, then the representational deficit in modern

[27] See ETH: 676. Arendt stresses there that precisely 'the belongingness to a class and the forms of representation developed in this system' (ETH: 676) ensured political and social stability to a certain extent.

[28] For a balanced and prudent critique of Arendt's understanding of representation as a presentation of identity, see also Thaa 2011b. While Winfried Thaa criticises Hannah Arendt for her action-oriented critique of representation, it is Arendt, at the same time, who focuses and guides Thaa's view with regard to a new version of political representation as a 'condition of possibility for political freedom' (Thaa 2008: 619).

mass societies radiates across the entire form of government. Arendt therefore concludes that under the

> condition of a *mass* society … democratic institutions such as democratic freedoms [lose] their meaning; they cannot function, because the majority of the people is never represented in them and they become incredibly dangerous when that part of the people that is not represented, which constitutes the true majority, rebels against being ruled by a supposed majority. (ETH: 672, emphasis added)

Leaving aside for a moment the question as to where exactly Arendt sees the dangers of a 'gigantic massing of individuals' (OT: 316) for the parliamentary system, and turning instead to the conditions under which the 'massing' occurred, the parliamentary system of the Continental European state itself becomes the object of critique. For Arendt, 'massing' is not the consequence of the capitalistic structure of modern societies alone. Arendt also notices tendencies in the representative system that politically support a *massing*, thus cementing institutionally the society-wide feeling of being superfluous. Arendt argues that even where 'the communication between voters and the elected' (ÜR: 356) still works in principle—she refers in this context to the Anglo-Saxon two-party system—one can by no means speak of a dialogue between equals. Every representative democracy perpetuates the confrontation between rulers and ruled. While the revolutions of the modern age included those people into the institutionalised political sphere who had been previously excluded—because of gender, birth or possessions—the structural 'relationship between a ruling élite and the people' (OR: 281) nevertheless remains. Even more, it has been the cornerstone of the structural composition of any democratic polity to date. By these means the majority of the population remains in a passive condition and in the awareness that their concrete opinion is politically irrelevant. In this way the representative system strengthens the 'massing of individuals' in the political sphere too, instead of 'breaking up "the many" into assemblies where everyone could count and be counted upon' (OR: 257). Arendt's argument, therefore, is that on the one hand the representative principle can no longer find those prerequisites in a mass society that can guarantee the continued cohesion of the state community. On the other hand, representative democracy for its part encourages by political means the phenomenon of massing and thus facilitates the spread of an apolitical mentality. Admittedly, the problem of the lack of interest and materiality does not result entirely from the lack of opportunities for political participation in the modern state. But Arendt certainly believes that active political participation could counteract the feeling of individual superfluity and meaninglessness when it comes to key political issues of the day.[29]

[29] The content of Arendt's argument is similar to that of Hirschman, who in his essay *Shifting Involvements* also detects a source of frustration in the institutionally 'forced underinvolvement', and also in the 'overinvolvement' (Hirschman 1982: 103). In contrast to Hirschman, however, Arendt does not pay attention to those '*push* factors' (Hirschman 1982: 5) of political action that

Now, a parliamentary democracy need not necessarily plunge into crisis because of some sort of mentality on the part of broad layers of society. However, the system is confronted by a legitimation problem: on the one hand, the mentality reveals the fact that parts of the community no longer consider themselves to be part of the political demos, thus contradicting the self-description of parliamentary democracy. The practice of power by political elites, on the other hand, is likely to gradually lose a normative foundation, leading to a legitimatory deficit. Moreover, if one argues, like Arendt, that the representative system itself promotes or upholds the mentality just outlined, then a key resource of legitimation becomes at the very least questionable with this form of parliamentarianism. In chapter one, on the paradoxes of the nation-state, I suggested that the question of legitimation, especially with democratic forms of government, can become a question of their political stability. The atrophy of legitimation is usually accompanied by the fact that the political elites of the parliamentary democracy lose the power of persuasion among wide sections of society in the political battle for the explanation, interpretation and evaluation of events and developments—a circumstance that has always been grist to the mill of populists of all kinds.

Arendt's critique of the Continental European state and its institutions is spurred even further by the fact that a mass society *also* contains a wide range of different life plans, values and ideals, and identities. Therefore in her view (and due to an unenforceable understanding of representation) it becomes increasingly impossible in a mass society to represent the interests of very different people thoroughly, comprehensively and permanently. This is one of the reasons why the establishment of discursive-democratic decision-making places is a political necessity, and with it the search for 'a new form of government that would permit every member of the modern egalitarian society to become a "participator" in public affairs' (OR: 268).

## B. Mistrust and Authority

Along with the preservation of a mentality of individual superfluity and meaninglessness, Arendt also considers the structural composition of the modern parliamentary state to be responsible for the fact that the citizens gradually develop a 'mistrust of all institutions which were supposed to represent the people' (ETH: 532). This mistrust undermines a cornerstone of the modern Continental European state: the citizens' 'belief in legality' (WuG: 19). But what exactly is meant by a belief in legality?

could lead specifically to political disaffection and disenchantment—and which are discussed at length by Hirschman. For Arendt, political action per se serves as a normative point of reference; any internal potential for disappointment must be borne.

The term 'belief in legality' comes from Max Weber. Weber uses it to express the fact that while the monopoly of physical violence lies as *ultima ratio* at the core of law and administration in the modern state, no modern state can function solely and exclusively on the basis of this monopoly. Precisely in contrast to the traditional and charismatic forms of domination of the past, it is the 'belief in legality' that prompts citizens to obey resolutions, laws and decisions. Weber understands 'belief in legality' as comprising

> belief in the validity of legal statute and functional 'competence' based on rationally created rules. In this case, obedience is expected in discharging statutory obligations. This is domination as exercised by the modern 'servant of the state' and by all those bearers of power who in this respect resemble him. (PaB: 507)

According to Weber, the 'submissiveness' of the citizens under the law lies in their belief that the decisions and resolutions are 'formally correct and … have been made in the accustomed manner' (EaS: 37), are therefore compatible with the basic order of the community, and have not been reached as a result of corruption or nepotism. The 'belief in legality' thus expresses trust in the fact that the state deploys its means impartially and independently of the interests of the ruling elite, solely in the common interest. This impartiality and independence is manifested and personalised in the form of the state bureaucracy.

Arendt now argues that the loss of reputation suffered by the party and parliament among wide sections of society can also extend to the remaining institutions of the state. In this way, the state in modern societies faces the danger of increasingly losing authority and consent. The reason for this loss of reputation and the mistrust shown to parties in modern society is due to its organisational type. For, over time, the party as an organisation of representation became an 'organisation of representatives … whose approach to the people is from without and from above' (OR: 251). Arendt writes on this point:

> Be that as it may, neither the people in general nor the political scientists in particular have left much doubt that the parties, because of their monopoly of nomination, cannot be regarded as popular organs, but that they are, on the contrary, the very efficient instruments through which the power of the people is curtailed and controlled. (OR: 273)

The development of parties into an 'organisation of representatives' is due above all to the systemic requirements for an internal differentiation of this form of organisation. The task of the political representation of interests must be mastered with limited resources—which also leads to an internal rationalisation of the parties. From an organisational-sociological perspective, the parties transform into party bureaucracies, the primary task of which is 'to recruit from among themselves their own élites' (OR: 281). According to Arendt, these elites are party elites; and this reveals the fact that the modern party is no longer a 'popular organ', but that only those party members who subject themselves to the party-political 'spirit of the guild' (PuR: 348) can hope to gain admission to a political career. As well as the compulsion to the internal rationalisation of this type of political organisation, Arendt—in line with Weber—points to the fact that 'spirit of the guild' and factional discipline could also be a consequence of 'negative politics'[30] to which parties are condemned in the everyday operation of modern parliamentarianism. These 'negative politics' would then be the result of a shifting of political power from the legislative to the executive. In any case, against this background, 'true political talent' only rarely has the opportunity to unfold, in Arendt's view. This talent is usually crushed by the 'petty manoeuvres of party politics' (ÜR: 357). Thus recruitment is conducted solely according to how convincingly one can prove one's attachment to the party. The fact that it is so obvious that 'politics has become a profession and a career' (OR: 282) means that any belief or confidence that the established world of politics could involve something like solidarity, communality and cohesion beyond the logic of 'buying and selling' (ÜR: 356) is lost. The less it is believed by vast parts of the public that political leaders can conduct politics in the interests of the nation and the common good as soon as they enter government, the greater the decline in confidence in the impartiality and independence of the state and its civil servants. In an age in which, politically, it is generally believed that only particular, private interests are being pursued, it is difficult for every group of people or professions to convince others that they exercise neutrality in term of interests and impartiality in the case of everyday political matters. Arendt concludes that the authority of the democratic constitutional state is then in decline when 'the general conviction' gains ground 'that civil servants are in the pay, not of the state, but of the owning classes' (OT:154) and are therefore just as corrupt as all the others.

Yet it is not the political apparatus alone, in the form of party, parliament and bureaucracy, that assumes the central focus of Arendt's criticism, but also and particularly the citizen's transfigured view of these institutions. For what does it mean to be 'convinced' that civil servants are not obligated to the state? What would the normal citizen of a parliamentary state consider to be an attitude that might indicate an attachment to the state? By questioning the very 'general conviction' of large sections of the citizenry, Arendt penetrates to the pathologies that constitute the Continental state and which can be seen in its citizens: Arendt argues that the 'isolation and lack of normal social relationships' (OT: 317) of the citizen in the political system, ie the insufficient

[30] PuR: 351. According to Weber, negative politics means that the parties are only in a position to exercise 'criticism, complaints, advice, alteration and execution of drafts of the government' (PuR: 351), and do not have the competence to introduce statutory submissions into parliament.

opportunity to involve oneself in a politically effective manner, leads to the fact that one remains bound by the isolation of one's particular interests. The consequence is the formation of a specific political mentality for which neither solidarity nor loyalty has an immediate relevance. Embedded in the logic of the life processes of a modern mass society, the 'world' is revealed to the individual only from his own subjective need. At best he might categorise talk of solidarity and communality as 'unworldly'; but usually he believes that he sees deception and hypocrisy behind it all.[31] Paradoxically, on the other hand, 'patriotism meant an abandonment of one's party and partial interests in favour of the government and the national interest' (OT:255). Solidarity and a civic ethos are thus equated with the waiving of one's own interests. Measured by this standard, the day-to-day business of political affairs must inevitably fail. The 'disparity' (Hirschman 1982: 96)[32] between expectation and experience becomes the source of the disappointment. While from the perceptive perspective and mentality of an individual of mass society there can be no such thing as solidarity in the political sphere, from the analytical perspective solidarity is attached to criteria that can never be fulfilled in everyday politics. When evaluating political debates, this false normative standard on the part of citizens of modern mass democracies leads to a so-called *self-fulfilling prophecy*: the political elites are already interested solely in their own welfare, and are therefore discredited before they even begin to act. The result is that one is always disappointed by the political apparatus—and is confirmed at the same time in one's own prejudices and attitudes. This double articulation marks the ideal breeding ground for political disenchantment and mistrust.

According to Arendt, mistrust and this specific kind of perception emerges from the lack of political experience on the part of the citizens in modern representative democracies. For they never have the opportunity to test their views and interests in a political dialogue, to discuss them with other viewpoints and to thus transform them into a political opinion.[33] There is no place

[31] There is an almost irreconcilable contradiction between the mentality of modernity and Arendt's thoughts on the plurality of interests and values of a mass society. As is known, the mentality leads to the fact that the individual subjects himself to a life process that equalises everything. Seen from the perspective of the mentality, it is considered, also according to Arendt, to be 'impertinence' for the individual mass person 'to say I' (Adorno [1951] 1997b: 55). Party-political promotion then becomes an 'advertising technique' (ÜR: 356). This term is of course the very opposite of a plurality of values and interests—and thus can be controlled best by an administrative machine. The only way out that Arendt seems to see is probably the point that this entire life process is not in fact as total as she describes elsewhere.

[32] 'Disappointment', according to Hirschman, 'arises from the disparity between expectations of a pleasurable activity and actual experience' (Hirschman 1982: 96).

[33] Seyla Benhabib pointed to the difference between Arendt's emphasis of the public space and Habermas's thoughts on the *Structural Transformation of the Public Sphere*: 'There is a shift from the model of an *ocular* to an auditory public; the public is no longer thought of as a group of humans seeing each other, as in the case of the united *demos*. Rather, the public is increasingly

where they can gather the practical experience that allows them to get to know the essence of democratic politics as a justified conflict between contradictory interests, as a struggle about specific problems, issues and positions, which can be observed and discussed in various different ways. The citizen of modern parliamentary mass democracies suffers from 'Praxisentzug, the suspension of action' (MuG: 80), which leads to the fact that one always looks at party political and parliamentary work only 'from the outside', from an extra-political position, warily and full of mistrust. Disenchantment with politics and politicians is (also) the consequence of an unrealistic 'adjustment of expectation' (Hirschman 1982: 10). From the perspective of the isolation of one's own subjectivity, the world of politics appears to be a deception in which the elite push through their interests at the expense of my needs. If we look at it from the radically opposite viewpoint, that of selflessness as a criterion for a type of politics which is truly oriented towards the common good, then every form of the representation of interests becomes a betrayal. From either perspective the word 'interests' is understood in 'absolute' terms, as either absolutely idiolised or absolutely condemned, instead of being understood as a signifier for the positioning of each individual speaker. Such a positioning is a prerequisite for the political negotiating process to be anchored in the specific and concrete conditions of existence. The pathologies of modern parliamentary mass democracy are manifested in the inconsistency within the citizens' level of expectation.[34]

If we consider both absolute interests against the background of the remarks on the *volonté générale*, it becomes clear how closely they are connected to each other: for only the absolute private lack of interest, the *aliénation totale*, to the benefit of the absolute *union sacré*, for example in the form of the nation,

formed through impersonal means of communication such as the printing press, newsletters, novels, and literary and scientific journals.' (Benhabib 2003: 200) Added to this is the change from the public sphere as a topographical description to a 'virtual community of readers' (Benhabib 2003: 200). Benhabib certainly makes a valid point here with regard to the different view of the public sphere held by Habermas and Arendt. However, I shall show in ch 5 that Arendt does take this step towards a structural transformation of the public sphere at the level of the analysis of modern mass democracies. Her theory of the decline of the public space, on the other hand, argued at a normative level, looks at phenomena such as massing, mistrust and meaninglessness, and labels these as a consequence of the political suspension of action.

[34] We encounter here a well-known methodical approach in Hannah Arendt's thought: conceptual content analysis. As exemplified in ch 1 with the concept of minority, in ch 2 with the concept of virtue, and in ch 3 with the concept of law, here with the concept of interest we find an analysis of each definition of the conceptual content. It is less the case, as Benhabib argues, that a fixed conceptual content is assumed and any deviation is criticised (see Benhabib 1995a: 100). It is more that each definition of content forms a new starting point for Arendt's political-theoretical reflection. The yardstick of Arendt's critique is not the deviation from the origin, but rather the question as to which consequences arise from these deviations for political togetherness.

seems to be able to pull the isolated individual out of his subjectivity. Only by means of the absolute condemnation of all private interests in political action can the individual be brought together with the other isolated citizens and mobilised for political action. Thus the yearning of citizens in a modern society for solidarity and belongingness can be discerned from the plea for all to renounce their private interests. However, due to the lack of opportunities to participate, this yearning only ever appears in the form of an unworldly renunciation of all interests. The fact that the total renunciation of one's own interest is declared to be the foundation of patriotism, and *aliénation* or selflessness to be a cardinal virtue, means that the feeling of community thus created loses all contact with the actual living situation of the people and the specific political conditions. This feeling of community can quickly take the form of a 'fanatical and chauvinistic nationalism', which then becomes the only 'means of connection' (ETH: 682) between the people of modern mass democracies. Such an abrupt turnaround from radical subjectivity on the one hand to *aliénation totale* on the other results from the fact that most citizens have never taken part in a political negotiating process that requires them to formulate and discuss interests within a community in a responsible manner. Almost incapable, as 'job holders' (VA: 410), of seeing the viewpoint of the other as legitimate and worthy of consideration, in times of crisis they seek, unconditionally and without reflection, solidarity with the greatest number, the national mass; they speak of the 'readiness of the people for self-sacrifice' and allow themselves to be mobilised to the extreme by the arousal of 'nationalistic passions' (ETH: 539; see also OT: 255). In this way Arendt makes it clear that nationalism is *also* a consequence of the 'non-political character of the nation-state form of government',[35] as it presents selflessness as the only way to generate a feeling of community among the citizenry.

If we return to the question of mistrust, it becomes clear just how much the loss of reputation and authority is a result of both the specific form of key institutions of the modern state and the hierarchical state structure. For this hierarchical structure is responsible for the suspension of action (*Praxisentzug*) of the citizens, as it 'does not provide any public spaces anywhere outside the party bureaucracies to which the people at large would have entrance' (ÜR: 357). By explaining the mistrust as being due to this suspension of action, Arendt breaks fundamentally with Weber, indeed opposes him completely. How and in what manner?

Weber assumes that in the course of the processes of rationalisation and the implementation of the idea of sovereignty, 'true domination' (WuG: 825) falls into the hands of the civil servants. For, as is generally known, the modern

[35] ETH: 676. In the English version Arendt writes, on the other hand, of the 'apolitical character of the nation-state's populations' (OT: 314), which is an important difference.

state is a 'bureaucratic state that passes judgement and administers according to rationally made laws and rationally conceived regulations' (PuR: 322). For Weber, rational law-finding and law-making are equated with the taking of an objective viewpoint which, beyond all influence and above all political factionalism, applies formally correct rules on the basis of purely objective competence. This rationality of rule and domination, which is nothing other than the rule of formal-rational law, is guaranteed precisely by the integrity of the civil servants, their expertise, their competence and their 'pride ... in protecting impartiality' (WuG: 854), and thus surrenders the basis for the 'belief in legality' to the citizens.[36] Although Arendt admits that the idea of the equality of all citizens before the law is expressed in the rationality of the law, she doubts that this normative content, or the reliability of the political order, can be permanently realised in the manner envisaged by Weber. Arendt's assumption is that because law-making processes remain impenetrable to the citizens in the *Rechtsstaat*—due to the idea of sovereignty and the hierarchical structure of the state—the citizens perceive rationalised legalised law to be external 'violence ... necessary to execute the law' (ETH: 540). This, however, increases their mistrust of the entire apparatus of the state and its elites. Arendt's opposing point of view is, thus, based on a political-theoretical consideration: she delineates the consequences that a Weberian account of legal rationality would have for the political culture and mentality of the citizens. She deduces that the participation of the citizens in the political decision-making process must be minimised for the sake of this (Weberian) kind of legal rationality and belief in legitimacy. Furthermore, the course of justice and the creation of laws must be detached completely from public opinion, and must remain solely the concern of administrative and legal elites. Arendt fundamentally doubts that such a finding of justice is capable of generating a belief in legality among the citizenry to the degree necessary to stabilise the political order. Rather, such an understanding of legal rationality leads to the juridification of public-political life (see OT: 314); it undermines the political meaning of those public spaces and debates where citizens come together and engage in a process of opinion formation. In other words, political mistrust is precisely the consequence of that which the citizens' 'belief in legality' was supposed, according to Weber, to have generated. Arendt seeks to elaborate the causes for the citizens' doubts that there is such a thing as impartiality in the sphere of politics—and although this doubt is justified, at the same time she points out how much the pathological form this doubt assumes results, in turn, from the composition of the modern state itself.

[36] Although Weber draws attention to the irrational countermovement to the rationalisation of domination, this does not change his idea of how a modern state should be structured. His 'leadership democracy with a "machine"' (PaB: 544) also adheres to the Continental European state structure.

With respect to our discussion about the relation between law and politics, it becomes clear once again at this point how much rational law *also* depends on the political. There is an internal connection between politics and law. The precondition for law to be rational in the Continental European state leads to the fact that the legitimacy of the law is questioned by the citizenry itself. Weber, too, noticed some kind of connection between law and politics. This can be seen from the fact that he linked the domination of formal-rational law itself to systemic prerequisites, provided by the structural composition of the modern institutional state. These systemic prerequisites themselves are already an expression of a very particular understanding of the political, which I called the formal-rational paradigm of the political in section III.A of this chapter. What is now decisive is that Weber does not draw any consequences from this internal connection for his understanding of law and politics. However, he fails to grasp this connection conceptually. The result is that the Weberian approach continues the dichotomy of law and politics. Accordingly, he is able merely to plead for a 'leadership democracy with a "machine"' (PaB: 544), as his concepts of the political and of the law are incompatible. For Weber, politics means rule. Ideally, in a leadership democracy, the *substantiated* expression of a will rules, which is formed by the higher art of reasons of state. At the same time, however, the 'machine' should rule as well and produce rational law. Rational law is ideally the *substantiated* expression of will of an independent, impartial, objective and competent judicial elite. The law achieves its reliability and verifiability from the fact that law-finding and law-making adhere solely to the logic of the legal sphere. Weber knows that the logic within the legal sphere is quite different from that within politics. As a result, all of his considerations about law and politics imply that two *substantiated* expressions of will, of 'divergent qualitative dignity' (WuG: 397), are directly opposed to each other. The result of this dichotomy of law and politics in Weber's thoughts is either the materialisation of the law, or the formalisation of politics. In Arendt's view, each of these is detrimental to the stability and permanence of the political order.

While the materialisation of the law was an object of criticism above, I shall now turn to the formalisation of politics: with Weber, rational rule demands precisely that the material postulate of a political public sphere, or 'public opinion' (WuG: 565f), is kept away from the law (see WuG: 507). But this can be realised only if the citizens remain deprived of active access to law-finding and law-making. Yet precisely this deprivation, in other words the prerequisite for rational law, is what contributes to massing, forces a lack of political experience and incites mistrust of the entire world of politics. The fact that the conditions of rational law lead in this way to the questioning of the authority of the law means that the concept of law itself becomes questionable. More precisely, it becomes questionable whether the law can be rational if it is solely the expression of the substantiated will, which was formed by a judicial elite with legal-technical means. This scepticism is increased even further when, as the next section shows, this mistrust against the political elites threatens to change suddenly to an antidemocratic attitude. Accordingly, in chapter five I shall demonstrate that for Arendt, 'rational law'—in the sense of an 'impartial' legal sphere—needs not only a new, different understanding of the political, but also a different understanding of the law, namely one that does not follow any anti-political logic and which must not materialise against the political. We can conclude with Arendt that law (or an understanding of law) that prevents the unfolding of a vibrant public-political life cannot be rational. For it calls for conditions that lead to the undermining of the very order that rational law is actually meant to preserve.

## C. Mass Movement and Power

According to Arendt, the political meaninglessness of the masses, their feeling of being 'superfluous' and their mistrust of state institutions represent a danger to the basic democratic order in so far as they encourage the rise of antidemocratic mass movements.[37] For Arendt, a key characteristic of modern mass movements—which should not be confused with democratic-political movements, such as the American civil rights movement—is their '"power propaganda"' (ETH: 540; see also OT: 340). This claims and promises to use the political power granted to the movement by its social support solely in the interest of all. In Arendt's view, the common rhetoric and slogans of mass movements that they stand 'above the parties', their appeal to 'men of all parties', and the boast that they would 'stand far removed from the strife of parties and represent only a national purpose' (OT: 250) have always had good chances of success. Why is that the case? What is the connection between the political pathologies of a mass democracy and the power propaganda of mass movements?

Without explaining in detail the conditions in which populist movements emerge, Arendt's analysis of mass movements should be read solely in the context of her critique of the state. Her remarks are certainly not complex

[37] Mass movements owe their 'actual attraction' to 'the people's suspicion and hostility against the existing party system and the prevailing representation in parliament' (OR 274), among other things. Not every mass political protest is a mass movement. With the term 'mass movement' Arendt means in the first instance a specific 'form of organisation' which, as I shall show below, can be characterised by its own kind of propaganda and its own type of political action. Although Arendt distinguishes between three different forms of movement—the 'parties above the parties', the pan-movements and the totalitarian mass movement—she detects the ideological substructure of the German students' movement as an element that is typical for mass movements.

enough for anything more than that, ie for a satisfying and comprehensive analysis of mass movements.[38] However, if we concentrate on the political-theoretical content of her thoughts, a further criticism of the structural composition of the modern state can be detected. According to Arendt, the power propaganda of the movements finds such fruitful ground in modern mass democracies because the suspension of political action and the citizens' lack of political experience is accompanied by a '*Machtfremdheit* (unfamiliarity with power) that formed the political ways of life of the Continental states, despite democratisation' (ETH: 540). According to Arendt, this unfamiliarity with power is expressed in two different ways: first, as *unfamiliarity with the phenomenon of political power*; and, secondly, as *alienation from the political process of power formation*. Although both aspects of *Machtfremdheit* are closely connected with the pathologies broached above, her confrontation with the power propaganda of mass movements opens up another view of modern democracies.

The *unfamiliarity with the phenomenon of power* dwells on the fact that the majority of citizens have no idea how political power arises at all, what constitutes it and which role interest plays in the formation process of power. One indulges in private 'speculations about Power' (OT: 252), understands political power as a substance 'beyond human reach', as a 'metaphysical entit[y] independent of the will and action of the citizens' (OT: 252), and is convinced that the 'deployment' of power for the common good must always be free of interest. This inexperience with the conditions that create power leads to the fact that the empty phrases of populist speeches, which merely seek to disguise the fact that these populists only wish to 'to promote one particular interest until it had devoured all others, and to make one particular group the master of the state machine' (OT: 256), are not exposed. Instead they are held up against the serious reform proposals of party politicians. Party politicians usually cannot prevail in this unequal battle, as their integration in parliamentary work dictates that they must argue along the lines of a specific programme and therefore cannot withdraw to the *specific mobilisation moment of propaganda* of mass movements.[39] It is here, in this specific mobilisation moment, that the

[38] An analysis of mass movements would have to operate in many different scientific fields and address not only political but also socio-psychological, cultural-psychological, socio-economic and socio-cultural questions. None of this is done by Arendt. Her view is 'restricted' to the political-theoretical sphere.

[39] Nevertheless Arendt points to the fact that a certain fanaticism in political confrontation, a transformation of political questions into ideological ones, could arise in the parties as a reaction to the spread of mass movements. This results from the fact that the parties try to deflect attention from the particularity of their interests by presenting their interests as the actual interests of all true patriots, reasonable people, responsible citizens and so on. According to Arendt, they believe that they can gain political support for their policies only by stating these policies in absolute terms. Thus they therefore fulfil those 'requirements' for mobilising the modern mass person, but at the same time they submit to the rules of the movements—and thereby undermine the parliamentary system. (See on this point ETH: 537f or 676f.)

other side of *Machtfremdheit* is revealed: *the alienation of the citizen from the political process of power formation.*

Mass movements use propaganda in response to a central vacancy in the everyday political life of modern mass democracies: the giving of meaning. What finds such a favourable reception among the masses in speeches and appeals to a 'general mood and a vague sentiment of belongingness' (ETH: 547) is the ideological message contained therein of (potentially) being part of a historically significant project. For this purpose, populist leaders revert deliberately to the 'most abstract slogans, which correspond only to the "general" historical moment, but not to any specific political situation' (ETH: 675). In contrast to planned reform proposals, adopted guidelines or detailed programmes—the tools of modern parliamentarianism—the 'most abstract slogans' try to hinder any opportunity for citizens to relate their specific living conditions in the social structure on the one hand, to the real consequences of these political slogans on the other. For each specific reform proposal involves the 'danger' that political attention could shift to the level of needs that can be provided for by the life process of a mass society, thus causing citizens to remain in the isolation of their private sphere, no longer open to being mobilised politically. Naturally, from the perspective of the mass movement and its populist leaders, this must be avoided. To this purpose they agitate in the language of absoluteness, totality and wholeness, and thus try to generate in the citizen the emotional prerequisite that is necessary for their *aliénation totale*—the only way to motivate the modern citizen to engage in political action. Just like the power propaganda, this kind of rhetoric, which Arendt calls an 'ideological mystification of power',

> can flourish only where citizens are removed from the sources of power, so that power confronts them … as in the *Rechtsstaat*, as the power that is necessary for executing laws and which, precisely for that reason, must therefore remain impartial and removed beyond the reach and the practical experience of the 'citizen'. (ETH: 540; see also OT: 248 and 256)

For Arendt, the rise of very different mass movements in modern democracies shows how the citizens' unfamiliarity with political power—understood both in the sense of the unfamiliarity with the conditions in which power is created and in the sense of an alienation from the political process—finds expression in a behaviour that questions the stability of the political order. At first glance Arendt therefore seems to follow Weber, who described the mass 'flight into the irrationalities of apolitical emotionalism' (WuG: 362) as a countermovement to total bureaucratisation.[40] The rationality of the modern

[40] Weber always refused to relate irrationality to the nation and nationalism. In this context Andreas Anter points to the fact that Weber 'does not want to link the nation, his "last value", with sheer irrationalism' (Anter 1995: 208). Ziegler takes a different approach: he argues that it was the 'rationalisation process of society' that 'released the new myth of the nation' (Ziegler 1931: 258).

constitutional state—Arendt seems to point explicitly to this rationality in the quotation displayed above by using the adjective 'impartial'—capsizes suddenly into the irrational behaviour of the people. Against this background, Weber declares, in his reflections on parliamentarianism, the search for a political form of organisation that can 'constrain and effectively control' (PuR: 333) the 'advance of bureaucratism' (PuR: 321) to be the vital question of his age. The path-breaking aspect of this is that his critique of the parliamentary system of the Weimar Republic complains of the poor conditions for the development of leadership qualities and charismatic political leadership personalities. Thus Weber does not call for the political participation of the people, but rather his goal is the 'plebiscitarian leadership democracy'.[41] The charisma of the democratic leader should prevent the switch to irrationality as a result of total bureaucratisation by addressing, assimilating and stabilising the emotions that have been neglected in the process of rationalisation of rule (see PuR: 382–406 and PaB: 541–51).

Arendt, on the other hand, lays her finger in the open wound of the lack of possibilities for participation and a lack of involvement of the citizens in the political decision-making process. For what makes the mass movement so attractive as a new form of political organisation—an organisational form that is diametrically opposed to the parties—is precisely its plea to establish the masses as a supra-state power (see OT: 258f). In a pseudo-active manner—for example by turning the assembly or demonstration into an *event*—it generates meaning in the sphere of politics and political affairs, and satisfies the need for belongingness and communality: all the things that the citizen hopes in vain to receive from a parliamentary mass democracy. In brief, mass movements are successful because they hold out the prospect of an end to passivity and isolation. In her numerous thoughts on the nature of mass movements, Arendt leaves no doubt that this promise is *falsches Glück*, a false happiness (see Benjamin [1936] 1980: 506): populist leaders allow the uprooted and contactless people on the street to express themselves—which is the reason for their usually great popularity—but without granting them their right to active political participation in discursive-democratic spaces.[42] For of course it is also

[41] WuG: 157. In *Politics as a Vocation*, Weber concludes that the alternative could only be 'leadership democracy with a "machine" or leaderless democracy, namely: the rule of "professional politicians" without a calling, without the inner charismatic qualities that make a leader' (PaB: 544).

[42] Weber's reference to the leadership democracy can also be addressed from a constitutional-theoretical perspective. What then emerges is the belief that to ensure the 'integrity of the whole' (OT: 252), one person or institution is necessary that can establish itself at the head of the state, where necessary in defiance of petty party conflicts, and which is interested solely in the preservation of the state and its power. These thoughts appear in Carl Schmitt's *Der Hüter der Verfassung*. There Schmitt argues that in exceptional cases the president of the Reich can intervene in the '"interest of the state"' by means of a 'state decision whose impartiality is based only on

true of mass movements that individual opinion does not count; in a mass movement, each acts 'for each other',[43] so that power is based precisely on the mass nature of the people. However, this does not change the fact that mass movements are certainly in a position to endanger the democratic order.

If we integrate Arendt's thoughts on discursive-democratic spaces into the context of her critique of the state, it stands out once again that her critique of the modern state, including that of the idea of popular sovereignty, is formulated as a critique of the specific bearing and the political consequences of this claim to sovereignty. It becomes clear here that Arendt *also* adjudges the political to have a dimension of meaning—but that does not mean that only political participation can give meaning to human life. Such an erroneous conclusion could be reached at best based only on a one-sided, exclusive and exaggerated interpretation of the *Vita activa/Human Condition.* Although Arendt demands quite a lot of the participation concept,[44] this dimension of meaning of the political is not set *a priori.* This dimension of meaning does not result from a normative-ontological or normative-anthropological concept of politics. Rather, Arendt derives her conviction that the political *also* has a dimension of meaning from the political-theoretical analysis of antidemocratic mass movements—and this means, from a fundamental analysis of everyday political phenomena. In my view the so-called normative-ontological interpretation of her political thought is a great intellectual-historical fallacy.

political unity and wholeness' (Schmitt [1931] 1996: 148). Almost all of the elements discussed above reappear in this passage: talk of a wholeness, the idea of an impartiality and a state interest that, far from discourse, relies on the 'other powers in a people' (Schmitt [1931] 1996: 148f). Arendt replies to these thoughts in the course of her critique of the state when she refers to the fact that 'it should be easier for a one-party dictatorship to seize the state machinery in countries where the state is above the parties, and thereby above the citizens' (OT: 255), than if the state, through the relevant institutions, is in the hands of a politically organised citizenry and power remains 'within the grasp of the citizens' (OT: 252). In this context Arendt points to the British two-party system. There one generally speaks of a '"party government"' (Rohe 1998: 239), implying that the governing party temporarily becomes the state, and even the Opposition is 'a kind of government institution' (ÜR: 345). A fundamental aspect of her thought is that the army, as the final guarantor of the monopoly of violence for the state, must not be immune to the loss of authority of the state as a result of massing, meaninglessness, mistrust and unfamiliarity with power. Not only in the Weimar Republic was its status challenged increasingly by paramilitary organisations, which were not only armed, but also in uniform. For Arendt, merely observing France or the history of revolutions shows that there is an internal connection between the confidence of citizens in the state on the one hand and the exercise of the monopoly of violence on the other.

[43] VA: 220. In *Vita activa/Human Condition*, Arendt differentiates between three different forms of action. 'Acting with one another' is set against both 'acting for one another' and 'acting against one another'. (*Cf* section on the 'Forms of Consensus and Modes of Action in the Political' in ch 5)

[44] In ch 5 I shall show that Arendt, in addition to the participation concept, certainly also looks at the institutional framework as a guarantor of order. Nevertheless, her critical remark remains that the lack of political participation is a risk to order in modern mass democracies.

Arendt's thinking does not have its normative origin in Athens but rather in the downfall of a European order based on the nation-state, the collapse of the Weimar Republic, and the rise of National Socialism. The beginning of her political-theoretical reflections is not marked by the work of Aristotle but by the abyss and 'remnants of Auschwitz' (Agamben 1999). Besides the fact that a normative-ontological interpretation of her work does not stand up to a thorough political-philosophical interpretation of the work, like those provided by Tsao, Tamineaux or Hammer, its greatest deficit lies in the fact that it does not take Arendt's thoughts on real political phenomena such as parties, mass movements, constitutions, parliaments, etc seriously. Such an interpretation sees only the polis citizen of antiquity behind her critique. This robs Arendt's thought of its critical-theoretical perspective, and reduces it essentially to a fairytale-like story of alienation and decline.

However, what has been shown in the context of the reconstruction of her critique of the state, parliament and parties, and what is decisive for the rest of our thoughts on the law and politics, is that the supposedly rational law cannot uphold its ordering function. The modern Continental European state itself, and thus the guarantee of how law can be rational in the Continental European tradition of political thought, triggers the suspension of political action, the unfamiliarity with power and a lack of political experience of its citizens. This political alienation (not *aliénation*) serves all kinds of antidemocratic mass movements as an ideal breeding ground, and is therefore an essential risk to the stability of the political order. Law that wants to be considered rational must therefore be of a very different nature. It must be able to respect the needs of an active democratic public sphere and enable political participation.

# 5

# *The Order of Freedom*

## On the Dehierarchisation of the Relationship Between Law and Politics

> No civilization—the man-made artifact to house successive generations—would ever have been possible without a framework of stability, to provide the wherein for the flux of change. Foremost among the stabilizing factors, more enduring than customs, manners, and traditions, are the legal systems that regulate our life in the world and our daily affairs with each other.
>
> Hannah Arendt, 'Civil Disobedience'

### I. INTRODUCTION

THE QUESTION OF the adequate relationship between law and politics in a democratic community is the subject of numerous debates. These debates repeatedly discuss possible answers to the two 'complementary pathologies' (Gerstenberg 1997: 11) of modern legal systems: while giving priority to politics can lead to the fact that individuals are subsumed in collective social objectives of whatever kind, the danger in giving priority to the law is that key social and political questions are decided upon by a juristic-administrative elite instead of being left to an active citizenry.[1] Many authors have become involved in this debate about the relationship between politics and the law. Although most of these authors probably agree in principle with Frank Michelman's dictum that 'nobody who participates seriously in constitutional discussions [can] overlook or paper over one of the two viewpoints, the rule of the people or the rule of the law, in the long term' (Michelmann 1994: 61), a rough distinction can nevertheless be made between three lines of argument. First, there are authors such as Wolin, Mouffe or Rancière, who argue—to a greater or lesser degree—in favour of a radical-democratic

[1] See on this point Gerstenberg 1997: 13f, Frankenberg 2003: 13, Preuß 1994: 117 and Preuß 1990: 76.

version of the political and the 'ontological primacy of the politics' (Laclau 1996: 62). In contrast, Ronald Dworkin advocates the supremacy of the law over politics. He is joined in his plea for a '*Justice in robes*' (Dworkin 2006) in different ways by authors such as John Ely (2002) and Bruce Ackerman—at least 'during periods of normal politics' (Ackerman 1989: 94). A third way is proposed by authors like Michelman, with his concept of 'jurisgenerative politics' (see Michelman 1988 and 1994), or Jürgen Habermas, with his co-originality thesis (FuG: 135). According to Habermas's approach, a democratic community is based on (*de facto* level) and should be based on (normative level) an equally-ranked relation between jurisdiction and legislation, between constitution and democracy, between private and public autonomy, between law and politics.

The question of the adequate relationship between the law and politics—as I have attempted to demonstrate during the course of this work—is also a central concern in Arendt's thought. Angelica Bernal is right when she states that 'Arendt for too long has been ignored as an important constitutional thinker' (Bemal 2009: 4). Arendt's starting point is the decline of Europe's nation-state order in the inter-war period. Chapter one showed how for Arendt the assumption of 'the decline of the nation-state' (OT: 267) is equivalent to the decline of the political and legal order, as well as the annulment of the rule of law. In her analysis of the refugee and minority problems of the European inter-war period, she reveals how government action 'undermines legality in the internal affairs of the affected states and their international relations' (ETH: 592); she diagnoses a spread of illegality in society and a 'defiance of the authority of laws', which are an 'explicit sign of the inner instability and vulnerability of existing governments and legal systems' (Arendt 1972a: 69). The consequence is a dynamic of an inability on the part of individual states to act, coupled with ethnic conflicts within states, the decline of the 'spirit of unorganized solidarity and agreement' (OT: 278) between states, and the loss of authority on the part of a democratic form of government. Moreover, with the 'collapse of the system of nation-state' (OT: 22) as a form of government, moral standards and values begin to disappear from public life. In brief: the stability, safety and reliability of the political order can no longer be guaranteed.

Arendt's account of the European inter-war period brought the issue of the interrelationship between law, politics and order—the triad of constitutionalism—to the fore. Inspired by this account, I have worked out two political-theoretical discourses in her work, proving in a more systematic manner the inappropriateness of both the understanding(s) of politics and the understanding(s) of law that—though incompatible with one another—had become paradigmatic for the European nation-state. The purpose of this endeavour was to point out the internal interrelatedness of law and politics in Arendt's thought.

For Arendt, the normative content of rational law cannot be realised without the connection to the political. That is the quintessence of her engagement with Weber and with the position of a dominance of the law over politics. What becomes clear in this discourse is that Arendt appreciates the verifiability and political independence of rational law as an important contribution to a reliable political order. But that is just one side of the coin. Arendt doubts that the reliability of the political order can be realised permanently through such a (Weberian) notion of legal rationalisation. If rule of law means that the involvement of the citizens in political processes of opinion formation and decision making is at best restricted for the sake of the rationality of the results, if this concept of law and understanding of rule of law demands that law finding and law making is separated from the process of public-political opinion formation and lies solely in the hands of an administrative and juristic elite, then for Arendt this concept of law becomes questionable. It becomes questionable because Arendt is convinced that a law understood in this way cannot fulfil its purpose for the political community: the safeguarding of order. Such a concept of law leads to the bureaucratisation and juridification of public life. Both are accompanied directly by the suspension of political action, an unfamiliarity with political power and a lack of political experience on the part of the citizens. The consequences are a feeling of political meaninglessness, as well as a rise of 'mistrust' against the political-legal elite among greater parts of society. According to Arendt, this either leads to political apathy, or serves as a breeding ground for antidemocratic mass movements. Neither of these contribute to the stability of the democratic order, but instead undermine the citizens' belief in legitimacy, meaning that Weber's project of deriving legitimacy from legality is doomed to failure.

Weber famously hoped to absorb these threatening 'irrationalities' deriving from the formalisation of politics by means of a plebiscitary leadership democracy; the charisma of the leader should add a vital element to the cold rationality of the 'machine'. If we ignore the fact that he misjudges, from an Arendtian perspective, the actual core of the 'irrational' mass impulse (see chapter four, section C), Weber's 'leadership democracy with a "machine"' (PaB: 544) perpetuates the tradition of a dichotomous, unmediated relationship between politics and the law: either the democratic leader ignores the formal postulates of his administrative-juristic elite with reference to the material imperatives of *raison d'état*; or the parliamentary representatives, under the dictate of social tensions and conflicts, fundamentally question the 'formalism of the law' with 'pathetic, moral postulates ("justice", "human dignity")' (WuG: 507). By appearing to approve the materialisation of the law in the first case but flatly rejecting it in the second instance, Weber's political preferences are clearly shown. Furthermore, it also becomes clear that politics, for Weber, can keep its autonomy only at the expense of the law, and vice versa. Both spheres, with their different forms of rationality, are directly opposed to each other.[2]

Yet Arendt's criticism is also directed at that position which, like the radical-democratic version shaped by Rousseau, demands the primacy of politics over the law. The conventional criticism is not only that such a position endangers individual legal rights, but that the entire legal system becomes fragile under the dictate of the claim to sovereignty by a general will. For this claim to sovereignty can be expressed legally only if the law turns into a commandment and central parts or fundamental principles of the legal system are composed in general clauses. (Arendt uses examples such as laws on asylum, minorities and immigrants.) If that is the case, and key elements of the legal system are covered by general clauses, then reliability, predictability and stability are lost. As Arendt writes, this 'played havoc with justice and made light of laws' (OR: 86). Such an understanding of the political is incompatible with an autonomous legal sphere.

For Arendt, law and politics are interrelated and thus refer internally to each other. Accordingly, both spheres, the legal sphere and the political sphere, must take the requirements of the other sphere into consideration and include the needs of the respective other. If this is not the case but instead one sphere is given primacy over the other, ie sovereignty of law or sovereignty of the people, and if the dichotomy between law and politics is maintained, the stability of the political order is at risk. Therefore, I shall point out in this chapter that Arendt argues for the 'dehierarchisation'[3] of the relationship between law and politics. This dehierarchisation marks the political-normative core of Arendt's constitutional-theoretical thought.

In order to develop, explain and justify this thesis in detail, I have divided the chapter into two further large sections. The first is concerned with Arendt's idea of successful political practice. In brief, I shall tease out Arendt's understanding of the political here. My claim is that whenever Arendt speaks of successful political practice, ie in those passages of her work that praise the sections and popular societies of the French Revolution, acknowledge the town hall meetings in North America or the council system of the Hungarian

[2] The problem of such a kind of materialisation of the law was described in ch 3: the law becomes 'situational law' (Schmitt [1922] 2004: 19). Its verifiability and stability is replaced by the arbitrary imposition of a sovereign power. In his *Homo sacer* project, Giorgio Agamben examines this type of criticism of modern democracies. The concentration camp, in Agamben's theory, becomes the 'paradigm of political space of modernity' (Agamben 1999: 123) because the law is designed from a state of emergency (see Agamben 2005: 1–31.).

[3] Kupka 1998: 265. Kupka argues in this essay for an understanding of democratic politics that attempts to abandon any natural-law remnants. In his analysis of Aristotle, Kant and Habermas he addresses, in the final section, the 'possibilities of dehierarchisation' in the relationship between the law and politics.

Revolution, etc, she is referring to 'structured politics' (Waldron 2005: 210). The structural principles expressed there—Arendt speaks of the 'syntax and grammar' (see OR: 173) of political action—are not only the product of 'acting with one another' (see HC: 180), but also its prerequisite. By pursuing Arendt's examples of successful political practice and working out the structural principles I shall demonstrate how the law is given space in Arendt's understanding of the political, and to what extent Arendt's concept of the political contributes to the dehierarchisation of the relationship between the law and politics. The second section is then concerned with Arendt's understanding of the law. In contrast to the legal-philosophical tradition (Hobbes, Bentham, Austin, etc) that advocates an 'imperative conception of law' (OV: 41), Arendt *de-substantialises* the concept of law and conceives of it as a concept of relationship. Starting from this fundamental change in perspective as regards the law, the question of the legitimacy of the law poses itself anew. My answer, which I derive from Arendt's thought and apply to the new question of the legitimation of law, is: the law is legitimate when it allows and enables political action to take place. In this way Arendt attempts to grant the requirements of an active and democratic public a constitutive place in her understanding of legitimate law. In her view, the task of the law is to secure and preserve the rules of an intact political public sphere. I shall show, however, that a number of pitfalls can be found in this viewpoint, and ultimately it remains unclear with Arendt how precisely the law should serve the needs of the political. A future theory of constitutionalism, inspired by an Arendtian perspective and rooted in her thoughts, should start here and develop from this point.

At the beginning of this chapter I referred to Habermas's co-originality theorem, which inevitably comes to mind when addressing the dehierarchisation of law and politics as a constitutional theorem. Habermas's critique of the dichotomy of the law and politics also originates from his analysis of Weber. In his *Tanner Lectures* he formulates—from a moral-philosophical perspective—three criticisms of Weber's understanding of the law. First, Weber misjudges the moral implications in the processes of law finding and law making he describes. In this case, according to the main point of Habermas's critique, Weber's considerations suffer from a misinterpretation of the formal properties of law. The reason for Weber's deficit is explained by Habermas as follows: 'Weber did not recognize this moral core of civil law because he qualified moral insights as subjective value orientations. Values counted as contents incapable of further justification and seemingly incompatible with the formal character of law.' (FuG: 549) Besides this interpretative deficit, Habermas remarks—secondly—that the procedures are only rational when they are based on moral principles. In this case, Habermas aims to criticise Weber's concept of rationality. In contrast to Weber's 'functionalist argumentation', laws can 'be justified as rational only in light of these morally substantial principles' (FuG: 548). Thirdly, Habermas formulates a criticism against the background of democratic demands for legitimation. In modern mass democracies, constitutionally legal processes must be based on moral principles in order to be able to claim any legitimation at all. Here Weber is criticised for misconceiving the democratic requirements of modern societies. All three criticisms amount to the tenor that 'legality can derive its legitimacy solely from a morally substantial procedural rationality' (FuG: 542). Weber rightly recognised that the 'autonomy of the law' (FuG: 573) could be considered to be safeguarded only under 'consideration of the rationality intrinsic to the form of law itself'; '[b]ut since law is internally related to politics, on the one side, and to morality, on the other, the rationality of law is not only a matter of law' (FuG: 580). Based on this necessary restriction of law, politics and morality, Habermas recapitulates the history of state and the law, and arrives by these means at a new interpretation of the idea of the social contract. In the course of this new interpretation, Habermas departs from Rousseau and Kant in so far as he breaks with their rootedness in the tradition of a philosophy of mind and composes a theory of communicative reason. The popular will is also not conceived of in a 'concretist' manner by him, but rather liquefies into 'subject-less forms of communication' (FuG: 365). Nevertheless, Habermas seeks to preserve the 'procedural rationality' embedded in the Rousseauian and Kantian version of social contract theory. Even more, this endeavour forms the starting point for his discourse theory of the law and his claim about the 'co-originality of private and public autonomy' (FuG: 135). It becomes clear to what extent his thinking is rooted in the Kantian tradition and that it is, first and foremost, a great philosophical project to ground politics (and democracy) on moral-philosophical foundations.

In contrast, Arendt's theorem of dehierarchisation represents a different approach and formulates—in an endeavour to distinguish politics from (any forms of) domination—an alternative to Habermas's co-originality.[4] Arendt was an excellent connoisseur of Kant's philosophy. This claim is supported not only by the Kant notebooks in the *Denktagebuch* (see DT: 807–24) or the numerous references and analyses in her published work, but also by a glance at her library in *Bard College*.[5] That is precisely why it is so astonishing to some

[4] In addition, the objection has been raised repeatedly from various sides against Habermas that his theory of co-originality represents in principle the dominance of the law. See on this point section III.B.ii.a in this chapter.

[5] One of many lasting impressions from my visit to the Arendt and Blücher collections in *Bard College* was Arendt's handwritten comments in the various editions of Kant's works—and at times her smug corrections of the English editions.

readers that she does not, at any stage, address what Habermas refers to as the 'ethical formalism'[6] of Kant's moral philosophy, on the basis of which Habermas developed his discourse theory of the law. In Arendt's view, moral questions are questions of the conscience—and, hence, impossible to generalise or even universalise.[7] However, as I shall elaborate during the course of my reflections on Arendt's concept of politics, *a mode of political action* can be discerned from her considerations, which follows principles that should safeguard the acknowledgement of the other and the respect for his opinion. This demand for acknowledgement does not originate in 'ethnic formalism', and therefore cannot stake any universal claim in the style of moral-philosophical justification. Instead, I argue that with Arendt, the acknowledgement of the other is the substratum of an 'ethics of power developed on the basis of the power of judgement',[8] as she writes in her intellectual diary (*Denktagebuch*). Yet if one questions why the other should be acknowledged in the political sphere, one finds 'only' a political argument: exclusion generates powerlessness—and in the short run or the long run, powerlessness is the central cause of the decline of a political order. I refer to these thoughts of Arendt as the 'stability theorem', and shall explain this theorem in detail in section II.A.iii below. What becomes obvious from these remarks, however, is that the durability and stability of political order form Arendt's point of reference—and not, as in the Kantian moral-philosophical tradition, the individual human being as 'an end in itself' (Kant [1785] 1999b: 53). According to Arendt, however, such a durable and stable order can only be a free one, ie one in which political action can be experienced by everybody. Yet it is important to note that Arendt's justification is 'only' based on a historical narrative, which seeks approval. While Habermas represents a theory of democracy grounded on moral-philosophical premises, 'power' and 'order'—two key political categories—mark the core of Arendt's political theory. This characterises essentially the

[6] FuG: 549. Habermas explains in *Eine genealogische Betrachtung zum kognitiven Gehalt der Moral*, 'It is no accident that the categorical imperative is directed to the second person singular and that it creates the impression that each individual could undertake the required test of norms for himself *in foro interno*. But in fact the reflexive application of the universalisation test calls for a form of deliberation in which each participant is compelled to adopt the perspective of all others in order to examine whether a norm could be willed by all *from the perspective of each person*. This is the situation of a *rational discourse* oriented to reaching understanding in which all those concerned participate.' (Habermas 1999a: 48)

[7] *Cf* on this point the remarks by Saavedra 2002: 153–89. Arendt stresses repeatedly in different passages that the problem of morality lies in the fact that it is a matter of conscience, and that whatever I cannot endure in order to be able to continue to live with myself can certainly be endured by others. (See Arendt [1975] 2003c.)

[8] DT: 818. The German text reads, 'Die Frage ist: Lässt sich eine Ethik der Macht aus der Urteilskraft entwickeln'.

difference between both thinkers and their distinctive focus: practical reason, knowledge and the epistemic function of democratic discourse on the one side; political power of judgement, experience and the emphasis on the dimensions of meaning of political action on the other.[9]

## II. ARENDT'S UNDERSTANDING OF THE POLITICAL

> In political philosophy the dominant discourse about democracy presupposes this freedom as power, faculty or the ability to act, the force or strength, in short, to do as one pleases, the energy of an intentional and deciding will. It is thus difficult to see—and this is what remains to be thought—how another experience of freedom might found in an immediate, continuous and effective way what would still be called a demo*cratic* politics or a demo*cratic* political philosophy.
>
> Jacques Derrida, *Rogues*

In this chapter I examine Arendt's understanding of the political. The focus is on demonstrating that Arendt appreciates the examples of successful political practice she presents precisely because a very specific mode of political action becomes reality in such practice. In order to explain this thesis in detail, I shall first recap Arendt's distinction between power and violence, and in doing so, reveal the normative substructure of her understanding of the political. Many authors query critically how Arendt justifies respecting the other in his otherness. What are the justification-theoretical foundations of Arendt's political thinking? What is, with respect to her postulate of plurality, Arendt's answer to Kant's *quaestio juris*? I argue that one can find in Arendt's work only a political justification for the treatment of human plurality. However, I do not consider this primarily to be a deficit, but rather explicit proof that she is more of a political thinker than a political philosopher. In this sense, I shall unfold a *political normativity* inherent to Arendt's political thought, which is realised in the formation of the political power of judgement. For Arendt, the political power of judgement is a cipher for a distinctive type of political rationality that is fundamentally different from raison d'état, bargaining, rational choice approaches or consensus orientation. Arendt develops and spells out this new type of political rationality in concrete terms, particularly in her analysis of the American Republic. This 'rationality of the power of judgement' (Vollrath 1987: 253) is formed on the basis of procedural rules within the institutions, between the institutions, and between the political system and the public sphere. Arendt's thoughts on the (foundation of the) American Republic are particularly significant in so far as they provide us with an insight into the treatment of the

[9] For a similar critique see Zerilli 2005:160.

tension between ideal and reality. Just as the constitutional state of the Federal Republic represented the real background against which Habermas could develop his normative thoughts in *Facts and Norms*, Arendt's analysis of the American Republic is central to the genesis of her understanding of the law and politics.

## A. Arendt and the Normativity of the Political

### *i. Power and Violence—A New Accentuation*

According to Arendt, every political community is founded on power. 'Power', she argues, 'is the essence of all government, indeed of all groups organised in some way'.[10] Every state, every political community and every organised group 'is essentially organised and institutionalised power' (OV: 51). With this assumption, Arendt opposes a traditional line of political thought that regards the essence of the political as lying in violence or, to be more precise, the violent enforcement of will. From Plato to Machiavelli, via Hobbes and Marx, and on to Weber and Schmitt, power has been associated with violence and conceived as the foundation of every form of political rule. This equation of power with violence begins with the ancient equation of forms of state with those of dominance, is reflected in the Judeo-Christian idea of the 'imperative character of the laws', and ultimately gains the decisive impulse with the formation of (modern) statehood from the seventeenth century. For Arendt, however, power and violence have nothing in common. Violence is always instrumental and without communication. Accordingly, she writes:

> [P]olitically speaking, it is insufficient to say that power and violence are not the same. Power and violence are opposites; where the one rules absolutely, the other is absent. Violence appears where power is in jeopardy, but left to its own course it ends in power's disappearance. This implies that it is not correct to think of the opposite of violence as nonviolence; to speak of nonviolent power is actually redundant. Violence can destroy power; it is utterly incapable of creating it. (OV: 56)

But what is power? For Arendt, '[*p*]*ower* corresponds to the human ability not just to act but to act in concert' (OV: 44). Power is generated from the common actions of many; it disappears as soon as those that constitute this 'many' go their own separate ways. Thus in contrast to violence, power is never held by an individual but only ever by a group. Since violence, on the other hand, relies on tools, Arendt believes that it is independent (for the most part) of the number of its supporters.

[10] MuG: 52. The phrase 'indeed of all groups organised in some way' is omitted from *On Violence*.

Yet we should now be careful here of interpreting Arendt's distinction between power and violence as a moral condemnation of violence.[11] Rather, Arendt writes of a certain 'rationality of violence' (see OV: 79), and explicates further that violence is sometimes necessary or even justified as a means in order to draw attention to intolerable political, social, economic or other conditions (see OV: 79). Instead of conceiving of it in terms of condemnation, the distinction between the conceptual features of power and violence is a preparatory step towards her claim that '[n]o government exclusively based on the means of violence has ever existed' (OV: 50). According to Arendt, the tradition of political thought is based—with a few exceptions—on a fallacy: power is the essence of the political.

Before addressing Arendt's concept of power in detail, we should remain for a moment with the distinction itself: what prompted Arendt's efforts in unhinging the fundamental stronghold of a tradition of political thought that had lasted more than 2,000 years? Arendt's deconstruction of this tradition must be interpreted as a reaction to the 'rupture of civilization' (Diner 1988). What Arendt seeks to develop is a new understanding of the political that reflects the experience of terror and violence and which rejects any instrumental access. For this purpose, her search takes two different directions, one of which I would like to call political-philosophical, and the other political-theoretical: the first is expressed in Arendt's philosophical recourse to the roots of our consideration of the political. In the foreground here is the analysis of ancient authors and the 'actual' experience within Athenian democracy. The core of her critique is that the retrospective philosophical analysis of the polis brings a concept—rule—into play, which is contrary to the actual substantial experience.[12] This exploratory movement is reflected in Arendt's political-philosophical work *Vita activa/Human Condition*, as well as in the numerous reflections in *Between Past and Future*. In 2007 Jerome Kohn published two treatments from Arendt's estate in *Social Research* with the title *The Great Tradition*, which once again illustrated this critique. Here, Arendt holds up the experience-based reports of Herodotus

[11] McGowan interprets the distinction in moral terms and speaks, accordingly, of 'Arendt's Utopian Vision' (McGowan 1997: 264). Keith Breen claims erroneously that Arendt derives violence from moral reasons, and believes that he can detect in her concept of power a plea for friendship and love (see Breen 2007: 343). Yet according to Breen, the history of the 20th century shows that we cannot dispense violence as a petty evil in order to prevent an even greater evil (Breen 2007: 348). My deliberations here will show that Arendt's distinction between power and violence should not be understood as a moral condemnation of violence.

[12] Seen from the perspective of the history of philosophy, the case against Socrates is decisive here. Arendt writes, as an example, that 'the gulf between philosophy and politics opened historically with the trial and and condemnation of Socrates, which in the history of political thought plays the same role of a turning point that the trial and condemnation of Jesus plays in the history of religion.' (Arendt [1954] 1990: 73)

and Thucydides against the later political-philosophical interpretation of the polis by Plato and Aristotle:

> That the whole organization of polis-life did not permit the distinction between ruler and subjects is quite manifest in Herodotus's famous discussion of forms of government where the defender of the Greek polis finally, after he is defeated in a contest, demands to be permitted to retire from political life altogether, because he neither wants to rule or to be ruled. The fact was, of course, that Greek polis-life did not know of any such division among its citizens. The rulership on which it was based, as is indicated more than once in Aristotle, was primarily experienced not in the public-political realm, but in the strictly private sphere of the household, whose head ruled over his family and slaves. (Arendt [1953] 2007b: 943)

This political-philosophical reinterpretation of the political was widely endorsed and is now also considered—thanks to excellent works by Tsao, Tamineaux, Hammer, etc—as a deconstruction of the Hellenistic period, as well as of Aristotle's interpretation of the Athenian democracy—and not, as O'Sullivan believed, as its affirmation (see on this point O'Sullivan 1975).

Her political-theoretical searching, on the other hand, refers to the rich experience of the revolutions of the modern age as a source for a reinterpretation of the political. It is precisely the revolutions of the last 200 years that reinforce Arendt's view that political power can only ever be about consent and support. For it is only when the old order and authority no longer find either consent or support that revolutions occur at all. For this reason, according to Arendt, revolutions are usually non-bloody in their early phases and merely illustrate the massive loss of legitimisation on the part of the *ancien régime* (see OV: 48f). Arendt describes vividly the moment at which it became unmistakeably clear in France that this was not simply a revolt but rather a revolution. 'The king, we are told, exclaimed, "*C'est une révolte!*", and Liancourt corrected him: "*Non, Sire, c'est une révolution.*"' (OR: 41) A revolt emphasises explicitly that the means of violence are still in the hands of, and available to, the state. But because, as in the scene described between Louis XVI and Liancourt, the soldiers did not obey the order to shoot, it became more than apparent that not even the last trump of the old order, the cannon, would prevail. The police, army, etc, no longer obeyed orders because the 'instruments of authority' no longer functioned. In this manner Arendt arrives at her key insight:

> Where commands are no longer obeyed, the means of violence are of no use; and the question of this obedience is not decided by the command-obedience relation but by opinion, and, of course, by the number of those who share it. *Everything depends on the power behind the violence.* The sudden dramatic breakdown of power that ushers in revolutions reveals in a flash how civil obedience—to laws, to rulers, to institutions—is but the outward manifestation of support and consent. (OV: 49, emphasis added)

The Revolution makes it clear that in case of doubt, everything depends on power.[13] These lines almost read like a parody of Schmitt's dictum from his *Political Theology*, according to which 'the normal' proves nothing and 'the exception proves everything' (Schmitt [1922] 2004: 21). If, says Arendt, almost as a retort to Schmitt, we turn our attention to the true state of emergency, the 'phenomenon of revolution' (OV: 47), we soon see just how unconvincing it is to reduce the political to violence—to violent will enforcement. The loss of authority by the old order in the eyes of the citizens also infects the police and the army. The deconstruction of political-philosophical thought on the one hand and the analysis of the revolutions on the other can be regarded as important sources that lead Arendt to proclaim power as the essential feature of the political. But this is nothing more than the starting point in relocating the consideration of politics. Until now nothing has been said about what power is, how it is formed, how it is preserved or how it relates to other concepts in Arendt's thinking.

### *ii. Forms of Consensus and Modes of Action*

Power is based on consent and support, and thus corresponds with the two types of activity, speaking and acting, which Arendt identifies as being paradigmatic for politics. If power is the essence of the political, then speaking and acting are no less significant. Since supportive action implies consent, for Arendt power is based on consent. But to Arendt—in contrast to Habermas—consent means nothing that is primarily rational: 'Consent entails the recognition that no man can act alone, that men if they wish to achieve something in the world must act in concert.' (LoM/W: 201) This says nothing about the content and manner of the consensus. Rather, the 'form of consent … can be constituted in many different ways' (LoM/W: 201). To give just a few examples: Arendt explains with the French Revolution and the scene of the Tennis Court Oath how consent was expressed by shouts, whistles, inarticulate bawling, by 'uplifting emotions' and 'wild applause' (OR: 116). In democracies, the level of consent is usually determined by means of elections. Even totalitarian rule, of which the key means of domination, according to Arendt,

[13] Arendt's thoughts on power and violence sometimes appear inconsistent. For example, one can read here and there that violence can destroy power, but is incapable of generating power (see OV: 56). One could argue that if violence can destroy power, then ultimately violence is what matters the most. However, if one were to interpret this passage against the background of her attempt to make a conceptual distinction between violence and power, it becomes clear that Arendt is concerned with showing that violence and power are fundamentally different phenomena. Power is also always behind the exertion of violence, ie the consent and support of the persons holding the weapons. What destroys violence is the power of the 'opposing group', and thus the entirety of possible power within a community.

are camps and police terror, 'needs a power basis', which is created in this case by 'the secret police and its net of informers'.[14] These few examples alone illustrate clearly that for Arendt the concept of power per se is undefined as regards any concrete content, and that power is therefore *not* 'absolutely positive',[15] 'emancipatory' (Meints-Stender 2012: 199),[16] 'radically normative' (Göhler 2009: 32) or as 'intrinsically normatively positive' (Allen 2010: 143), as many authors believe. Quite the opposite : Arendt even refers to power constellations, ie to forms of consent, which undermine the key categories of her political thought:

> A democracy ..., that is, a simple majority rule based solely on power, can be very formidable in the suppression of the rights of minorities and very effective in the suffocation of dissent without any use of violence. Undivided and uncontrolled power can generate uniformity of opinion that is scarcely less 'coercive' than violent suppression. But that does not mean that violence and power are the same. (MuG: 43; see also OV: 42)

Although it is a contested academic question as to how the acknowledgement of plurality and the recognition of other persons are justified in Arendt's work—I shall return to this point at the end of this chapter—it is a commonplace that Arendt '"augmented" the world by one word: the word "plurality"' (Canovan 1992: 281). The central question therefore is that of a form of consensus or constellation of power that also politically reflects and enables plurality. If every form of consensus and power constellation arises from speaking and acting, the pressing question is how political acting should be conducted in order to give rise to forms of consent and support that can realise plurality politically. Arendt's thoughts on power suggest that the *political-normative quality of a power constellation* depends not so much on acting and speaking as such, as on the *manner and ways in which acting and speaking are conducted.*[17] Accordingly,

[14] OV: 50. Once again Arendt is contradictory on this point. On the one hand she claims that totalitarian rule needs a power base; on the other hand she states that at the point in time when terror reaches its peak, 'power disappears entirely' (OV: 55). Given serious consideration, this statement is true from only one perspective, which I have referred to elsewhere as the 'ethical dimension of the Shoah' (Volk 2007: 71). This means that the Nazi concentration camps were aimed principally at the elimination of humans as humans. They wanted to change the nature of the human itself; the Muselmann represented the prototype of such a form of domination, the 'model of the citizen of a totalitarian state' (ETH: 936). Because in this case the self of the human was eliminated, the meaning of concepts such as consent and support dissolve. One can certainly try to interpret the statement that power left the country in the system of totalitarian rule in a less dramatic manner. One can state, for example, that terror leads to 'social atomization' (OV: 55) by means of its 'iron band' (OT: 473). But in order to uphold this apparatus, the support of the secret police and informers is required—and this is the support of a few.

[15] Anter 2012: 97. See also Young-Bruehl 2006: 92.

[16] See also Parekh 1981: 160; Luban 1979: 82.

[17] A word on the ways of acting and their relationship to the political: according to Arendt, there is only action in the political. Since the political is based on power, it is only ever concerned

Arendt distinguishes between distinct forms of action in *The Human Condition*, and even writes of 'perverted form(s) of "acting together"' (HC: 203). She contrasts 'acting with one another' with 'acting for one another' and 'acting against one another' when she writes that the 'revelatory quality of speech and action comes to the fore where people are *with* others and neither *for* nor *against* them' (HC: 180, emphasis added). While all three modes of action lead to the development of power, they involve key differences in terms of their normative content:

> Without the disclosure of the agent in the act, action loses its specific character and becomes one form of achievement among others.... This happens whenever human togetherness is lost, that is, when people are only for or against other people, as for instance in modern warfare, where men go into action and use means of violence in order to achieve certain objectives for their own side and against the enemy. In these instances ... speech becomes indeed 'mere talk,' ... whether it serves to deceive the enemy or to dazzle everybody with propaganda ... In these instances action has lost the quality through which it transcends mere productive activity. (HC: 180)

When acting for or acting against one another, the act of speaking loses its meaning in so far as it does not provide any real information about the person speaking, and the person acting as such is no longer relevant. Arendt refers to goodness as an example of 'acting for one another', tracing it back to the Christian traditional line that has won a place in the modern age via moral philosophy, at least in terms of its mode of action.[18] For Rousseau's ideas and the *volonté générale* in particular derive their alleged moral content from the fact that the individual abandons all of his personal interests and devotes himself to the good of the community, that is, 'for' others. The internalisation of the political in the course of the French Revolution and the birth of the nation receive a Christian complexion by means of the postulated mode of action.

'Acting against one another' comes to the fore most clearly in the political in the agonal spirit of the Greeks, especially in the figure of Achilles. The war and the 'acting against one another' became a means of 'self-disclosure at the expense of all other factors' (HC: 194). With the exception of Achilles—who provides the famous exception to the rule—this kind of self-disclosure is

with speech and action—as long as human plurality is a basic prerequisite of our coexistence on Earth. One can contrive the political in the philosophical spirit as 'working', as political philosophy has always done since Plato, according to Arendt, and attempt to replace action with 'an activity in the mode of working' (VA: 279). In Arendt's view, however, this will fail in practice as long as there is human plurality. The elimination of action as the quintessence of the political is preceded by the *de facto* elimination of human plurality.

[18] See WiP: 61f. *Cf* on this point also Kalyvas 2004: 327.

always only strategic and solely directed towards the opponent.[19] Captured in such a mode of action, one cannot 'risk the disclosure' (HC: 180) and reveal 'the "who", the unique and distinct identity of the agent.' (HC: 180) This mode of action also misses the 'actual goal of action'; and 'this concept of action is highly individualistic' (VA: 243; see also HC: 194). If political power is generated in a mode of 'acting for one another' or in the mode of 'acting against one another', then the criteria of inter-subjectivity derived from the principle of plurality as a condition of human action remains unrealised. The moment of subjectivity, the individual perception of the world, is either dissolved or hypostasised. Either that person is considered to be politically virtuous who stands up passionately and selflessly for the other and abandons his personal interests; or the 'self-disclosure' becomes an end in itself. The fact that the self-disclosure is hypostasised means that, in return, the relationship to the other, that is the *inter*-subjectivity, takes on a purely instrumental character. With acting against one another as a political mode of action, the acting 'we' is constituted by the opposition and the fight against an imagined and constructed 'them'. In such a scenario, objections and suggestions of political opponents, however legitimate or justified, are not taken into consideration. The articulation and formation of power of a 'we' generated in this mode is always strategic in nature and aimed primarily at the opponent. It is quite similar when political power is generated in a mode of acting for one another: since each person identifies with the principle of 'for one another', and sacrifices himself completely 'for' the group or community, the space between individuals dissolves and diversity of opinion is sacrificed to the unifying principle. Thus the moment of *inter*-subjectivity that is supposed to guarantee plurality in the political sphere is lost.[20]

Power for Arendt is not per se an "intrinsically normatively positive' (Allen: 2010: 143), 'radically normative' (Göhler 2009: 32) or 'emancipatory' (Meints-Stender 2012: 119) concept—as is generally claimed.[21] For Arendt there is only *one form of political action*—namely, 'acting with one another'—which leads to the formation of a normative substantial concept of power. When power

[19] The special thing about Achilles in Arendt's view is that he was the only person involved in 'acting against one another' who 'delivers into the narrator's hand the full significance of his deeds, so that it is as though he had not merely enacted the story of his life but at the same time also "made" it' (HC: 194). Achilles, in other words, is the exception to the rule that states that nobody knows who he actually reveals when he acts.

[20] In her work Arendt gives countless examples of power constellations that were generated in the modes of 'acting for one another' or 'acting against one another'. Worth mentioning are antidemocratic, pan-Germanic, nationalistic mass movements in the Weimar Republic, Jacobin rule, the Black Panther movement or the ideological German students' movement.

[21] I seek to provide a comprehensive and general analysis of Arendt's concept of power in Volk 2013a and Volk 2015.

is generated in the mode of acting with one another, then people assemble together freely, appear in person, represent their point of view on a specific topic, have the right to make their views public, and allow themselves to hear and be challenged by other views. Acting with one another does not mean rational action that is oriented towards reasonable consensus. Rather, it is about listening and being listened to, about the clarification of political alternatives, about responsiveness and expressiveness in a serious discourse, and a strong debate between conflicting and perhaps even incompatible opinions. Acting with one another stands for the integration of other positions in a political process of opinion-making, with the goals of strengthening the political power of judgement of all involved and contributing to a formation of political awareness through public discourse, and thus—possibly—establishing individual 'islands of conviction' (Deitelhoff 2007: 32) in a sea of uncertainty. Acting with one another means agreeing on issues of political conflict in which consensus is neither probable nor intended as a normative vanishing point. Agreement can also mean to agree that we disagree, for it is not the other who stands at the centre of such a *political* agreement, 'but rather the common world as it appears to the other' (DT: 451).

Therefore, although 'acting for one another' and 'acting against one another' arise repeatedly in the political sphere, generating consensus and thus generating power, according to Arendt only 'acting with one another' can produce a form of power in which plurality can be realised politically. In Arendt's view, being able to participate in this 'acting with one another' means being free. However, what is decisive is that 'acting with one another' means that plurality and the possibility of political freedom can be preserved *only* based on a *specific mode or procedure* in which political action is conducted. Only in addressing and fulfilling certain principles in its performance, ie by acting, does 'acting with one another' secure plurality in the political sphere. In her later writings, Arendt connects this mode of acting with the concept of judgement in so far as this mode is required in order for the power of judgement to be capable of manifestation in public political matters (in the *Human Condition/ Vita activa*, however, the power of judgement does not really play a part and does not even appear in the index): 'acting with one another' is an action based on the power of judgement. In her *Denktagebuch* she writes of an 'ethics of power developed on the basis of the power of judgement' (DT: 818). This means specifically that the 'methodical procedure' (Vollrath 1987: 271)[22] of the power of judgement is applied in speech and action, and that a specific political rationality is formed in this manner. What makes this political rationality, the 'rationality of the power of judgement' (Vollrath 1987: 253), normatively substantial is that it seeks to realise both the 'individuality of the individual' (Meints-Stender

[22] See also the knowledgeable work by Meints-Stender 2011.

2012: 120) and the political experience of freedom. I shall address this in detail below and present the power of judgement as a political concept of practical wisdom that is conceived first at the level of the individual. However, I shall argue that the political power of judgement stands for the 'methodical procedure' (Vollrath 1987: 271) of a form of rationality whose principles can be found as procedural norms in those institutions that allow, according to Arendt, plurality in the life of a polity in the first place. Beforehand, however, we shall turn to the question as to why plurality should be acknowledged in the political. How can the acknowledgement of the other, which characterises 'acting with one another' as the mode of political action favoured by Arendt, be justified at all?

### *iii. The Acknowledgement of the Other: An Attempt at a Political Answer to the 'Normative Lacuna'*

Within the field of Arendt research there is a broad discourse about the justification of the acknowledgement of plurality. It is hardly surprising that this debate has ignited primarily with regard to the guarantee of human rights. On the one side, authors like Canovan, Kateb, Villa, Lefort and Benhabib argue that there is 'a normative lacuna' (Benhabib 2003: 193) in Arendt's thinking. Benhabib argues that Arendt's work lacks a philosophical foundation for *how* one can move from plurality as a human condition to the 'the moral and political equality of human beings in a community of reciprocal recognition'. Arendt answers the question, on what basis and *why* we should care for one another, with a 'factual-seeming description of the human condition' (Benhabib 2003: 193).[23] The price that she pays for this, according to Benhabib, is a deficit in legitimacy (see Benhabib 2003: 193). Although there are fundamental differences between Benhabib and Villa in the interpretation of the overall work, Villa also assumes that Arendt 'devotes little attention to the liberal tradition and the theory of rights which animates' (Villa 1999: 199) the human rights discourse. Claude Lefort also formulates similar doubts (Lefort 1988: 54).

On the other side, authors such as Birmingham, Bernstein, Parekh, Michelman and Hansen believe they can identify in Arendt's work ontological, anthropological, moral or ethical arguments for the acknowledgement of

[23] In her deliberations 'Another Universalism: On the Unity and Diversity of Human Rights', Benhabib describes the discourse-theoretical answer to the question of the acknowledgement of the other as follows: 'By contrast, in the discourse model we argue that the recognition of *your* right to have rights is the very precondition for you to be able to contest or accept *my* claim to rights in the first place. *My* agent-specific needs can serve as a justification for *you* only if I presuppose that *your* agent-specific needs can likewise serve as a justification for *me*. And this means that you and I have recognized each others' right to have rights.' (Benhabib 2007: 16)

the other and the political realisation of plurality. In her book *Hannah Arendt and Human Rights*, published in 2006, Birmingham claims that most Arendt readers 'have failed to grasp that one of her primary concerns, beginning with the *Origins of Totalitarianism*, is the working out of a theoretical foundation for a reformulation of the modern notion of human rights' (Birmingham 2006: 3). This 'reformulation' assumes the 'principle of common humanity' which comes from the 'anarchic and unpredictable event of natality' (Birmingham 2006: 3). An ontological justification for human rights can be gleaned from the principle of natality. Richard Bernstein assumes that without the acknowledgement of the other and without the opportunity to participate in political events, no 'fully human life' (Bernstein 2005: 58) can be lived. According to Serena Parekh, Arendt's understanding of human rights is rooted directly in 'our very nature as a political being' (Parekh 2004: 49), which can be derived from our actions. A similar argument is presented by Frank Michelman, who writes that Arendt trusted in 'humanity as its own last best hope' (Michelman 1996: 207) for the guarantee of human rights. In contrast, Phillip Hansen argues that the acknowledgement of the other is precisely not a 'contingent feature of human existence', but is instead an 'essential element of our existence as plural beings' (Hansen 2004: 10).

The problem of previous attempts at justification, as I see it, is exemplified nicely by Birmingham herself:

> By providing a new principle of humanity, Arendt is able to distinguish between legitimate and illegitimate shapes of power and political action without having to invoke the ethical. Power, which is synonymous with acting politically with others, must be inspired by the categorical imperative of the political: the principle of plurality provides us with a new law of humanity, demanding that each actor, by virtue of the event of natality itself, has the right to appear with others, the right to act and speak within the political space. (Birmingham 2006: 60)

Although I agree with Birmingham that the observance of plurality must be the litmus test of every power constellation, it remains unclear to what extent her reasoning of the guarantee of human rights reacts to the political problem of its non-realisation, as outlined by Arendt. Without doubt, the history of philosophy contains many sound contributions that provide reasons and seek to justify why the other should be acknowledged in his otherness.[24] Even more, with my remarks in chapter one I agree with Birmingham's assessment

[24] For example, Benhabib speaks of the 'essentialist universalism' of the 18th century, in which the conviction was expressed that there is a 'fundamental human nature or human essence which defines who we are as humans' (Benhabib 2007: 11). But attempts are also made from the perspective of classical moral universalism or rational universalism to answer the Kantian *quaestio juris*. (see Benhabib 2007: 11ff.)

that 'Arendt places the responsibility of the death camps squarely at the feet of a philosophically invalid and politically impotent notion of human rights' (Birmingham 2007: 270). However, I do not see how Birmingham's justification by means of the concept of natality can provide human rights with the missing political clout. As Wellmer rightly stresses in another context, it is the 'problem of application'—and precisely not the 'problem of justification' (Wellmer 1986, 137)—that Arendt draws into focus in the discourse on human rights. In my view, Birmingham's ontological justification of human rights fits seamlessly into the tradition of the '*politically impotent notion of human rights*'. For example, in a central passage of the book she makes reference to a common Greek phrase used frequently by Arendt, 'wherever you go, you will be a polis' (VA: 192). Birmingham interprets this phrase so 'that wherever one goes, one has the right to belong to a political space ... This is because each human being is an appearance who requires a public space in order to truly appear' (Birmingham 2006: 59).

As I have said, by no means do I dispute the fact that philosophy can offer good reasons for securing a place in the world for the other. The key question is to what extent it can do so with the necessary political argumentative strength and cogency. For, as is known, all knowledge is transformed into opinion in the political. As a philosophical contribution I find Birmingham's remarks on 'beginning and givenness', the dual structure of natality, very inspiring, but it remains unclear to what extent this justification can be 'politically more potent' than the existing moral-philosophical justification. Even more, by burdening Arendt's ontological description of the human condition with having to serve as a criterion of legitimation, her thinking is drawn unintentionally towards the realm of metaphysics. As with Heidegger in *Being and Time*, the essence and the existence of humans become identical through the hypostatisation of ontology. But in contrast to Heidegger, Arendt precisely does not seek to define the 'meaning of existence' (Heidegger [1927] 2001: 17) with her ontological considerations, but rather to work out the conditions to which both existence and political action are exposed.[25] Answering the *quaestio juris* with her ontological description, therefore, turns Arendt's political thinking into political metaphysics—an undertaking that, as Birmingham herself rightly states, is diametrically opposed to Arendt's thought.[26] The question as to 'with what right' something should be as it is (or dealt with as it is) is answered simply by stating that it is. In this manner, however, one transforms a description of the condition into a normative claim.

[25] *Cf* on this point Arendt's Heidegger critique in Arendt [1948] 1990a: 31 and in Arendt [1954] 1994e: 436ff.

[26] See Birmingham 2007: 269. See also Vollrath 1979a: 19.

## a. The Stability Theorem and the Question of Justification

In Arendt's work, one looks in vain for modes of argumentation in the style of the foundational universalism of moral philosophy, in which the recognition of others derives from the language of reciprocity. In this respect, I agree with Benhabib's observation. Nevertheless, what can certainly be found is a specific theorem that runs through all of Arendt's work, and which 'suggests' the acknowledgement of the other and of plurality—'justifies' is not quite the right word. A central role in this theorem is played specifically by the durability and stability of the political order, ie the power constellation. Or, to put it another way, general statements are made about the 'inevitable loss of power' (HC: 222), 'the sudden dramatic breakdown of power' (OV: 49) or 'powerlessness' (ÜR: 113). This theorem, which I would like to call the 'stability theorem', is as follows: exclusion generates powerlessness, and powerlessness leads to a collapse in the political order in the short or the long term. Plurality is a 'fact' (WiP: 9), and a stable constellation of power cannot avoid recognising and working through this fact. The *political normativity* thus formulated, which is what Arendt's stability-theorem stands for, is constituted entirely differently from the Kantian *quaestio juris* of demanded moral justifications. This theorem is the starting point for Arendt's consideration of historical-political questions, as well as the theoretical position from which Arendt approaches contemporary American social issues and foundational questions of intellectual history. What Arendt identifies and traces through all of these considerations and contexts are the negative consequences that follow when a political order arises out of a politics of exclusion or non-recognition.

The stability theorem is embedded in her *historical narrative of the political events and incidents of the twentieth century*. As we have seen in the first chapter, for example, in Arendt's analysis of the European inter-war period, not only did the policies of the European nation-states regarding refugees and minorities lead the refugees themselves into a precarious humanitarian situation, but the factual policy of exclusion also had negative effects, in her analysis, on the stability of the political order of the European nation-states. Arendt writes of the 'decline of the nation-state' (OT: 267), or of the 'collapse of the system of nation-states' (OT: 22). Here, what Arendt is referring to is the way in which the political measures undertaken to ensure national security massively undermined the legal and constitutional order of democratic nation-states and poisoned international relations. The politics of exclusion negatively affects the constitutional order, contradicts fundamental and even essential norms and values of a legal-democratic political order, and can develop negative consequences, particularly in a globalised world (see Volk 2010: 27–67). In brief: Arendt's political narrative here is that this policy of exclusion precisely did not lead to a durable and stable order, but rather to its decay.

From a *political-philosophical* perspective, the stability theorem is encountered in Arendt's thoughts on the political significance of plurality. The conceptual starting point here is, as Patchen Markell pointed out, 'the existence of others—as yet unspecified, indeterminate others—[that] makes unpredictability and lack of mastery into unavoidable conditions of human agency' (Markell 2003: 180). What follows from this unpredictability and lack of mastery is that the structural or individual inability or unwillingness to take others' political standpoints and opinions into account, scatters 'germs of its own destruction' (HC: 203)[27] within political coexistence. This decay materialises in two ways: first, a power constellation is formed that is not concerned—structurally—with the inclusion and consent of all, but is rather from the outset based on the exclusion of the 'other'. For Arendt, it is more than questionable whether this sort of political order will find even tacit approval from the marginalised. Whether quickly or over a longer period of time, the marginalised 'others' will create radical ways in which to resist the current political order. Secondly, the political denial of plurality deprives *everyone* in a society of the opportunity to take the 'reality of the world' into account. Such a system reinforces one's own limited perspective on the world and corresponds solely to one's own idiosyncrasies, rather than taking into account the multitude of standpoints and opinions that in fact constitute society. As a result, one fails to recognise the potential for conflict altogether, or until it is far too late.

In terms of *intellectual history*, Arendt locates the stability theorem with Montesquieu: according to Arendt's interpretation of Montesquieu, he was convinced that tyranny—in contrast to monarchy—is supported by only a small number of people. Thus, although tyranny is the most violent form of government, it is, according to Montesquieu, the most powerless one.[28] Leading on from her Montesquieu interpretation, Arendt then states that a policy of exclusion 'pave[s] the way to an inevitable loss of power, even though the actual disaster may occur in a relatively distant future' (HC: 222). And as long as 'robot soldiers' (OV: 50) do not replace humans—one of her objections—and the world is not transformed into a concentration camp, a durable and stable order can be based only on the acknowledgement of plurality.

Measured against the requirements profile of the Kantian *quaestio juris* and the moral-philosophical justification of rights, this stability theorem is not really satisfactory. (Moreover, it is telling that Arendt's references on this point

[27] See also Young 2002: 267.

[28] On these thoughts see Montesquieu [1748] 1992: 104–16.

are Montesquieu and Machiavelli—and not Kant.)[29] The stability and 'great durability', which she considers to be the 'promise' (OR: 227)[30] of the republican form of government, are Arendt's criteria for assessing a political order. Yet in a society marked by the plurality of conflicting perspectives, only a constellation of power which emanates from 'acting with one another' can enable political freedom to be experienced and give justified hope that stability and durability can be preserved. Against this background, that which enables political freedom is *politically rational.* In this spirit, Ernst Vollrath described the principle of such an understanding of politics as follows: 'Act in such a manner that your actions and those of others remain possible at all times, ie that a human world is preserved.' (Vollrath 1977: 215)

These reflections do not formulate any claim to truth, as they quite obviously lack any 'epistemic connotation' (Habermas 1999b: 85). At the same time, however, the foundational-theoretical lacuna in Arendt's thinking indicates that Arendt chooses a different starting point for her kind of political theory from those scholars who follow the tradition of moral-philosophical foundationalism. What can be derived from this fact is the insight that if the question of justice is the first question of political philosophy, then the question of freedom—and how to order and institutionalise that freedom—is the first question of political theory. In this sense, Arendt must be considered a political theorist.

### b. A Cautious Outlook: Republican Cosmopolitanism

For Arendt, human plurality is a 'fact' (WiP: 9). And political actors are confronted with this fact—whether they want to be or not, whether they react to it or not, or whether or not they indeed should react to it. In the globalised age this plurality is expressed in the fact that a number of political problems and conflicts do not end at the state border, are very likely to affect the political and legal order of all states, and concern humanity as a whole. In her thoughts on refugee and minority problems, on the Israeli-Palestinian conflict, on the Cold War (Vietnam, Cambodia, Hungary) etc, Arendt reflects on this new

[29] It is notable here that Arendt does not refer to Kant's thoughts on political freedom, but rather those of Machiavelli: 'For Machiavelli it was less a question of whether one loved God more than the world, than whether one was capable of loving the world more than oneself. And indeed has always been a key question for those who are, in fact, political. Machiavelli's objections to religion are generally directed at those who love themselves, ie their own salvation more than the world; they do not concern, or not generally, those who truly love God more than the world and themselves.' (ÜR: 366) *Cf* on this point also Bluhm 2011: 198f, Förster 2009: 61–63 and Baluch 2014.

[30] She writes, 'Hence, the republican form of government recommended itself to the prerevolutionary political thinkers not because of its egalitarian character … but because of its promise of great durability.' (OR: 227)

political reality of the twentieth century. But humanity becomes a political concept only when political structures are created in which this reality can be expressed. Some specific examples certainly include her thoughts on the establishment of an International Criminal Court (EJ: 393), on a European confederation,[31] on the 'right to have rights' and on the institutionalisation of a fair, non-exploitative economic order.[32]

Her key contribution, however, is surely the reinterpretation of the political itself, which is directly linked to the experience of founding the American Republic. Arendt is convinced that the foundation of America contained 'in fact an instruction for a political organisation of humanity'.[33] Nation-state sovereignty is replaced by a federal network of different centres of power, in which all communities remain in relation to one another at all times and in all political matters.[34] Such a federation, 'whose internal structure predetermined them [...] for a constant enlargement whose principle was neither expansion nor conquest but the further combination of powers' (OR: 167), establishes the 'right to have rights' both locally and globally at the same time. Locally, because that is where a right to have rights gets its specific form and content in the first place. Globally, because this right is an expression of the fact that the power and rationality of the entire order is based on the possibility that every person *may* have a say within it. This puts an end to the nationalisation of citizenship, including its corresponding constructs of identity and solidarity. In such a 'political organisation of humanity', the 'right to have rights' has become the condition for the possibility of political freedom. Under such conditions the promise of human rights, ie to guarantee a place in this world for every person, would no longer run contrary to the established political structures, but would instead be their genuine expression. At the same time, the concept of human *rights* changes: the individual is no longer protected as an abstract individualistic 'human being', but rather as a world

[31] See on this point also her comments in 'Foreign Affairs in the Foreign-Language Press' (Arendt [1944] 1994b: 100–04), 'Power Politics Triumphs' (Arendt [1945] 1994c: 156f) and the 'Rand School Lecture' (Arendt [1948/1949] 1994d: 222f), all of which were published in *Essays in Understanding*.

[32] See JW: 423–50 and the comments by Birmingham 2006: 141f.

[33] DT: 131. I disagree with Stefan Ahrens's view that the American foundation experience cannot, for Arendt, be generalised theoretically (see Ahrens 2005: 262). In the founding of America and its republic, Arendt does not merely identify a new type of political rationality, setting it against the *raison d'état*-styled or party political version of the European nation-state.

[34] This should not be confused with Arendt's scepticism of a world government. Arendt includes the idea of a world government in the tradition of Continental European constitutional state thinking. In her view, the idea of a world government completes the concept of the hierarchical structure of political community. In a world organised in such a manner, according to Arendt's horror scenario, all power and violence would be monopolised and all means of escape would be blocked.

citizen. Human rights become the rights of world citizens, which contains, per definition, the 'plurality of human beings in themselves'.[35] That is the core of Arendt's republican cosmopolitanism. Arendt has no moral argument with universal validity to hand as to what right one might have to demand such a 'political organisation of humanity'. Instead she relies on a political narrative that is intended to make clear and generate affirmative support for the fact that exclusion generates powerlessness. In the following section we shall take a closer look at the political rationality type, which Arendt considers to lie in the systemic structure of the American Republic. At the same time, more evidence is produced in this manner to support the thesis that for Arendt, successful political practice means a kind of 'structured politics'.

## B. From the Power of Judgement to the Procedural Rules of the Political System

'The condition of the possibility of the power of judgement is the presence of the other, the public.'

Hannah Arendt, *Denktagebuch*

The theoretical foundation for Arendt's understanding of political rationality is provided by the concept of 'enlarged mentality' (Kant 2001: 158) from Kant's critique of judgement. The 'enlarged mentality' of 'reflective judgements' (Kant 2001: 294) describes a form of rationality that differs both from the material rationality of Weber's statesman and from the formal rationality of the judicial elite. Although formal rationality demands from Weber's civil servants merely the correct recognition of the matter to be negotiated, while the statesman, in contrast, requires 'determinant judgement' (Kant 2001: 293) in order to establish the relationship between the specific situation and the rational canon of the *raison d'état*, for both mental activities a general rule is given in which to subsume the specific judging case.[36] There is no such general

[35] ETH: 604.

[36] Weber conceives the judicial civil servant as a 'paragraph machine' (PuR: 323). If we completely ignore the fact that this is an antiquated assumption, then in the case of Weber's judicial civil servant 'logical reasoning' (HC: 171) is required, which places the correct recognition in the foreground. In contrast, the statesman must demonstrate that which, following Kant, is called 'determinant judgement'. In contrast to logical reasoning, determinant judgement has always operated in a weightless space, for the relationships to be established between the specific and the general are by no means obvious with the determinant judgement. Precisely for this reason the responsibility to be borne by the statesman is not only greater than, but also of a nature completely different from that of the civil servant. One side's procedural error is the other side's political misjudgement. Arendt's thoughts on the political, in contrast, detach themselves from the *raison d'état*—and thus from any idea that there is any such thing as an objective general in the political.

rule in the case of 'reflective judgement'. The validity of the verdict cannot be determined by a supposedly impartial standpoint outside the political debate, but only from that standpoint formed by all other standpoints in their relationship to one another. With Kant, and as long as one remains at the level of the individual, a certain willingness must also be summoned—Kant called it the 'inactive delight (*untätiges Wohlgefallen*)' (Kant cited according to LoK: 13)—to be open to this 'operation of reflection' (LoK: 68) in reaching judgement. This 'operation of reflection' then secures a different kind of 'impartiality' (LoK: 68) from that proposed by Weber. Impartiality towards events and occurrences in the political sphere then means that a position is aspired to that results from the context of these events and occurrences themselves (*cf* Vollrath 1979b: 62f; Vollrath 1979c: 103ff).

By reinterpreting Kant's theory of judgement, Arendt develops a new and different type of political rationality. In this chapter I shall show that in Arendt's view, this other kind of 'impartiality' and rationality in the political sphere is realised precisely in and by institutionalised political acting. Political institutions can contribute to the spread of this new type of political rationality whenever their internal procedures are structured in the sense of the 'operation of reflection'.[37]

Yet if we remain at the level of the individual for a moment and work out these internal procedures in detail, we see that impartiality is achieved when one allows the standpoints of others to flow into one's own opinion. Judging persons free themselves from self-centred concentration on their own private living conditions and consider other possible views on the same issue. In order to be able to envision the other perspectives—at least mentally—an 'operation of imagination' is required: one makes present that which is absent. Alongside the operation of imagination, an operation of reflection is also necessary for reaching judgement. It is divided into two phases. At the beginning of the judgement process the 'inner senses' (LoK: 66), the core of subjectivity, make a distinction: this pleases me or it does not. The 'inner sense' that leads to this distinction is called taste. But one can approve or disapprove the instance of pleasing or displeasing. Taste itself is, in turn, subject to approval or disapproval.[38] But how can one decide between approval and disapproval

[37] Although Ernst Vollrath does not take the step suggested by me of tracing the procedural rules within the political institutions themselves, but instead develops the power of judgement further 'merely' as an (individual) concept of practical wisdom, yet he clearly stresses the procedural character of the power of judgement (see Vollrath 1987: 279) and serves as my source of inspiration in this case.

[38] According to Arendt, this is the difference between taste and judgement, ie between the statements 'This pleases me' and 'That is beautiful'. If no reason can be given why one likes something, the item remains pleasing but not beautiful—the adjective 'beautiful' already denotes that I appeal to the agreement of the other.

in matters of taste? The criterion for approval or disapproval is 'communicability' (LoK: 40). One must give an account, ie not prove, but be able to argue why one has reached an opinion. The measure of communicability is the '*sensus communis*':

> This *sensus communis* is what judgment appeals to in everyone, and it is this possible appeal that gives judgments their special validity. The it-pleases-or-displeases-me, which as a feeling seems so utterly private and non-communicative, is actually rooted in this community sense and is therefore open to communication once it has been transformed by reflection, which takes all others and their feelings into account. The validity of these judgments never has the validity of cognitive or scientific propositions, which are not judgments, properly speaking. (LoK: 72)

In the judgement one has abandoned the egoism of taste and considers the feelings, opinions, etc of other persons. Thus something non-subjective is found in the midst of the apparently invariably private and most subjective sense, the sense of taste, which makes it possible to reach a judgement that is understandable and acceptable to others. Though every judgement retains its subjective content, for the sake of the other one overcomes the *purely* subjective bias of 'taste' by considering the possible judgements of others (see LoK: 67f).

While it might suffice for aesthetic matters merely to imagine this process of judgement, this is certainly not the case with political matters. The subject-object separation alone—here the judge, there the image—can no longer be guaranteed in questions of human coexistence. Without the confrontation with the specific opinion of the other, the 'object' of political considerations loses its consistency. Accordingly, Arendt writes: 'For the reality in which we live requires language, if its influence on us is to outlive the moment of vital experience, it requires speech and disclosure, communication with others, *in order to prevail as reality*.' (DUR: 35, emphasis added)[39] Passing judgement in political matters requires addressing the concrete opinions of others. The variety of perspectives is necessary in order to be able to agree at all on what the world is as a human fabric of relationships in general, and what the public sphere is in particular. Thus Arendt argues that reality is conditioned by two things: without the diversity of perspectives from different people it is not at all possible to agree on what the world is; furthermore, it is necessary that the individual represents his standpoint in the world—if people are silent, reality remains worldless. When applied to the political sphere, the statements on reality suggest that an

[39] With individual judgements one wanders mentally and tries to think about the position of others. Arendt argues that this is advisable in general if we want to understand the '*reality of the world*' (HC: 50) at all. Only those things that are 'seen by many in a wide range of perspectives, without losing their identity', can inform us about 'worldly reality' (VA: 72). True discourse is essential for the continued existence of this reality, and thus for the political debate on it. (*Cf* also Curtis 1999: 23–65).

institutionalised space is required in which the appearance of persons is guaranteed. These spaces must be designed in such a manner that, in the process of opinion-forming, they take in precisely those principles that characterise the 'rationality of judgement' (Vollrath 1987: 253).

Arendt saw this rationality of a 'politics of judgement' (Howard 2001: 25)[40] realised in discursive-democratic spaces such as councils, sections, popular societies and town halls. If, however, one were to measure all political action solely against the ideal of the direct political participation of citizens in such spaces—quite apart from any possible constraints within these spaces themselves—then there would be no need in the first place for any critical analysis of the political actions of contemporary democracies. (At least if one were hoping for some kind of added institutional value from the critique.) No modern parliamentary democracy will ever be able to come even close to attaining the ideal of rationality that Arendt describes in her thoughts on the councils and town-hall meetings. Under such premises the result is clear before the analysis even begins. The interventionist criticism in everyday political matters would be strangely unworldly, as they would no longer reflect on the conditions.[41] Arendt never embarked on such a path. The 'presentness' of her political thought is her quality criterion. This becomes clear in her analysis of the political system of the United States. For this is not merely a simple comparison of ideal and reality. Quite the contrary: Arendt certainly sees this rationality of a politics of judgement laid out in the institutions of the American Republic, the Senate, the Supreme Court, the caucuses, etc, as well as in the structure of the political system—the principle of federalism, the division of powers, and the role of the judiciary. It is precisely this rationality that Arendt considers to be endangered by systemic shifts, by the undermining of and the loss of power and authority on the part of political institutions. In other words: Arendt's analysis of American politics and the American Republic is at the same time critical and affirmative. Affirmative in the sense that the analysis of the American Republic is the force behind Arendt's development

[40] By means of a determined analysis of the foundation of America, Howard attempts to prove that 'a new way … of thinking about political experience' (Howard 2001: 25) was formed in the institutions of the American Republic. In line with Howard, I also do not equate the power of judgement with the 'decision-making power of the Supreme Court or some other governmental power' (Howard 2001: 25), but understand in the first instance a different kind of political rationality.

[41] This is also the tenor of Wellmer's accurate criticism of Villa: the Heideggerian interpretation of Arendt's concept of politics that reduces politics to the event in revolutionary moment leads, according to Wellmer, to a 'depoliticization of the Arendtian concept of the political'. For Arendt's concept of the political would thus lose all 'recognizable connection to the political experiences and possibilities inherent in the everyday life of complex democratic societies: politics would become the "other" of the political as we know it' (Wellmer 2005: 226f). The results would surely be very similar if councils and town halls were the only true forms of the political.

of a new type of rationality, which she then sets up against the prevailing concept of politics and statehood in Continental Europe. Critical in the sense that she shows where and to what extent the United States has abandoned this rationality. Below I shall demonstrate that this new type does indeed also refer to the rationality of judgement—until now I have simply claimed that this is the case. I shall prove that Arendt identifies procedures of political interaction at all three levels[42]—within the discursive-democratic institutions, between the institutions of the political system, and between the political system and civil society/the public sphere—which realise the rational content of the power of judgement precisely due to their underlying rules and norms.

### *i. Political Rationality within Institutions*

In Arendt's view, councils and popular societies are those institutions that are paradigmatic for discursive-democratic spaces: Arendt favours these discursive-democratic spaces for the exchange of political views and the making of judgements precisely because it is here that the ideal of the political rationality of judgement finds its closest approximation. This becomes clear when we take a look at her thoughts on the Hungarian Revolution. In her own specific manner of exaggeration, Arendt states that in the different councils of the Hungarian Revolution 'the voice of the people' had been heard, 'unadulterated by the shouts of the mob and the squabbling of the fanatics' (DUR: 46). Why? How is this kind of 'purification' possible? It is and can be possible only when certain rules are followed during opinion-making, thus guaranteeing an all-round exchange of opinion. In *On Revolution* Arendt states accordingly that 'a *reasonable* formation of opinion' (ÜR: 303, emphasis added) can occur only where people can come together freely, where they can appear in person, advocate their standpoint on a specific topic, and have the right to represent their views publicly.[43] Only where they are open to other opinions and can test these can one speak of a 'truly' political formation of opinion and passing of judgement (see ÜR: 290f).

Jeremy Waldron has pointed to the fact that such a mode of political action can never function without certain rules; indeed, that these rules make the difference that separates 'structured politics' from every form of 'undifferentiated welling-up of mass opinion in an extra-parliamentary context that so worried

[42] Arendt actually names four levels: she argues that the peculiarity of the American Republic lies in the fact that it both converted foreign policy treaties into domestic laws and also appealed to the 'world's court of justice for the purpose of justifying' (ÜR: 166) its decisions. In my view it is not quite clear what exactly Arendt wishes to say with the second part, especially as judicial decisions by the highest foreign courts are scorned in the American legal tradition. Other supreme courts certainly do justify verdicts by referring to international legal practice.

[43] See Arendt [1964] 2000e: 350 and Arendt's thoughts on 'subjective truth' (Arendt [1964] 2000e: 352).

her'. For this reason, says Waldron, Arendt must also be concerned with these 'basic rules of political procedure', which determine things such as

> how debates are initiated and concluded; who has the right to speak, how often, and for how long; who may interrupt, who may exact an answer to a question, who has the right of reply; how a common sense of relevance is maintained; how deliberation is related to a community's powers of resolution and action. (Waldron 2005: 210)

Only a political process of opinion-making that is based on such rules can allow and guarantee equality in the political process of negotiation. If we look at Arendt's work from this perspective, it becomes clear that it is precisely this aspect of political self-organisation that she highlights with the revolutionary councils, popular societies, etc. For example, she refers to the fact that in the early phase of the French Revolution, one could see clearly 'from the statutes of one of the Paris sections … *how* the people go about organising themselves'. There the appointments of the 'president and vice-president [are regulated] (four secretaries, eight censors, the treasurers and the archivist)'. The 'frequency of sessions' is determined and the changes in office are monitored. The statutes stipulate that every opinion will be 'conscientiously respected', that a speaker 'may not be interrupted for any reason': 'If he [a speaker] digresses or gets tiresome, the audience will stand up. As soon as six have risen, the president must consult the assembly.' (ÜR: 311; see also OR: 246). In all of these discursive-democratic spaces, questions concerning the concrete implementation of '"freedom, equality, unity and the indivisibility of the Republic"' were addressed. There was a constant concern with '"discussing the laws to be passed, gaining clarity on existing laws, monitoring all public persons"'. Members were supposed to '"inform about the true principles of the constitution and to display the constitution openly"' (ÜR: 307). Such procedural norms can only be considered secure on the basis of a legal order; indeed they already imply such an order. That is the reason why Arendt argues that participants within the popular societies and sections always referred to the '"imperishable constitution"' and—something quite unique for France—referred to the constitution as '"holy"' (ÜR: 312).

Arendt made no great effort to work out at any length these procedural norms that a 'reasonable formation of opinion' should uphold. The main reason for this is probably the fact that most of her thoughts on judgement were directed at the individual person. For Arendt, the power of judgement is first and foremost a concept of practical wisdom.[44] A not insignificant part of her

[44] Vollrath claims that Arendt assumed in conversation with him that the power of judgment was an '"old practical wisdom"' (Vollrath 1987: 257), which must simply be reconstructed. Today it is clear to Vollrath that the power of judgement represents a new beginning, due to its radical nature. Accordingly, he now calls it a 'new wisdom' (Vollrath 1987: 256). In her most recent thoughts on *Phronesis bei Aristoteles und Hannah Arendt*, Helgard Mahrdt also believes that the 'solution [is] in the *attitude*' of the person (Mahrdt 2007: 598). However, I doubt that one can feel the force of the power of judgement for the political if one sees it solely as a concept of wisdom.

political thought is based on the idea that judicious persons in small groups such as councils, sections, popular societies or town halls come together freely and, on the basis of direct and immediate discourse with one another—*quasi of their own accord*—observe such rules that permit a 'fairly, fully, and peaceably expressed' discussion (OR: 237). In that respect political rationality is the result of judicious individuals and not of the institution.

Now Arendt, however, points to the fact that the Americans failed to institutionalise those local town and village councils constitutionally. In Arendt's view they therefore lost a key pillar of the 'spirit of the revolution' (ÜR: 277). In the age of modern mass societies this loss translates into conformism or political massing. Arendt creates the term 'unfamiliarity with power' for this phenomenon. Thus she underlines that the citizens' power of judgement is based on experience, and can dry up very easily without the necessary possibilities for political participation. According to Arendt, the danger of such developments towards massing and conformism is that they conceal 'totalitarian elements and tendencies' (ETH: 530) and (can) therefore undermine the stability and order of the community.

Just as we frequently detect thoughts that stress the possibilities of direct participation, we also find comments that stress precisely the structural composition of a 'successful' community. A key idea in Arendt's thoughts on totalitarianism, for example, is that it is due to the 'political structure' (ETH: 533) that no truly politically significant antidemocratic mass movement managed to establish itself in either the United States of American (USA) or in the United Kingdom—in contrast to Continental Europe. This illustrates clearly that the reason for the specific political rationality of the American Republic cannot be found *solely* at the level of small, direct citizen participation, but that the power of judgement must also be generated by the structural and institutional composition of the political system.

The problem now is that Arendt, in her comments on and references to judgements, does not distinguish adequately between the judgement of an individual, the judgement of the councils and sections, the processes of opinion making and judgement in the political-parliamentary decision-making arenas—that which is traditionally known as democratic policy making—or the judgments of the judiciary. Why is it justifiable to speak of judging or the power of judgement in all of these cases? It remains completely open as to what the rationality of judgement in the individual has in common with that of a small group, that of the parliament or that of the Supreme Court. The following quotation shows nicely just how unclear and inconsistent Arendt is in her use of the terms 'opinion' and 'judgement':

> In this scheme, opinion and judgement obviously belong among the faculties of reason, but the point of the matter is, that these two, politically most important, rational faculties had been almost entirely neglected by the tradition of political as well

> as philosophic thought. Obviously it was no theoretical or philosophical interest that made the men of the Revolution aware of the importance of these faculties ... What enabled the Founding Fathers to transcend the narrow and tradition-bound framework of their general concepts was the urgent desire to assure stability to their new creation, and *to stabilize every factor of political life into a 'lasting institution'*. (OR: 231f, emphasis added)

In the context under discussion here, this passage is revealing in two ways: first it underlines the fact that the American Republic managed to establish the power of judgement institutionally in the political system. Thus the rationality of judgement is indeed no longer a matter for the individual or for local councils. Secondly, however, the form of separation between opinion and judgement is confusing. In my view this separation is an expression of the fact that Arendt has not drawn together the different threads that run through her work, representing a 'politics of judgement'. For although this separation of opinion from judgement reflects something central, namely the distinction between the spheres of politics and law, it does not make any sense, in that we 'cannot move in the political sphere without judging, because political thought is based essentially on the power of judgement' (WiP: 19). The numerous criticisms and controversies within the secondary literature start from this contradiction between judicial judgment, which always judges a matter retrospectively, and political judgement, which looks to the future. Arendt takes on this contradiction because in her philosophical reflections—starting from the idea of the direct participation of the individual—she conceives the power of judgement primarily as a concept of practical wisdom. To a certain extent her philosophical thoughts on judgement thus limp behind the radical nature of her political thought, in so far as Arendt, in her concept of judgement, looks more at the judicious *person* than she considers what happens *between* persons. If she had placed more emphasis on the 'methodical procedure' and its principles, instead of focusing on the personal attitude of the person passing judgement, she might not have ended up in the dead-end of retrospective and forward-looking judgements.[45] For it behoves only these procedural principles to claim of an opinion-making process—in the individual, in the councils, in parliament or the Supreme Court—that it forms the political rationality of the power of judgement. Indisputably, the procedures are executed very differently at the different levels.[46] And yet only a political

[45] For this debate see Beiner 1985: 176. An opposing position is formulated by Hermenau (1999), Saavedra (2002) and Opstaele (1999), among others. For an overview see Volk 2005: 79 and 112.

[46] Thus at the level of the individual it is appropriate to speak of procedural principles when passing judgement. For the term 'principle' already contains a reference to the manner in which the individual approaches or 'begins' with a judgement. Moving to the level where different people come together and judge together, one might speak of procedural norms that are followed

process of opinion formation, which is oriented towards the 'principle' of the 'methodical procedure' (Vollrath 1987: 271) of judgement, comes close to the ideal of an 'enlarged mentality'.

In Arendt's councils, sections and popular societies this political rationality is developed in such a manner that the content of the 'operation of imagination' ensures that each person in these institutionalised political spaces can have his say, can express his opinions freely and informally, and can hear other opinions. The presence of the others, and the obligation to justify which they embody, means that each person is obliged to explain his position with credible reasons and by these means to convince. Opinions are oriented on the criterion of communicability. As the measure of communicability is the *sensus communis*, these must be opinions that both are capable of being acceptable to a majority and do not question the general rules of exchanging views. In brief, politically, *sensus communis* means the ability to attain a majority in conformity with the constitution—and not simply pre-political commonalities like those that come to mind with local associations such as village and town councils. The impartiality of the judgement, ie the aspiration that the judgement represents the position taken by all other positions in relation to the others, is realised by means of such a mode of acting and speaking 'in accordance with principle'. In other words, impartiality is the '*spirit*' that prevails in these discursive-democratic spaces, which should ensure that the judgement can claim 'subjective general validity' (Kant 2001: 63)—or, as Benhabib suggests, 'intersubjective validity' (Benhabib 1995b: 146).

The spaces formed according to the principles of rational judgement ensure reasonable opinion formation, but are of course, on the other hand, dependent on the formation of the power of judgement within the community.[47] For this reason, Arendt also describes these discursive-democratic spaces as a 'school of the people' (ÜR: 302).[48] By participating in such spaces the individual develops further his individual political power of judgement and 'practises' political thinking—as the power of judgement cannot be learned but only practised, the term 'school' in connection with the

when passing judgement. If a group, a section or a council has been established, one could speak of procedural rules. Within a community and at the level of each political institution, these procedural rules are legally guaranteed. The procedural norms have become legal norms, and can now be found legally positivised in the concrete statutes and procedural provisions.

47 In 'Kultur und Politik' Arendt reflects on the cohesion of an intact cultural scene (music, art, etc) for the formation of the power of judgement. See on this point especially her discourse on the 'socialisation of culture in mass culture' (Arendt [1958] 2000d: 278.) In 'Die Krise der Erziehung' she thinks about the relationship between political feelings of responsibility and the type of education. In her view this crisis in education is nothing less than a crisis of common sense (Arendt [1958] 2000c: 259f).

48 *Cf* on this point Tocqueville's thoughts on municipal codes in America (Tocqueville [1835] 2002: 57).

power of judgement is somewhat unfortunate (see Kant [1781] 1998: 236f). The greatest danger to such processes of opinion and judgement making in modern capitalist societies is massing and conformism. Without doubt, the political engagement of every individual is a powerful weapon against this (see on this point Tocqueville [1835] 2002: 489–92). As dependent as discursive-democratic politics might be on political culture, this political culture is equally not detached from legal-political institutions when it comes to opinion and judgement making. Accordingly, Arendt stresses that the institutionalised political spaces are not fully but still partially dependent on the power of judgement of the individual. Due to their statutes, democratic-political institutions secure procedures by which means the rationality of the judgements can be formed. This shows clearly why Arendt sees the councils, popular societies, sections, etc as 'organs of order' (OR: 266).[49] For a political order is characterised precisely by the fact that, while it is always connected to concrete life within the society, at the same time it develops such structures that help to regulate political life and emancipate it—in part—from moods, views, etc. Accordingly, Arendt writes:

> Had one taken notice of the history of the councils, there would have been no talk of the old adages of the anarchistic, lawless tendencies of the people; for wherever councils appeared, especially also in the Hungarian Revolution, they were concerned with the reorganisation of political and economic life; the last thing they wished was to welcome chaos, and nothing was more important to them than to establish *a new political order* as quickly as possible. (ÜR: 349, emphasis added; see also OR: 275)

Thus, the councils, popular societies, etc describe the 'physiognomy of the only democratic system' (DUR: 46), but also a procedure for the formation of opinion and judgement. Although the 'tragic oversights' (OR: 238) of the American Revolution lie in the fact that the town halls were not constitutionally institutionalised as arenas of political action, the mode of reasonable opinion making on which they are based has not disappeared from the political system as a whole. In the caucuses and as a jury member in court, the 'last remnant of active citizen participation in the Republic' (DïT: 90), the 'normal citizen' still has the opportunity to take part in and influence actively and directly—and not merely in the privacy of the poll booth—the political life of the country, albeit at the lowest level of the political system. Both forms indicate the rationality of political action and speech in the sense of the power of judgement (see PRPI: 104).

[49] Karl-Heinz Breier emphasises the aspect of order in Arendt's thought, but addresses it one-sidedly—instead of dialectically—in the direction of 'experience, attitude and … everyday habits' (Breier 2001: 132).

Yet apart from these important but still quite peripheral forms, Arendt is convinced that both the Senate and the Supreme Court are the 'American institutions of liberty' (Arendt [1964] 2003e: 260). What makes these institutions so special for the political process is that they prevent a 'chaos of unrepresented and unpurified opinions' (OR: 231). This, in turn, can be achieved only on the basis of the procedural rules that prevail in both institutions. This type of rationality generation can be seen quite nicely from Arendt's description of the Senate. To 'mediate their differences and conflicts' the manifold opinions that prevail in the political arena are passed 'through the medium of a body of men', the Senate.

> It is not that these representatives of opinion—the Senators—are themselves, as individuals, 'wise' or wiser than their fellow citizens, but they have been elected and are gathered in an institution whose purpose it is to secure a place in political life for the possible *wisdom in public matters; and the institution itself takes account of the conditions of the fallibility and frailty of the human mind.* (ÜR: 293, emphasis added)[50]

Two aspects from the quote above are of interest to our discussion. First, Arendt speaks of 'wisdom' and not of the balancing of interests. However, 'wisdom' expresses a political rationality, the achievement of which is the 'purpose' of the whole institution. In the political sphere 'wisdom' cannot mean anything else but the power of judgement. However, and secondly, this power of judgement is not attached to the persons within the institution, the senators, but to the institution itself. Nevertheless, to claim that the power of judgement is attached to the institution only makes sense when the political exchange of opinions within these institutions is based on those procedural norms necessary for the rationality of judgement to develop. Otherwise the entire political process would indeed be dependent solely on the integrity of the representatives. In other words, for Arendt the political rationality of judgement is realised to a certain degree also at the level of the institutionalised political system of the USA. The rules in the political process guarantee the exchange of different opinions and prevent an 'hysterical, unanimous "public opinion" … which is the death of all opinions', from making laws.

> Technically speaking, the alternative to a purified and represented diversity of opinion is the plebiscite, which indeed corresponds closely to the rule of public opinion. And just as the public opinion is, in truth, the death of all opinions and opinion-making, the plebiscite puts an end to the citizens' right to vote, on the basis

[50] The English version reads: 'Since opinions are formed and tested in a process of exchange of opinions against opinion, their differences can be mediated only by passing them through the medium of a body of men, chosen for this purpose; these men, taken by themselves, are not wise, and yet their common purpose is wisdom—wisdom under the conditions of the fallibility and frailty of the human mind.' (OR: 230)

> of which the citizens at least have the right to choose and control the government. (ÜR: 294; see OR: 231)

Arendt assumes that, in terms both of her ideal of discursive-democratic spaces and of American parliamentarianism, the making of a decision must revert ultimately to the principle of majority (see OR: 163). From Arendt's perspective this is not a disadvantage or deficit of the political process, but rather the realisation of political equality and democracy: '*One man, one vote*!' However, it should be guaranteed—and here we see Arendt's anti-party attitude, which is not anti-parliamentarian (see DUR: 42)—that the majority is formed anew for each question; thus opinion-making may not be determined by any kind of party-based coercion, neither should it be possible for the majority to remove from the outset certain opinions from the future political exchange of opinions. Here, too, the issue is one of procedural postulates, which can be attained only on the basis of (legally secured) rules. But the fact that the principle of majority should determine the decision means at the same time that the 'politics of the power of judgement' cannot be completely independent of the political judgement of the individual citizen. While the institutionalised democratic procedural rules are definitely of great importance, 'reasonable' opinion and judgement making *also* depends on the political culture of a community to realise a 'politics of the power of judgement'.

### *ii. Political Rationality Between Institutions*

Arendt argues that the rationality of political action is not only realised in the aforementioned institutions, but also results from the relationship of the institutions with one another. As I mean to examine specifically the relationship between the sphere of law and that of politics below, I shall concentrate my brief comments here primarily on the legislative and executive branches.

Ideally, Arendt imagines a systemic structure in which the different discursive-democratic spaces stand 'in relation to each other … and elect from their midst the representatives for the higher government organs … right up to the supreme national council, somewhat similar to the state government' (DUR: 46). Besides Arendt's conviction that only participation can counter the negative consequences of political massing, political rationality should be guaranteed by such an interweaving of relationships. Arendt outlined the genesis of this rationality in an interview with Adelbert Reif:

> But when even only ten people sit at a table, everyone says his opinion, everyone hears the opinions of the others, a *reasonable opinion can be formed* through the exchange of opinions. It will also emerge in the discussion which of us is best suited to represent our opinion at the next highest council, where our opinion is then once more clarified, reshaped or proved to be false under the influence of other opinions. (Arendt [1970] 1998e: 132f, emphasis added)

If we force ourselves to address these comments at their strongest argumentative point and ignore the romanticising idea of a 'ten-man circle',[51] we see that a three-stage process of reflection is implied. Through the exchange with others the individual views and attitudes of the single person are transformed at the first level into an opinion. Arendt omitted this step in the quotation set out above. It is obvious from her writings, however, that she makes a distinction between an undiscussed 'individual opinion', the mood, view or attitude, and a discussed and reflected opinion. At this point she concentrates on the 'reasonable formation of opinion' within the discursive-democratic space, the second level so to speak. Reasonableness can claim this 'exchange of opinions' only when it is conducted in accordance with the principles discussed in detail above. At the third level the rationality potential of each discursive-democratic space is now increased by mediation with other democratic-political spaces (sections, councils, wards, etc). For at this third level the opinion is 'clarified', 'reshaped' and rejected as 'false', ie as undifferentiated, or as incapable of attaining a majority, or as not in conformity with the constitution or similar. It is very likely that both the clarification and reshaping, as well as the rejection of an opinion at the next highest level of such a political system, will be accepted by the previous level only if the rules for reasonable debate and opinion formation have been followed and respected there as well.

What Arendt describes here with the multi-staged structure of the interwoven relationships of discursive-democratic spaces can be found once more in her thoughts on American federalism. There, too, the 'central power' does not eliminate the power of the federal states, but rather is in a relationship with them. The dependencies and interdependencies of the different levels in the American political system not only create a 'radically different concept of power' (OR: 272), which is diametrically opposed to that of Continental Europe, but also a different type of political rationality. It is crucial that Arendt, in her writings from the 1960s and 1970s on the political situation in America, repeatedly refers to the consequences of 'the enormous growth of federal power at the expense of states' rights' (CD: 75) for the rationality of political decisions. Arendt's accusation is that the USA is getting ever closer to the centralism of the European nation-state model, and is therefore committing itself to the nation-state idea of sovereignty. From Arendt's perspective this idea of sovereignty is questionable for a number of reasons. In 'Civil Disobedience',

[51] *Cf* on this point Bhikhu Parekhs' criticism that Arendt's assessment of the revolutionary elites in those council systems is 'romantic and rather naive' (Parekh 1981: 170). Canovan states that Arendt's council idea excludes specifically the elderly, the sick, the workers and those who cannot articulate themselves from the political process (Canovan 1978: 19). A defence of the council idea is provided by Heuer (Heuer 1992: 332). By placing the focus of my interpretation of the councils on the aspect of rationality, I remove Arendt's council idea at least partially from the firing line of this justified criticism.

for example, she is concerned that the Supreme Court is condemned to silence by the so-called 'political question doctrine' (CD: 100), and that disputed laws or ordinances cannot be examined for their constitutionality.

A further aspect is of decisive significance for our discussion: Arendt warns that the shifts within the political system mean that a certain type of rationality—new to America, but certainly known in Continental Europe—begins to penetrate political operations: the 'reason of state doctrine' (CD: 100). Yet under the conditions of modern capitalist societies, Arendt claims, this new, though in some respects old type of rationality will lead inevitably to irrational politics. This warning is stated most urgently in her thoughts on the Pentagon papers: because the 'image' of a government or a politician has become so centrally important in modern societies, so-called 'public-relations managers' and 'problem-solvers' (LiP: 9) exert an increasing influence on political decisions. These 'modern varieties of the art of lying' undermine a reasonable political process of judgement making by creating an 'Alice-in-Wonderland atmosphere' (LiP: 20). For image reasons, therefore, one's own lies threaten to form the basis of political decisions, with the result, ultimately, of landing in the realm of completely irrational politics, which exclude reality. While politics in modern societies are always faced with this danger, the procedures between the different political organs, institutions, etc and levels of the political system at least maintain a certain rationality and increase the chance that political operations are not completely absorbed by such image-related practices. But if these procedures are circumvented or disabled by means of shifts within the political system, the irrationalisation of politics threatens to occur.[52] In her thoughts on the Pentagon papers, Arendt states that the President (and with him the executive branch) becomes 'an ideal victim of complete manipulation' by public relations managers and image compulsion. She argues that this is the consequence of the executive branch's cutting itself off from contact with the legislative power of Congress. For Arendt, 'it is the logical outcome in our system of government when the Senate is being deprived of, or is reluctant to exercise, its powers to *participate and advise*'

[52] Probably the most urgent example of the irrationalisation of political decisions provided by Arendt in the course of her analysis of the Pentagon papers is the status and significance of the domino theory in political decisions. Although very few people in the CIA and the administration saw anything more than a theory in the domino theory, it became a guideline for action in politics. The reason, says Arendt, was that this theory condenses complex political circumstances to such a degree that it can convince a broad mass of politically uninterested citizens. The problem, however, is that due to the systemic shifting and reinforcement of the executive, this theory also replaces political reality for those who have to decide. Arendt writes, 'According to the Pentagon papers, "only the Joint Chiefs, Mr [Walt W] Rostow and General [Maxwell] Taylor appear to have accepted the domino theory in its literal sense," and the point here is that those who did not accept it still used it, not merely for public statements, but as part of their own premises as well.' (LiP: 25)

(LiP: 9, emphasis added) in the political decision-making process. The procedural exchange between the different organs of state is inhibited, with the result that the rationality of the political decision sinks and 'deception' becomes 'chronic' (CD: 93).

Against the background of order-threatening phenomena such as a political massing and conformism, the American Republic has lost a large part of its rationality potential. Neither federalism nor the quality of the democratic political output can compensate for this loss. That is *Arendt's thorn*, stuck in every modern capitalist democracy, which makes it clear that her political thought is one of crisis. At this point an important difference becomes quite clear between her political philosophy and that of Jürgen Habermas, who unavoidably comes to mind with all this talk of procedures and procedural rules. Habermas pursues his analysis of the political everyday life of complex democratic societies primarily from a legitimisation-theoretical perspective. That means that he examines—and where necessary criticises—political decisions with respect to their (moral) validity. In brief, he is primarily concerned with the moral normativity of political-democratic decisions. Arendt, in contrast, is not really engaged in scrutinising the moral validity of political decisions. Rather, she is concerned with the question of the durability and stability of the political order. However, by seeing the political stability as threatened, both by the systemic shifts towards strengthening the central power and by the lack of participatory opportunities for the citizens, it shows that the durability of a political order is necessarily connected to the enabling and realisation of plurality in the process of opinion and judgement formation. Summing up, one can say that Arendt is concerned with the political normativity of political-democratic decisions.

### *iii. Political Rationality Between the Political System and the Public Sphere*

Arendt laments that both the transformation of views into opinions and a reasonable process of opinion-making are guaranteed only insufficiently due to the disappearance or the loss of political significance of the town halls. Opinions are formed solely from a 'lively exchange of opinion' and come about 'only in a process of public discussion': 'Wherever there is no space for such an exchange of opinion, there may be moods of all kinds …, but no opinion.' (ÜR: 346) Arendt verifies, however, the 'structural transformation of the public', in so far as she identifies the press as 'the only public organ' in modern mass democracies in which at least 'some kind of representation of opinion' takes place. In her view, the press is rightly termed 'a kind of fourth estate, almost equal to the executing, legislating and judicial powers' (ÜR: 346). The media represent only a makeshift replacement for the lack of institutionalised discursive-democratic spaces—makeshift not only due to systemic compulsions, but also because they cannot replace the disappearance of concrete participation. The tasks of the press include 'examining opinions, discarding the arbitrary or purely individual matters and allowing only those opinions to reach the public that can claim a certain validity' (ÜR: 292). Quite in line with the 'operation of imagination', the press delivers a potpourri of different reflected opinions on matters requiring regulation. Indirectly, parliament picks up on some of these opinions, and tests their political plausibility in its committees and panels. The opinions or decisions represented in parliament or by parliamentarians are discussed once again in the press, and must prove their ability there to represent the *sensus communis*. (If that is not the case, a charge of unconstitutionality is possible.) In this manner, too, public communications processes are initiated, which generate 'attention to and the feeling of the importance' (Thiel 2012: 204) of political matters.

In her writings on the situation of America's political system, Arendt repeatedly criticises the fact that the system-immanent mediation, communication and reflection process is suspended or circumvented. In her thoughts on the Pentagon papers she places strong emphasis on 'the integrity and the power of the press' (LiP: 45)—a press that she appraised quite differently during the Eichmann controversy—but especially against the background of the Vietnam War, she doubts whether the right to non-manipulated opinion can be guaranteed by a constitutional article alone (see LiP: 45). For this reason Arendt increasingly supports political protest by civil society.

Jean Cohen accused Arendt of ignoring the agents of civil society. Cohen believed to have identified in Arendt a 'sociological deficit' that was expressed in particular by the fact that she could give no 'satisfactory account of the source of basic or "fundamental" rights' (Cohen 1996: 164f). This 'sociological deficit' is the 'great lacuna' (Cohen 1996: 180)[53] in Arendt's thinking:

> Civil as distinct from political society plays a crucial role in asserting and protecting rights because it is a locus for the spontaneous development of free association, civil publics and powers alongside of political institutions and structures. In the sense of civil society, the social is distinct from the political, but it is politically relevant. Social life in modern civil society is hardly reducible to wordlessness, atomism, or the unnatural expansion of the natural. On the contrary, civil society establishes connections and relations, as the proliferation today on the national and international levels of a wide and highly articulated range of associations, nongovernmental organizations, committees, interconnected publics, and social movements witness. These can produce recognition and trust by creating contexts in which individuals can act in concert as peers, exchange opinions, and develop the civic competence needed for exercising influence on political entities, administrative bodies, and courts, on the national and supranational level. (Cohen 1996: 180f)

[53] In her most recent thoughts on Arendt, Cohen revises her praise of civil society and announces that her 'optimism is gone and things look rather different' (Cohen 2007: 292).

But Cohen overlooks a central work that certainly can be considered a foundation stone of Arendt's thoughts on what one now calls civil society: her piece 'Civil Disobedience'. Here Arendt goes well beyond a form of political articulation that chooses to break the law in order to highlight grievances. This can be outlined based on no more than three key characteristics of her treatment of the concept: *first*, Arendt includes in the term 'civil disobedience' things that can nowadays be attributed without hesitation to civil society—such as the American civil rights movement. Furthermore, Arendt refers to the resistance to compulsory military service, which together with the anti-war movement is considered, especially in the European post-war societies, to be the beginning of civic activity. It is even more marked when she refers to the rights to tariffs, strikes and organisation, all of which in her view were the result of civil disobedience. Today these rights belong to the inventory of debates on social and employment policy, and provide negotiating room for trade unions as agents of civil society (see CD: 80.). *Secondly*, Arendt states that civil disobedience is voluntary, is neither state not economically motivated, and always forms whenever 'a significant number of citizens' (CD: 74) join together in movements or groups because parliament fails to address certain topics, or does so inadequately. But that is precisely the 'spontaneous development of free association, civil publics and powers alongside of political institutions and structures' which Cohen claims Arendt misjudges. Arendt concludes that these agents of civil society are attaining an ever greater importance in modern democracies, and these democracies are no longer conceivable without them. Although the civil movements, ie the 'voluntary associations … have been the specifically American remedy for the failure of institutions, the unreliability of men, and the uncertain nature of the future' (CD: 102), Arendt states that a legal background is also required here. It becomes clear exactly at this point just how far her comments go beyond the narrow definition of civil disobedience. For, *thirdly*, she pleads in favour of providing those groups with opportunities to dock on to the political system, giving them the same recognition as the lobbyist of the 'pressure groups' (CD: 101). It is of course debatable whether it makes sense in the course of a discussion of the concept of civil society to distinguish between politically motivated agents on the one hand and corporate lobbies on the other. But Arendt's primary concern in her plea for 'the establishment of civil disobedience among our political institutions' (CD: 101) is that these agents receive the legally guaranteed right 'to establish themselves as a power that is not only "seen from afar" during demonstrations … but is always present and to be reckoned with in the daily business of government' (CD: 101). This very clearly goes well beyond spontaneous, disorganised and anti-institutional protest. In contrast to her thoughts on discursive-democratic spaces in the form of councils, which are conceived systemically from within and are certainly granted decision-making competencies,[54] the agents of civil society rampage around the corridors and entrance halls of parliament. There they try, using 'means of persuasion, qualified opinion and the numbers of their constituents', which are the tools of agents of civil society in modern democracies, 'to influence and 'assist' Congress' (CD: 101). Or they aim to mobilise a political public by means of assemblies, demonstrations, etc. However, in each case the political decision-making power remains the preserve of the parliamentary representation.

How 'reasonably' opinion is formed within the different groups or movements of civil society varies from agent to agent and from topic to topic.[55] Irrespective of this, the contribution of civil society lies in the fact that it advocates 'necessary and desirable change or [the] necessary and desirable preservation or restoration of the status quo' (CD: 75), and thus exposes grievances to the public. For Arendt, civil society is an essential part of the political public. This interdependence of the political system, civil society and the public sphere results in increased degree of political rationality for the community. Regarding the problem of corruption, Arendt describes the importance of an intact public as follows:

> The only remedies against the misuse of public power by private individuals lie in the public realm itself, in the light which exhibits each deed enacted within its boundaries, in the very visibility to which it exposes all those who enter it. (OR: 256)

Agents of civil society draw attention to the actual behaviour of political agents. In other words: they examine the communicability of a certain political practice and confront it with the *sensus communis* of a community. This *sensus communis* is reflected not only in the constitution, or parts thereof, but also in political culture. By means of a policy of 'blaming and shaming', such political practices that are (supposedly) incompatible with the prevailing public culture are branded publicly—with the aim of delegitimising these practices. In terms of her works, Arendt hits upon the political potential of civil society in the section of *Crisis of the Republic* that covers the Watergate scandal, the Pentagon papers, racial and student upheavals, and the Vietnam War.

In conclusion, Arendt's 'ethics of power developed on the basis of the power of judgement' means implementing the 'methodical procedure' of the

[54] Albrecht Wellmer overlooks this difference between councils and civil society. Instead he argues that Arendt's plea for the councils only makes sense if we interpret it as a contribution for the strengthening of civil society—'in *contrast* to the actual political institutions' (Wellmer 1999: 131). Instead, Arendt's thoughts on the councils are the expression of a specific institutional rationality.

[55] Arendt refers here to Tocqueville, who stressed that these societies exercise a 'tyrannical control' (CD: 97) in their internal relations.

power of judgement within political institutions, between political institutions, and between the institutionalised political system and the public. In this way we arrive at an understanding of political rationality with Arendt that differs fundamentally from the traditional understanding. For Arendt, political rationality is realised when the political institutions and political action both enable and stabilise the other in the sense of an order of freedom. The core criterion for political rationality is the preservation of an order of freedom. By this means it has become possible to take a different view of Arendt's concept of the political and to roughly outline how this concept could contribute to the dehierarchisation of the relationship of law and politics. Now, in the section III. of the chapter, I shall turn my attention to the law.

## III. ARENDT'S THEORY OF LAW

So far we have worked out the interrelation between acting and power in Arendt's thoughts. In this manner we explained how an Arendtian understanding of politics is internally linked with the preservation and enabling of a logic of law—or, to be more precise, how legally secured procedural rules lead to an accommodating condition of successful political practice and a vital democratic public, and mark the *conditio sine qua non* of a durable, stable and free political order. Aside from the fact that this finding must be explicated further, the prevailing question in this chapter now is how the concept of law needs to be reconceptualised in order to be applicable to a constitutional theory based on the criterion of dehierarchisation.

First I shall examine how Arendt, in her thoughts on law, turns away from the '"command" theory of common and statute law' (Dewey [1927] 1985: 269). By placing herself in the Roman tradition, she attempts to *desubstantialise* the concept of law, to highlight its relationship-establishing dimension and to conceive law as a relational concept. In a second step I scrutinise how this legal-philosophical change in perspective regarding the essence of law aims to overcome the dichotomy between law and politics and leads to a different kind of legitimisation. Legitimate law, I argue, is that law which enables the political acting of a democratic political public. Despite this fertile legal-philosophical reconceptualisation of law, however, it remains unclear how Arendt translates this legal-philosophical account into an appropriate and corresponding understanding of jurisdiction, and what the legal-theoretical consequences are of such a claim that the legal system should help to preserve the syntax and grammar of an active public-political sphere. What does this mean for the practice of jurisdiction, the course and finding of legal justice, and the (possible) status of judicial review within a political order? What are the contours of a legal theory compatible with a version of constitutionalism for which the theorem of dehierarchisation is centre-stage? What are the contours of a legal theory compatible with the requirements of the public-political sphere? Answers to these questions are more or less missing. But these answers would have been necessary in order to corroborate Arendt's critical perspective on the interrelation between law and politics in general, and the dehierarchisation theorem as the vanishing point of her thoughts in particular.

## A. The Concept of Law: Relationship versus Substance

The internal connection between law and politics, the constitutional theorem of dehierarchisation which is derived from that connection, and Arendt's departure from the identification of politics with rule and domination, make it necessary also to rethink the concept of law. A first step in this process of reconsideration is to apply her thoughts on the nature of political power to law, and thus refer to the supposed will to dominate behind the law as a 'delusion' (OV: 97). The reason for this is that power, as the nature and essence of every political community, refers to some kind of consensus between people. In short: it indicates reciprocity. The revolutions in particular revealed for Arendt that ultimately 'everything depends on power'. In her view, the collapse in power presented by revolutions proves just how much the supposed obedience to laws is contingent on public opinion, and is an expression of positive support and general consent (see OV: 48f). This shift in perspective makes it clear that the law is not the expression of a command, not the legally attained will of the ruler(s), but rather that the essence of law is to describe, register and regulate the relationship that exists between people in a political community.[56] Against the background of Arendt's reinterpretation of the political, every law within a community is the legally formalised expression of the existing relationships of consent. The law does not become an expression of power, and certainly not identical with power, but the law provides insights into the underlying power constellation of a community.[57] My argument that Arendt conceives the law as a relational concept, as a relationship-establishing concept that elucidates the existing power constellation, can also be drawn from her thoughts on criminals or rebels. In Arendt's view, the power of the police in domestic affairs and in the combatting of crime

> functions as the last resort of power against criminals or rebels—that is, against single individuals who, as it were, refuse to be overpowered by the consensus of the majority. It is normally the superiority of this majority and its 'opinion' that charges the police with or empowers them to exert violence against those who withdraw from their claim to power. (MuG: 52; see also OV: 51)

[56] A similar account is given by John Dewey. See Dewey [1927] 1985: 269f.
[57] Along these lines Dworkin refers to the law as a '*revealing social institution*' (Dworkin 1998: 11).

All others who comply with the laws, irrespective of whether or not they agree with these laws, give them their implicit consent. They thus acknowledge that the relationship between them is regulated in the manner written in the law. For Arendt, obedience towards commands and laws in the political always means consent.[58]

Against this background, the social contract theories of Kant and Rousseau have become stuck half way. Without a doubt, Arendt takes on board essential parts of Kant's and Rousseau's contractual ideas for her political thought. For what gives the contractual idea such compelling plausibility is that it seeks to constitute a political community on the basis of the relationship of citizens and thus dispenses with all forms of foreign domination. That is the emancipatory and democratic core of the contractual idea as represented by Kant and Rousseau. Yet the problem of both contractual theories is that they fall in with a tradition that equates politics with rule. This means that the contractual theory searches desperately for a new subject of rule, which is then conceived either in the direction of law or in the direction of politics. How should we understand this? Kant and Rousseau reconceived the form of rule in the political; but the equation of politics and rule remained untouched by both thinkers. This endows the contractual idea with the very dichotomy between politics and law that Arendt aims to avoid. Accordingly, the only matter of concern in the liberal, Kantian version is whether the government in question complies with the laws (republican) or not (despotic)—irrespective of how many participate in the ruling authority. In his work *Zum ewigen Frieden*, Kant distinguishes between the 'form of domination (forma imperii)' and the 'form of government (forma regiminis)' (Kant [1795] 1999a: 13). Whereas in the first case one, some or all can rule, in the second case there can be only republican or despotic systems. Kant leaves no doubt that republicanism is the only sensible form of government. However, for this form of government it is not really important how many people rule—though Kant states that he prefers only a few to rule (see Kant [1795] 1999a: 14f).

The contractual-theoretical alternative is presented by Rousseau's republicanism, in which the rule of the community cannot and may not be bound by any law in the world (see Rousseau [1762] 2012: 52).[59] While in the Kantian

[58] See Arendt [1964] 2003e: 43ff. The entire Eichmann discourse provides an example of this. See on this point Volk 2005: 16–46; 81–91; 113–38.

[59] Arendt herself often speaks of the 'rule of the law' in a republic; but, as I shall demonstrate below, even that is at least ambiguous from her political-theoretical perspective. Arendt most likely means that political action should follow a certain grammar and should embody the spirit of fundamental constitutional principles. Thus she joins the tradition of the *rule of law*. At the same time, however, the 'rule of law' naturally can also mean law-rule and refer to a state dominated by an administrative and judicial elite, which was also a subject of criticism in the previous chapter. Rather, Arendt's political thought should be read and understood as an attempt to depart from the concept of rule and domination.

case the law is given priority, in the Rousseauian case this priority is assumed by politics. The order-endangering potential of both is well known. As far as our discussion of the concept of law is concerned, in both cases the law is conceived and *substantiated* from the perspective of the will through the continuation of the tradition of the political idea of domination: either, as with Kant, by means of the individual will (or individual arbitrariness and the accompanying dissociation of claims to freedom), or, as with Rousseau, as an expression of the general will (see Kant [1797] 1977: 337 and Rousseau [1762] 2012: 67).

In Arendt's view only Montesquieu recognised that the law is not a substance of the will to dominate, but rather an expression of the relationship that exists between the people in a governmental system. Montesquieu advanced to this insight because his entire political thinking was rooted deeply in the Roman tradition. His considerations on law, on *loi*, are in line with Roman legal thinking and its idea of *lex*—and not in the Greek tradition of *nomos*. The difference between *lex* and *nomos* is crucial when developing Arendt's legal-philosophical thinking:[60] while the Greek *nomos* expresses the idea of demarcation, the Roman *lex* stands for relationship:

> For the Roman lex, which was very different from and even contrary to what the Greeks understood by nomos, actually means 'lasting tie' and very quickly came to mean 'contract', whether between private citizens or as a treaty between nations. Consequently *a law is something that links human beings together, and it comes into being not by diktat or by an act of force but rather through mutual agreement....* For the Greeks, law is neither an agreement nor a contract; it certainly does not arise between men in the back-and-forth exchange of words and action ... [The Greeks seek] to set limits to action by means of the nomos and to interpret the law not as a link and a relationship, but rather as an enclosing border that no one should overstep. (Arendt [1950] 2007c: 184, emphasis added)

Arendt juxtaposes the political experiences of the Romans, embedded in their concept of *lex*, against the Greek *nomos*. While stressing the notion of mutual agreement as the crucial feature of law, the Roman *lex* demonstrates the relation-establishing dimension of law. Arendt, therefore, explicitly talks

[60] In my interpretation of Arendt's legal thought as a shift from *nomos* to *lex*, I disagree with Hans Lindahl's reading. Lindahl is convinced that for Arendt '*nomos* deserves conceptual and political priority over other, derivative conceptions of law.' (Lindahl 2006, 884) In Lindahl's view, this is the case because Arendt's 'strong claim that the legal closure of space is constitutive for political community as such.' (Lindahl 2006, 884) Lindahl, in my view, not only misses the fact that Arendt argues in favour of a relational conception of law but also that she understands space in terms of relational space—a notion of space that corresponds to her concept of the political—and, therefore, departs from the notion of a political community still rooted in container space thinking with its strong emphasis on boundaries.

about the 'contractual character of law' and characterises the Roman concept as a 'political concept of law' (ÜR: 244). To be sure, what makes the Roman concept of law a political one is its relation-establishing character. Such a concept of law perfectly suits a notion of the political which emphasises 'acting in concert'. The purpose and rationality of the legal system, in her view, is to preserve the syntax and grammar of democratic political acting and to maintain the rules of an active public-political sphere.

Although Arendt is convinced that the Greek concept of law is 'pre-political', in the sense that the laws, designed by a lawgiver, are there first and foremost to establish the political realm—like the walls of the city—in which further political action and interaction can take place, it is crucial to emphasise that, for her, the relation-establishing dimension of law is also present in the idea of *nomos*. In contrast to the Roman concept, however, this relation-establishing dimension is far from obvious; rather, it becomes apparent only by means of the pre-philosophical writings of the Hellenistic city-states. According to these writings, it was the pursuit of immortality which motivated people to engage in political affairs. This also explains the central function poets and historians took within the Hellenistic city-states. For the Hellenistic pursuit of immortality, however, laws were by no means of less importance:

> The great advantage of the polis organization of public life was that the polis, because of the stabilizing force of its wall of law, could impart to human affairs a solidity that human action itself, in its intrinsic futility and dependence on the immortalizing praise of poets, can never possess. Because it surrounded itself with a permanent wall of law, the polis as a unity could claim to ensure that whatever happened or was done within it would not perish with the life of the doer or endurer, but live on in the memory of future generations. (Arendt [1953] 2007a: 716)

The Greek concept of law was unable to establish relationships between the city-states. This is what distinguishes it from the Roman *lex*. However, due to its 'stabilizing force' and 'permanent wall', the Greek *nomos* guaranteed that political agents would stay 'in the memory of future generations'; and by doing so, within the Greek political patterns of thought, the laws helped to establish a relation between the citizens of the polis. Thus, similar to the Roman *lex*, we can also unpack the relation-establishing dimension within the Greek notion of *nomos*. However, this forces us to reconsider the idea of demarcation and the notion of boundary anew, which we mainly ascribed to the Greek concept of law. What becomes apparent, then, is the fact that even the Roman concept of *lex* is ambivalent with respect to boundary and demarcation. To illustrate the ambivalence, Arendt refers to ancient Carthage as an example. With respect to military force, Carthage was on par with Rome, 'and simultaneously embodied a principle opposed to Rome's' (Arendt [1950] 2007c: 181). What the history of the two empires reveals is that the Roman political principle of contract and relationship between partners could not be applied everywhere. Therefore, Arendt concludes:

> The price the Greeks paid for this form-giving power of their *nomos* was their inability to build an empire, and there is no doubt that all Hellas ultimately perished because of the *nomos* of the poleis, the city-states, which though they were able to proliferate as colonies could never join together and unite in a permanent alliance. But we can say with equal justification that the Romans were also victim of their law, of their *lex*, which, although it allowed them to establish lasting ties and alliances wherever they went, was in itself unlimited and thus forced them against their own will—indeed absent of any will to power or lust for domination—to rule the entire globe, a dominion that once achieved could only collapse. (Arendt [1950] 2007c: 187)

This passage underlines that the horizon of political experiences and the pattern of political thoughts manifest themselves within the respective concepts of law and, by doing so, point to the internal relationship between law and politics. At the same time, the respective paradigm of the political is closely interconnected with culture, religion, society and so on. Therefore, even if Arendt points out that the Romans lack 'any will to power or lust for domination', their understanding and notion of law sought to establish a 'relationship between partners' (Arendt [1950] 2007c: 186). Carthage, however, was not willing to enter into such a relationship, and therefore became a 'rogue state' in the eyes of Rome, which had to be destroyed.[61]

In his article 'Law beyond command?', Keith Breen addresses this problem and poses the question whether Arendt's shift from *nomos* to *lex* has 'in fact freed law from the problems of sovereignty' (Breen 2012: 16). Breen acknowledges Arendt's attempt to conceive law 'simultaneously in terms of boundaries and relationships', and to free politics and law from the shackles of rulership and coercion. In his view, however, Arendt ultimately fails. Although Breen agrees with Arendt that neither politics nor law can be reduced to relations of command and obedience, he claims that both, politics and law, cannot be completely divorced from these relations. Breen argues forcefully that 'to the extent that she does try to divorce them, Arendt shies away from driving home the unsettling implications of both *nomos* and *lex*, misrepresents the

[61] Ulrich Preuß describes this danger, which is inherent to the idea of a global juridification, as the 'Achilles' heel of what is actually a likeable project' (Preuß 2007: 332). This danger highlights the fact that although the law must not necessarily be the expression of rule, there is nevertheless no such thing as neutral law. Every law, regardless of its type, transports its own version of a good life—and although one might find good reasons not to do so, one must ultimately accept that its enforcement can never be possible 'without ambivalence and with a completely clear conscience' (Wellmer 1998: 288) towards other cultural circles.

course of historical events and hides realities that ought to, indeed must, be acknowledged' (Breen 2012: 32).

While I agree with Breen that Arendt gives us too little detail about how her understanding of law could be grounded in legal theory, we do not have to follow Breen's assumption that any law needs to be based on command and obedience. An important counterargument is that the punchline of Arendt's political-theoretical consideration is to argue that obedience is a term that we should ban from our *political* vocabulary. For her, the breakdown of public authority in the moment of revolution stresses the fact that, in the end, the alleged obedience to the law mainly depends on public opinion and general consent. This brings her to the conclusion that law should not be seen as an expression of command or as the legal will of the sovereign, but rather as describing, revealing and arranging the relations among people within a political community. That is the reason why she compares law to the rules of a game which establish relations between people. Against this background, laws are the legally formalised expression of agreements—or at least of tacit consent (see Volk 2010: 775f).

Besides the reference to the general thrust of Arendt's project, there is a second, somewhat weightier counterargument: as Stefanie Rosenmüller has established (see Rosenmüller 2013a: 158, or Rosenmüller 2013b: 410ff), there is a third concept of law in Arendt's work—*rapport*—which seeks to combine the defensive function of *nomos* with the enabling dimension of *lex* and which Breen overlooks or overrides. Law as *rapport* can be traced back to Montesquieu. For Arendt's Montesquieu, *rapport* means 'the relation subsisting between different entities'. This lays the foundation for a concept of law which is 'relative by definition' (Arendt [1950] 2007c: 183).[62] In Arendt's interpretation, Montesquieu came to this conclusion because he differentiated between philosophical and political freedom. While the first is based on the individual 'I will', the second refers to an 'I can', that is, to being empowered by others. Thus, according to Montesquieu, one can be politically 'free' only where 'one cannot be coerced to perform an act that the law does not prescribe' (Montesquieu [1748] 1992: 232). Only where people are reciprocally empowered to act, where 'civil laws' (Montesquieu [1748] 1992b: 232) regulate life,

[62] Right at the beginning of the first book of *Vom Geist der Gesetze*, Montesquieu describes laws as relationships: 'Laws in the broadest sense of the word are relationships that emerge necessarily from the nature of things.' (Montesquieu [1748] 1992: 9) Montesquieu also writes 'of a "Creator and Preserver" of the universe', of the '"state of nature"' and of '"natural law", by which he understands the laws of nature' (ÜR: 243). But for Arendt these laws describe, in his view, merely 'the references between the creator and creation or also between humans in their natural state'. What the laws reveals in Arendt's interpretation of Montesquieu are the '"rules" or règles which determine the government of the world and without which a world would not exist at all' (OR: 189).

can one speak of political freedom. To be reciprocally empowered to act means to regard one another as political persons. According to Arendt, the word person, *persona*, originates from the language of the theatre and denotes the mask of the actor. As such it always had two functions. On the one hand, the mask had to hide the natural face of the actor—or rather replace it—but on the other hand, it had to be designed in such a way that the natural voice could be heard (OR: 97). Thus the status that subjects mutually guarantee to one another enables participation and protection simultaneously. On the one hand, it shields the area of subjectivity, possession, cultural origin, private preferences, etc. On the other hand, by means of the mask, this status enables one to speak as an equal to other equals (Volk 2010: 268–79).

## B. What is Legitimate Law?

### *i. Neither Foundation nor Promise*

Although the relationship character of Arendt's concept of law is based on the by-all-means ambivalent idea of a 'relationship between partners', and thus demands a cooperative opposite number, it has become clear that law is something relative, ie it concerns 'relations which exist and preserve different realms of being' (OR: 189). As yet, however, nothing substantial has been said about one of the key questions of the whole chapter, namely, the legitimacy of law. This question arises not only against the background of parliamentary legislation and a political public sphere, but also at the basis of modern criminal law (see DT: 244).[63] At the outset I presented the argument that legitimate law, according to Arendt, is the law that enables political acting. In order to explain this claim step by step, I shall first turn to two other views.

In his work *Die Gründung der Freiheit*, Stefan Ahrens argues that with Arendt, legitimacy results from the possibility for political action experienced in the act of foundation. At the moment of foundation the 'elementary grammar of political action as such' (Ahrens 2005: 261) is expressed, and that means, in Ahrens' view, the will to begin and its creative spontaneity. Only such political action is able to 'guarantee legitimacy … It is neither legalistically nor institutionally definable, and it is unpredictable.' (Ahrens 2005: 261) It always conceals within it the 'danger of the retraction of gains in rationalisation'

[63] In *Macht und Gewalt*, Arendt hints at the question of the legitimacy of law when she writes: 'If the essence of power exists in the effectiveness of the command, then there is in fact no greater power than that which comes "from the barrel of a gun", and the only difficulty would be that it is now impossible to say "how the commands of the police differ from those of an armed criminal"' (MuG: 38). But what is the difference if we conceive law differently? What constitutes legitimate law?

(Ahrens 2005: 270f), and Arendt therefore could not name any 'barrier against the influence of undesired social movements' (Ahrens 2005: 271).

Yet Ahrens becomes increasingly tangled up in contradictions: on the one hand he assumes that political freedom and action are the only reference points of all legitimate politics, and as such cannot be 'fundamentally limitable'. On the other hand he emphasises, however, that 'plurality and the reference back to foundation' represented 'limiting dimensions' (Ahrens 2005: 271) for Arendt, and stresses the significance of the power of judgement. If we ignore the fact that it remains unclear whether Ahrens believes that political action can be limited or not, then the required reference back to foundation and the observance of plurality can hardly be achieved by the will. For within Arendt's terminology, at least, the will is either free or there is none (see LotM/W: 140f). The concept of the will is characterised for Arendt precisely by the fact that it does not allow itself to be bound or obligated in any way, regardless of how liberally the act of foundation has occurred. It also remains unclear with Ahrens how the will and the power of judgement should go together. Within Arendt's conceptual horizon, at least, an understanding of the political that is based on free will is totally different in character from that which refers to plurality and judgement. Arendt never ceases to stress the differences between politics of the will and politics of the power of judgement.[64] It can therefore be said that Stefan Ahrens does not address the theoretical content of Arendt's plurality postulate for the political. Had he done so, he might well have taken into account that the realisation of political plurality requires an institutional order. Instead, however, he assumes that in 'Arendt's theory of the act of foundation … the decisive turning point does not lie in the creation of the institutions' (Ahrens 2005: 261).

In his work *Die Sorge um die Welt und die Freiheit des Handelns*, Jürgen Förster tackles this point and attributes the inconsistency of Ahrens' thoughts to his fixation with the will as the source of political freedom. Förster argues against Ahrens that if

> the will [were] the only organ of freedom, then humans would be hopelessly at the mercy of the sea of uncertainty and politics would be impossible. But political freedom is not identical to the contingency. Politics tries to contain this quasi prepolitical freedom, which is not viable in its absoluteness, by founding 'islands in the sea of uncertainty'. (Förster 2009: 317)[65]

[64] See on this point inter alia FuP: 216; ÜR: 96; VLG: 425f; WiP: 48–53. Ahrens is aware of these passages and stresses therefore that the will is one of the 'most dubious terms' (Ahrens 2005: 77) for the political. Yet strangely he draws no consequences from that fact. A similar treatment of the will can also be found in Kalyvas 2004.

[65] *Cf* also the comments by Canovan, who also sees the faculty of making promises as a guarantee of 'predictability' (Canovan 1992: 192; Calhoun 1997: 246). Alan Keenan also addresses Arendt's thoughts on the power of promise. He represents the argument that political freedom

With a view to the American Revolution, it becomes clear, according to Förster, that the American beginning was precisely not, as Ahrens believes, based 'on *archein*, here in the meaning of "to rule", and also not on *archestai*, to be understood here as the obedience of the ruled as enforced by the rulers'. According to Förster such a new beginning is 'possible only insofar as there is a beginning that is not motivated by an act of will' (Förster 2009: 318).

Instead of reducing and narrowing the American foundation to the will to begin and spontaneity, Förster uses a completely different terminology in his interpretation of Arendt's reading of the American foundation. The core of the American experience of foundation lies in the discovery of the faculty of making promises as an order-establishing and 'world-forming institution per se' (Förster 2009: 480). The history of the American foundation encourages Arendt to regard the faculty of making promises as the world-forming institution per se, and also to see the foundation of 'the political and also the law' (Förster 2009: 480) in the promise. For Förster, every claim to legitimacy within the community originates in the promise. By replacing the will with the promise, Förster gets a view of the reciprocity of politics and law. In contrast to the commanding nature of the will, the promise is in line with Arendt's theory of the 'contractual character of the law'. In this sense Arendt assumes that 'contract theory is a theory of the promise' (DT: 338).

One must, however, be aware of the fact that for Arendt *all* law means relationship—and accordingly that the command theory does not express any truth about the essence of law, but is rather a legal-philosophical fallacy. And no matter how the laws have been established, 'maintaining the laws … can be seen as maintaining the promise' (DT: 338). This is precisely the point of her claim that the supposed dilemma between natural law and legal positivism is based on 'a delusion':

> The common dilemma—either the law is absolutely valid and therefore needs for its legitimacy an immortal, divine legislator or the law is simply a command with nothing behind it but the state's monopoly of violence—is a delusion. All laws are 'directives' rather than 'imperatives'. They direct human intercourse as the rules direct the game. And the ultimate guarantee of their validity is contained in the old Roman maxim Pacta sunt servanda. (OV: 98)

So although Förster's reference to the concept of the promise brings up both the relationship-establishing character of the law and also the internal

is 'inevitably' lost with the foundation, the promise, and the legal order. He considers the faculty of making promises and the foundation to be '*non-political activities*' (Keenan 1994: 299). With this in mind he argues that a constitution 'can effectively lay down the law of freedom only by immediately violating that same law' (Keenan 2003: 89; very similar also Honig 1991: 111). This is an example of the fact that Keenan neither recognises the political nature of the promise nor has he been able to liberate himself from the classic dichotomy of law and politics.

connection between law and politics, the concept of the promise does not provide any criteria that would enable a differentiation between 'right' and 'wrong', or between just law and unjust law.[66] If we reflect Förster's thoughts on the promise in the light of the comments in section II above, their lack of a political-normative foundation becomes clear. The promise can only claim 'order-establishing' and 'world-forming' qualities if it has come about in a very specific manner, in a very particular mode, and if the observance of this mode is also expected for future political action. In other words, if the promise does not come about in a manner which realises the principles of the power of judgement, it might well be a promise but the force of the promise cannot claim *order-establishing* and *world-forming* qualities in a free democratic and Arendtian sense. To illustrate this it is not even necessary to take the extreme example of a Nuremberg Rally by the NSDAP, with its collective promise, 'Führer, command! We shall follow!' Arendt's comparison of the French and American drafting of the constitutions, which is in fact a comparison of the forms of consensus and promise, is sufficient. For this comparison makes sense only when the mode of promise itself is once more scrutinised. Only then does the hue and cry at the drafting of the constitution in France sound 'like mockery' when one 'thinks of the extensive debates in the people's assembly that preceded the ratification of the constitution in America' (ÜR: 161; see also ÜR: 154). What differentiates the *union sacrée* of the French from the *de pluribus unum* of the Americans is not the promise as such—or at least only when the concept of promise is grounded or has already been prepared in normative terms. In brief, only that kind of promise that is preceded by a free process of opinion and judgement making, and which expects the observance of these rules for the future, can claim to establish legitimate law.[67] Only

[66] Arendt returns repeatedly at various points to the question of the 'injustice of the laws' (CD: 60), but never spells out a clear answer.

[67] For Rousseau, too, the complete submission to the general will is possible only if there was a 'prior convention' (Rousseau [1776] 2012: 49); Rousseau famously calls it the 'first convention' (Rousseau [1762] 2012: 48). The 'first convention' means that the people promise one another to follow the general will. Here too, reciprocity, equality, affiliation and commitment, ie the central features of the promise, are fulfilled. I do not dispute the fact that Arendt contributed to the confusion in matters concerning the nature and the political power of the promise: she never fully realised the normative foundation of her concept of promise; or rather she never spelled out this foundation. This can be seen, for example, in the fact that she sometimes interpreted Rousseau's social contract in tradition of the theories of promises (DT: 135, 338) and sometimes did not (CD: 94). The normative framework of the whole concept becomes clear whenever she disputes the promise character of certain forms of the social contract. The examinations in ch 2 in particular attempt to do justice to the depth of Arendt's Rousseau discourse. The study makes clear the complexity of Arendt's argument and underlines the fact that Arendt's differentiation—here the promise, there none—was preceded by massive theoretical conceptual work. It is clear from Förster's thoughts that he revolves his mind around this normative core of the concept of promise, referring always to principles of action or the power of judgement. In his last chapter, he argues for the rationality of judgement: 'The power of judgement', writes

such a promise reflects the key central thought that emerges in the American experience of foundation: the dehierarchisation of the relationship between political 'acting with one another' and law.

### *ii. Enlargement and Preservation: Arendt's Understanding of Political Order*

Arendt illustrates this dehierarchised relationship between politics and law with her thoughts on the settlers, who, 'almost by inadvertence, discovered the *elementary grammar of political action and its more complicated syntax, whose rules determine the rise and fall of human power*' (OR: 173, emphasis added). It should first be noted that Arendt leaves a false trail here with the verb 'discover'. In the field of moral-philosophical, legal-philosophical and political-theoretical foundation discourse, the term 'discovery', as Michael Walzer outlined, refers implicitly to the 'revealing God'. God revealed the moral laws to Moses, who then brought them to the people. Political philosophy, which argues with the termini of discovery, has always been aimed at revelation, says Walzer:

> Religious morality commonly takes the form of a written text, a sacred book, and so it requires interpretation. But we first experience it through the medium of discovery. The moral world is like a new continent, and the religious leader (God's servant) is like an explorer who brings us the good news of its existence and the first map of its shape. (Walzer 1993: 4)[68]

Although Arendt assumes that this grammar and syntax of political action concerns 'the few elementary truths' (OR: 173),[69] in many aspects this classic, natural-law approach is incompatible with her thinking. First, *On Revolution* can be read as an exploration to find sources of political coexistence beyond any divine absoluteness. In addition she stresses in *Elemente/Origins* that 'the absolute and transcendent measurements of religion or the law of nature have lost their authority' (OT: 299) and that human rights cannot be justified on their basis. Probably the most important argument in this context, however, is—thirdly—that the natural-law reference to God as the highest authority continues the tradition of political ideas of rule, and for precisely this reason is incompatible with the thoughts outlined above about law as a

Förster, 'guarantees political decisions with a sense of proportion and plausibility.' (Förster 2009: 483) Yet the relationship between judgement and promise remains unclear. This could be due to the fact that he too sees the power of judgement ultimately as a concept of practical wisdom and not as a procedural norm materialised in the political institutions themselves.

[68] In *Three Paths in Moral Philosophy*, Walzer distinguishes the ways of justifying moral norms according to whether one discovers, invents or interprets these norms from the social context.

[69] Arendt explains elsewhere in the *Denktagebuch* precisely what she means by elementary truth: 'Only the opinion can rule in the political; in it there is only perspective! Precisely that is its "truth".' (DT: 375) The German text reads: 'Im Politischen kann nur die Meinung herrschen; in ihr gibt es nur Perspektivisches! Gerade das ist ihre "Wahrheit".'

relationship. Nevertheless, where the natural-law justification of law succeeds in comparison to legal positivism is in the authorisation of a certain unavailability, the sacralisation of law. Although Arendt states that this unavailability and its protection against arbitrariness can no longer be upheld in the political with recourse to God, reason or nature, this feature of natural law also holds a certain attractiveness for her thought. This attractiveness is thus reflected in expressions such as 'elementary grammar' or in the previously cited term 'few elementary truths' (OR: 174). What is attractive about natural law from an Arendtian perspective is that it outlines a way of political acting that is pre-legal in the sense of positive law, yet not without any attachment to the (natural) law.

The grammar, syntax and the elementary truths of political action are not discovered by the settlers, however—then that would mean that there is an author of law beyond politics, whose imperative would then become effective in the political. And they are also not 'invented' (see Walzer 1993: 11), as Walzer claims in the context of Habermas's discourse theory. Arendt states that 'neither grammar nor syntax [was] a true innovation in western history'. The novelty of the American experience of foundation lay rather in the fact that grammar and syntax were *'experienced' in the execution* of the 'acting and speaking with one another':

> The United States owes its origin to the American Revolution, and this revolution carried within it a *new, never fully articulated concept of law*, which was the result of no theory but *had been formed by the extraordinary experiences* of the early colonists. (CD: 83, emphasis added)

The passage underlines not only that the experience of the settlers was relevant as a new mode of understanding political acting, but also that the manner of action meant at the same time that a new understanding of law found expression. This experience of a simultaneity of 'law' and 'politics', ie the insight that action can lead to a durable and stable power constellation only when a certain grammar and syntax, a certain mode of action, is considered in the execution, describes in Arendt's view the characteristic trait of the American experience of foundation and the normative core that is expressed in this version of republican politics (*cf* Canovan 1992: 201). If we spell out the systematic political-theoretical consequences of such an interpretation, we need to distinguish Arendt's constitutional-political thought from discourse-theoretical as well as from radical-democratic premises.

### a. Dehierarchisation, Co-originality, and the Question of Political Freedom

In contrast to Habermas's theory of co-originality, the idea of dehierarchisation does not serve Arendt as a yardstick for legitimate politics, ie this idea is not inspired by moral philosophy but rather emerges from the experience that power 'perishes' without the upholding of this grammar and syntax. Whereas Habermas construes—or in Walzer's language 'invents'—co-originality because he believes that democratic decisions should not be independent of moral claims to validity, Arendt is interested in the question of the conditions under which political power is sustained.[70] If we examine Arendt's interpretation of the pre-colonial and pre-revolutionary experience from this perspective, it soon becomes clear than the 'elementary grammar of all political action' and the 'complicated syntax' mean precisely that structure of order that allows 'acting with one another'. Arendt explains how this 'pre-revolutionary and even precolonial experience' of the principles of political rationality was able to develop further in the centuries of self-administration, thus shaping the 'essential character of the revolutionary spirit', which was later reflected—legally positivised—in the American constitution.[71] In her view the key 'lesson' was that political action and speech exert their 'balancing effect' (ÜR: 225) when they follow a certain 'grammar and syntax' in their execution. In other words: when only the 'joint effort' counts in political action; when the action 'involves the many', leaves aside questions of 'motivation—whether they are eg an "undesired lot"—' and does not consider the 'uniformity of motives, past and origin':

> The joint effort cancels out any differences in origin or in personal quality *in a highly effective manner; all truly are equal in this effort.* The roots of the frequently and rightly admired realism of the founding fathers in relation to human nature can be found in this trust in the equalising effect of action itself. They could afford to simply ignore the French revolutionary hope of meeting the 'good person' outside of society in an imagined state of nature—after all, this was the hope of the Enlightenment, to which they also belonged. In other words they could afford to be without illusion and even pessimistic in their estimate of humans as individuals, because they relied on the fact that a community of 'sinners', as long as it has constituted itself *according to the right principles*], need not necessarily reflect the sinful side of human nature. (ÜR: 225, emphasis added)

The 'highly effective' equalisation depends on the 'right principles' that determine the 'internal structure' of a political space and form 'a political realm *that enjoyed power and was entitled to claim rights without possessing or claiming sovereignty*' (ÜR: 218; see also OR: 167). By converging power and rights, Arendt attempts

[70] According to Habermas, the legitimatory power of discursive opinion and will forming results precisely from the fact that 'the illocutionary binding power of the agreement-oriented linguistic use is used to bring together reason and will—and to reach convictions in which every individual can agree without constraint' (FuG: 134). Under the conditions of modern democracy, the legitimacy of law is based (merely) on a 'communicative arrangement: as participants in rational discourse the legal parties must be able to test whether a contentious norm finds or could find the agreement of all those possibly affected' (FuG: 134).

[71] At the same time, however, Arendt speaks of the 'failure of post-revolutionary thought to remember the revolutionary spirit and to understand it conceptually' (OR: 234).

to overcome the dichotomy of law and politics, which is expressed negatively either in the materialisation of the law or in the formalisation of politics. Whereas in the first case guarantees believed to be safe become questionable, political business that is remote from the citizen in the second case generates political disaffection, disenchantment and disengagement, mistrust and the downfall of the belief in legitimacy.

In addition to the different approaches to the question of co-originality or dehierarchisation, there is another point that should be considered in this discussion. Thomas Kupka has shown in an analysis of Habermas that his postulate of co-originality essentially supports the predominance of the law and is—to some extent at least—paternalistic towards political action. Habermas's moral-philosophical account spells out basic moral rights, which he calls 'unsaturated rights' (FuG: 159; *cf* also Kupka 1998: 259). These unsaturated rights not only set the benchmark for every political process in its quest for democratic legitimacy, but they must also be transformed into fundamental rights of a democratic polity (see Habermas 1998: 159f). By these means the law is 'informed', as Kupka criticises, by morality, instead of representing only an '"expectation-stabilising supplement to morality"' (FuG: 151; *cf* also Kupka 1998: 259). For if citizens wish to live under legitimate law, they must acknowledge precisely those basic rights that were drafted in the Habermas system of rights (see Kupka 1998: 258). If this is the case, we can no longer speak of co-originality; instead the relationship between politics and moral-legal norms tilts clearly in favour of a primacy of law and morality. Admittedly this Habermas interpretation is exaggerated, and surely does not adequately appreciate the contingency that lies between the moral-philosophical postulate and legal materialisation (*cf* Günther 1994: 478). Nevertheless, in the context under discussion here it helps us to illustrate Arendt's constitutional theorem of dehierarchisation and her concept of political order. Arendt's idea of order is not static in space and time. 'Syntax and grammar' do not stand for pre-political or moral norms and basic rights, which then must merely be interpreted and developed, sometimes in this manner, sometimes in another. By the 'syntax and grammar' of political action Arendt means norms that originate and are experienced in the first place only through political action; they can be understood only through political action in its whole meaning as a condition of political freedom. In contrast to Habermas's claim, they also lack all 'epistemic connotation', because they make sense only where political power is generated. Richard Bellamy summarised this idea as follows in his thoughts on a 'pre-sovereign notion of democratic politics':

> Being essentially an argument from democracy, it must surely rest on both a set of constitutional democratic rights and a *demos*. But the norms do not in any sense precede or frame the practice of dialogue, they are intrinsic to it and only emerge within it. Thus, there is no pre-existing consensus on rights. (Bellamy 2006: 184)

In the same sense Arendt is concerned with 'experiencing', and not with 'discovering' or 'inventing', norms and rights in the course of political action. This gives us a deep insight into Arendt's idea of order. For Arendt, a durable and stable political order is characterised by its dialectic of 'enlargement and preservation'. Something can be preserved only by means of its enlargement, ie in political action that propels us into the future. Because it is only in the moment of acting that one experiences what the meaning and impact of that which is to be preserved has for ones life in concrete terms. To put it in a nutshell, to uphold a democratic polity is only possible through experiencing political acting. Only by politically acting with one another can one experience the political meaning of the constitution and the rules of a democratic public sphere. Enlargement is possible only when one is aware, during enlargement, that the constellation of political power, which is formed at the moment of action between people, disintegrates as soon as they no longer observe the rules of its creation. Seen from this perspective, Arendt tries to integrate the awareness of the need for enlarging and for preserving simultaneously. This integrative approach reproduces the core idea of an Arendtian Constitutionalism, where the relationship between law and politics gets de-hierarchised, and constitution and democracy, preservation and enlargement are interrelated in the moment of acting.

As I have argued, Arendt is concerned with 'experiencing' and not with 'inventing' or constructing norms and rights. At this point, therefore, my reading of her work also differs from that of Jeremy Waldron, who interprets Arendt's claim for rules, procedures and the guarantee of individual rights in a constructivist light, ie rules and rights as the *precondition* for constituting political power. Similar to Habermas, but also to Pettit's neo-republican 'freedom as non-domination' (see Pettit 1999: 21),[72] Waldron thereby tacitly continues the

[72] Essentially, the difference between Pettit's freedom as non-domination and my reading of Arendt's account of political freedom can be narrowed down to the fact that one must experience the enabling power of the political order; it is not enough for it to be legally codified in a merely protective sense. One could now object that Pettit does not even dispute this. For example, in his democratic-theoretical considerations he argues that it is necessary to establish a contestatory democracy that goes beyond an electoral democracy. The former is characterised precisely by the fact that possibilities for action are presented both to the individual and to groups (Pettit 2000). But this still takes the classical liberal view: Pettit needs this (at least potential) moment of political action in order to be sure that arbitrary power is uncovered and a distinction can be made between the condition of benign hegemony and a condition of the greatest possible freedom (see here the pointed critique by Patchen Markell (2008) and Thorsten Thiel (2013). However, this means that political action is, on the one hand, curtailed instrumentally: neo-Roman republicanism needs political action *only* in order to uncover arbitrary power. The fact that democracy is a whole and distinctive way of life is not considered. On the other hand—and much more importantly—Pettit fails to grasp the preconditions of such political acting, of a contestatory democracy in theoretical, conceptual terms. He does not address the question regarding under which conditions political action occurs in the first place, under which conditions the various different forms of arbitrary power can actually be uncovered at all. Pettit looks

tradition of the negative freedom/positive freedom binary (see Berlin 2006 and Taylor 2008) in so far as he fails to acknowledge Arendt's main argument about the 'coincidence of politics and freedom' (Arendt [1961] 2006b: 147): only the *making of the experience* of political acting *will keep our awareness* of the fact that the legally guaranteed possibility to act politically is the *conditio sine qua non* of any freedom. This Arendtian perspective on the 'coincidence of politics and freedom' challenges the negative freedom/positive freedom binary. It does so by arguing that the decline of an active citizenry, the rise of the depoliticisation of public-political life, and the loss of the experience of acting politically in concert in a political community leads to a decline in our freedom in general, as it triggers both the degeneration of the democratic-political culture and processes of disintegration—even though the legal and constitutional order may stay intact (for a while). What Arendt refers to at this point is the problem, as Rahel Jaeggi calls it, of the ossification *of* political institutions and the negation of the element of political practice *within* political institutions (Jaeggi 2009: 542). Both developments result in the fact that rights and institutions which should enable political action become foreign to the citizens and are perceived as having grown apart from them.

### b. Arendt's Constitutional Theorem of Dehierarchisation and the Tradition of Radical Democracy

Arendt's political thinking needs to be distanced not only from the natural-law remnants of Habermas's co-originality theorem, but also from the agenda of 'radical democracy' (see Laclau and Mouffe 2001). From the perspective of radical democracy, (real) politics is not a practice of everyday life (see Rancière 2002: 29) but solely a mode of acting that arises in 'fugitive' (Wolin 1994: 11) moments.[73] For authors like Abensour, Rancière or Mouffe, democratic politics

only at the enabling of political action, which can then occur or not. Yet the central challenge of modern democracies lies precisely in this gap between enabling and occurring—and also the central problem of political freedom.

[73] Without being able to do justice here to the wide range of radical-democratic thought, radical democracy is characterised in my view by three central democratic-theoretical components. These components are: *first*, 'dynamisation' (Buchstein and Jörke 2003: 490), ie the emphasis on conflictive, agonistic political action; *secondly*, talk of the 'irreducability of antagonism' (Mouffe 2005: 12), which leads to considering the political from the perspective of the 'shareless' (Rancière 2002: 24); *thirdly*, politics as the politics of collective identities. However, in view of the political-theoretical consequences derived by the aforementioned authors from these components, a large degree of heterogeneity can be identified. Thus, for example, the relationship between institutions and politics is treated very differently by radical-democratic thinkers. While a commitment to democratic-institutionalised procedures can be found with Mouffe—not, however, reflected by Mouffe in democratic-theoretical terms—authors such as Žižek place the revolutionary act at the centre.

require the old order to be 'interrupted by a freedom which modernizes the equality on which every social order centers' (Rancière 2002: 29). Accordingly, authors like Ronald Beiner, Dana Villa, Andreas Kalyvas, Sheldon Wolin or Bonnie Honig, who have worked on Arendt intensively, point out those passages in her work that seem to highlight the importance of 'liberation' (Kalyvas 2004: 340), of 'initiatory, agonistic action' for which 'the ability to shine forth, to be glorious' (Villa 1996: 55) matters most—those passages that appear to appraise the 'radical break with our ordinary expectations' (Beiner 1984: 355) and which seem to argue that 'the moment of intervention is … the moment of politics' (Honig 1991: 111).[74] Although such a reading of her work finds some textual evidence, it neglects the order-preserving aspects in Arendt's work, and also fails to think them through conceptually or integrate them argumentatively. Arendt's political thoughts go beyond the radical-democratic agenda.

As inspiring as the radical-democratic perspective might be in detecting elements of depoliticisation within modern political systems, it is also problematic.[75] From my reading of Arendt's work, two major objections must be raised to the radical-democratic account—both of which help to specify the meaning of Arendt's constitutional-theoretical approach for political theorising. The first objection addresses the mode of political action that underlies radical-democratic theory; the second one questions the perception of political order and introduces an alternative understanding of politicisation.

### c. Arendt's Critique of Agonistic Understanding of Political Action

The radical-democratic perspective alleges the necessity and facticity of a political antagonism in terms of an 'us-them distinction'. An 'us' against the established order, an 'us' against the hegemonic powers. In this reading, every political order is conceived first and foremost as an order of domination; laws are primarily seen as an expression of the command of an established hegemonic power. The purpose of each and every 'democratic moment', therefore, is to break with this traditional order and 'the profound transformation of the existing power relations and the establishment of a new hegemony' (Mouffe 2005: 52). This results in an endless spiral of order and destruction. Durability is not the goal. Therefore, the radical-democratic emphasis on antagonism and the 'us-them distinction' refers to a mode of acting which is best described as 'acting against one another'.

As we have seen above, the problem with this mode of acting is that the 'we' is only constituted by an enmity against someone or something. Bound

[74] Bonnie Honig revised her position to some extent. See Honig 2007: 14.
[75] See, eg, Mouffe 2005 or Rancière 2002.

by this instrumental rationality, the 'revelatory quality of speech and action', which only 'comes to the fore where people are *with* others and neither *for* nor *against* them' (HC: 180), disappears. In addition, it is very likely that such a 'we' ignores even justifiable objections, proposals or critique from 'them'. Quite aside from the fact that this theoretical position cannot explain what holds a community together, such a political mind set emphasises assertiveness, rigidity and a certain degree of ignorance, rather than public and civic spirit and a sense of solidarity accompanied by the power of political judgement. Such thinking therefore contributes precisely to that 'loss of responsiveness' which in Patchen Markell's view represented for Arendt 'the most fundamental threat to democratic political activity' and advanced 'the erosion of the contexts in which action makes sense' (Markell 2006: 12 ).

In contrast, for Arendt democratic politics means the orientation towards understanding and the involvement of the other in a political process of opinion and judgement making. Consequently Arendt decisively rejects an agonal understanding of the political, because 'the commonness of the political world [is] not seen or experienced in the relationships between the citizens':

> In this agonal spirit, which eventually was to bring the Greek city states to ruin because it made alliances between them well-nigh impossible and poisoned the domestic life of citizens with envy and mutual hatred (envy was the national vice of ancient Greece), the commonwealth was constantly threatened. *Because the commonness of the political world was constituted only by the walls of the city and the boundaries of its laws, it was not seen or experienced in the relationships between the citizens*, not in the world which lay *between* them, common to them all, even though opening up in a different way to each man. (Arendt [1954] 1990b: 82, emphasis added)

If we apply these thoughts to the question discussed in section III.B.i. above with Ahrens and Förster of the basis of legitimacy of the (American) constitution, the result is as follows: the source of legitimisation for the (American) constitution lies less in the foundation and the promise than in the enabling of an 'acting with one another', which is developed in the execution of the power of judgement. The content of the reciprocal promise—the pre-colonial, the pre-revolutionary and the constituent—was the formal recognition of the grammar and syntax of 'acting with one another', ie the principles of the power of judgement and thus their simultaneous transformation into legal norms. The rationality of judgement, in turn, by no means results from its competence in solving problems—although Arendt trusts it more in political affairs than any other type of rationality. Its potential for rationality comes from the fact that it refers to an 'acting with one another' in which political freedom can become reality, thus preserving a durable and stable political order. If the 'meaning of politics is freedom' (WiP: 28), if political freedom can be *experienced* only in the execution of 'acting with one another', then the power of judgement is the condition for the possibility of this freedom. For Arendt it is by no means sufficient for the realisation of political freedom to rely solely on an intact political culture and to trust that citizens will not exaggerate with agonistic politics. Rather, the principles of the power of judgement must be integrated into the constitution as legal norms and inspire the formation of political institutions, thus preserving that 'context' in which 'acting with one another' can be experienced.

This connection outlined above marks the core of probably one of the most central passage of her work, in *Freiheit und Politik*,[76] where she discusses Montesquieu's distinction between philosophical and political freedom. In the course of this discussion Arendt focuses on Montesquieu's statement that 'political liberty consists in security' (*la liberté politique consiste dans la sûreté*) (Montesquieu [1748] 2002: 188); that this political liberty is not always and everywhere present, but rather only in political communities that have been defined by laws; without this security there is no political freedom, whereby freedom 'can consist only in having the power to do what one should want to do' (*la liberté ne peut consister qu'à pouvoir faire ce que l'on doit vouloir*) (Montesquieu [1748] 2002: 155). In order to understand the statement properly, which at first glance sounds like Hobbes and an upholding of the philosophical tradition of freedom of the will, and to reveal Montesquieu's 'real intention' (FuP: 216), Arendt argues that we need to 'read these sentences in a manner that puts emphasis *not* on the *power* (*pouvoir*) [emphasis added]—that one must have the *power* to do what one wants or ought to will—but on the *doing* (*faire*) [emphasis added]' (FuP: 216). And additionally we need to add that *doing* means much more in this context than merely executing one's will. If we do so, we arrive at a completely different understanding of political freedom from those with which the philosophical tradition provides us. Arendt writes accordingly:

> *Being free itself is inherent to acting, and the power to do so is guaranteed by the others as a security*. Freedom does not consist in an 'I will', which, as the case may be, can mean or contradict an 'I can', yet without questioning human freedom; being free only manifests itself with acting, so that not-having-the-power-to-act and not-being-free means the same thing, even if the (philosophical) freedom of will remains intact. In other words, political freedom is not identical with 'inner freedom' …; it [political freedom] depends on the fact that a free nation grants the space in which acting can have an impact and can become visible. (FuP: 216, emphasis added)

I have indicated elsewhere that I do not share the normative-ontological and anthropologising interpretation of Arendt's concept of politics, according to

[76] 'Freiheit und Politik' differs fundamentally from the version 'What is freedom', which was published in *Between Past and Future* and is merely an early version of Arendt's thoughts on the connection between freedom and politics. 'Freiheit und Politik' is a revised version of a lecture Arendt gave in May 1958 in Zurich. The passage I refer to is missing from 'What is Freedom' (Arendt [1961] 2006b) as well as from 'Freedom and Politics: A lecture', published in the *Chicago Review*. For the history of this paper, see the cogent comments by Ursula Ludz (FuP: 410).

which a person is free only when he actually acts. Being free begins with the fact that a person receives the constitutional guarantee from the other members of a community that he is allowed to act—if he likes; being unfree in political terms means that a person is denied of the power to act by other members of the polity, but it does not mean that he *does not act.* If a person does not act, he does not *experience* the full content of political freedom in the first instance—and in the long run this lack of political experience yields negative consequences. A free, durable and stable order depends precisely on an active and democratic public—also because by these means people learn about the significance and impact of basic political rights for their own lives.

The security derived from law lies in the fact that the possibility to act is guaranteed to each person—where necessary also by means of external coercion against those who wish to deny this right. When the law is understood in this manner, the demand for plurality in political affairs takes on a concrete form in space and time. Accordingly, Ernst Vollrath states that 'legitimate coercion'—in contrast to illegitimate coercion—serves 'the enabling of being able to act'. Laws are 'not boundaries …, but enabling reasons' (Vollrath 1977: 211): 'All individual laws of such a constitution enable room for acting, referring back to the constitution' (Vollrath 1977: 215). In other words: legitimate law opens up an enabling space in which political 'acting with one another' *can* be realised.

### d. Order and Politicisation

These last remarks point to another key difference between Arendt and the radical-democratic tradition: radical democratic theory also differs from an Arendtian view of politics with respect to the perception of political order. From an Arendtian perspective, radical-democratic theory does not take account of the enabling character of a democratic legal order. In the view of the radical democrats, rights and laws are conceptualised only as limitations of political action and political freedom. Laws and the legal order are interpreted only as an expression of hegemony. An example can be found with Sheldon Wolin: 'Thus a constitution in setting limits to politics sets limits as well to democracy, constituting it in ways compatible with and legitimating of the dominant power groups in the society.' (Wolin 1994: 14) Due to this assessment and evaluation of law and legal-political order, radical-democratic theorists argue for the 'interruption of order' and the 'ontological primacy of politics' (Laclau 1996: 62).

With Arendt, I consider this assessment of law and political order to be exaggerated and implausible. One crucial feature of democratic-political communities is that their constitutional order also seeks to preserve durable and reliable political 'contexts' (Markell 2006: 12) in which 'acting with one another' can happen. In this sense, law safeguards parts of the conditions that allow for an active citizenry. On this account, protest and resistance in democracies do not necessarily need to be great heroic deeds or a matter of life and death. But this is precisely what protest and resistance are in dictatorships, authoritarian and even totalitarian regimes, which beat down any sort of protest with violence and terror (EJ: 221). Michael Greven therefore writes of the 'possibility to politicize' (see Greven 2010: 68), guaranteed in democratic orders as their distinctive feature.

The possibility to politicise is the other side of the coin of a political-democratic legal order, and it reveals the facts both that a democratic legal order cannot be simply identified with hegemony, and that it is not plausible to reduce law to its restrictive and imperative account. Rather, we need to acknowledge the enabling dimension of a democratic legal order as *conditio sine qua non* for experiencing political freedom. Within democratic political orders, law *also* establishes an enabling space in which political clashes can be dealt with and the conflictive plurality appear. Radical democratic thinkers may concede this, but they fail conceptually to grasp the enabling dimension of order—especially with regard to the question of how to preserve the awareness of the significance of such a legal democratic order. Or, to phrase it in the words of Claude Lefort, some radical-democratic thinkers lack a proper sense of how much they and their thoughts owe to the 'democratic experience' (Lefort 1986: 20).

In contrast to the radical-democratic fundamental critique of political order, the possibility to politicise marks the distinctive feature of a free and reliable political order in the Arendtian sense. Themes, facts or existing regulations are seen as politicised when they can be traced and referred back to publicly and controversially discussed opinions. In this sense, politicisation is the constant updating of differences, the conversation with others, a discourse on differences and similarities (Thiel 2012: 204). The 'performative dynamics' which arise in the process of politicisation uphold political struggle and debate, and 'prevent the closure of the political system' (Thiel 2012: 179); instead they encourage reflection. Such a concept of politicisation must be positioned against the bureaucratisation, informalisation, economisation and juridification of the political decision-making process; the management jargon and the necessity-and-functionality talk alongside presentations of political programmes; a media landscape which depicts and helps to produce citizens as consumers, who are monadic and fundamentally politically disinterested; and a political culture which ignores not only the expressive and creative elements of political freedom, but also the public's desire for these elements. These factors all contribute to the depoliticisation of democracy, while strengthening the impression that there is no longer anything contingent in the political process—nothing that can be changed through democratic means of political engagement.

Furthermore, it is not the objective of politicisation to form a general will, but rather to initiate public awareness processes that create attention, a feeling of importance for political issues, and which, in the process, seek to counter the political disenchantment of broader parts of society. Such a concept of politicisation modelled in an Arendtian sense, therefore, differs fundamentally from the liberal notion of politicisation that reduces (and empties) its meaning to tough lobbying and mere interest politics; but it also differs from the radical-democratic variation of politicisation, which equates the term with the genuine reconstruction of the social and political framework (Žižek 2009: 48). In contrast to a radical-democratic version of politicisation, Arendt conceives the constitutional democratic-political order not as something that is opposed to politicisation; and therefore politicisation is not understood as a process that refers to something that lies beyond the existing order or is external to it. Rather, it is the democratic order itself, based on abstract normative principles such as political equality, political freedom and visible alternativity and conflictuality that enables politicisation as its inherent principle. To the degree to which a democratic-constitutional order is based on these abstract principles, it enters into promises that are meant to be realised within its framework. It is the distinctive feature, therefore, of a democratic-political order that these promises can be reclaimed and that these principles can be interpreted in new and differing ways in the course of political conflicts.

### e. Arendt and the Source of Authority of the Constitution

Additionally, only this enabling endows the constitution with its authority—and that in turn, finally, indicates another important difference from Habermas's thought: compared to the discourse-theoretical approach of Habermas, for whom the authority of the constitution is rooted in the fact that it is based on principles to which everyone, in principle, must be able to consent, Arendt takes a different path. The constitution symbolises a kind of consensus of a community. This consensus is not based solely on the generalised values and principles of a political way of life, but on the history of a republican-political dialogue that is remembered, presented and narrated as such (*cf* Michelman 1988: 1513). Through this manner of remembering and narrating, history becomes *our* history. Authority, Arendt now argues, is recognised 'wherever one feels that one owes one's existence to another (author, founder, engenderer, propagator)' (DT: 299). However, it is precisely for this reason that Arendt, in her writings about the political situation in America in the 1960s and 1970s, was convinced that the battle of the black population for equal rights is and must be a battle against the constitution. For in her view, the 'original crime' committed by the foundation of the American Republic is the '*tacit* exclusion' of the black population 'from the *tacit* consensus' (CD: 90f). All immigrants were welcome, but not the blacks. Since the black population had no political alternative to this battle for equal rights, the authority of the constitution was called massively into question and the Republic was in crisis. The possible way out sketched by Arendt is characteristic of her understanding of authority: racial segregation must be suspended and banned immediately at all levels of political and public life. At the same time, however, Arendt does not believe that the solution can be found solely by simply extending the *consensus universalis* to the black population in retrospect—as the Fourteenth and Fifteenth Amendments suggest. Too many times has the Supreme Court presented a different interpretation of the constitution, as she shows with reference to the case of *Dred Scott vs Sandford* in 1857. With respect to this case, she quotes from the verdict, which states explicitly that "'Negroes are not and cannot be citizens in the meaning of the federal constitution'" (CD: 91). The only thing that could help, in Arendt's view, would be 'an explicit constitutional amendment' that is 'addressed specifically to the Negro people of America', and which bluntly admits and condemns the past injustice and inhumanity, and, in doing so, underlines and assures the 'great change' (CD: 91).[77] Only by these means can the constitution become the symbolic expression of a new common consensus, including those who were formerly excluded, and thus develop into a history that also makes sense for those who were previously excluded. What gives the constitution authority, in Arendt's view, is not so much the supposed universalisation potential of its principles, but rather the degree to which the constitution as a whole symbolises a common, meaningful historical experience and empowers each person to act politically.

## C. Arendt's Demanding Concept of Political Enabling

### *i. On the Dialectic of Subjective and Objective Rights*

What precisely is meant by the enabling of political participation? If we ignore the fact that the question of law in Arendt's work has been neglected for a long time, her thinking is generally categorised as republican. Previous accounts appear to correspond with this image, in so far as they reach the conclusion that a constitution is legitimate when it safeguards the conditions of the possibility of political freedom. For Arendt, however, political freedom is not yet secured where one is guaranteed objective rights, including those of participation, but only where also subjective and fundamental rights can

[77] See also the thoughts of Bell and Bansal (1997). At the same time certain parallels can be drawn to those debates ignited by Ackermann's book *We the People*. The question that arises concerns the extent to which the civil rights movement was a 'constitutional moment' or not. (See Ackerman 1998, McMahon 2003, Graham 1990, Smith 1999.)

be considered guaranteed. Arendt's concept of enabling is a demanding one. This can be seen clearly from the fact that she describes the political realm upon which political freedom relies as a 'realm that *enjoyed power and was entitled to claim rights without possessing or claiming sovereignty*' (ÜR: 218; see also OR: 167). Power is based on consent and support; it is therefore dependent on the classic participatory rights of republicanism. Within that republican tradition, which represents a milestone for Rousseau, this participation is given priority over fundamental rights. An example of this is Rousseau's *aliénation totale.*

With reference to the American founding experience, Arendt speaks explicitly of an equality that abstains from any kind of subjectivity (see OR: 174). In acting, the agents assure each other of their status as legal subjects, ie they recognise each other as a *person.* I have already pointed out that the concept of 'person' originates from the language of theatre and refers to the masks of the actors. As such it has always had a double function. It hides the actor's own face, but it also makes it possible for the voice to sound through (see OR: 102). The status as a legal subject, which each guarantees mutually, thus enables participation and defence at the same time. It protects the area of subjectivity, private property, cultural origin, personal preferences, etc, on the one hand, and ensures by means of the mask, on the other hand, the freedom to speak as equal to equal. Without the protection of that which is hidden behind the mask and which characterises precisely the subjectivity of the individual, it is not possible for any sound emitted by one to reach the other.

If we attempt to specify these subjective rights, the first thing to mention would be the protection of the private sphere. In this context Arendt speaks generally of the fact that nobody can expose himself to public view at all times. The retreat into the private sphere is an elementary basic condition for political participation.[78] The protection of the private sphere is the condition for 'personal integrity', and thus secures the 'untaught and natural feeling of identity with whatever we happen to be by the accident of birth' (RoLR: 193). In social coexistence, the personal integrity of the individual is not only endangered by social conformism, but is also permanently exposed to the social potential for discrimination. Arendt believes that the phenomenon of discrimination in particular is typical of the social sphere and is explained by the simple fact that people separate themselves from others in the form of different groups for very different reasons, at times even for their own enjoyment:

> In any event, discrimination is as indispensable a social right as equality is a political right. The question is not how to abolish discrimination, but how to keep it confined within the social sphere, where it is legitimate, and prevent its trespassing on the political and the personal sphere, where it is destructive. (RoLR: 51)

[78] See inter alia ÜR: 121, as well as Moruzzi's work on the meaning of the mask for Arendt's thinking (Moruzzi 2000: 137ff) and van der Walt's considerations on the law and the space of appearance (Walt 2012: 63–66).

Arendt argues that social discrimination towards other social groups must be condemned and legally prohibited only when it occurs in the public sphere and shapes those 'public services ... that everyone needs in order to pursue his business and lead his life' (RoLR: 52). Arendt's examples are public buses, trains, squares, markets, hotels and restaurants. (Her example of discrimination discussed in 'Reflections on Little Rock', which extends into the private sphere, is the prohibition of mixed marriage, which she criticises vehemently (see RoLR: 53).)

But this prohibition of discrimination in the purely negative form outlined here is not sufficient as a condition for participation in political life. As Arendt makes clear, using the example of poverty, not only the negative protection against discrimination is required, but also positive enabling rights. She writes:

> So if we talk about equality, the question always is: how much have we to change the private lives of the poor? In other words, how much money do we have to give them to make them capable of enjoying public happiness? Education is very nice, but the real thing is money. Only when they can enjoy the public will they be willing and able to make sacrifices for the public good. To ask sacrifices of individuals who are not yet citizens is to ask them for an idealism which they do not have and cannot have in view of the urgency of the life process. *Before we ask the poor for idealism, we must first make them citizens: and this involves so changing the circumstances of their private lives that they become capable of enjoying the 'public'* (PRPI: 106f, emphasis added)[79]

The last sentence of the quotation in particular makes it clear that equality and civil rights must be accompanied directly by liberation from poverty. Civil rights can be fully used only on the basis of social rights. Participation is possible only where poverty has been 'repelled'. On the other hand, however, subjective rights can be considered to be secured only when one has the right to campaign publicly for their maintenance. According to Arendt, these fundamental civic rights are 'never realised where citizens are not guaranteed the right to active participation in public matters' (ÜR: 281).[80] This is directed just as much against republicanism—at least in its Rousseauean version—as it is against liberalism. I tried to illustrate clearly in chapter four how the *internalisation of the political* replaces the concept of *persona* in the course of the Rousseauism of the French Revolution, how ideas of morality and virtue take the place of law and end the determinate nature of law. But in Arendt's view the liberal reduction of politics as a guarantee of negative freedom is no less

[79] This no longer has anything to do with an 'elitist' concept of the public sphere in so far as the social prerequisites for political engagement are also reflected, as it were, by Arendt. (But *cf* Brunkhorst 2005: 178 and Brunkhorst 1994: 153.)

[80] John Sitton did not notice this merging of participatory and fundamental rights in his thoughts on council democracy in Arendt. He therefore concludes that Arendt 'did fail to recognize distinctions among the negative liberties and accordingly underestimated the importance of certain civil liberties for maintaining the possibility of participation' (Sitton 1987: 93).

dangerous. Not only does it lead to the self-declared autonomy of the state-political sphere, which develops a logic under the auspices of modernity, gathering up, step by step, negative freedoms that were once believed to be secure. Moreover, such a liberal approach triggers the depoliticisation of public life and the loss of the experience of political acting. This results in processes of disintegration and degeneration of the democratic-political culture, which have a negative impact on the stability of the legal order itself. Political participation cannot be secured without the rights of defence and withdrawal; fundamental basic rights without the right of participation are a chimera.

### *ii. On the Internal Reference of Constitution and Democratic Politics*

Law and politics are by no means made identical to each other by the dehierarchisation postulate, but rather continue to follow their own functional logic. The enabling of political freedom does not represent political freedom itself. Nor is the *enabling* the *guarantee* of political freedom. Arendt argues that there can be no guarantee of political freedom because the implementation of these supposed guarantees would smother the last remnants of 'unpredictability inherent in the very concept of freedom' (Arendt [1954] 1994f: 420).[81] Politics is about negotiation, compromise, dispute, rhetoric—and, of course, the organisation of majorities. A culture of debate and the occurrence of political discourse is neither unconditional nor the condition itself. Arendt makes it explicitly clear that the consent on the procedures of political debate does not extend to 'specific laws or even specific policies, even if they are the result of majority decisions' (CD: 88). Politics and political freedom do not resolve into law and legislation (*cf* also Heuer 1992: 339). The same is true conversely. The 'grandeur of court procedure' results precisely from the fact 'that it is concerned with meting out justice to an individual, and remains unconcerned with everything else—with the Zeitgeist or with opinions that the defendant may share with others and try to present in court' (CD: 99). A considerable part of the integrity of trials, therefore, is grounded on the norms of the court procedures, and on the legal means used to interpret the constitution and to

[81] Albrecht Wellmer pinpoints it very incisively when he stresses that political freedom includes 'moments of desire, experience, judgement and happy circumstances … which cannot—like the demand for general and equal rights—be universalised by a normative principle' (Wellmer 1999: 141). With a distinction between enabling and guarantee I agree with Wellmer's observation, but one objection I have to his interpretation is that he criticises this guarantee so radically that he loses his grip on Arendt's enabling postulate. (*Cf* on this point also Heuer 1992: 331.) The consequence is that Wellmer can only refer to Arendt's supposed 'anthropologically-founded universalism' (Wellmer 1999: 130) in order to hope that political acting is taking place at all. What he neglects, however, are Arendt's considerations on the enabling dimension of law itself.

solve legal issues.[82] In other words, the rationality of law is *also* guaranteed by the independence and autonomy of law itself and a juridical understanding of law (see also Rosenmüller 2013a: 358–93).[83]

However, from an Arendtian point of view, politics and law are interrelated. This interrelatedness has major consequences for the normative foundation of an Arendtian notion of constitutionalism. In contrast to Weber, the rationality does not originate in the law itself alone.[84] An essential part of the rationality of both spheres depends on the exchange and connection with the other in each case: the judiciary can only scrutinise legislation and, where applicable, declare its incompatibility with the constitutional principles; but it can never suggest laws itself or modify them. The law has authority only, but no power (see ÜR: 229ff). In addition, legal decisions must always be made on the basis of the constitution, whose authority, as worked out above, derives from its enabling character of political freedom. Arendt states that the 'Supreme Court decisions are constitutional interpretations' (CD: 91). This direct reference to the constitution results in the legitimacy of judicial decisions for the political process. Conversely, Arendt points out that decisions of the legislative and the executive branches must also be related to the constitution—otherwise people will lose their 'confidence in constitutional processes … [and] that is the withdrawal of consent' (CD: 89). For her, the constitutionality of political action(s) serves as a criterion of legitimacy, and in this manner points once again to the internal connection between law and politics.

How seriously Arendt takes this demand about the constitutionality of all political action can be seen from a central discussion in her thoughts on 'Reflections on Little Rock': there she explicates an argument made by the 'liberals' (RoLR: 53) which holds that the Confederate states' reference to their constitutionally guaranteed legislative competences is a 'ready-made subterfuge'(RoLR: 53). The legislative competences of the individual states should be curbed in order to strengthen Washington's competences, so that an end can be put to the legal racism of the Confederate states. Arendt also

[82] Arendt hints at this rationality of the law in a letter to Jaspers, in which she reports on her activity as a juror in court. Arendt writes, 'What is decisive is always what the facts say and the appropriate law, which the judge explains to the jury. The judge says repeatedly: "If you don't like the law, you as a juror cannot do anything; you must still decide in accordance with it. You can change the law as a 'citizen'; but not now, while you are a *juror*".' (Arendt/Jaspers: 701)

[83] In her Eichmann book in particular, Arendt defends the Jerusalem court against all demands made from the political sphere. A closed documentation neither of the National Socialist system nor of Jewish history can form the object of proceedings; rather, the function of the court is simply to 'pass judgement and to render justice' (EJ: 373).

[84] With reference to Arendt's Eichmann book, Linda Maxwell elaborated 'Arendt's affirmation of law's dependence on political action' (Maxwell 2012: 104.) I agree with this account, but I seek to demonstrate that there politics are *also* dependent on law in Arendt's thoughts.

finds the legal racism in the Confederate states unbearable. Yet she contends, against the 'liberals', that such a shift within the political system can be justified, if at all, 'only on grounds of legal argument and constitutional history' (RoLR: 54). Such arguments are neither 'abstruse' nor 'subterfuges', but 'are based on a principle which indeed was uppermost in the minds of the founders of the Republic' (RoLR: 54): governmental political actions are legitimate only when they are compatible with the rules of opinion and decision making as defined in the constitution. *Mutatis mutandis*, such measures can only ever be legitimised legally if one can present sound constitutional arguments. Otherwise these measures take an axe to liberal federalism and strengthen in a dangerous manner the already growing power at federal level.

However, in order to reveal the constitutional-theoretical account of her thoughts, we must also consider the bits and pieces of Arendt's 'constitutionalized extraordinary politics' (Kalyvas 2004: 15) and her 'agonistic understanding of law'—'an understanding that portrays contestation of legal rules and constraints as enabling of, not debilitating to, law's authority and responsiveness' (Maxwell 2012: 104). Such an 'agonistic understanding' is also traceable in 'Civil Disobedience', where Arendt discusses the question as to whether resistance against laws is justified when persons believe that these laws are unjust (see CD: 99). From the perspective of the judicature, 'freedom riders' break traffic laws just as much as the civil rights campaigners broke the laws of the Confederate states with their actions. According to Arendt, it lies in the 'nature of the law' (CD: 99) that it cannot allow such practices. At the same time, however, she states that such practices of breaking the law are legitimate when they comply with the 'spirit of the constitution'—even if not with its wording. At first glance, and reverting back to the American founding experience, it now appears as if the 'spirit of the constitution' is fulfilled when '*associations*' come about. In line with Tocqueville, one could argue that these 'associations' reflect the spirit of the constitution and must therefore be permitted (see Tocqueville [1835] 2002: 485–500). Stefan Ahrens argues along these lines, and assumes accordingly that Arendt could not formulate any barriers against undesirable social movements (see Ahrens 2005: 270).

From my point of view, this argument misses the key point of her thoughts in 'Civil Disobedience'. It is clear, precisely from her thoughts on totalitarianism, which potential for danger Arendt attributes to mass movements. The account in chapter four demonstrated the scepticism with which she viewed such movements. Now, in addition—and this is decisive for the further argumentation—political movements, according to Arendt, are no longer in compliance with the 'spirit of the constitution' when they force themselves into the public sphere with 'vandalism, violence, bad temper, and worse manners', but also when 'the growing infection of the movement with ideologies' (CD: 98) occurs. The politics-destroying content of ideologies lies in the fact that ideologies know and can explain everything before anyone has even expressed an opinion. Clinging to one or two axioms, they not only profess to explain the world but also consider all discourse to be superfluous. Instead of any form of political closure, civil disobedience should trigger public-political debate and bring dilemmas into the open (see CD: 81). The idea of political protest is to question the status quo and to start a political debate including many different perspectives and dissenting voices—and not just to undermine political order but to realise a free and equal one.[85] Accordingly, Arendt pronounces that political movements such as the civil rights movement are so 'important, not merely in numbers, but in quality of opinion' (CD: 76), that they cannot be disregarded even though they may break the law and contest it. However, political movements that *per se* distance themselves from the rules of the game of public debate, and which do not want to commit themselves to a political and subject-related discussion, are not compatible with the 'spirit of the constitution' (CD: 67). For Arendt, the 'right to dissent' is based on the consent to democratic-political means of working out conflict, which is necessary for upholding a political context in which a controversial public debate can take place. It is this consensus regarding the rules to which the public discourse should orient itself—and not the mere association as such—that is the expression of the 'spirit of American laws [and the] American legal system' (CD: 99). Therefore, from an Arendtian perspective, the political dimension of protest neither manifests itself in the moment of interruption, nor is protest within a democracy condemned to stick stubbornly to the letter of the law in order still to be called legitimate.

Undoubtedly, protest movements often have a confrontational, and even violent, side because—and Robin Celikates has rightly pointed to this in his work—protest frequently cannot develop its symbolic significance without factual confrontation (see Celikates 2013: 225): if one plans to erect a camp on a public square (to highlight the precarious situation of refugees and asylum seekers, or to demonstrate against global capitalism), or if one wishes to set up an autonomous centre in a building, which should convey a certain political symbolism, then one must also be prepared to defend this square or this building. Otherwise it remains merely an empty and ineffective expression of will. This is not a justification of violence and militancy, but simply addresses the misgivings about goodwill and the willingness to convert on the part of those who govern.

However, the confrontation may not represent the sole moment of the movement. Arendt argues that a willingness to engage with the political opponent with a view to reaching an understanding also needs to be part

[85] See here also Patchen Markell's reading of Arendt and his emphasis on political practices of responsiveness, by which I am inspired and with which I agree (Markell 2006: 12).

of the political repertoire. Otherwise, this opposition is absolute. And such an absolute opposition usually results in a political climate that undermines the reflective democratic practices within the protest movements. Discussion and debate then become a juggling of platitudes and ideological stereotypes that merely serve to reinforce one's own position, instead of contributing to the development of a political power of judgement. Furthermore, a political attitude is then formed that is *no longer able* to accept possible justified objections, compromises or alternative suggestions from the opposing side. Dispute, discourse and debate then become not only unnecessary, but also impossible. Instead of contributing to a public discourse and to political awareness building through protest, the conflict threatens to escalate. Thus, protest movements should also consider the democratic experience on which their practices are based. This experience is fuelled by the fact that a democratic political order is *also* characterised by its enabling character. In other words, it is characterised by the fact that it can interpret and realise acts of civil disobedience as acts of re-politicisation. That is of fundamental importance in so far as that in democracies, civil disobedience must not immediately become a great act of heroism or a question of life or death. But civil disobedience in dictatorships and authoritarian or even totalitarian regimes is precisely of this nature. The fear here is that every act of political protest will be stifled with violence and terror. Therefore, Arendt should be understood as a thinker of political order, who seeks to examine conceptually the importance of a durable and free political order in and through which political struggle and dissent can happen and be experienced.

### *iii. The Incomplete Dehierarchisation*

When Arendt states that the law should guarantee and preserve the rules of an intact political public, this might at first recall John Ely's pluralistic process theory. According to Ely, the courts must intervene when political minorities of whatever hue are threatened with being excluded from the political process. Ely calls this view of the courts a 'representation-reinforcing theory of judicial review' (Ely 2002: 181). I argued above that it is not sufficient for the enabling of political participation to secure access to the political arena in the negative sense of a prohibition on exclusion. Arendt has a much more demanding concept of enabling in her sights. Political equality as a condition of the possibility of political participation means more than the guaranteeing of equal political rights. Arendt argues for social rights, the protection of the private sphere and a prohibition on the discrimination of groups in the public space.

In his discussion with Ely, Ronald Dworkin raises a similar point and also argues for a more substantial concept of enabling political participation. Individuals, argues Dworkin, participate in the political sphere only if their moral and ethical independence is legally protected (see Dworkin 1994: 187–91). What is crucial now for our discussion is that Dworkin argues that only the judiciary can guarantee this enabling, because (i) only the judiciary has the necessary independence to decide on questions of moral value, and (ii) only it knows how to interpret the constitution correctly. An example that helps to illuminate Dworkin's position is the discussion on abortion, and the question as to who may decide whether a foetus is a 'constitutional person' and how. Dworkin argues that there are lobby groups that can better organise their interests and thus influence the political process. This can lead to decisions that are not in the interests of all citizens. Furthermore, the question under discussion regarding the legal status of a foetus is not a metaphysical or theological question but solely a juristic one. Judges must decide in cases of juristic dispute, because they are after all the ones who know the constitution best. (see Dworkin 1990: 69f.) The judge is the 'Hercules' (Dworkin 1994: 337f),[86] Dworkin writes, who knows how to find the right answer to a legal dispute. And Dworkin believes that this circumstance justifies the expansive role of the courts—also when it comes to guaranteeing the conditions of political participation. In brief: a plea for a 'strong judicial review' (Waldron 2006: 1350 and 1353).

Richard Bellamy disagrees with this view, arguing that Dworkin blurs the boundaries between law and legislation. Bellamy accuses Dworkin of turning judges and courts into superior participants in the political process. Dworkin's concept is therefore a prime example of 'legal constitutionalism' (Bellamy 2007: 13), which deprives politics of the air it needs to breathe and replaces the democratic process with the 'rule of judges' (Bellamy 2007: 79). Leaving aside the question of whether Bellamy's alternative model of 'democratising the judiciary' (Bellamy 2007: 83) is more convincing, this brief discussion exemplifies how the legal enabling of political participation can itself become a problem. Bellamy's objection is that Dworkin's claim for enabling political participation is implemented *in such a way* that it negates the autonomy of the political. Specifically, therefore, the problem is the manner in which so-called 'law rule' is understood and practised. How does Arendt approach this problem?

For American authors such as Dworkin, Michelman, Ackerman and Ely, the period of the Warren Courts, from 1953 to 1969, is of key significance. At this time the American Supreme Court, under Chief Justice Earl Warren, initiated important political reforms, or supported their progress by means of progressive constitutional decisions—that, at least, is a common interpretation.

86 For a balanced critique of Dworkin's description of the judge as Hercules, see also Cornell 1988: 1177ff.

Arendt's political-theoretical works fall precisely within this period, and she even makes references in some passages to the Warren Courts—most explicitly in 'Civil Disobedience' and 'Reflections on Little Rock'.[87] However, contrary to Dworkin and others, Arendt argues that 'it is now widely held that changes can be effected by law'. This opinion, for Arendt, seems 'to be based on an error about what the law can achieve and what it cannot. The law can indeed stabilize and legalize change once it has occurred, but the change itself is always the result of extra-legal action.' (CD: 80) 'Extra-legal' means that the changes do not occur as a result of judicial decisions, but rather as a result of political decisions or in terms of a transfer from the public sphere into the political-systemic sphere. The task and the function of jurisdiction are to serve justice and 'to act *intra vires*' (Goldoni and McCorkindale 2012: 122).

Yet this is the very core of the problem: how can a court render justice and *at the same time* respect the autonomy of the political sphere? Given the fact that for Arendt the preconditions for enabling people to participate in the political-democratic process are substantive and demanding, courts and judges need to be equipped to some extent with respective competences. On the one hand, therefore, jurisdiction and judicial review must result in more than just a mere 'testing whether legislation and administrative action had, indeed, come about in the right manner' (Klabbers 2007: 21). On the other hand, 'strong judicial review', ie the courts' 'authority to decline to apply a statute in a particular case … or to modify the effect of a statute … or to actually strike a piece of legislation out of the statute-book altogether' (Waldron 2006: 1354), would lead to a situation in which crucial political problems are decided by an administrative and juridical elite rather than by an active citizenry. The juridification of public-political life and the depoliticisation of democracy would be the negative consequences.

There is no doubt that Arendt gives us little by way of detail about how to solve this constitutional-theoretical puzzle and how she believes the dangers outlined can be avoided. Nevertheless, from the perspective of the postulate of dehierarchisation, it seems that Arendt argues for a 'system of weak judicial review', ie a system where the court's declaration of the incompatibility of a statute could 'initiate a fast-track legislative procedure to remedy the

[87] The core of her criticism of the judgment of the Supreme Court on the prohibition of racial segregation in public schools is that the burden is placed on the children to solve a social and political problem, an act that their parents and grandparents have failed to do. Furthermore, the law infringes the right of parents—in both black and white families—to select a school of their choice for their children. The prohibition of mixed marriages, on the other hand, remains incomprehensibly untouched, argues Arendt, even though this is a monstrosity of racial segregation that does indeed contravene human rights. Arendt's essay *Little Rock* provoked a wave of protest as soon as it was published, and indeed remains contentious to this day. For a detailed overview of the controversy, see Benhabib 2003: 146–55.

incompatibility' (Waldron 2006: 1354f). This at least corresponds to her conception of the Supreme Court as a common point of reference and avoids embracing a 'constitution of judges' (Arato and Cohen 2010: 161). The different political camps or parties involved in a conflict should not be simply overruled, outvoted or silenced by the court's decision. There are many legitimate and justifiable perspectives in a legal dispute, and the decisive question for the stability and durability of the political order is how to mediate between them. From an Arendtian perspective, therefore, it is highly questionable whether a form of legal constitutionalism and a system of strong judicial review is able to do so. Such an approach towards legal disputes upholds the sovereigntist tradition of the 'imperative conception of law', in this case the commands of the administrative and juridical elite, and ignores the demands of a vivid public-political life.

In contrast to strong judicial review, a supreme court's declaration of incompatibility seeks to actualise a common democratic consensus. This common consensus could be the new starting point for once again engaging in the issue of political debate. At least this is the kind of interpretation one can get from Arendt's thoughts on jurisdiction, found scattered throughout her work, and her strict distinction between power and authority. What Arendt regards 'as characteristic of' the Supreme Court is 'its being the seat of authority, and neither the locus of power (people) nor the source of law (the written constitution)' (Goldoni and McCorkindale 2012: 119). The people have power, but authority is with the courts. If both coincide, there will be despotism. The courts, therefore, use their authority in order to introduce a new level of debate to the conflicting parties, and by doing so, establish a new kind of relationship between them. And only such an understanding of justice and jurisdiction can uphold law as a relationship. In this case, the rationality of law does not result merely from the will of a well-educated administrative elite sticking to the rules of legal formalism, but from the ability of a legal decision to open up a new political space in which acting together can be realised and the 'syntax and grammar' (see OR: 165) of an active public-political sphere can be preserved. This seems to be more in line with Arendt's political-theoretical thinking, her scattered constitutional-theoretical remarks and the theorem of dehierarchisation, derived from her analysis of the decline of the European nation-state.

Nevertheless, my thoughts remain sketchy here and are more speculative and explorative in nature; there is not enough substantial information in her work for a genuine Arendtian answer to the question of how to translate her legal-philosophical and political-theoretical account into an appropriate and corresponding understanding of jurisdiction and juridical review—an understanding which would meet the requirements for a vivid public-political sphere and avoid the danger of ignoring the plurality and the connectivity of the political. Such deliberations would have been necessary in order to corroborate her claim for a dehierarchised version of constitutionalism in legal-theoretical terms. Certainly, it was never Arendt's concern to spell out such a legal theory. Nevertheless, it should have been, if she had taken the normative implications of her critical evaluations of political events more seriously and followed up on the diverse aspects of her thoughts on the relation between law and politics, constitution and democracy, order and freedom, preservation and action. A future theory of constitutionalism, however, inspired by Arendt's thoughts on politics and the political—and there are some good reasons for such a theory—needs to approach these legal-theoretical questions.

# *Conclusion*

IN RECENT DECADES, different interpretations of Arendt's work have competed with each other: a deliberative interpretation, an agonistic interpretation, or even a decisionist interpretation.[1] Paradigmatically, different concepts are drawn to the centre of each interpretation as key concepts: discourse and deliberation, intervention, responsiveness, the extraordinary and the self-institution of society. In this book I have argued for a new and different interpretation: Arendt as a thinker of political order. I have argued that her thoughts highlight the importance of a durable, stable and free political order in and through which political struggle, debate and 'acting with one another' can happen, appear and be experienced. In order for political freedom to become reality, it is essential to participate in these debates and public controversies. The history and present of political thought has produced different conceptions and understandings of political freedom. Political freedom as defined by Arendt means making the experience of 'having the power to act politically'. In order to be able to perpetuate such an experience of freedom, a corresponding institutionalised political order is required. The object of this book was to outline this order of freedom. The modern sovereign state cannot realise such an order. For this reason Arendt reflected throughout her life about an alternative form of political organisation, in and through which an order of freedom could be realised.

I have argued throughout this book that in such an institutionalised order, the concepts of law and politics are not only reconfigured but also stand in a dehierarchised relation to each other. They are connected in such a manner that political action is considered as legitimate when it is conducted in the mode of 'acting with one another', thus observing Arendt's 'syntax and grammar'. The task of the law is to ensure and to perpetuate these rules in the execution of political opinion and decision making. This does not make the law and politics identical. The *autonomy of the law* consists in the fact that only legal-technical means are allowed to be used in law finding, and only the statutory law is taken as a basis for decision. Conversely, the *autonomy of the political* results from the fact that the postulated mode of action is practised in a manner that corresponds with the conflict-ridden nature of political debates and controversies. 'Acting with one another' as a specific mode of political action

[1] For a decisionist interpretation see Jay (1978), as well as the profound critique of such an account by Honig (2007).

realises the 'methodical procedure' of the power of judgement. My remarks have shown that Arendt does not locate the power of judgement solely with the individual, but rather argues that it must be extended to political institutions in particular. This change in perspective is made possible by working out that the execution of the method of the 'operation of reflection' is the *conditio sine qua non* for the formation of the power of judgement. Only where the procedural steps of the power of judgement are followed can there be justifiable hope that the 'rationality of the power of judgement' will be accounted for in the political sphere as well. Yet the power of judgement is not identical to these procedural steps or principles. They cannot guarantee any power of judgement, but what they can do is *enable* the development of the power of judgement in the political. Without these procedural steps and principles, the 'politics of the power of judgement' must remain an illusion. Thus political freedom does not mean acting against or beyond the order; political freedom can only flourish where the ability to act is guaranteed by the others. The law is a central medium by which to express the guarantee, to perpetuate and to stabilise this ability. Arendt derives this political-normative backdrop not only from her analysis of the American political system, but also from her interpretation of those political institutions that were of paramount importance in the course of revolutions—the councils, sections, popular societies and town halls—all of which she refers to as 'organs of order' (OR: 275). It might well be the case, therefore, that a beginning is possible everywhere, but one can speak of a *free beginning* only where political action is exercised in the mode of 'acting with one another'.

The central purpose of my study was to show that Arendt—although she is critical of the modern state as a form of political organisation—is concerned with rethinking the idea of political order: the examination of the 'paradoxes of the nation-state' establish that the question of legal-political order is a key question in Arendt's thought. Arendt's theory of the decline of Europe's nation-state order means the collapse of the rule of law. In her view, therefore, the problem of order is also a problem of law. The inadequate treatment of minorities and the stateless in the inter-war period leads to the dissolution of the rule of law and constitutional statehood of the nation-states. The consequence is that authoritarian regimes take the place of democratic constitutional states, and moral standards and values begin to disappear along with the 'downfall of the nation-state' as a form of government. The decline of political and moral culture in Europe is therefore directly connected to the decline of the political-legal order of the nation-state. That is an initial, decisive step in the rather lengthy process of preparing for the extermination of human beings.

Two lines of argumentation lead from here, which are united once again in chapter four on the critique of popular sovereignty. The first line analyses the nation as a political idea of order. At the centre of this is the critique of Rousseau's *volonté générale*. The Rousseau discourse is an analysis of the understanding of the political that sees the solidarity and identity of the community arising from the moral integrity of the individual. This *internalisation of the political* is expressed most clearly in the 'patriotism of the heart', the nucleus of the nation. The second line is formed by the Weber discourse: the intention here is to reveal Weber's legacy in Arendt's considerations of the modern Continental European state and to discuss the concept of rational law. Arendt's critique of the imperialistic apparatuses of rule shows that she by no means wishes to dispense with the verifiability and reliability of the rational law of a modern constitutional state. At the same time, however, her thoughts on the political-institutional composition of the state make it clear that the rationality of law in the Continental European tradition, as outlined exemplarily by Weber, is based on systemic preconditions that promote a political culture and mentality within the citizenry that undermine precisely that which the rational law is supposed to preserve: the political order.[2] Since, with Weber, the rationality of the law depends on the law finding and law making being completely isolated from 'public opinion',[3] political massing, lack of experience and mistrust are strengthened, which then provides the perfect breeding ground for antidemocratic mass movement. Here the problem of order reveals itself in the form of a depoliticised political culture. At the same time it becomes clear that the modern state, as a form of political organisation, is unsuitable and incapable of realising the order of freedom. Thus Arendt considers the political order to be conceived against the modern state as a hierarchically structured and centralised power complex.

Law and politics are connected to each other internally. If, against this background, the law is supposed to be in a position to fulfil its order function, then it must reflect the needs of an active, democratic public sphere. Legitimate law is law that enables political action. Conversely, Arendt's Rousseau discourse reveals the dangers that occur when the law is equated to 'public opinion'. A legal order such as that described by Rousseau creates law with undefined content—law as commandment—and can be founded only on general clauses. Due to its supposedly moral supremacy of the highest sovereignty, the general will is *potestas legibus soluta*. This claim to sovereignty can be trans-

[2] Given Arendt's Weber discourse, we see how mistaken Jean Cohen and Andrew Arato are to assume that Arendt argues in favour of a 'constitution of judges' (Arato and Cohen 2010: 161) and for the primacy of law or even legal sovereignty. Instead, Jan Klabbers is right to argue that for Arendt, the idea of 'getting judges to solve political debates or fix political outcomes under the heading of judicial review would run into serious difficulties' (Klabbers 2007: 22). For a comparison of Arato and Cohen versus Klabbers, see also Goldoni and McCorkindale 2012: 118.

[3] A similar critique of the process of global governance has been set out recently by Jan Klabbers, with reference to Arendt. See Klabbers 2012.

lated into legal codes and anchored in the legal system *only* with the help of general clauses. A legal order in which key parts or fundamental principles are contained in general clauses is neither reliable nor trustworthy, and it is not rational. The rationality of law cannot be realised on the basis of any 'politics of the general will'. The law can unfold its order function only against the background of an accommodating understanding of the political, which respects the autonomy of the law. So while Arendt's political critique of popular sovereignty switches to a critique of the concept of law, her legal-political critique demands another, different concept of the political.

At the beginning of this book, I mentioned that the phrase 'order of freedom' is borrowed from Walter Benjamin's considerations in *Critique of Violence* (*Zur Kritik der Gewalt*). There Benjamin argues that a profound and fully-bodied critique of law could only be developed from a 'higher order of freedom' (Benjamin [1920–21] 1965: 41). A characteristic of Benjamin's political metaphysics is that he believes this higher order to lie in divine justice. If we ignore the apolitical monism of Benjamin's thought which, firm in the belief that 'divine justice' (*cf* Benjamin [1920–21] 1965: 57) truly is just, blends out human plurality, his thoughts flee into a metaphysical hope, as he thinks of the law as a substance. For Benjamin, each human law is the legally congealed expression of rule and domination. That is precisely why he reverts to the idea of divine justice, which should establish a kind of zero point of justice, into whose service all order-preserving forces of law could enter. The 'holy manifestation' (Benjamin [1920–21] 1965: 60) of the pure divine violence, which is obligated solely to the principle of justice, thus supposedly creates the way out of the eternal recurrence of repression and violence.

By comprehending—by means of her deconstruction of the concept of domination—power, and thus consent and support, as the core of the political, Arendt succeeds in thinking of the law as a relationship. For Arendt, the law is not the substance of the will to rule, but rather the formal-juristic description of relationships of consent. This makes it possible for her to differentiate forms of consent and support, and that means forms of speaking and acting—and thus of power—according to whether they help to establish a space in which political 'acting with one another' is possible and human plurality can be expressed and experienced politically—or not. In this way, Arendt frees herself from Benjamin's fatalism, which perceives only the force of domination behind every law.

Not even the punishment for the 'normal criminal' changes in any way the relationship character of the law. For precisely because of the fact that the criminal makes a deliberate exception for himself and also judges his crime as a crime, he agrees with the consensus of what is and what is not allowed in a community. Only when this consensus breaks does 'the penalty [become] an act of revenge or self-defence or the interest of a majority' (DT: 244).

Adolf Eichmann personifies such a breach. From Eichmann's perspective, the punishment is an act of revenge, and law is merely violence (*cf* EJ: 93f). The decisive aspect in the case of Eichmann is not that the supposed rules of the international community were broken—Arendt's thoughts on the interwar period in Europe have underlined all too clearly how far the European states were removed from a common consensus. Of much greater importance, according to Arendt, is the circumstance that the National Socialist policy of extermination attempted to establish completely new rules.[4] Because Eichmann contributed to this project, Arendt believes that he has forfeited his life. This is clear from her ideal judgment on the final pages of *Eichmann in Jerusalem*:

> And just as you supported and carried out a policy of not wanting to share the earth with the Jewish people and the people of a number of other nations—as though you and your superiors had any right to determine who should and who should not inhabit the world—we find that no one, that is, no member of the human race, can be expected to want to share the earth with you. That is the reason, and the only reason, you must hang. (EJ: 279)

This is not a final moral verdict, but rather a political-legal plea for the consensus of a future international community. The purpose of this ideal judgment is that Arendt wanted to make a political norm out of plurality as a 'fact' of human coexistence. This norm should express the consensus of a future international community and represent the first step in turning humanity into a political concept. Only against the background of such a consensus and the development of corresponding political institutions can one speak of the 'right to have rights' as a lived reality.

Authors such as Seyla Benhabib have rightly pointed to the fact that Arendt presents no morally reasonable argument as to why the individual might have any right to claim the 'right to have rights'. One can see a deficit here, but should be aware of the circumstance that the question of the moral reason for human rights is not Arendt's question. Arendt is concerned with the political conditions under which any 'right to have rights' can be secured at all. She is not concerned with the reason for, but rather with the working out of that political context in which each person is guaranteed a place in the world. Accordingly, we will not find modes of argumentation in the style of the foundational universalism of moral philosophy, in which the recognition of others

[4] In *Personal Responsibility under Dictatorship* she argues that the political-legal dimension of the National Socialist policy of extermination can be understood only when one recognises that the crimes of the National Socialists were committed within the framework of a lawful order. A juristic cornerstone of the Nazi order was, simply put, '"Thou shalt kill", not thy enemy but innocent people who were not even potentially dangerous' (Arendt [1964] 2003e: 42). Her argument is that the Nazis gave their juristic blessing to a policy of extermination and eradication, indeed established extermination as a legal standard.

derives from the grammar of reciprocity. What can be found with Arendt, as I have attempted to show, is a political normativity that describes the acknowledgement of the other as *conditio sine qua non* of a stable, durable and free political order. With this in mind, it should have become clear that, according to Arendt, the Continental European tradition of the idea of state and popular sovereignty is not in a position to preserve a permanent and stable order precisely because it can neither realise nor legally secure the acknowledgement of the other. Identity and solidarity within a community organised on the principle of sovereignty can be generated only via the mechanism of inclusion and exclusion. The consequence is that the acknowledgement of the other as the other cannot be reflected in everyday political life. The other finds acknowledgement only as my image. With such an understanding of the political, 'a secure peace is as utopian as the squaring of the circle' (TPR: 229) in a globalised world. According to Arendt, in contrast, a permanent and stable order can be based only on the acknowledgement of plurality. And even though the exclusion of the other, indeed his extermination, is a fact documented by the twentieth century like no century before, this exclusion and extermination has never led to a durable and stable order. A durable and stable order can only be a free one. That is the core of Arendt's political normativity. But this is not a truth, rather a possible narrative of a common conviction.

# *Bibliography*

## WORKS OF HANNAH ARENDT


Arendt, H (1946) 'The Nation' 1 *The Review of Politics* 8, 138.

—— (1958) *Die ungarische Revolution und der totalitäre Imperialismus* (München, Piper).

—— (1960) *Von der Menschlichkeit in finsteren Zeiten. Rede über Lessing* (München, Piper)

—— (1963) *On Revolution* (New York, NY, Viking).

—— (1970) *On Violence* (New York, NY, Harvest Books).

—— (1972a) 'Civil Disobedience' in H Arendt, *Crises of the Republic* (New York, NY, Harvest Books).

—— (1972b) 'Thoughts on Politics and Revolution. A Commentary' in H Arendt, *Crises of the Republic* (New York, NY, Harvest Books).

—— (1972c) 'Lying in Politics' in H Arendt, *Crises of the Republic* (New York, NY, Harvest Books).

—— (1977) 'Public Rights and Private Interests' in M Mooney and F Stuber (eds), *Small Comforts for Hard Times: Humanists on Public Policy* (New York, NY, Columbia University Press).

—— (1989 [1968]) 'Walter Benjamin' in H Arendt (U Lutz ed), *Menschen in finsteren Zeiten* (München, Piper).

—— (1990a [1948]) *Was ist Existenz-Philosophie?* (Frankfurt, Hain). Arendt, Hannah. 1990. "Philosophy and Politics." *Social Research* 57 (Spring), 73–103.

—— (1990b [1954]) 'Philosophy and Politics' *Social Research* 57 (Spring), 73–103.

—— (1994a [1951]) *Origins of Totalitarianism* (New York, NY, Harvest Books).

—— (1994b [1944]) 'Foreign Affairs in the Foreign-Language Press' in H Arendt (J Kohn ed), *Essays in Understanding 1930–1954. Formation, Exile, and Totalitarianism* (New York, NY, Schocken).

—— (1994c [1945]) 'Power Politics Triumphs' in H Arendt (J Kohn ed), *Essays in Understanding 1930–1954. Formation, Exile, and Totalitarianism* (New York, NY, Schocken).

—— (1994d [1948/1949]) 'Rand School Lecture' in H Arendt (J Kohn ed), *Essays in Understanding 1930–1954. Formation, Exile, and Totalitarianism* (New York, NY, Schocken).

—— (1994e [1954]) 'Concern with Politics in Recent European Philosophical Thought' in H Arendt (J Kohn ed), *Essays in Understanding 1930–1954. Formation, Exile, and Totalitarianism* (New York, NY, Schocken).

—— (1994f [1954]) 'Europe and the Atom Bomb' in H Arendt (J Kohn ed), *Essays in Understanding 1930–1954. Formation, Exile, and Totalitarianism* (New York, NY, Schocken)

—— (1998a [1958]) *The Human Condition* (Chicago, IL, Chicago University Press).

—— (1998b [1979]) 'Diskussionen mit Freunden und Kollegen in Toronto (November 1972)' in H Arendt (R Beiner and U Ludz eds), *Ich will verstehen. Selbstauskünfte zu Leben und Werk* (München, Piper).

—— (1998c [1964]) 'Fernsehgespräche mit Günter Gaus (Oktober 1964)' in H Arendt (U Ludz ed), *Ich will verstehen. Selbstauskünfte zu Leben und Werk* (München, Piper).

—— (1998d [1970]) *Macht und Gewalt* (München, Piper).

—— (1998e [1970]) 'Interview mit Hannah Arendt. Von Adelbert Reif' in H Arendt (ed), *Macht und Gewalt* (München, Piper).
—— (2000a [1963]) *Über die Revolution* (München, Piper).
—— (2000b [1956]) 'Was ist Autoriät?' in H Arendt (U Ludz ed), *Zwischen Vergangenheit und Zukunft. Übungen im politischen Denken I* (München, Piper).
—— (2000c [1958]) 'Die Krise in der Erziehung' in H Arendt (U Ludz ed), *Zwischen Vergangenheit und Zukunft. Übungen im politischen Denken I* (München, Piper).
—— (2000d [1958]) 'Kultur und Politik' in H Arendt (U Ludz ed), *Zwischen Vergangenheit und Zukunft. Übungen im politischen Denken I* (München, Piper).
—— (2000e [1964]) 'Wahrheit und Politik' in H Arendt (U Ludz, ed), *Zwischen Vergangenheit und Zukunft. Übungen im politischen Denken I* (München, Piper).
—— (2002 [1958]) *Vita activa oder Vom tätigen Leben* (München, Piper).
—— (2003a [1951]) *Elemente und Ursprünge totaler Herrschaft. Antisemitismus, Imperialismus, totale Herrschaft* (München, Piper).
—— (2003b) 'Some Questions of Moral Philosophy' in H Arendt (J Kohn, ed), *Responsibility and Judgement* (New York, NY, Random House).
—— (2003c [1975]) 'Home to Roost' in H Arendt (J Kohn ed), *Responsibility and Judgement* (New York, NY, Random House).
—— (2003d [1959]) 'Reflections on Little Rock' in H Arendt (J Kohn ed), *Responsibility and Judgement* (New York, NY, Random House).
—— (2003e [1964]) 'Personal responsibility und dictatorship' in H Arendt (J Kohn ed), *Responsibility and Judgement* (New York, NY, Random House).
—— (2006a [1963]) 'Nationalstaat und Demokratie' in 2 *Hannah Arendt.net-Zeitschrift für politisches Denken* 1.
—— (2006b [1961]) 'What is Freedom?' in H Arendt (ed), *Between Past and Future* (New York, NY, Penguin Classics.
—— (2006c [1963]) *Eichmann in Jerusalem. A report on the banality of Evil* (New York, NY, Penguin).
—— (2007a [1953]) 'The Great Tradition I. Law and Power' 3 *Social Research* 74, 713.
—— (2007b [1953]) 'The Great Tradition II. Ruling and Being Ruled' 4 *Social Research* 74, 941.
—— (2007c [1950]) (J Kohn ed) *The Promise of Politics* (New York, NY, Random House).
Arendt, H and Jaspers, K (L Köhler and H Saner eds) (2001 [1985]) *Briefwechsel 1926–1969* (München, Piper).
Arendt, H (J Kohn and RH Feldmann eds) (2007) *The Jewish Writings* (New York, NY, Schocken).
Arendt, H (U Ludz, ed) (2003 [1993]) *Was ist Politik. Fragmente aus dem Nachlaß* (München, Piper).
Arendt, H (U Ludz and I Nordmann eds) (2003) *Denktagebuch*, vols 1 and 2 (München, Piper).

## SECONDARY LITERATURE AND OTHER WRITINGSS

Abensour, M (2012) 'Die rebellierende Demokratie' 5 *Blätter für deutsche und internationale Politik* 57, 90.
Ackerman, B (1989) 'Constitutional Politics/Constitutional Law' 3 *Yale Law Journal* 99, 453.
—— (1998) *We the People. Transformations*, vol 2 (Boston, MA, Harvard University Press).

Adorno, TW (1997a [1931]) 'Die Aktualität der Philosophie' in R Tiedemann (ed), *Philosophische Frühschriften, Gesammelte Schriften*, vol 1 (Frankfurt, Suhrkamp).
—— (1997b [1951]) 'Minima Moralia. Reflexionen aus dem beschädigten Leben' in TW Adorno (R Tiedemann ed), *Gesammelte Schriften*, vol 4 (Frankfurt, Suhrkamp).
—— (1997c [1966]) 'Negative Dialektik' in TW Adorno (R Tiedemann ed), *Gesammelte Schriften*, vol 6 (Frankfurt, Suhrkamp).
—— (1997d [1958]) 'Der Essay als Form' in TW Adorno (R Tiedemann ed), *Noten zur Literatur, Gesammelte Schriften*, vol 11 (Frankfurt, Suhrkamp).
Agamben, G (1999) *Remnants of Ausschwitz* (New York, NY, Zone York).
—— (2002) *Homo sacer. Sovereign Power and Bare Life* (Stanford, CA, Stanford University Press).
—— (2005) *State of Exception* (Chicago, IL, The University of Chicago Press).
Ahrens, S (2005) *Die Gründung der Freiheit. Hannah Arendts politisches Denken über die Legitimität demokratischer Ordnungen* (Frankfurt, Peter Lang Publishing).
Allen, A (2010) 'Power, Subjectivity, and Agency: Between Arendt and Foucault' 2 *International Journal of Philosophical Studies* 10, 143.
Alte. Synagoge (ed) (1997) *Hannah Arendt. Lebensgeschichte einer deutschen Jüdin* ... (Essen, Klartext Verlagsgesellschaft).
Anderson, B (1996) *Die Erfindung der Nation. Zur Karriere eines erfolgreichen Konzepts* (Frankfurt, Campus).
Anter, A (1995) *Max Webers Theorie des modernen Staates. Herkunft, Struktur und Bedeutung* (Berlin, Duncker & Humblodt).
—— (2004) 'Modernität und Ambivalenz in Georg Jellineks Staatsdenken' in A Anter (ed), *Die normative Kraft des Faktischen. Das Staatsverständnis Georg Jellineks* (Baden-Baden, Nomos).
—— (2007) *Die Macht der Ordnung. Aspekte einer Grundkategorie des Politischen* (Tübingen, Mohr Siebeck).
—— (2012) *Theorien der Macht. Zur Einführung* (Hamburg, Junius).
Arato, A and Cohen, JL (2010) 'Banishing the Sovereign. Internal and External Sovereignty' in S Benhabib (ed), *Politics in Dark Times: Encounters with Hannah Arendt* (Cambridge, Cambridge University Press).
Baehr, P (2001) 'The Grammar of Prudence. Arendt, Jaspers, and the Appraisal of Max Weber' in SE Aschheim (ed), *Hannah Arendt in Jerusalem* (Los Angeles, University of California Press).
—— (2005) 'Personal Dilemma or Intellectual Influence? The Relationship between Hannah Arendt and Max Weber' 1 *Max Weber Studies* 5, 125.
Balibar, É (2004) 'Is a Philosophy of Human Civic Rights Possible? New Reflections on Equaliberty' 2–3 *The South Atlantic Quarterly* 103, 311.
—— (2007) '(De)constructing the Human as Human Institution. A Reflection on the Coherence of Hannah Arendt's Practical Philosophy' in Heinrich-Böll-Stiftung (ed), *Hannah Arendt: Verborgene Tradition—Unzeitgemäße Aktualität?* (Berlin, Akademie Verlag).
Baluch, F (2014) 'Arendt's Machiavellian moment' in 2 *European Journal of Political Theory* 13, 154.
Barley, D (1990) *Hannah Arendt. Einführung in ihr Werk* (München, Alber).
Beiner, R (1984) 'Action, Natality, and Citizenship: Hannah Arendt's Concept of Freedom' in Z Pelczynski and J Gray (eds), *Conceptions of Liberty in Political Philosophy* (New York, NY, Continuum International).
—— (1985) 'Hannah Arendt über das Urteilen' in H Arendt (R Beiner ed), *Das Urteilen. Texte zu Kants Politischer Philosophie* (München, Piper).
Bell, D and Bansal, P (1988) 'The Republican Revival and Racial Politics' 8 *Yale Law Journal: Symposium on the Republican Revival* 97, 1609.

Bellamy, R (2006) 'Sovereignty, Post-Sovereignty and Pre-Sovereignty: Three Models of State, Democracy and Rights within the EU' in N Walker (ed), *Sovereignty in Transition* (Oxford, Hart Publishing).

—— (2007) *Political Constitutionalism. A Republican Defence of the Constitutionality of Democracy* (Cambridge, Cambridge University Press).

Bemal, A (2009) 'A Revolution in Law's Republic: Arendt and Michelman in Dialogue' 1 *HannahArendtNet* 5, 1–19.

Benhabib, S (1992a) *Kritik, Norm und Utopie. Die normativen Grundlagen der Kritischen Theorie* (Frankfurt, Fischer).

—— (1992b) 'Models of Public Space' in S Benhabib (ed), *Situating the Self: Gender, Community and Postmodernism in Contemporary Ethics* (Cambridge, Polity Press).

—— (1995a) 'Modelle des "öffentlichen Raums". Hannah Arendt, die liberale Tradition und Jürgen Habermas' in S Benhabib (ed), *Selbst im Kontext* (Frankfurt, Suhrkamp).

—— (1995b) 'Über das Urteilen und die moralische Grundlagen der Politik im Denken Hannah Arendts' in S Benhabib (ed), *Selbst im Kontext* (Frankfurt, Suhrkamp).

—— (2003) *The Reluctant Modernism of Hannah Arendt* (Lanham, Rowman & Littlefield).

—— (2004) *The Rights of Others* (Cambridge, Cambridge University Press).

—— (2006) *Hannah Arendt. Die melancholische Denkerin der Moderne* (Frankfurt, Suhrkamp).

—— (2007) 'Another Universalism: On the Unity and Diversity of Human Rights' 2 *Proceedings and Addresses of the American Philosophical Association* 81, 7.

Benjamin, W (1961 [1943]) 'Geschichtsphilosophische Thesen' in W Benjamin and S Unseld (eds), *Illuminationen. Ausgewählte Schriften* (Frankfurt, Suhrkamp).

—— (1965 [1920–21]) 'Zur Kritik der Gewalt' in W Benjamin (ed), *Zur Kritik der Gewalt und andere Aufsätze. Mit einem Nachwort versehen von Herbert Marcuse* (Frankfurt, Suhrkamp).

—— (1980 [1936]) 'Das Kunstwerk im Zeitalter seiner technischen Reproduzierbarkeit' in W Benjamin (R Tiedemann and H Schweppenhäuser eds), *Abhandlungen, Gesammelte Schriften,* vol 1 (Frankfurt, Suhrkamp).

—— (P Demetz ed) (1986 [1978]) 'Reflections: Essays, Aphorisms, Autobiographical Writings' (New York, NY, Schocken).

—— (R Tiedemann and H Schweppenhäuser eds) (1991 [1928–1929, 1934–1940]) *Das Passagen-Werk. Aufzeichnungen und Materialen, Gesammelte Schriften,* vol 1 (Frankfurt, Suhrkamp).

Berlin, I (2006) *Freiheit: Vier Versuche* (Frankfurt, Fischer).

Bernstein, RJ (1986a) 'Judging—the Actor and the Spectator' in RJ Bernstein (ed), *Philosophical Profiles: Essays in a Pragmatic Mode* (Philadelphia, PA, University of Pennsylvania Press).

—— (1986b) 'Rethinking the Social and the Political' in RJ Bernstein (ed), *Philosophical Profiles: Essays in a Pragmatic Mode* (Philadelphia, PA, University of Pensylvania Press).

—— (2005) 'Hannah Arendt on the Stateless' 1 *Parallax* 11, 46–60.

—— (2007) 'Sind Hannah Arendts Reflexionen über das Böse noch relevant?' 4 *Deutsche Zeitschrift für Philosophie* 55, 573.

Bielefeldt, H (1993) *Wiedergewinnung des Politischen. Eine Einführung in Hannah Arendt* (Würzburg, Königshaussen & Neumann).

Bilsky, L (2001) 'Between Justice and Politics: The Competition of Storytellers in the Eichmann Trial' in SE Aschheim (ed), *Hannah Arendt in Jerusalem* (Los Angeles, CA, University of California Press).

—— (2004) *Transformative Justice. Israeli Identity on Trial* (Ann Arbor, MI, The University of Michigan Press).

Birmingham, P (2006) *Hannah Arendt and Human Rights. The Predicament of Common Responsibility* (Bloomington, IN, Indiana of University Press).

—— (2007) 'The An-Archic Event of Natality and the "Right to have rights"' in Heinrich-Böll-Stiftung (ed), *Hannah Arendt: Verborgene Tradition—Unzeitgemäße Aktualität?* (Berlin, Akademie Verlag).

Bluhm, H (2002) *Die Ordnung der Ordnung. Das politische Philosophieren von Leo Strauss* (Berlin, Akademie Verlag).

—— (2011) 'Niccolò Machiavelli' in W Heuer/B Heiter/S Rosenmüller (eds): *Arendt-Handbuch. Leben—Werk—Wirkung* (Stuttgart, Metzler Verlag), 198–99.

Bobbio, N (1987) 'Max Weber und Hans Kelsen' in M Rehbinder and KP Tieck (eds), *Max Weber als Rechtssoziologie* (Berlin, Duncker & Humblodt).

Bowen-Moore, P (1989) *Hannah Arendt's Philosophy of Natality* (New York, NY, St Martin's Press).

Bradshaw, L (1989) *Acting and Thinking: The political thought of Hannah Arendt* (Toronto, University of Toronto Press).

Breen, K (2007) 'Violence and power: A critique of Hannah Arendt on the "political"' 3 *Philosophy and Social Criticism* 33, 343.

—— (2012) 'Law beyond Command? An Evaluation of Arendt's Understanding of Law' in M Goldoni and C McCorkindale (eds) *Hannah Arendt and the Law* (Oxford, Hart Publishing), 15–34.

Breier, KH (2001) *Hannah Arendt zur Einführung* (Hamburg, Junius).

Breuer, S (1993) 'Max Webers Staatssoziologie' 2 *Kölner Zeitschrift für Soziologie und Sozialpsychologie* 45, 199.

—— (1998) *Der Staat. Entstehung, Typen, Organisationsstadien* (Reinbeck, Rowohlt).

Breuer, S, Treiber, H and Walther, M (1982) 'Entstehungsbedingungen des modernen Anstaltsstaates. Überlegungen im Anschluss an Max Weber' in S Breuer and H Treiber (eds), *Entstehung und Strukturwandel des Staates* (Opladen, Westdeutscher Verlag).

Brubaker, R (1994) *Staats-Bürger* (Hamburg, Hamburger Edition).

Brumlik, M (2007) 'Zwischen Polis und Weltgesellschaft. Hannah Arendt in unserer Gegenwart' in Heinrich-Böll-Stiftung (ed), *Hannah Arendt: Verborgene Tradition—Unzeitgemäße Aktualität?* (Berlin, Akademie Verlag).

Brunkhorst, H (1994) 'Brot und Spiele? Hannah Arendts zweideutiger Begriff von der Öffentlichkeit' in U Kubes-Hofmann (ed), *Sagen, was ist. Zur Aktualität Hannah Arendts* (Wien, Verlag für Gesellschaftskritik).

—— (1996) 'Sind Menschenrechte Aporien? Kritische Bemerkungen zu einer These Hannah Arendts' 3 *Kritische Justiz* 29, 335.

—— (1999) *Hannah Arendt* (München, CH Beck).

—— (2005) 'Equality and elitism in Arendt' in DR Villa (ed), *The Cambridge Companion to Hannah Arendt* (Cambridge, Cambridge University Press).

Buchstein, H and Jörke, D (2003) 'Das Unbehagen an der Demokratietheorie' 4 *Leviathan* 31, 470.

Calhoun, C (1997) 'Plurality, Promises, and Public Spaces' in C Calhoun and J McGowan (eds), *Hannah Arendt and the Meaning of Politics* (Minneapolis, MN, University of Minnesota Press).

Canovan, M (1978) 'The Contradictions of Hannah Arendt's Political Thought' 1 *Political Theory* 6, 5.

—— (1990) 'Socrates or Heidegger? Hannah Arendt Reflections on Philosophy and Politics' 1 *Social Research* 57, 135.

—— (1992) *Hannah Arendt: A Reinterpretation of Her Political Thought* (Cambridge, Cambridge University Press).

—— (1998) 'Lasting institutions. Arendtian Thoughts on Nations and Republics' 2 *Graduate Faculty Philosophy Journal* 21, 133.

Castoriadis, C (1990) 'Gesellschaft als imaginäre Institution. Entwurf einer politischen Philosophie' (Frankfurt, Suhrkamp).

Celikates, R (2013) 'Ziviler Ungehorsam zwischen Gewaltfreiheit und Gewalt' in F Martinsen and O Flügel-Martinsen (eds), *Gewaltbefragungen. Beiträge zur Politischen Philosophie der Gewalt* (Bielefeld, transcript).

Cohen, JL (1996) 'Rights, Citizenship, and the Modern Form of the Social: Dilemmas of Arendtian Republicanism' 2 *Constellations* 3, 164.

—— (2007) 'Sovereignty and Rights: Thinking with and beyond Hannah Arendt' in Heinrich-Böll-Stiftung (ed), *Hannah Arendt: Verborgene Tradition—Unzeitgemäße Aktualität?* (Berlin, Akademie Verlag).

Coing, H (1969) *Grundzüge der Rechtsphilosophie* (Frankfurt, De Gruyter).

Cornell, DL (1988) 'Institutionalization of Meaning, Recollective Imagination and the Potential for Transformative Legal Interpretation' 4 *University of Pennsylvania Law Review* 136, 1135.

Curtis, K (1999) *Our sense of the Real. Aesthetic Experience and Arendtian Politics* (Ithaca, NY, Cornell University Press).

D'Entrèves, MP (1994) *The Political Thought of Hannah Arendt* (London, Routledge).

Deitelhoff, N (2007) 'Was vom Tage übrig blieb. Inseln der Überzeugung im vermachteten Alltagsgeschäft internationalen Regierens' in P Niesen and B Herborth (eds) *Anarchie der kommunikativen Freiheit. Jürgen Habermas und die Theorie der internationalen Politik* (Frankfurt, Suhrkamp), 26.

Delos, J-T (1944) *La Nation*, 2 vols (Montreal, Edition de l'Arbre)

Derrida, J (1991) *Gesetzeskraft. Der 'mystische Grund der Autorität'* (Frankfurt, Suhrkamp).

Dewey, J (1985 [1927]) 'The Public and its Problems' in JA Boydston (ed), *John Dewey. The Later Works 1925–1935*, vol 2: *1925–1927* (Carbondale, IL, Southern Illinois University Press).

Diner, D (ed) (1988) *Zivilisationsbruch: Denken nach Auschwitz* (Frankfurt, Fischer).

Disch, L (1994) *Hannah Arendt and the Limits of Philosophy* (Ithaca, NY/London, Cornell University Press).

—— (2011) 'How could Hannah Arendt glorify the American Revolution and revile the French? Placing On Revolution in the historiography of the French and American Revolutions' 3 *European Journal of Political Theory* 10, 350.

Dolan, FM (2005) 'The paradoxical liberty of bio-power. Hannah Arendt and Michel Foucault on modern politics' 3 *Philosophy and Social Critism* 31, 369.

Dworkin, R (1990) 'Taking Rights Seriously in the Abortion Case' 1 *Ratio Juris* 3, 68.

—— (1994) 'Gleichheit, Demokratie und die Verfassung: Wir, das Volk, und die Richter' in UK Preuß (ed), *Zum Begriff der Verfassung. Die Ordnung des Politischen* (Frankfurt, Fischer).

—— (1998) *Law's Empire* (Oxford, Harvard University Press).

—— (2005) *Taking rights seriously* (Cambridge, Harvard University Press).

—— (2006) *Justice in robes* (Cambridge, Harvard University Press).

Elias, N (1997 [1939]) *Über den Prozess der Zivilisation. Soziogenetische und psychogenetische Untersuchungen*, 2 vols (Frankfurt, Suhrkamp).

Ely, JH (2002) *Democracy and Distrust. A Theory of Juridical Review* (Cambridge, Harvard University Press).

Euben, PJ (2005) 'Arendt's Hellenism' in DR Villa (ed), *The Cambridge Companion to Hannah Arendt* (Cambridge, Cambridge University Press).

Febbrajo, A (1987) 'Kapitalismus, moderner Staat und national-formales Recht' in M Rehbinder and KP Tieck (eds), *Max Weber als Rechtssoziologie* (Berlin, Duncker & Humblodt).

Fehrenbach, E (1997) 'Nation' in E Fehrenbach, HW Hahn and J Müller (eds), *Politischer Umbruch und gesellschaftliche Bewegung. Ausgewählte Aufsätze zur Geschichte Frankreichs und Deutschlands im 19. Jahrhundert* (München, Oldenbourg).

Förster, J (2008) 'Leben im Ausnahmezustand—Über den Widerspruch zwischen Freiheit und Sicherheit' in M Biegi *et al* (eds), *Demokratie, Recht und Legitimität im 21. Jahrhundert* (Wiesbaden, VS Verlag für Sozialwissenschaften).

—— (2009) *Die Sorge um die Welt und die Freiheit des Handelns. Zur institutionellen Verfassung der Freiheit im politischen Denken Hannah Arendts* (Würzburg, Königshausen & Neumann).

Foucault, M (1994) *Überwachen und Strafen. Die Geburt des Gefängnisses* (Frankfurt, Suhrkamp).

—— (M Sennelart ed) (2004) *Geschichte der Gouvernementalität I. Sicherheit, Territorium, Bevölkerung, Vorlesung am Collège de France, 1977–1978* (Frankfurt, Suhrkamp).

—— (2006) 'What is Enlightenment?' in M Foucault (Paul Rabinow ed), *Ethics: Subjectivity and Truth* (New York, NY, The New Press).

Frank, JA (2010) *Constituent Moments: Enacting the People in Postrevolutionary America* (Durham, NC, Duke University Press).

Frankenberg, G (2003) 'Feindes Wiederkehr? Zur Verfassung des unbequemen Verhältnisses von Recht und Politik' in G Frankenberg (ed), *Autorität und Integration. Zur Grammatik von Recht und Verfassung* (Frankfurt, Suhrkamp).

Fraser, N (2004) 'Hannah Arendt in the 21st Century' 3 *Contemporary Political Theory* 3, 253.

Freud, S (1999a [1920]) 'Jenseits des Lustprinzips' in S Freud (A Freud ed), *Gesammelte Werke*, vol 13 (Frankfurt, Fischer).

—— (1999b [1930]) 'Das Unbehagen in der Kultur' in S Freud and (A Freud ed), *Gesammelte Werke*, vol 14 (Frankfurt, Fischer).

—— (1999c [1939]) 'Der Mann Moses und die monotheistische Religion' in S Freud (A Freud ed), *Gesammelte Werke*, vol 16 (Frankfurt, Fischer).

Freund, J (1987) 'Die Rationalisierung des Rechts nach Max Weber' in M Rehbinder and KP Tieck (eds), *Max Weber als Rechtssoziologie* (Berlin, Duncker & Humblodt).

Gadamer, HG (1975) *Wahrheit und Methode. Grundzüge einer philosophischen Hermeneutik* (Tübingen, Mohr Siebeck).

Gellner, E (1995) *Nationalismus und Moderne* (Berlin, Rotbuch Verlag).

Gerstenberg, O (1997) *Bürgerrechte und deliberative Demokratie. Elemente einer pluralistischen Verfassungstheorie* (Frankfurt, Suhrkamp).

Göhler, G (2009) '"Power to" and "Power over"' in R Stewart and M Haugaard (eds), *The SAGE Handbook of Power* (London, SAGE), 32.

Goldoni, M and McCorkindale, C (2012) 'The Role of the Supreme Court in Arendt's Political Constitution' in M Goldoni and C McCorkindale (eds), *Hannah Arendt and the Law* (Oxford, Hart Publishing), 117–32.

Gosepath, S (2007) 'Hannah Arendts Kritik der Menschenrechte und ihr "Recht, Rechte zu haben"' in Heinrich-Böll-Stiftung (ed), *Hannah Arendt: Verborgene Tradition—Unzeitgemäße Aktualität?* (Berlin, Akademie Verlag).

Graham, HD (1990) *The Civil Rights Era. Origins and Development of a National Policy 1960–1972* (Oxford, Oxford University Press).

Gray, G (1979) 'Die Winde des Denkens' in A Reif (ed), *Hannah Arendt: Materialien zu ihrem Werk* (Wien, Baulino Verlag).

Greven, MT (2010) 'Verschwindet das Politische in der politischen Gesellschaft? Über Strategien der Kontingenzverleugnung' in T Bedorf *et al* (eds), *Das Politische und die Politik* (Frankfurt, Suhrkamp).

Guggenberg, B (1993) 'Das Ende der Arbeitsgesellschaft und die Erosion des Politischen: Eine Erkundung mit Hannah Arendt' in P Kemper (ed), *Die Zukunft des Politischen: Ausblicke auf Hannah Arendt* (Frankfurt, Fischer).

Günther, K (1994) 'Diskurstheorie des Rechts oder Naturrecht in diskurstheoretischem Gewande?' 4 *Kritische Justiz* 27, 470.

Habermas, J (1977) 'Hannah Arendt's Communication Concept of Power' 1 *Social Research* 44, 3.

—— (1981) 'Die Geschichte von den zwei Revolutionen' in J Habermas (ed), *Philosophisch-politische Profile* (Frankfurt, Suhrkamp).

—— (1990) *Strukturwandel der Öffentlichkeit. Untersuchungen zu einer Kategorie der bürgerlichen Gesellschaft* (Frankfurt, Suhrkamp).

—— (1994) *Faktizität und Geltung* (Frankfurt, Suhrkamp).

—— (1998) 'The European Nation-State: On the Past and Future of Sovereignty and Citizenship' in J Habermas (ed), *The Inclusion of Other: Studies in Political Theory* (Boston, MA, MIT Press).

—— (1999a) 'Eine genealogische Betrachtung zum kognitiven Gehalt der Moral' in J Habermas (ed), *Die Einbeziehung des Anderen. Studien zur politischen Theorie* (Frankfurt, Suhrkamp).

—— (1999b) 'Versöhnung durch öffentlichen Vernunftgebrauch' in J Habermas (ed), *Die Einbeziehung des Anderen. Studien zur politischen Theorie* (Frankfurt, Suhrkamp).

Hammer, D (2002) 'Hannah Arendt and Roman Political Thought: The practice of theory' 1 *Political Theory* 30, 124.

Hansen, P (2004) 'Hannah Arendt and Bearing with Strangers' 3 *Contemporary Political Theory* 13, 3.

Hayes, C (1949) *The Historical Evolution of Modern Nationalism* (New York, NY, The MacMillan Company).

Hegel, GWF (1986 [1820]) *Grundlinien der Philosophie des Rechts oder Naturrecht und Staatswissenschaft im Grundriss*, works vol 7 (Frankfurt, Suhrkamp).

Heidegger, M (2001 [1927]) *Sein und Zeit* (Tübingen, Mohr Siebeck).

Heller, H (1971 [1927]) 'Die Souveränität. Ein Beitrag zur Theorie des Staats- und Völkerrechts' in H Heller (ed), *Gesammelte Schriften. Recht, Staat, Macht*, 2 vols (Leiden, Sijthoff).

Hennis, W (2003) *Das Problem der Souveränität. Ein Beitrag zur neueren Literaturgeschichte und gegenwärtigen Problematik der politischen Wissenschaften* (Tübingen, Mohr Siebeck).

Herb, K (1989) *Rousseaus Theorie legitimer Herrschaft. Voraussetzungen und Begründungen* (Würzburg, Königshausen & Neumann).

Hermenau, F (1999) *Urteilskraft als politisches Vermögen. Zu Hannah Arendts Theorie der Urteilskraft* (Lüneburg, Zuklampen).

Heuer, W (1992) *Citizen. Persönliche Integrität und politisches Handeln. Eine Rekonstruktion des politischen Humanismus Hannah Arendts* (Berlin, Akademie Verlag).

—— (2007) 'Europa und seine Flüchtlinge. Hannah Arendt über die notwendige Politisierung von Minderheiten' in Heinrich-Böll-Stiftung (ed), *Hannah Arendt: Verborgene Tradition—Unzeitgemäße Aktualität?* (Berlin, Akademie Verlag).

—— (2011) 'On Revolution/Über die Revolution' in W Heuer/B Heiter/S Rosenmüller (eds), *Arendt-Handbuch. Leben—Werk—Wirkung* (Stuttgart, Metzler Verlag), 84–91.

Heuer. W and Rosenmüller. S (2011) 'Between Past and Future/Zwischen Vergangeheit und Zukunft' in W Heuer/B Heiter/S Rosenmüller (eds), *Arendt-Handbuch. Leben—Werk—Wirkung* (Stuttgart, Metzler Verlag), 70–84.

Hirschman, AO (1982) *Shifting Involvements. Private Interests and Public Action* (Princeton, Princeton University Press).

Hobbes, T (1984 [1651]) *Leviathan. Oder Stoff, Form und Gewalt eines kirchlichen und bürgerlichen Staates* (Frankfurt, Suhrkamp).

Hobsbawm, EJ (1977) 'Hannah Arendt on Revolution' in EJ Hobsbawm (ed), *Revolutionaries* (London, Quartet Books).

—— (1991) *Nationen und Nationalismus* (Frankfurt, Campus).

Höffe, O (1993) 'Politische Ethik im Gespräch mit Hannah Arendt' in P Kemper (ed), *Die Zukunft des Politischen: Ausblicke auf Hannah Arendt* (Frankfurt, Fischer).

Hofmann, H (1964) *Legitimität gegen Legalität. Der Weg der politischen Philosophie Carl Schmitts* (Neuwied, Luchterhand).

Honig, B (1988) 'Arendt, Identity, and Difference' 1 *Political Theory* 16, 77.

—— (1991) 'Declarations of Independence: Arendt and Derrida on the Problem of Founding a Republic' 1 *American Political Science Review* 85, 97.

—— (2007) 'Between Decision and Deliberation: Political Paradox in Democratic Theory' 1 *American Political Science Review* 101, 1.

Howard, D (2001) *Die Grundlegung der amerikanischen Demokratie* (Frankfurt, Suhrkamp).

Hume, D (1988 [1748]) 'Über den ursprünglichen Vertrag' in D Hume (U Bermbach ed), *Politische und ökonomische Essays*, vol 1 (Hamburg, Meiner).

Ignatieff, M (2001) *Human Rights as Politics and Idolatry* (Princeton, NJ, Princeton University Press).

Isaac, CJ (1992) *Arendt, Camus and Modern Rebellion* (New Haven, CT, Yale University Press).

Jacoby, R (2007) 'Wege des Ruhms. Hannah Arendt war keine bedeutende Philosophin, aber eine große Essayistin' 3 *Merkur* 695, 263.

Jaeggi, R (1997) *Welt und Person: Zum anthropologischen Hintergrund der Gesellschaftskritik Hannah Arendts* (Berlin, Lukas).

—— (2009) 'Was ist eine (gute) Institution' in R Forst *et al* (eds), *Sozialphilosophie und Kritik* (Frankfurt, Suhrkamp).

Jay, M (1978) 'The Political Existentialism of Hannah Arendt' 3 *Partisan Review* 45, 2.

Jonas, F (1979) 'Hannah Arendts Theorie der Revolution' in A Reif (ed), *Hannah Arendt: Materialien zu ihrem Werk* (Wien, Europaverlag).

Jonas, H (1979) 'Handeln, Erkennen, Denken: Zu Hannah Arendts philosophischen Werk' in A Reif (ed), *Hannah Arendt: Materialien zu ihrem Werk* (Wien, Europaverlag).

Kalyvas, A (2004) 'From the act to the decision: Hannah Arendt and the Question of Decisionism' 3 *Political Theory* 32, 320.

—— (2008) *Democracy and the Politics of the Extraordinary: Max Weber, Carl Schmitt, and Hannah Arendt* (Cambridge, Cambridge University Press).

Kant, I (1977 [1797]) *Die Metaphysik der Sitten*, volume VIII (Frankfurt, Suhrkamp).

—— (1998 [1781]) *Kritik der reinen Vernunft* (Hamburg, Meiner).

—— (1999a [1795]) Zum ewigen Frieden (Stuttgart, Reclam).

—— (1999b [1785]) 'Grundlegung zur Metaphysik der Sitten' in I Kant (B Kraft and D Schönecker eds), *Grundlegung zur Metaphysik der Sitten* (Hamburg, Meiner).

—— (2001 [1790]) 'Kritik der Urteilskraft' in I Kant (HF Klemme ed), *Kritik der Urteilskraft* (Hamburg, Meiner).

Kateb, G (1984) *Hannah Arendt. Politics, Conscience, Evil* (Oxford, Robertson).

Keenan, A (1994) 'Promises, Promises: The Abyss of Freedom and the Loss of the Political in the Work of Hannah Arendt' 2 *Political Theory* 22, 297.

—— (2003) *Democracy in Question: Democratic Openness in a Time of Political Closure* (Stanford, CA, Stanford University Press).

Kelsen, H (1994 [1934]) *Reine Rechtslehre. Einleitung in die rechtswissenschaftliche Problematik* (Aalen, Scientia-Verlag).

—— (2002 [1934]) *Pure Theory of Law*, translation from the second German edition by Max Knight (Berkeley, CA, University of California Press).

Kersting, W (1996) *Die politische Philosophie des Gesellschaftsvertrags* (Darmstadt, Primus-Verlag).

Klabbers, J (2007) 'Possible Islands of Predictability: The Legal Thought of Hannah Arendt' 1 *Leiden Journal of International Law* 20, 1.

—— (2012) 'Hannah Arendt and the Languages of Global Governance' in M Goldini and C McCorkindale (eds), *Hannah Arendt and the Law* (Oxford, Hart Publishing).

Knott, ML (2011) 'The Human Condition/Vita activa oder Vom tätigen Leben' in W Heuer, B Heiter and S Rosenmüller (eds), *Arendt-Handbuch. Leben—Werk—Wirkung* (Stuttgart, Metzler Verlag), 61.

König, H (2008) *Politik und Gedächtnis* (Weilerswist, Velbrück Wissenschaft).

Kristeva, J (1991) *Strangers to Ourselves* (New York, NY, Columbia University Press).

—— (1993) *Nations without Nationalism* (New York, NY, Columbia University Press).

—— (2001) *Hannah Arendt* (New York, NY, Columbia University Press).

Kupka, T (1998) 'Demokratie ohne Naturrecht. Eine rechtsphilosophische Entwicklungsskizze in vier Schritten und einem Ausblick' in H Brunkhorst (ed), *Demokratischer Experimentalismus. Politik in der komplexen Gesellschaft* (Frankfurt, Suhrkamp).

Laclau, E (1996) 'Deconstruction, Pragmatism, Hegemony' in C Mouffe (ed), *Deconstruction and Pragmatism* (London, Routledge).

Laclau, E and Mouffe, C (2001) *Hegemony and the Socialist Strategy. Towards A Radical Democratic Politics* (London/New York, NY, Verso).

Lefort, C (1986) *The Political Forms of Modern Society* (Cambridge, MA, MIT Press).

—— (1988) *Democracy and Political Theory, translated by David Macey* (Minneapolis, MN, University of Minnesota Press).

—— (1990) 'Die Frage der Demokratie' in U Rödel (ed), *Autonome Gesellschaft und libertäre Demokratie* (Frankfurt, Suhrkamp).

Lindahl, H (2006) 'Give and take. Arendt and the nomos of political community' 7 *Philosophy and Social Criticism* 32, 881.

Lindner, B (1997) 'Derrida. Benjamin. Holocaust: Zur politischen Problematik der Kritik der Gewalt' 5 *Zeitschrift für Kritische Theorie* 5, 65.

Luban, D (1979) 'On Habermas, on Arendt, on Power' 1 *Philosophy and Social Criticism* 6, 80.

Ludz, U (2000) 'Nachwort der Herausgeberin' in H Arendt (U Ludz ed), *Zwischen Vergangenheit und Zukunft* (München, Piper), 371.

Machiavelli, N (2001 [1532]) *Der Fürst* (Frankfurt, Insel-Verlag).

Mahrdt, H (2007) 'Phronesis bei Aristoteles und Hannah Arendt. Von der Sorge um das Leben und das Selbst zur Sorge um die Welt' 4 *Deutsche Zeitschrift für Philosophie* 55, 587.

Manthe, U (2003) *Geschichte des Römischen Rechts* (München, CH Beck).

Markell, P (1997) 'Contesting Consensus: Rereading Habermas on the public sphere' 3 *Constellations* 3, 377.

—— (2000) 'Making affects safe for democracy?' 1 *Political Theory* 28, 38.
—— (2003) *Bound by Recognition* (Princeton, NJ, Princeton University Press).
—— (2006) 'The Rule of the People: Arendt, Archê, and Democracy' 1 *American Political Science Review* 100, 1.
—— (2008) 'The Insufficency of Non-Domination' 1 *Political Theory* 36, 9.
Marrus, M (1985) *The Unwanted. European Refugees in the Twentieth Century* (Oxford, Oxford University Press).
Marx, K (1961a [1842]) 'Verhandlungen des 6. Rheinischen Landtags. Debatten über das Holzdiebstahlsgesetz' in Institut für Marxismus-Leninismus des ZK der SED (ed), *MEW*, vol 1 (Berlin, Dietz).
—— (1961b [1844]) 'Zur Judenfrage' in Institut für Marxismus-Leninismus des ZK der SED (ed), *MEW*, vol 1 (Berlin, Dietz).
Massing, O (1993) 'Souveränität—ein unverzichtbarer Anachronismus' in R Voigt (ed), *Abschied vom Staat—Rückkehr zum Staat?* (Baden-Baden, Nomos).
Maus, I (1994) *Zur Aufklärung der Demokratietheorie. Rechts- und demokratietheoretische Überlegungen im Anschluß an Kant* (Frankfurt, Suhrkamp).
Maxwell, L (2012) 'Toward an Agonistic Understanding of Law. Law and Politics in Hannah Arendt's Eichmann in Jerusalem' 1 *Contemporary Political Theory* 11, 88.
McGowan, J (1997) 'Arendt's Utopian Vision' in C Calhoun and J McGowan (eds), *Hannah Arendt and the Meaning of Politics* (Minneapolis, MN, University of Minnesota Press).
McMahon, KJ (2004) *Reconsidering Roosevelt on race. How the Presidency paved the road to Brown* (Chicago, IL, University of Chicago Press).
Meinecke, F (1929 [1924]) *Die Idee der Staatsräson in der neueren Geschichte* (München, Oldenbourg).
Meints, W (2003): 'Globalisierung und Menschenrechte. Zur Aktualität der Krisendiagnose von Hannah Arendt' 5 *Mittelweg* 36, 53.
Meints-Stender, W (2007) 'Hannah Arendt und das Problem der Exklusion—eine Aktualisierung' in Heinrich-Böll-Stiftung (ed), *Hannah Arendt: Verborgene Tradition—Unzeitgemäße Aktualität?* (Berlin, Akademie Verlag).
—— (2011) *Partei ergreifen im Interesse der Welt. Eine Studie zur politischen Urteilskraft im Denken Hannah Arendts* (Bielefeld, transcript).
—— (2012) 'Reflektierende Urteilskraft als Ethos der Macht—eine Annäherung an einen emanzipatorischen Begriff von Macht' in K-H Brier and A Gantschow (eds), *Politische Existenz und republikanische Ordnung* (Baden-Baden, Nomos).
Meuter, G (1994) *Der Katechon. Zu Carl Schmitts fundamentalistischer Kritik der Zeit* (Berlin, Duncker & Humblot).
Michelman, FI (1988) 'Law's Republic' 8 *Yale Law Journal* 97, 1493.
—— (1994) 'Kollektiv, Gemeinschaft und das liberale Denken in Verfassungen' in G Frankenberg (ed), *Auf der Suche nach der gerechten Gesellschaft* (Frankfurt, Fischer).
—— (1996) 'Parsing "a right to have rights"' 2 *Constellations* 3, 200.
Mill, JS (2006 [1879]) *On the Liberty and Subjection of Women* (New York, NY, Penguin).
Minnich, EK (1989) 'To judge in freedom: Hannah Arendt on the relation of thinking and morality' in GT Kaplan and CS Kessler (eds), *Hannah Arendt—Thinking, Judging, Freedom* (Sydney, Allen & Unwin).
Möllers, C (2000) *Staat als Argument* (München, CH Beck).
Montesquieu, CL de (1992 [1748]) *Vom Geist der Gesetze*, volume 1 & 2 (Tübingen, Mohr).
—— (2002 [1748]) *The Spirit of the Laws* (Cambridge, Cambridge University Press).

Moruzzi, NC (2000) *Speaking through the Mask: Hannah Arendt and the Politics of Social Identity* (Ithaca, NY, Cornell University Press).

Mouffe, C (1992) *Dimensions of radical democracy. Pluralism, Citizenship, Community* (London, Verso).

—— (1999) 'Dekonstruktion, Pragmatismus und die Politik der Demokratie' in C Mouffe (ed), *Dekonstruktion und Pragmatismus: Demokratie, Wahrheit und Vernunft* (Wien, Passagen-Verlag).

—— (2000) *The Democratic Paradox* (London, Verso).

—— (2005) *On the Political* (London, Routledge).

—— (2007) *Über das Politische. Wider die kosmopolitische Illusion* (Frankfurt, Suhrkamp).

Mumford, L (1966) *The City in History* (London, Harcourt Brace Jovanovitch)

Neumann, F (1970) 'Der Funktionswandel des Gesetzes im Recht der bürgerlichen Gesellschaft' in F Neumann (ed), *Demokratischer Staat und autoritärer Staat. Beiträge zur Soziologie der Politik* (Frankfurt, Europäische Verlagsanstalt).

Nietzsche, F (1972a [1878]) 'Menschliches, Allzumenschliches' in F Nietzsche (K Schlechta ed), *Werke vol 1* (Frankfurt, Ullstein).

—— (1972b [1881]) 'Morgenröte. Gedanken über die moralischen Vorurteile' in F Nietzsche (K Schlechta ed), *Werke vol 2* (Frankfurt, Ullstein).

—— (1972c [1882]) 'Die Fröhliche Wissenschaft' in F Nietzsche (K Schlechta ed), *Werke vol 2* (Frankfurt, Ullstein).

—— (1972d [1886]) 'Jenseits von Gut und Böse' in F Nietzsche (K Schlechta ed), *Werke vol 3* (Frankfurt, Ullstein).

Nisbet, R (1979) 'Hannah Arendt und die amerikanische Revolution' in A Reif (ed), *Hannah Arendt: Materialien zu ihrem Werk* (Wien, Europaverlag).

Noiriel, G (1994) *Die Tyrannei des Nationalen* (Lüneburg, zu Klampen).

Nussbaum, MC (2000) 'Toleranz, Mitleid und Gnade' in R Forst (ed), *Toleranz. Philosophische Grundlagen und gesellschaftliche Praxis einer umstrittenen Tugend* (Frankfurt, Campus-Verlag).

O'Sullivan, NK (1973) 'Politics, totalitarianism and freedom: The political thought of Hannah Arendt' 2 *Political Studies* 21, 183–98.

—— (1975) 'Hellenic Nostalgia and Industrial Society' in A de Crespigny and K Minogue (eds), *Contemporary Political Philosophers* (New York, NY, Dodd, Mead).

Opstaele, DJ (1999) *Politik, Geist und Kritik: Eine hermeneutische Rekonstruktion von Hannah Arendts Philosophiebegriff* (Würzburg, Königshausen & Neumann).

Otten, HR (2001) 'Befehl und Gebot? Über Carl Schmitt, das Gesetz und die Gewalt' in U Erzgräber and A Hirsch (eds), *Sprache und Gewalt* (Berlin, Berlin Verlag).

Owens, P (2008) 'Humanity, Sovereignty and the Camps' 4 *International Politics* 45, 522.

Palonen, K (2006) 'Was hätte Max Weber zu Hannah Arendt gesagt? Reflexionen zu Hannah Arendts Kritik der repräsentativen Demokratie' in H Buchstein and R Schmalz-Bruns (eds), *Politik der Integration. Symbole, Repräsentation, Institution* (Baden-Baden, Nomos).

Parekh, B (1981) *Hannah Arendt and the Search for a New Political Philosophy* (Atlantic Highlands, NJ, Humanities Press).

Parekh, S (2004) 'A meaningful place in the world: Hannah Arendt on the nature of human rights' 1 *Journal of Human Rights* 3, 41.

Parvikko, T (2004) 'A Note on Max Weber's Impact on Hannah Arendt's Thought' 2 *Max Weber Studies* 4, 235.

Pearson, R (1983) *National Minorities in Eastern Europe 1848–1945* (London, Macmillan).

Pettit, P (1999) *Republicanism. A Theory of Freedom and Government* (Oxford, Oxford University Press).

—— (2000) 'Democracy: electoral and Contestatory' in I Shapiro and S Macedo (eds), *Designing Democratic Institutions* (New York, NY, New York University Press).

Pitkin, HF (1972) *The Concept of Representation* (Berkeley, CA, University of California Press).

—— (1998) *The Attack of the Blob. Hannah Arendt's Concept of the Social* (Chicago, IL, University of Chicago Press).

Preuß, UK (1990) *Revolution, Fortschritt und Verfassung. Zu einem neuen Verfassungsverständnis* (Berlin, Wagenbach).

—— (1994) 'Zu einem neuen Verfassungsverständnis. Wie kann der Geist der Revolution institutionalisiert werden?' in G Frankenberg (ed), *Auf der Suche nach der gerechten Gesellschaft* (Frankfurt, Fischer).

—— (2006) 'Constitutional Powermaking for the New Polity: Some Deliberations on the Relations between Constituent Power and the Constitution' in R Bellamy (ed), *Constitutionalism and Democracy* (Aldershot, Ashgate).

—— (2007) 'Souveränität—Zwischenbemerkung zu einem Schlüsselbegriff des Politischen' in T Stein *et al* (eds), *Souveränität, Recht, Moral. Die Grundlagen politischer Gemeinschaft* (Frankfurt, Campus Verlag).

Rancière, J (2002) *Das Unvernehmen. Politik und Philosophie* (Frankfurt, Suhrkamp).

—— (2004) 'Who is the Subject of the Rights of Man?' 2–3 *South Atlantic Quarterly* 103, 297.

Rawls, J (1998 [1971]) *Eine Theorie der Gerechtigkeit* (Frankfurt, Suhrkamp).

Renan, E (1995 [1882]) 'Renan an Strauß, Briefe vom 29. September 1870 und 15. September 1871' in E Renan (ed), *Was ist eine Nation? und andere politische Schriften, mit einem einleitenden Essay von Walter Euchner und einem Nachwort von Silvio Lanaro* (Wien, Folio-Verlag).

—— (1996 [1882]) *Was ist eine Nation? Rede am 11. März 1882 an der Sorbonne. Mit einem Essay von Walter Euchner* (Hamburg, Europäische Verlagsanstalt).

Richter, E (2008) *Die Wurzeln der Demokratie* (Weilerswist, Velbrück Wissenschaft).

Rödig, J (H Kindermann ed) (1986) *Einführung in die analytische Rechtslehre* (Berlin, Springer).

Rohe, K (1998) 'Parteien und Parteiensysteme' in H Kastendiek *et al* (eds), *Länderbericht Großbritannien. Geschichte, Politik, Wirtschaft Gesellschaft* (Bonn, Bundeszentrale für politische Bildung).

Rosenmüller, S (2009) '"Rechte als Zäune"? Hannah Arendt und das Problem des Urteilens' in C Kupke and B Heiter (eds), *Andersheit, Fremdheit Exklusion* (Berlin, Parodos).

—— (2013a) *Orte des Rechts. Gemeinsinn und richterliches Urteilen nach Hannah Arendt* (Baden-Baden, Nomos).

—— (2013b) 'Recht kraft Urteilens: zum Recht im Denken Hannah Arendts' in J Schulze Wessel, C Volk and S Salzborn (eds), *Ambivalenzen der Ordnung. Der Staat im Denken Hannah Arendts* (Wiesbaden, Springer VS).

Rossi, P (1987) 'Die Rationalisierung des Rechts und ihre Beziehung zur Wirtschaft' in M Rehbinder and KP Tieck (eds), *Max Weber als Rechtssoziologe* (Berlin, Ducker & Humblot).

Rousseau, JJ (M Halbwachs ed) (1976 [1762]) *Du Contrat Social, Introduction, notes, commentaire par Maurice Halbwachs* (Paris, Aubier).

—— (1979 [1762]) *Emile: Or On Education* (New York, NY, Basic Books).

—— (1981 [1753]) 'Versuch über den Ursprung der Sprachen, in dem von der Melodie und der musikalischen Nachahmung die Rede ist' in I Fetscher (ed), *Sozialphilosophie und politische Schriften* (München, Artemis & Winkler).

—— (1995 [1755]) 'Abhandlung über den Ursprung und die Grundlagen der Ungleichheit unter den Menschen' in K Weigand (ed), *Schriften zur Kulturkritik* (Hamburg, Meiner).

—— (2012 [1762]) 'The Social Contract' in V Gourevitch (ed), *The Social Contract and Other Later Political Writings.* (Cambridge, Cambridge University Press).

Saavedra, EM (2002) *Die deliberative Rationalität des Politischen: Eine Interpretation der Urteilslehre Hannah Arendts* (Würzburg, Königshausen & Neumann).

Schieder, T, Dann, O and Wehler, HU (eds) (1991) *Nationalismus und Nationalstaat. Studien zum nationalen Problem im modernen Europa* (Göttingen, Vandenhoeck & Ruprecht).

Schluchter, W (1979) *Die Entwicklung des Okzidentalen Rationalismus* (Tübingen, Mohr).

Schmid, B (1983) *Sittliche Existenz in Entfremdung. Eine Untersuchung zur Ethik Jean-Jacques Rousseau* (Düsseldorf, Patmos-Verlag).

Schmitt, C (1914) *Der Wert des Staates und die Bedeutung des Einzelnen* (Tübingen, Mohr).

—— (1991 [1923]) *Die geistesgeschichtliche Lage des heutigen Parlamentarismus* (Berlin, Duncker & Humblot).

—— (1993 [1934]) *Über die drei Arten des rechtswissenschaftlichen Denkens* (Berlin, Duncker & Humblot).

—— (1996 [1931]) *Der Hüter der Verfassung* (Berlin, Duncker & Humblot).

—— (2002 [1932]) *Der Begriff des Politischen* (Berlin, Duncker & Humblot).

—— (2004 [1922]) *Politische Theologie. Vier Kapitel zur Lehre von der Souveränität* (Berlin, Duncker & Humblot).

Schöttker, D and Wizisla, E (2006) 'Hannah Arendt und Walter Benjamin. Konstellationen, Debatten, Vermittlungen' in D Schöttker and E Wizisla (eds), *Arendt und Benjamin. Texte, Briefe, Dokumente* (Frankfurt, Suhrkamp).

Seelmann, K (2001) *Rechtsphilosophie* (München, Beck).

Sieyès, EJ (O Dann ed) (1988 [1789] ) *Was ist der dritte Stand?* (Essen, Hobbing).

Simpson, SIR JH (1939) *The Refugee Problem. Report of a Survey* (Oxford, Oxford University Press).

Sitton, JF (1987) 'Hannah Arendt's Argument for Council Democracy' 1 *Polity* 20, 80.

Skran, C (1995) *Refugees in Inter-War Europe. The Emergence of a Regime* (Oxford, Oxford University Press).

Smend, R (1994 [1945]) 'Staat und Politik' in R Smend (ed), *Staatsrechtliche Abhandlungen und andere Aufsätze* (Berlin, Duncker & Humblot).

Smith, RM (1999) *Civic Ideals. Conflicting Visions of Citizenship in US History* (New Haven, CT, Yale University Press).

Speth, R (2000) *Nation und Revolution. Politische Mythen im 19. Jahrhundert* (Opladen, Leske + Budrich).

Springborg, P (1989) 'Hannah Arendt and the classical republican tradition' in GT Kaplan and CS Kessler (eds), *Hannah Arendt—Thinking, Judging, Freedom* (Sydney, Allen & Unwin).

Sternberger, D (1979) 'Metamorphosen der Bürgerschaft' in A Reif (ed), *Hannah Arendt: Materialien zu ihrem Werk* (Wien, Europaverlag).

—— (1980) 'Hannah Arendt—Denkerin der Polis' in E Nordhofen (ed), *Physiognomien. Philosophen des 20. Jahrhunderts in Portraits* (Königstein, Athenäum-Verlag).

Strauss, L (1956) *Naturrecht und Geschichte* (Stuttgart, Koehler).

Tamineaux, J (2000) 'Athens and Rome' in DR Villa (ed), *The Cambridge Companion to Hannah Arendt* (Cambridge, Cambridge University Press).

Taylor, C (2002) 'Wieviel Gemeinschaft braucht die Demokratie?' in C Taylor (ed), *Wieviel Gemeinschaft braucht die Demokratie?* (Frankfurt, Suhrkamp).

—— (2008) *Negative Freiheit?: Zur Kritik des neuzeitlichen Individualismus* (Frankfurt, Suhrkamp).

Thaa, W (1997) 'Hannah Arendt: Politik und Weltentfremdung' 4 *Politische Vierteljahreszeitschrift* 38, 695.

—— (2008) 'Kritik und Neubewertung politischer Repräsentation: vom Hindernis zur Möglichkeitsbedingung politischer Freiheit' *Politische Vierteljahresschrift* 49, 618.

—— (2011a) 'Die Krise politische Repräsentation—eine Folge der Auflösung gesellschaftlicher Großgruppen und sozio-kultureller Milieus?' in W Thaa and M Linden (eds), *Krise und Reform politischer Repräsentation* (Baden-Baden, Nomos).

—— (2011b) *Politisches Handeln. Demokratietheoretische Überlegungen im Anschluss an Hannah Arendt* (Baden-Baden, Nomos Verlag).

Thiel, T (2012) *Republikanismus und die Europäische Union* (Baden-Baden, Nomos).

—— (2013) 'Politik, Freiheit und Demokratie—Hannah Arendt und der Moderne Republikanismus' in J Schulze-Wessel, C Volk and S Salzborn (eds), *Ambivalenzen der Ordnung. Der Staat im Denken Hannah Arendts* (Wiesbaden, Springer VS).

Tocqueville, A de (JP Mayer ed) (1969 [1856]) *Der alte Staat und die Revolution* (Reinbek bei Hamburg, Rowohlt).

—— (2002 [1835]) translated, edited and with an introduction by Harvey C Mansfield and Delba Winthrop (eds), *Democracy in America,* (Chicago, IL, University of Chicago Press).

Tsao RT (2002) 'Arendt against Athens. Rereading the Human Condition' 1 *Political Theory* 30, 97.

—— (2004) 'Arendt and the modern state: variations on Hegel in The Origins of Totalitarianism' 1 *The Review of Politics* 66, 105.

Villa, DR (1996) *Arendt and Heidegger. The Fate of the Political* (Princeton, NJ, Princeton University Press).

—— (1999) *Politics, philosophy, terror: essays on the thought of Hannah Arendt* (Princeton, NJ, Princeton University Press).

Volk, C (2005) *Urteilen in dunklen Zeiten. Eine neue Lesart von Hannah Arendts 'Banalität des Bösen'* (Berlin, Lukas Verlag).

—— (2006) '"Wo das Wort versagt und das Denken scheitert". Überlegungen zu Hannah Arendts Eichmann-Charakterisierung' 1 *Aschkenas. Zeitschrift für Geschichte und Kultur der Juden,* 16, 195.

—— (2007) 'Hannah Arendt über das Böse und die Zukunft des Politischen' 1 *Internationale Zeitschrift für Philosophie* 16, 52.

—— (2008) 'Die Garantie der Menschenrechte als politisches Argument. Eine Skizze des Arendtschen Rechtsverständnisses' in M Biegi *et al* (eds), *Demokratie, Recht und Legitimität im 21. Jahrhundert* (Wiesbaden, Verlag für Sozialwissenschaften).

—— (2010) 'From nomos to lex. Hannah Arendt on law, politics and order' 4 *Leiden Journal of International Law* 23, 759.

—— (2013a) 'Hannah Arendt und die Kritik der Macht' 4 *Deutsche Zeitschrift für Philosophie* 61, 505.

—— (2013b) 'Hannah Arendt and the Law' 1 *International Journal of Constitutional Law* 11, 261.

—— (2015) 'Towards a critical theory of the political. Hannah Arendt on power and Critique' in *Philosophy and Social Criticism,* February 13, 2015, DOI 10.1177/0191453715568921.

Vollrath, E (1977) *Die Rekonstruktion der politischen Urteilskraft* (Stuttgart, Klett).

—— (1979a) 'Politik und Metaphysik: Zum Denken Hannah Arendts' in A Reif (ed), *Hannah Arendt: Materialien zu ihrem Werk* (Wien, Europaverlag).

—— (1979b) 'Hannah Arendt und die Methode des politischen Denkens' in A Reif (ed), *Hannah Arendt: Materialien zu ihrem Werk* (Wien, Europaverlag).

—— (1979c) 'Hannah Arendt über Meinung und Urteilskraft' in A Reif (ed), *Hannah Arendt: Materialien zu ihrem Werk* (Wien, Europaverlag).

—— (1987) *Grundlegung einer philosophischen Theorie des Politischen* (Würzburg, Königshausen & Neumann).

—— (1993) 'Hannah Arendts "Kritik der politischen Urteilskraft"' in P Kemper (ed), *Die Zukunft des Politischen: Ausblicke auf Hannah Arendt* (Frankfurt, Fischer).

—— (1996) 'Revolution und Konstitution als republikanische Grundmotive bei Hannah Arendt' in B Baule (ed), *Hannah Arendt und die Berliner Republik* (Berlin, Aufbau-Verlag).

Waldron, J (2005) 'Arendt's constitutional politics' in DR Villa (ed), *The Cambridge Companion to Hannah Arendt* (Cambridge, Cambridge University Press).

—— (2006) 'The Core of the Case Against Judicial Review' *Yale Law Journal* 115, 1346.

Walt, J van der (2012) 'Law and the Space of Appearance in Arendt's Thought' in M Goldoni and C McCorkindale (eds), *Hannah Arendt and the Law* (Oxford, Hart Publishing), 63.

Walzer, M (1993) *Kritik und Gemeinsinn. Drei Wege der Gesellschaftskritik* (Frankfurt, Fischer).

—— (1993) *Interpretation and Social Criticism* (New Haven, CT, Harvard University Press).

Weber, M (1924 [1923]) *Wirtschaftsgeschichte* (München, Duncker & Humblodt).

—— (1972a [1920]) 'Vorbemerkung zu den "Gesammelten Aufsätze zur Religionssoziologie"' in M Weber, *Gesammelte Aufsätze zur Rechtssoziologie*, vol 1 (Tübingen, Mohr).

—— (1972b [1915–1919]) 'Die Wirtschaftsethik der Weltreligionen. Vergleichende religionssoziologische Versuche' in M Weber, *Gesammelte Aufsätze zur Rechtssoziologie*, vol 1 (Tübingen, Mohr).

—— (1973 [1922]) 'R. Stammlers "Überwindung" der materialistischen Geschichtsauffassung' in J Winckelmann (ed), *Gesammelte Aufsätze zur Wissenschaftslehre* (Tübingen, Mohr).

—— (1976 [1921]) 'Wirtschaft und Gesellschaft. Grundriss der verstehenden Soziologie, 1. und 2. Halbband' in J Winkelmann (ed), *Gesammelte Politische Schriften* (Tübingen, Mohr).

—— (1980a [1918]) 'Parlament und Regierung im neugeordneten Deutschland' in J Winckelmann (ed), *Gesammelte Politische Schriften* (Tübingen, Mohr).

—— (1980b [1919]) 'Politik als Beruf' in J Winckelmann (ed), *Gesammelte Politische Schriften* (Tübingen, Mohr).

Wellmer, A (1986) *Ethik und Dialog. Elemente des moralischen Urteils bei Kant und in der Diskursethik* (Frankfurt, Suhrkamp).

—— (1998) 'Menschenrechte und Demokratie' in S Gosepath and G Lohmann (eds), *Philosophie der Menschenrechte* (Frankfurt, Suhrkamp).

—— (1999) 'Hannah Arendt über die Revolution' in H Brunkhorst *et al* (eds), *Recht auf Menschenrechte. Menschenrechte, Demokratie und internationale Politik* (Frankfurt, Suhrkamp).

—— (2000) 'Arendt on revolution' in DR Villa (ed), *The Cambridge Companion to Hannah Arendt* (Cambridge, Cambridge University Press).

Wolin, SS (1994) 'Fugitive Democracy' 1 *Constellations* 1, 11.

Young, IM (2002) 'Power, Violence and Legitimacy: A reading of Hannah Arendt in an Age of Police Brutality and Humanitarian Intervention' in M Minow (ed), *Breaking the Cycles of hatred: memory, law and repair* (Princeton, NJ, Princeton University Press).

Young-Bruehl, E (1991) *Hannah Arendt: Leben, Werk und Zeit* (Frankfurt, Fischer).

—— (2006) *Why Arendt Matters* (New Haven, CT, Yale University Press).

Zerilli, LM (2005) '"We feel our freedom." Imagination and Judgment in the Thought of Hannah Arendt' 2 *Political Theory* 33, 158.

Ziegler, HO (1931) *Die moderne Nation. Ein Beitrag zur politischen Soziologie* (Tübingen, Mohr).

Zimmermann, R (2005) *Philosophie nach Auschwitz* (Reinbek bei Hamburg, Rowohlt).

Žižek, S (2009) *Ein Plädoyer für die Intoleranz* (Vienna, Passagen Verlag).

Zolberg, A (1983) 'The Formation of New States as a Refugee-Generating Process' 24 *The Annals of the American Academy of Political and Social Science* 467, 24.

# Index

www.ingramcontent.com/pod-product-compliance
Lightning Source LLC
LaVergne TN
LVHW050302210926
848481LV00014BA/372